"Startlingly good."
Peter C. Newman, *Maclean's*

"An informative and enjoyable piece of reading. In the
annals of business, the like of the old CPR will never be
seen again. Cruise and Griffiths are to be congratulated for
giving the story of this historical phenomenon an intimate
human dimension . . . . it may have some of the hard old
rogues who ran it turning uncomfortably in their graves."
The Gazette, Montreal

"*Lords of the Line* is colourful and anecdotal, but carefully
and extensively researched."
The Globe and Mail, Toronto

". . . never before has this intimate and interesting a book
been written on the politics, greed, vanity and manipulation
that surrounded the CPR and its top executives . . .
compelling Canadian history at its finest."
North Shore News, Vancouver

". . . the bleeding-knuckled account of the ego, occasional
corruption, high drama, gruelling work and intellectual
genius of business leadership."
The Calgary Sun

"*Lords of the Line* manages to animate the past. The men
they profile jump off the page and tell their own story to
the reader."
The Chronicle-Journal, Thunder Bay

PENGUIN BOOKS

LORDS OF THE LINE

David Cruise and Alison Griffiths are writers whose work has won them four national writing awards. Their acclaimed and bestselling books include *Fleecing the Lamb* and *Net Worth*.

Cruise and Griffiths live in Toronto with their two daughters.

LORDS OF THE LINE

THE MEN WHO BUILT THE CPR

**DAVID CRUISE
ALISON GRIFFITHS**

Penguin Books

PENGUIN BOOKS
Published by the Penguin Group
Penguin Books Canada Ltd, 10 Alcorn Avenue, Toronto, Ontario,
Canada M4V 3B2
Penguin Books Ltd, 27 Wrights Lane, London W8 5TZ, England
Penguin Books USA Inc., 375 Hudson Street, New York, New York
10014, U.S.A.
Penguin Books Australia Ltd, Ringwood, Victoria, Australia
Penguin Books (NZ) Ltd, 182-190 Wairau Road, Auckland 10,
New Zealand

Penguin Books Ltd, Registered Offices: Harmondsworth, Middlesex,
England

First published in Viking by Penguin Books Canada Limited, 1988
Published in Penguin Books, 1989
Published in this edition, 1996

10 9 8 7 6 5 4 3 2 1

Manufactured in Canada

Canadian Cataloguing in Publication Data

Cruise, David, 1950-
   Lords of the line

Includes bibliographical references.
ISBN 0-14-025473-0 (trade format)

1. Canadian Pacific Limited - Presidents. 2. Canadian Pacific Limited -
History. I. Griffiths, Alison, 1953-   . II. Title.

HE2810.C2C78 1989   385'.06'571   C90-001471-7

To Quinn and Claudia who, in their own way, worked every bit as hard as we did.

LORDS OF THE LINE

Acknowledgements

The Canadian Pacific has a reputation as a tightly shuttered, secretive corporation. As we did the research for this book, we found the company unfailingly cooperative and helpful — often as curious to find out about its past as we were. The company officers weren't always happy with our line of questioning but never tried to influence us. Our official Canadian Pacific contact, Bob Rice, a former journalist and currently vice-president of corporate communications and public affairs, was professional in all his dealings with us and offered his own insights into the company. Because we couldn't spend the many weeks necessary to read Edward Beatty's letterbooks in Montreal, CP microfilmed the more than 90,000 letters so we could read them in Vancouver. This was an extraordinary service not only to us but also to subsequent researchers and historians.

We are particularly indebted to the living presidents of Canadian Pacific, Buck Crump, Ian Sinclair, Fred Burbidge and Bill Stinson, for giving up their valuable time and providing unprecedented access to company documents. Buck Crump and Ian Sinclair made themselves available for long interviews and to answer endless small questions. As well, they offered us photos and family documents which have hitherto been private. They both also encouraged us not to hesitate in making tough judgments of the company and the men who led it.

We would also like to thank Susan Morton, Donald Sinclair and Ruth Sinclair for providing helpful background. The current Lord Shaughnessy allowed us to view his grandfather's papers and gave us access to photographs that had never been seen outside the family. He also spent many hours talking to us, providing his unique view of the CPR and its presidents. His cousin Thomas Shaughnessy also recounted his childhood memories for us. Similarly, Alexis Reford showed us documents and material that added immeasurably to our knowledge of George Stephen.

Hundreds of present and past Canadian Pacific company directors and employees shared recollections of "their" company. Paul Nepveu, Graham MacMurray, Barry Scott, Ron Swan, Don Bower, Fred Stone, Rolly Wilkes, David Flicker, Jack Anderson, Tommy Lawson, Florence Evans, Paul Jolicœur and the late John Shearer submitted uncomplainingly to our initial interviews and our numerous follow-up questions. Canadian Pacific secretaries Pat Brock and Mary Johnston were also enormously helpful. Many company outsiders provided important background information: Mitzi Dobrin, Jack Pickersgill, Bob Bandeen, Marc Lalonde, Matthew Hannon, Hazel Mclean, Calvert Knudsen, Edgar Andrew Collard and Jean Marchand, to name a few.

In St Andrews, New Brunswick, Willa Walker, Margot Mais, Wade Veniot, Richard Wilbur, Carol-Ann Nicholson and Eddy Williamson gave us a wonderful tour of their town and fascinating first- and second-hand accounts of the wealthy who lived there. Renaldo Rinaldi, the manager of the Mount Stephen Club in Montreal, gave us an exhaustive tour of the immaculately preserved Mount Stephen House.

We are grateful to historians W. Kaye Lamb, Peter Waite, Heather Gilbert and John Eagle for sharing their professional knowledge and insights. Scott McIntyre generously supplied us with reference books from his backlist. Amanda Valpy of the *Globe and Mail* and Agnes McFarlane of the Montreal *Gazette*, kindly gave us access to their newspaper libraries.

Jack Cruise provided interim financing. Bob and Julie Inness shared their home on several occasions. Pat Griffiths came up with a title when everyone else had failed. Special thanks to Fiona Griffiths for all her help. Kathryn Dean, our skilful editor, operated under extreme time pressure and put up with endless last-minute changes. We also thank David Kilgour, former senior editor; Iris Skeoch, senior editor; Cynthia Good, vice-president and editor-in-chief; and Morty Mint, president, of Penguin Books Canada for their faith in the project.

David Colbert, our agent, suggested the original idea for the book and Pat Anderson, then editor of *Executive* magazine, allowed us to perform a small journalistic coup by flying two western writers east to interview Ian Sinclair. At just the right moment, John Cox encouraged us to consider writing a book on Canadian Pacific.

There exists in this country, stretching from the Atlantic to the Pacific and from the Arctic to the forty-ninth parallel, an unofficial club whose members number in the tens of thousands. They are CPR fanciers and railroad buffs. In researching *Lords of the Line* we tapped this informative gold mine and wish to thank the hundreds of people who happily talked trains and presidents with us. There also exist in this country the unspoken heroes of railway history. They are the librarians, archivists and researchers who labour to preserve this part of our heritage. We thank in particular Jim Shields, Canadian Pacific's archivist, who searched for documents, maps and information and gave us the benefit of his vast knowledge and years of experience.

We are grateful to Dave Jones and Omer Lavallée (former archivist) of Canadian Pacific, David Monaghan of the Canadian Railroad Historical Association, Kenneth S. Mackenzie of CN Archives, Neil Forsyth, Andrew Rogers and Andris Kesteris of the National Archives of Canada and the staff at the Glenbow Archives, Calgary, Alberta, for the invaluable assistance they gave us. Stanley Triggs of McCord Museum, McGill University, provided photographs on very short order. Tom White and Bob Frame of the James Jerome Hill Reference Library in St Paul, Minnesota, were intensely interested in the project and guided us through J. J. Hill's papers. Doreen Sullivan and Steve Williams of the West Vancouver Public Library gave us the run of their reference section. And, without Nancy Williatte-Battet's dedicated search of the CP Rail

Corporate Archives, we simply would not have the quantity of rare photographs that enhance this book.

Many more people contributed to this book than can be named in a brief section such as this. We hope the book, which you are all a part of, measures up to your expectations.

David Cruise
Alison Griffiths
West Vancouver, B.C.
July 8, 1988

CONTENTS

Maps

PROLOGUE

I n the spring of 1891 William Van Horne, president of the
Canadian Pacific Railway, made a blunder. It was only a
medium-sized blunder as blunders go, but because Van
Horne was Van Horne and the CPR was the CPR it changed the
result of an election. Partial to extravagant gestures and
hyperbole, Van Horne wrote a highly critical letter about
Wilfrid Laurier's Liberal party. Somehow the letter made its
way into the newspapers, and the Liberals, favoured to win
the forthcoming federal election, were outraged.

Concerned that the party would seek revenge against the
CPR if it came to power, Van Horne met with his second-in-
command, Thomas Shaughnessy, a former politician, to do
some damage control. Instead of issuing a simple statement of
retraction or explanation, the pair decided to throw the massive weight of the CPR and its purse behind the Conservatives,
both publicly and covertly. "Through various channels of the
Company we organized a most far-reaching and effective bit
of election machinery," Shaughnessy later boasted, "to which,
in my mind, Sir John Macdonald owed his success in that
campaign."[1]

It wasn't the first "effective bit" of electioneering by the CPR, nor would it be the last. During the construction years, George Stephen greased the wheels of Parliament with $1 million in bribes, or "bonifications," as he called them. It was widely rumoured that he gave Lady Macdonald a £40,000 necklace — a gift many believed saved the railway from bankruptcy. Such high-handed tactics, together with nationwide resentment of the CPR's early monopoly and massive land grants, have made "Goddamn the CPR" the nearest thing to a national curse that exists in this disparate country. Still a powerful presence, the company, with more than $20 billion in assets and over 105,000 employees, ranks as the second-largest corporation in Canada.*

Lords of the Line is about the six men who have dominated the Canadian Pacific Railway† for 91 of its 107 years.‡ Corporate titans whose power at times rivalled and even surpassed that of the country's prime ministers, they have been over-shadowed by the company's historical importance.

Unmasking these men became a passion. In the two years of research and writing, we crisscrossed the country a dozen times, sniffing out clues. We washed century-old grit, and not a few cobwebs, off our hands at a dozen archives, where we read nearly 300,000 letters. We uncovered plots and counterplots and schemes within schemes as complicated and cruel as any concocted by Nicolò Machiavelli. We found Rockefeller-like feats of entrepreneurial daring and moments of touching

---

*The largest corporation in Canada is Bell Canada Enterprises, with $26 billion in assets and 117,000 employees. Canada's other fabled firm, the Hudson's Bay Company, has $3.2 billion in assets and employs less than 40,000 people. (The Canadian Pacific figures are estimates, which include the company's 1988 purchase of a controlling interest in Laidlaw Transportation Ltd. for $500 million in cash and shares. The figures also include the 1988 purchase of Canadian National's chain of nine hotels for $260 million. The purchase made Canadian Pacific the largest hotelier in the country, with 12,500 rooms and a total of 27 hotels, either owned or managed.)

†The CPR was officially renamed Canadian Pacific Ltd. in 1971, but most Canadians still think of it by its original name.

‡There have been fourteen presidents in all, including Father Lacombe, the "black robe voyageur," who did so much to ease relations between the Blackfeet and the company during the construction years. Lacombe reigned for a single hour when George Stephen temporarily handed over the presidency to him at a dinner held in his honour.

humanity. One particularly poignant visit was to William Van Horne's tragically neglected summer estate, Covenhoven, on Minister's Island near St Andrews, New Brunswick.

Another moving moment was our descent into the dank, stone CP vaults in the bowels of Windsor Station, the company's Montreal headquarters. Few outsiders have ever set foot inside these caverns which contain so much of our country's history. Long, grimy piles of documents and correspondence are heaped one upon the other beside dusty barometers, dishes, lamps, linen and other relics of train stations, telegraph offices and steamships. Eeriest of all are racks of still-pristine uniforms once worn by long-dead hotel, train and ship employees. They hang there as if their owners had just left work and expected to return for their next shift.

Lords of the Line isn't always a pleasant tale, as it ripples through bogs of corruption, greed and treachery, but it is often a story of great courage, foresight and self-sacrifice, with all the attendant humour and eccentricities of the human spirit. The Lords, though not always the paragons portrayed in history books, were all larger-than-life characters, who ruled with the kind of iron-fisted autocracy that may never again be possible.

CHAPTER 1

THREE MEN
AND A DREAM

*Stephen and Smith were master schemers who could
cruelly carve up an opponent but Hill revelled in
heavy punching . . . .*

A t 9:22 A.M. on the damp, cold Saturday morning of
November 7, 1885, a frail, silver-bearded gentleman in
top hat and morning coat strained to stand erect against the
heavy mallet held in his hands. Donald A. Smith was poised to
drive the last spike of the Canadian Pacific Railway at
Craigellachie, British Columbia. It was the most important
single event in Canadian history, fulfilling, at long last, the
articles of Confederation that promised British Columbia a
rail connection with the east.

Staggering slightly, Smith struck a feeble, glancing blow,
bending the spike and knocking it askew. The well-prepared
roadmaster quickly set up a spare one, which Smith attacked
with renewed precision, tapping it in with a series of carefully
measured blows. Silence followed, a short breathless moment
of disbelief that the job was actually done. Then, as the impact
of the occasion percolated through the disparate band of
rough-clad navvies, railway officials and curious onlookers, a
ragged cheer erupted into the winter mist. When the shouts
and back slapping died away General Manager William C.
Van Horne brusquely offered his fifteen immortal words: "All
I can say is that the work has been done well in every way."

1

There are no more evocative images of this country's heritage than pictures of the last spike. But, like everything to do with the formation and construction of the CPR, dark, unfathomable currents roiled beneath the surface. It was a curious and jarringly unpretentious ceremony to mark such a momentous event. In contrast, the last spike celebration at Promontory, Utah, on May 10, 1869, marking the completion of the first American transcontinental railroad, featured two gold and two silver spikes, each driven into a polished laurel cross-tie. The main spike was forged by a jeweller at a cost of $400. Every telegraph office was manned, and the spikes and silver maul were specially wired so that their contact could be "heard" across the country. When the governor of California hammered the spike home, spontaneous celebrations broke out from New York to Los Angeles. Drunken strangers embraced in the street, fire alarms and church bells rang endlessly, special church services were held and even the long-silent Liberty Bell was rung.[1]*

William Van Horne, the CPR's general manager, behaved as if any ceremony would overshadow the miracle he had accomplished in ramming the railroad through impenetrable mountain and across bog. He went to considerable lengths to downplay the entire event. "The last spike," he'd announced earlier, "will be just as good an iron one as there is between Montreal and Vancouver."[2] Normally extravagantly generous with free passes, he refused to grant any for travel to the last spike, cutting media attendance to a minimum. There was no royalty present, no head of state nor even a highly ranked

---

*The last spike ceremony of the Northern Pacific Railroad on September 7, 1883, at Goldcreek, Montana, was even more elaborate. Henry Villard, company president, brought ex-U.S. president Ulysses Grant to the ceremony, as well as a host of nobility and barons of business. An enormous, flag-bedecked pavilion was erected right over the track itself and a temporary spur line was built around it. The 1,000 invited guests quaffed gallons of champagne and nibbled their way through three hundred pounds of rare Beluga caviar. The dignitaries arrived in forty-three private cars requiring four separate trains to haul them. The whole event cost $250,000, the cheapest item being the spike itself, which was the first spike — hammered in fourteen years earlier.

political figure. Only two people of any real importance attended, Van Horne and Smith. During a short refuelling and revictualling stopover while en route to Craigellachie, Van Horne had bellowed at a reporter pestering him for details:

> OUR TRIP HAS NOTHING TO DO with the opening of the road. It is just the plainest kind of business trip. Just the usual trip of inspection before the winter sets in. There has always got to be a general clearing up before winter comes on. We intend going to British Columbia, but cannot say whether we will pass over the line before or after the last spike, about which you appear to be so anxious, is driven. No, I'm sure I can't say who will drive the last spike. It may be Tom Mularky or Joe Tubby, and the only ceremony I fancy may occur will be the damning of the foreman for not driving it quicker. There will be no concluding ceremony, no nonsense.[3]

Front and centre in the great Canadian picture is Donald A. Smith, a man who was far from what he seemed. Known for his quiet voice, humility and simplicity, Smith's grandfatherly façade and oriental inscrutability masked virulent ambition and great cunning. Though Smith had spent twenty of his sixty-five years isolated in a Labrador fur-trading post, he was a controlling figure in two of North America's most profitable companies, the Hudson's Bay Company and the Bank of Montreal, as well as a major shareholder in two significant railroads, the CPR and the St Paul, Minneapolis and Manitoba. At the same time, Smith had engineered a stunning political career.

There were seven* original investors in the syndicate that built the CPR, but Smith was the first to see the true potential of the enterprise. He had been dreaming of a transcontinental line for two decades. With the patience of drops of water eroding rock he relentlessly pursued his vision, even bringing down Sir John A. Macdonald's Conservative government in

---

*George Stephen, James Jerome Hill, R. B. Angus, Duncan McIntyre, John S. Kennedy, Morton Rose and Company and Kohn, Reinach and Company. (Other investors, not officially listed, included Norman Kittson and Donald A. Smith.)

The last spike. Donald Smith is looking at the camera. Sir William Van Horne is to his right.

1873 to prevent it being built by others. Smith had often spoken of a Canadian railroad to his cousin George Stephen and was delighted when Stephen put together a syndicate in 1880 to take on the challenge. But his delight turned to bitterness when Macdonald, re-elected in 1879, insisted that Smith's name not appear on the contract between the CPR and the government. It was cruel revenge on a man who craved the spotlight almost as much as money and power.*

During the construction years, Smith was kept in the background by Stephen, called upon only to exert his considerable political influence and repeatedly pledge his fortune as the railroad faced one financial crisis after another. A few months before the last spike, when the government had rescued the CPR for a final time, a humiliated rumour sprang up that Macdonald had agreed to the assistance only if Smith would run as a Conservative in the Montreal riding in the next federal election and promise to endorse the prime minister, his hated enemy. Despite the slights and insults of his CPR experience and the meagreness of the final ceremony, Smith was thrilled to be the man to drive home the last spike.

More curious even than the understated ceremony was the absence of two key men, the Scottish financier George Stephen and the American railroader James J. Hill. Together with Donald Smith they comprised the triumvirate that formed and controlled the original syndicate of investors in the CPR. It was a team which was to persist through thirty years, weathering treachery, duplicity and deceit. At their peak these three associates individually and collectively wielded unmatched financial and political power in North America. A few short years after the last spike, they would be among the richest men

*Careful examination of the various pictures of the last spike reveals an amusing fact. In the minutes before the event, several pictures were taken. Though the other spectators are captured in various postures and looking in different directions, Donald Smith's eye is always fixed firmly on the camera, as if he thought a second's straying of attention might cost him his moment of immortality.

not just in North America, but in the entire world. But that day, neither Hill nor Stephen was present. Hill was back in St Paul, temporarily alienated from his partners and well on his way to becoming the CPR's most hostile and implacable foe. He would spend the rest of his life warring with the railroad he had helped to build.

Most conspicuous by his absence was George Stephen, first president of the CPR and its major shareholder. Even as Donald Smith lined up his first blow, Stephen, known as "Boss" to his intimates, was turning his back on Canada and the Canadian Pacific Railway. Considered to be Canada's most influential financial figure, Stephen was a man of intrigue and ambiguous loyalty. His businesses were a labyrinth of conflicting interests and he took care that no one understood more than slivers of his many schemes.

George Stephen was a charmed figure, who inspired life-long reverence among his acquaintances, even those he had victimized. Part of his allure lay in his calm, aristocratic, almost aloof demeanour and his assiduously cultivated appearance. Tall and lean, with a wide, smooth brow, long slender fingers and a neatly trimmed, spade-shaped beard, George Stephen was so striking that men and women would turn and openly stare when he passed in the street. His handsomeness was complemented by apparel that was the benchmark of understated elegance in young Canada. Attended by the first personal valet to be employed in Montreal, Stephen was always immaculately and appropriately turned out. Even more compelling was his deeply resonant voice, which easily convinced friend or foe that his confidences were meant for them alone.

But Stephen's confidences belonged to no one except himself — and they stayed that way even after his death. Before he left Canada, the railway magnate systematically destroyed his files, even ones that were railroad property. And though he was a prolific correspondent, often penning six or seven long letters a day, no business records exist documenting the thirty years he worked in England. Most attribute the destruction of his papers to a lifelong aversion to publicity. In fact, Stephen knew that his papers would reveal just how carefully partitioned and duplicitous his life was. By the time he died, Stephen was the object of much affection throughout the British Empire. Revelations, particularly about the construction of the CPR, for which he had received his peerage, certainly would have changed all that.

GEORGE STEPHEN'S EARLY YEARS were as ordinary as his later ones were exceptional. The oldest of eight children, he was born on June 5, 1829, in the Scottish village of Dufftown, forty miles east of Inverness in the north of Scotland. The Dufftown countryside consisted of small, well-ordered farms carefully tended by the same families for generations, but a mushrooming birth rate placed enormous pressure on the country's already limited capacity to support its population. Hardly a cottage existed without at least one child who couldn't find work. But overpopulation was only one problem. Landowners attempting, often unscrupulously, to create efficient economic units out of the jumble of tenant farms and smallholdings forced an ever-increasing number of people off the land and into other countries.

George Stephen's father, William, was a carpenter, so his income wasn't tied directly to the land. Nevertheless, with eight children, "siller was very scarce — aye it was that — a shilling was about the size o' a cairt-wheel,"[4] as Stephen liked to recall in later years from the comfortable perch of his magnificent English mansion. The only real hint that there was something special about young George came from his schoolmaster John Macpherson, a vigorous outdoorsman who, with his great height, muscular build and loud, passionate manner, inspired and intimidated several generations of students to excellence. When William Stephen tried to take his ten-year-old son out of school to supplement the family's income,

George Stephen in 1871

Macpherson, who rated George as one of the three finest mathematicians he ever taught, interceded. He waived the school fee, which paid his own salary, in return for William Stephen's promise to let George continue taking classes.

In 1843, at the age of fourteen, George Stephen took a job as an ostler, or stable boy, at a local hotel and the next year was apprenticed to Alexander Sinclair, an Aberdeen draper and silk merchant. When his apprenticeship ended in 1848, George moved to London, where he landed a position with J. F. Pawson and Co., a wholesale drygoods merchant.

George advanced quickly in the firm, becoming a departmental senior within two years. Early in 1850 a man came into Pawson's, placed a large order and asked some unusually probing questions of the young clerk who served him. Further conversation revealed that the man, William Stephen, was George's father's cousin and a successful Montreal merchant/importer specializing in British and other foreign dry goods. Both professed amazement at the coincidence.* William Stephen's firm had prospered faster than he'd ever dreamt possible, forcing him to look for trustworthy help. Notoriously cautious, Stephen came into Pawson's with the express purpose of sizing up George. He was obviously impressed because he offered his cousin a job on the spot.

CANADA IN THE 1850S was a place of expansion and optimism, a good country for a young man full of ambition. Montreal had blossomed from a rag-tag polyglot of fur traders and colonial fortune seekers into Canada's premier city, outstripping both Halifax and Toronto. Thanks in part to the entrepreneurial wizardry of John Molson and his offspring, the city's industries were no longer mere suppliers of natural resources. Iron founding, engine manufacturing, distilling and ship building were beginning to flourish. Nowhere was expansion more

---

*This story, commonly told as a chance meeting between William and George Stephen, defies belief. It also has no documentation. George's parents had moved to Montreal, undoubtedly at the instigation of William Stephen, who was already a prosperous merchant there and it is unlikely to the extreme that they wouldn't have mentioned to him that their son was working at Pawson's, a firm William Stephen would have routinely done business with. An even livelier version, given wide play in George Stephen's obituaries, had Donald Smith cast as the relative who met George Stephen so fortuitously.

obvious than in the manufacturing and sale of textiles;* even so George Stephen's progress was little short of phenomenal.

His cousin William was so pleased with the young man that he soon promoted him to buyer. It was work Stephen loved and it suited him perfectly. He made frequent buying trips to London and because the transatlantic cable was not yet laid,† he had to make his own judgments on purchases. Soon his fastidiously maintained but simple clothes gave way to the latest fashions.

Stephen prospered as a buyer; he had a discerning eye for quality and made decisions quickly, which lent him an air of authority and experience far beyond his years. William Stephen relied ever more heavily on his young partner, but that dependence had its risks. "There are some still living in Montreal," wrote Beckles Willson, Donald Smith's official biographer, "who remember Mr. William Stephen and his uneasiness over some of his young relative's financial excursions. Not infrequently his consent to some arrangement or other would be prefaced by the half-serious comment, 'Well, it is clear George is going to ruin the firm, so it might as well come now as at a later time.'"[5]

By March, 1854, George Stephen felt secure enough to marry Anne Charlotte Kane, daughter of the controller of the Naval Arsenal at Portsmouth. It was a happy marriage, with the socially adept "Lady Boss," as she came to be called by George Stephen's business associates, becoming his only true confidant.

---

*The sewing machine, though still a new invention, had turned the home-centred industry on its ear. Textile manufacturers allied themselves with shops that produced finished products. By the mid-1850s, the Moss brothers, who were dominant in the field, employed eight hundred people to sew shirts in their factories. The knitting machine was making inroads too. By the time Stephen's land legs had returned after his voyage across the Atlantic, woven garments were being churned out by the thousands in Canadian mills, and the economy was booming.

†The first functional transatlantic cable began operation on July 27, 1866, signalling from Ireland to Newfoundland. It was the fifth attempt to operate such a line. One cable was in operation for less than a month in 1856.

Later in 1854, Stephen, only twenty-four, took his first big business gamble — and it was based on inside political information as so many of his later ventures would be. James Morrison,* a British merchant king and member of Parliament who had taken a liking to Stephen, suggested that the Crimean War between Turkey and Russia, then entering its third year, might interrupt the regular flow of shipping from England to Canada. Stephen's new father-in-law confirmed that more Canadian and British commercial ships would likely be commandeered before the conflict was over. Without a second thought, Stephen purchased as much woollen and cotton goods as his firm's credit allowed and he could cajole from the wholesalers. George worked so quickly that to William Stephen's bewildered horror, shipments began piling up on the Montreal docks even before his cousin returned to Canada to explain his purchases.

It was a bold risk, one that would certainly wipe the firm out if it failed. But the inside information paid dividends almost immediately. Consumer goods were soon shoved aside in the rush to transport troops and armaments. When the newly formed Montreal Ocean Steamship Company (later known as the Allan Line) cancelled its London-to-Montreal runs and steamed towards the Black Sea, shortages rapidly developed. George Stephen had the only stockpile of dry goods in Canada, and his firm could name its price. It was the beginning of his fortune and of the George Stephen legend.

By the time William Stephen died on July 8, 1862, George was the dominant partner in all but name. Shorn of the older

---

*Morrison, who was attracted to Stephen because of his quick mind and their similarly humble backgrounds, had taken the first step in his own ascent by accident. As a young apprentice, he lived in his master's house, where he became enamoured of a servant maid. She willingly encouraged caresses in darkened corners and often arranged to meet her suitor in the evening. One night, Morrison, who had been waiting for her on the back stairs, seized a passing female figure in a passionate embrace. To his horror he discovered he had assaulted the master's daughter, but the encounter was apparently anything but unpleasant — the two were shortly married.

man's restraint, Stephen unleashed his ambition. He had seen enough of it to know he wanted wealth, but it was the power to control entire domains that he hungered for. His quest couldn't have been planned for a better era.

In the first decades of the nineteenth century the small domestic Canadian market had been overrun by cheaper American consumer goods. When the Americans cancelled the Reciprocity Treaty with Canada in 1865, a new wave of nationalist fever injected fresh life into virtually every domestic industry. The American Civil War provided another boost, causing disruptions in the cotton trade, which made Canadian wool products more appealing. Stephen, who had begun to specialize in Canadian tweeds, seized the new opportunity.

In 1866, Stephen bought into a small, water-powered woollen mill in Almonte, Ontario, fifty miles southwest of Ottawa. By this time Stephen had met Donald Smith and, knowing that he had ready capital, suggested a profitable use for it. Their first investment was a joint stock company formed to incorporate the Paton Company of Sherbrooke, Quebec. It wasn't long before the company, under George Stephen's vice-presidency, had swallowed up the nearby Lomas Woolen Mill and the Quebec Worsted Company.

Stephen was rarely a passive investor, nor did he ever lose his penchant for bowel-knotting risks. On one occasion he was visiting shipping magnate John Redpath. As they were talking, Redpath "mentioned to Mr. Stephen that one of the firm's ships, then loaded with lumber for Buenos Ayres had, as yet, no return cargo arranged. Without a moment's thought Mr. Stephen said, 'Fill her up with wool, and I will take the whole.' The matter was arranged then and there. . . ."[6]

IN THE GANGLY SPRAWL of young Canada, transportation was critical to any business with aspirations beyond the city limits. Manufacturers and producers of primary goods like coal and lumber had to move their goods to sell them, a reality which put them completely at the mercy of profiteers who set the rates, totally unregulated by government. Even when they weren't being exploited by high rates, their businesses could be ruined by erratic schedules, lack of rolling stock and the regular disappearance of shippers into bankruptcy. Between 1850 and 1870 manufacturers and producers began protecting themselves by investing heavily in transportation. Though steamboats, wagon-freighters and canal boats were still widely used, the emerging giant was railroading. In 1848 only 22 miles of railroad track existed in the entire country and two years later the total had grown to only 66. But by 1860 there were 2,065 miles and at the time of Confederation in 1867 there were 15 different railway companies operating on 2,495 miles of non-overlapping track.

By the late 1860s George Stephen was a dominant force in Canada's textile industry; it was only natural that he protect himself by becoming a major player in railroading. Aside from the money to be made, if there was something George Stephen could never stomach it was paying the high cost of someone else's profit. And as a matter of practice, Stephen avoided unpleasant surprises by controlling anything or anyone he might be dependent on.

The Canadian business and political world of the 1860s and 1870s was a bare-knuckle, groin-kicking survival of the fittest. Self-interest was the lowest common denominator and bribes, kickbacks and blatant conflicts of interest were a matter of course, rather than the exception. Honesty was prized, though it was more the keeping of a handshake agreement than the ethical nature of the deal itself that anyone was concerned about. Separating railway entrepreneurs from politicians and determining whose hand was in whose pocket was a difficult task.

Francis Hincks, joint-premier of Canada, was caught accepting a £10,000 bribe to support the Northern Railway in 1854. His immediate successor, Sir Allan Napier MacNab, the longtime chairman of the powerful Canadian standing committee regulating and granting charters to railways and transportation, felt no need to hide his role in decisions favourable to the Great Western Railway — of which he was the president. It was

MacNab who authored, in 1853, one of Canada's most memorable quotations. "All my politics are Railroads, and I will support whoever supports railroads." The political arena was so corrupt that even the paid lobbyist of the Grand Trunk Railway, hardly an organization of vestal virgins, was disgusted. "Upon my word," he sighed after a tour in Ottawa, "I do not think that there is much to be said for Canadians over Turks when contracts, places, free tickets on railways or even cash was in question."[7]

George Stephen thrived in this cesspool, astutely using bribes — he called them "bonifications" — to smooth obstacles, be they government officials or competitors. He was ruthless in dispatching "enemies," as he habitually called competitors, while presenting an image of benign good will. It is a measure of Stephen's deviousness that his reputation as a paragon of rectitude remains unchallenged to this day. He cloaked his

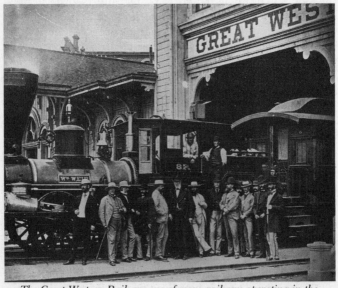

The Great Western Railway, one of many railways operating in the Canadas in the 1850s

predatory nature by working through a labyrinth of channels and using others to run interference for him. So skillful were Stephen's machinations that his victims often felt he'd done them a great favour. His subterfuges were so complicated that even his front men got confused. Years later, Stephen's associates found shares that he owned — $300,000 worth in one case — that they'd been secretly holding and had simply forgotten about.

Within his small circle of close acquaintances Stephen's hatreds were so legendary that even the most hagiographic writers referred to them. He trusted almost no one and kept his multiple projects isolated from one another, often playing his associates off against each other in such a way that each thought he alone possessed Stephen's confidence and allegiance. His "friends" would have been horrified to hear his denunciations of them. J. J. Hill, Donald Smith, R. B. Angus and William Van Horne were all mocked when they turned their backs.

By the early 1870s George Stephen was a powerful and wealthy man. The mere association of his name with an investment was enough to convince many people that they were onto a sure thing. But he would have remained just another rich man if his cousin Donald Smith hadn't visited him a few years earlier, in 1866. It was Smith who showed him where the real money and power was hidden. Though they'd grown up only a few miles from each other in Scotland and both had been in Canada for nearly two decades, it was their first meeting. Stephen was only thirty-seven and Smith, forty-six. Fresh from a fourteen-year stint in Labrador with the Hudson's Bay Company, Smith was a peculiar sight on the streets of Montreal. His "countrified appearance, with long sandy hair, a heavy red beard and bushy red eyebrows,"[8] contrasted sharply with Stephen's own discreetly fashionable apparel. One of Smith's fellow Hudson's Bay factors recalled the fateful meeting:

> I first saw Donald Smith on his visit to Montreal in 1866. He had been spending some days at Lachine, with his wife and two children, where his mother-in-law, Mrs. Hardisty then resided.

One morning he said, "I have a cousin in Montreal, Mr. George Stephen, whom I have never seen. Do you know anything about him? He's a prominent man in the woolen trade, I believe."

I said I had heard of Mr. Stephen, who had been a junior partner with his cousin William Stephen, in a firm of wholesale drapers, and was now established for himself.

As Mrs. Smith had some shopping to do, we all went into the city together. I gave him Mr. Stephen's address, and we parted company. A couple of hours later I met all the Smiths in St. James Street loaded down with parcels and Mr. Smith carrying a rather gaudy carpet bag. He stopped to show me the bag, and asked my opinion of it.

"It's just the thing for Labrador," I said, "It'll make a great hit with the Indians there." I enquired if he had met his cousin, Mr. Stephen.

"Oh, yes," he said, "I went in and had a few moments conversation with him."

"I suppose he was glad to see you eh?"

Mr. Smith seemed a little embarrassed at the question, but his wife burst forth, "He wasn't glad at all. Why should Mr. Stephen be glad to see country cousins like us — all the way from Labrador?" "I wish," she added shyly, "I wish he had waited until he had met Mr. Stephen before buying that red carpet bag. But he wouldn't let me carry it, and the rest of us waited outside."[9]

Stephen made no attempt to hide his disdain for his seemingly bucolic cousin. He failed to perceive the daring and cunning mind behind the backwoods demeanour.

The relationship between the two cousins never progressed much beyond their first meeting. Smith was always an enigma to Stephen. "What a strange creature he is," Stephen sighed more than thirty years later, "so Indian like in his love of mystery & secretiveness."[10] Though professing to admire the "pluck" that Smith showed in standing by him during financial crises, Stephen was cruelly inconsiderate of the older man's feelings. In 1889, when he was about to resign from the CPR presidency, he gave Smith no advance warning. Stephen merely made his announcement and bolted from the directors' meeting, leaving the bewildered Smith following in his wake pathetically calling, "George, George." When Smith protested about the poor treatment, Stephen mockingly called him "boyish" and a "baby."

No real intimacy ever developed between the two Scots, but they were held together by powerful complementary strengths, and their association was a convenient and extremely rewarding one. Where Stephen's temperament was mercurial — one minute grandly taking a great risk and the next fretting about the consequences — Smith was slow to come to a decision but totally resolute in carrying it through to the finish. While both had entrepreneurial traits, Smith was the instigator and catalyst and Stephen the consummate deal maker and financier who always knew how to capitalize on an opportunity. Underlining it all was Smith's rare sense of where to find the real money and power. His intuition led Stephen into his most profitable investments: the Bank of Montreal, the St Paul and Pacific Railroad and the CPR.

DONALD ALEXANDER SMITH was born in Forres, Scotland, about twenty-five miles northwest of Dufftown, on August 6, 1820. His father, Alexander Smith, was a congenial man more comfortable bending his arm or leading a rousing song at the pub than tending to business. But Smith's mother, Barbara Stuart, had more than enough backbone for two and her stoical reserve and patient determination were indelibly etched in Smith's soul. He even absorbed her habits of cleanliness and neatness and from a young age became known for his meticulous quarters.

Barbara Stuart's brothers led exciting lives in the fur trade working for the North West Company, the Hudson's Bay Company's rival in the North American colonies until the two were amalgamated in 1821. They returned periodically from the wilds of the new world to regale their nephew with stories of the far-off land. Completely smitten with the opportunities that beckoned on the other side of the Atlantic, the eighteen-year-old Smith left Scotland in 1838 for Canada, armed with a fistful of recommendations from his relatives.

Smith had barely been hired as an apprentice clerk when he ran afoul of the one man no HBC employee could afford to displease, George Simpson, justly known as the "Emperor of the Plains" for his tyrannical forty-year rule as the company's Canadian governor. Simpson's wife was an attractive English-woman, with plenty of time on her hands thanks to the gover-nor's frequent absences. She "always took a friendly interest in the 'indentured young gentlemen,'" and Smith in particular caught her eye because of his "simplicity and gentle address." Mrs Simpson and Donald Smith spent hours together walk-ing, boating and taking tea. It was probably an innocent flirta-tion, but Simpson, returning unexpectedly from a long trip, thought otherwise. "The Governor," recalled one of Smith's fellow apprentices, "in a highly pitched treble, declare[d] that he was not going to endure any 'upstart, quill-driving appren-tices dangling about a parlour reserved to the nobility and gentry.'"[11]

Simpson vengefully hobbled Smith's career for several de-cades, transferring him in 1841 to Tadoussac, an insignificant post located at the point where the Saguenay River joins the St Lawrence. Tadoussac was considered to be a burial ground where promotions were rare, provisions terrible and the fur supply meagre. Worst of all, those posted to Tadoussac usually ended up in Labrador.

But it was at Tadoussac that Smith first showed his potential. Shortly after his arrival rumours circulated that a notoriously ornery "half-breed" by the name of Dugas had some prize furs, including a coveted black fox, which he intended to sell in Quebec, bypassing the local HBC post. Smith was assigned to get the furs, a task complicated by the fact that the senior HBC officer had thoroughly antagonized Dugas in the past.

Dugas greeted Smith's arrival with a prolonged harangue about the grievous injustices committed against him. Smith blandly said he knew nothing about the matter and was simply stopping over on his way to visit another trapper. The at-mosphere lightened when he handed Dugas a pouch of to-bacco and a bottle of whiskey and distributed picture books and candy to the children. Without another word, Smith split sufficient firewood for dinner and began helping the trapper's

Indian wife, whom he respectfully called "Madame Dugas," prepare the meal. Every time conversation veered towards the Dugas furs, Smith redirected it by telling unflattering stories about the senior officer or imparting news of other traders.

The next morning Smith rose before the trapper, again collected firewood and caught a string of fish. After breakfast he shook hands all around and bid the family adieu.

> "Perhaps," he added, "you will still be here on my way back. If so, we may meet again — who knows?" He then shouldered his pack and was shaking hands, when Dugas, who had been standing by in a state of sulky astonishment, cried out, "You no want my furs?"
>
> "What!" exclaimed Smith. "Monsieur Dugas, you have furs to sell? Ah, that will make Mr. H. [the senior HBC officer] . . . sorry, very sorry to think that he should have lost his temper. What a pity!"[12]

After considerable discussion Smith allowed Dugas to persuade him to take the furs off his hands, including the prize black fox at a cost of £8 — a coup because the same pelt would earn the company at least £50 in London.

One of Smith's responsibilities at Tadoussac was keeping the post's books — a duty that gives the first indication of his almost obsessive secrecy. His accounts were so obscure to his successors that they jotted comments in the margin like "Hang Donald S." or "Damn Donald Smith! I can't make head or tail out of this!" Smith's accounting practices infuriated George Simpson. "Your counting house department appeared to me in a very slovenly condition, so much so, that I could make very little of any document that came under my notice."[13]

Smith's bookkeeping shortcomings have been often attributed to inexperience, but a close friend, George Miles, later revealed that Smith coded his entries to ensure that he was the only one who knew the exact financial state of the post. Smith's unwillingness to commit anything incriminating to paper was so great that he never once wrote George Stephen a letter during their forty-eight-year association — preferring to discuss important matters in person, even if it meant crossing the ocean to do so.[14]

In 1847 Donald Smith had another run-in with Governor

Simpson, now Sir George, which gave his career a decided turn for the worse. It was late November and Smith's eyes had been bothering him severely after a bout of snow blindness. He'd written three times to Simpson for permission to leave his post to have them examined but never got a reply. Finally, fearing he was going blind, he set out for Montreal without permission. The minute he arrived he called on Simpson, who treated his employee's unexpected appearance as an everyday event and calmly invited him in for dinner. At the same time, he called for his own doctor, who examined Smith after the meal.

> "No danger of blindness?" asked the Governor.
>
> "Oh dear, no, Sir George — none whatever," returned the doctor.
>
> "Then," continued the autocrat, more sternly than ever, ". . . this appears to me a serious case of indiscipline. It is now eight o'clock" — here he took out his watch. "I will give you thirty minutes to leave Montreal for your new post."
>
> "My new post?" faltered Smith.
>
> "Yes; you are appointed to the Esquimaux Bay District and will report yourself forthwith. . . . There will be no stage available at Quebec for Bersimits. You will proceed on foot . . . Good night sir," and the inflexible and inexorable Governor turned on his heel.[15]

Smith came close to throwing the job in Simpson's face, but instead acquiesced, setting off as ordered for the severe isolation of Labrador, where he was to spend the next twenty years. Labrador was an exile capable of disheartening and destroying even the strongest, but Smith, then nearly twenty-eight, used it as the launching pad for his remarkable career which led to control of the Hudson's Bay Company and far beyond.

All the same, being relegated to the northern wastes of Labrador was a heavy penalty for his youthful indiscretion and thereafter he strove mightily to avoid making enemies. "With opponents, or those who crossed his will," wrote W. T. R. Preston, one of Smith's biographers, "his method was to try first to win them over without any of the appearance of the mailed fist. Courtesy and gold were pressed into service to make rough places smooth and overcome opposition. But if the subjects of his consideration remained obdurate, then he crushed without delay, taking pains, however, that [his] hand was never seen in the matter. There were always others willing to accept the responsibility. He developed his power in this direction into a science. He never allowed himself to show resentment. So far as possible he avoided arousing thoughts of reprisals in the hearts of his opponents. However the end might justify the means was not in evidence — his hand was never visible. In fact, he more often than not tempered the wind to the shorn lamb, with an appearance of personal sympathy."[16]

In spite of his best efforts, Smith still accumulated more than any one man's share. But when he had to make an enemy, as he did in 1873 with Sir John A. Macdonald, he ensured there was something extremely valuable at stake.

SHORTLY AFTER SMITH'S ARRIVAL at the main Esquimaux Bay post in 1848, a new chief trader, Richard Hardisty, took over. Accompanying Hardisty was his eighteen-year-old daughter, Isabella. She became Smith's wife on March 9, 1853, after her marriage to a Mr Grant ended in mysterious circumstances. Rumours and gossip about their union hung like a pall over Smith's head until he died. Beckles Willson, who wrote two biographies of Donald Smith, the second financed and supervised by Smith's executor, claimed that Isabella's earlier marriage "was duly annulled."[17] But years later, freed from constraint, Willson stated that Smith "had run away with another man's wife" and that it was one of the most important events in his life, "tending to make a man who was naturally secretive, more secretive than ever."[18]

In 1852 Smith succeeded Richard Hardisty as chief trader and he recognized that the only way he could prosper in the company was to remove himself from George Simpson's control. He developed a strategy to draw the attention of the HBC's directors in England by boosting the district's lagging profits. As a first step, he befriended the Moravian missionaries in Labrador by building them a church and a house and offering to pay the mission a sizeable annual stipend. In return, the missionaries saw to Smith's spiritual health and made sure that all furs were directed to the HBC post.*

Though most of the HBC's revenue came from the fur trade, iced salmon, shipped to Europe and the United States, was a small source of additional income for the post. During the fishing season, Smith drove himself with a furious tenacity, overseeing packing during the day and working all night on the books — often going several days without sleeping or even changing his clothes. Bypassing Simpson, Smith wrote directly to London, suggesting that even larger profits could be earned by building a salmon-canning plant in Labrador — a project that turned out to be enormously profitable.† His plans bore fruit in 1859 when the Esquimaux Bay district was removed from Montreal's control and he was awarded the title of chief factor of the district. Along with greater freedom, the promotion gave Smith the opportunity to curry the board's favour personally when he made his annual progress reports in London.

Smith's painstaking construction of a pipeline to the company's headquarters was a marvel of patience and self-discipline. A year could pass before a decision on one of his ideas reached him. But patience was something Smith had in abundance. He became a voracious reader, consuming everything he could get his hands on, from thick medical texts to theoretical studies of economics. His real treasures were the London *Times* and Montreal *Gazette*, which were shipped in bulk on the semiannual supply ship. (If the papers missed the supply ship they could be as much as a year old.) Instead of

---

*There is also the suggestion that Smith, while in Labrador, was surreptitiously carrying on a great deal of private fur trade with the Indians. (Preston, *My Generation of Canadian Politics*, p. 51)

†In his quest for HBC profits, Smith investigated exploitation of Labrador's mineral potential, its cranberries, wild sarsaparilla and the abundant fish offal which he felt would be a perfect substitute for the rapidly depleting world supply of bird guano.

Donald Smith and other Hudson's Bay Company officials.
(Smith is seated second from the left.)

reading them all at once, or even the most recent issues, Smith disciplined himself to read, in chronological order, one and only one paper at breakfast. He also faithfully wrote a long letter to his mother every week, even though the letters couldn't be sent for six months.

Smith's greatest strength was an almost superhuman ability to set an impossible goal, and slowly, almost imperceptibly, bend the world to his will in order to reach it. There is no better example of his patience and determination than his Labrador farm. The very idea of a productive farm in the harsh climate of Labrador was a ridiculous notion that the locals and his colleagues derided. But once he conceived it, Smith nurtured it to astonishing completion. "Smith's Farm" reduced the post's expenses, making his profits appear even higher and providing a respite from the dreary winter diet of root crops and dried or salted game.

But more than anything, fashioning an Eden out of Labrador's barrenness gave Smith a sense of god-like power. His tools were two books on horticulture, the firm belief that fish offal would make an excellent fertilizer and whatever seeds and livestock he could import. Charles Hallock,* an eminent American scientist, led a party to Labrador in 1860 and was flabbergasted when he stumbled on Smith's re-creation of an English country farm in the middle of the wilderness. "The astonished ear is greeted with the lowing of cattle and the bleating of sheep on shore; and in the rear of the agent's house are veritable barns, from whose open windows hangs fragrant new-mown hay; and a noisy cackle within is ominous of fresh-laid eggs! Surely Nature has been remarkably lavish here, or some presiding genius, of no ordinary enterprise and taste, has redeemed the place from its wilderness desolation. . . ."

Smith had seven acres cultivated, much of it under makeshift greenhouses, where he grew turnips, peas, cucumbers, potatoes, pumpkins, oats and even melons. He also had a herd of twelve cows, six sheep, a goat and chickens. Surrounding the house was a cheerful flower garden of favourite English varieties. "Here too, is a carriage road, two miles long (strange sight in this roadless country!)," marvelled Hallock, "upon which the agent betimes indulges in the luxury of a drive. . . . There is no other place like Smith's in Labrador, in all its area of 420,000 square miles."[19]

Lacking expensive diversions and frivolous temptations, Smith rigidly saved half his salary. When he was made chief factor, his income was increased from one to two shares of the total trade income, netting him the handsome sum of £700 annually.† Keenly interested in the principles of investment, Smith could only wield so much power with the money he could accumulate personally. By guaranteeing a 3 percent return, he persuaded a number of fellow HBC officers to sign

---

*Hallock later became dean of the Smithsonian Institution in Washington, D.C.

†Hudson's Bay Company profits were divided into eighty-five parts, and incomes for the "wintering partners," as head traders were called, were portions or multiples of an eighty-fifth share.

over their salary cheques and savings to him, which he in turn invested, retaining the difference for himself.* By the time he left Labrador in 1868 to take charge of the Montreal department, which would include Labrador, Smith was worth $50,000, not much compared to other fortunes perhaps, but staggering in light of his isolation.

SHORTLY BEFORE HE MET GEORGE STEPHEN in 1866, Donald Smith began buying Bank of Montreal shares with his own savings and the pool of money he managed. Though their first meeting was inauspicious to the extreme, the cousins stayed in touch, and following Smith's lead, as he would so often do in the future, Stephen too began acquiring Bank shares. While Smith was content to be a passive investor in the bank, Stephen was determined to take control. Night after night he brought thick banking tomes home and sat utterly absorbed for hours as he systematically accumulated a vast knowledge of the intricacies of banking.

Not only did the bank offer major shareholders like Stephen and Smith a ready source of capital at the most favourable interest rates, but it was a wonderful investment in the bargain. In 1871, for instance, the dividend was an amazing 16 percent. Nonetheless, Smith, still running his HBC investment pool, passed on only the agreed-upon minimum of 3 percent to his fellow company officers. When one of them wanted to withdraw from the pool, Smith simply bought him out using the profit differential. By 1873, Smith was the single largest shareholder in the Bank and Stephen wasn't far behind.

Never content to attack an objective from only one direction, Stephen began cultivating Richard Bathgate (R. B.) Angus, a young man doggedly working his way to the top of the Bank. Slender and exceptionally handsome, Angus had been hired

---

*It is an exquisite irony that Smith used the salaries of its own employees to begin buying control of the Hudson's Bay Company.

away from the Manchester and Liverpool Bank in 1857 at the age of twenty-six. He assumed a stern mien and grew an officious-looking moustache — complete with bushy mutton chops — to mask the youthful softness and artistic pallor of his face. As a reward for the excellent job he did in establishing the new Chicago branch in 1861, he was promoted to the position of assistant general manager in New York, a prestigious location. In 1864 he returned to Montreal as manager of the local branch.

Not a creative financier himself, Angus's faculty was making social and business contacts, conciliating opposing viewpoints and seeing right to the heart of his own advantage in a financial matter. Stephen, knowing he could make use of the young man's pragmatism and raw ambition, began letting him in on investment opportunities, and by 1868 Angus was heavily, if silently, involved with George Stephen's companies. In 1869, with Stephen's and Smith's support, Angus, only thirty-eight, was elevated to general manager of the whole bank.

At first Stephen watched the banking industry from the sidelines, biding his time, absorbing the nuances of its operations. But as his confidence grew and his shares accumulated, his voice, backed by Smith, was heard more and more often until it carried the most weight on the board. In 1873 he was elected vice-president, and he succeeded President David Torrance, of the Dominion Line, on his death in 1876. Working closely with Angus, Stephen insinuated his influence into every aspect of the bank's affairs. Then, under Stephen's direction, the previously cautious Bank began embarking on riskier investments — including railways. When the "narrow views" of the bank's oldest directors got in his way, Stephen ruthlessly manœuvred those officers off the board.[20]

With Stephen and Angus in firm control, the Bank survived the depression of 1873-78* and by 1879 it was in a position of

---

*In 1877 the dividend was shaved to a still healthy 13 percent, which the press refused to consider suffering. "It shows . . . what a handsome return had grown to be expected from the

unassailable strength. While other banks and businesses were still scrambling simply to stay out of the clutches of receivers, the Bank of Montreal, with considerable unallocated capital, was ready to take on new investments — at bargain basement prices whenever possible. Unbeknownst to the Bank's common shareholders, Stephen, along with Smith and James Jerome Hill, an expatriate Canadian, had hatched a scheme that was rapidly soaking up the loose capital.

POWERFUL AND WEALTHY AS THE Stephen-Smith partnership already was, there was a critical element missing from their alchemy. Though both were master schemers who could cruelly carve up an opponent, neither of the cousins cared to sully his hands by personally doing the dirty work. Just as Smith led the partnership to their initial investments, so he was to provide the missing link. The man he produced was James Jerome Hill, someone who revelled in heavy punching and was quite comfortable simply giving his hands a thorough wash after a skirmish.

Donald Smith stumbled across J. J. Hill in the middle of a raging blizzard in 1870. Joseph Howe, Canadian secretary of state for the provinces, had asked Hill, still a Canadian citizen though he was living in St Paul, Minnesota, to travel to Fort Garry and report on the Riel Rebellion, which was then five months old. Donald Smith, by then chief factor of the Hudson's Bay Company, was already in Fort Garry acting as John A. Macdonald's personal emissary.

Hill set out for Fort Garry in March, an inopportune time to be travelling, as the countryside from St Paul to the Fort was still firmly held in winter's snowy grip. He completed the first part of his trek easily, riding for eighty miles on the St Paul and Pacific Railroad, but from there on, conditions deteriorated

---

institution when a 13 percent dividend was regarded as a result requiring to be excused . . . ," commented the *Monetary Times* on June 8, 1877.

rapidly. He travelled the next hundred miles by stagecoach, which had to be hauled out of snowdrifts at frequent intervals. Leaving the stage when it arrived at the trail along the Red River, Hill hired a dog sled, and a half-breed guide who soon abandoned him. Hill, far from an experienced woodsman, had an agonizing three-day ordeal on the trail. He was so concerned about chance encounters with hostile Indians or half-breeds that he risked freezing to death by twice crossing the Red River, stripped to his underwear and towing his clothes on a make-shift raft. At night he slept with the dogs to stay warm.

Hill's third day on the trail started with a further drop in temperature and a swirling snowstorm. The discouraged traveller couldn't see more than a few feet in front of him. Already nervous, he nearly fainted when another dog team materialized in front of him. It was Donald Smith returning from his own investigation of the Rebellion. Hill was delighted to see a white man, any white man, and he greeted Smith as a dear, long-lost friend. Smith, who had walked and canoed hundreds of miles from Labrador to Montreal to get his eyes examined, was most impressed by Hill's solo journey. It was precisely the kind of epic frontier adventure that Smith adored. The two men had briefly met in St Paul during the first leg of Smith's trip north, but both treated this fortuitous encounter as a sign of mystic destiny.*

That night they huddled together before a raging fire and, well fortified with brandy, discovered a common ambition. Although they had been living at different ends of the St Paul–Fort Garry trade route, Smith and Hill had come to the same conclusion: the Red River Valley was a ripe plum, and whoever could pick it would be rich beyond their wildest dreams. Seven years would pass before James J. Hill, Donald A.

---

*Donald Smith held the meeting very dear to his heart. In August, 1909, he gave a speech in Winnipeg which was attended by Hill, whom he extolled — to the intense annoyance of CPR officials — as the greatest railroader who ever lived.

Smith and George Stephen would do just that, but the first step had been taken. Together they were to become the Associates, and the fit was pure magic. Smith, Stephen and Hill comprised a powerful financial troika that was broken only by their deaths.

ONE OF THE GREAT IRONIES of North American history is that James J. Hill, the greatest American railroader, was born in Canada, and William C. Van Horne, the greatest Canadian railroader, was an American. Hill was born on September 16, 1838, into a Rockwood, Ontario, farming family whose land earned them a living but no more. Little distinguished the Hills from any other family, save, perhaps, the tradition of naming the first-born son "James," generation after generation. Hill kicked at many traditions during his long life and this was the first. He created a middle name for himself — Jerome — after the brother of the man who rearranged the map of Europe, Napoleon Bonaparte.

As with George Stephen, it was a teacher who kindled a spark within Hill. William Wetherald began operating a one-room school in 1849, and it was there that Hill's education began. The courses offered were an eclectic stew of algebra, geometry, bookkeeping and land surveying, leavened with a dose of great literature. Hill dreamed about becoming a doctor, a desire ended by the death of his father in 1852. But Wetherald's all-encompassing approach to education introduced a few more possibilities.

After leaving school J. J. Hill laboured for three years at a variety of jobs to support his family. The positions (clerk in a country store, for instance) were menial, but they introduced Hill to the practical rudiments of capitalism and helped form the business philosophy that made him such a formidable opponent in later commercial dealings. He developed a fanatical belief in the power of being the lowest-cost competitor in any contest.

In 1856, with commerce depressed in Canada, J. J. Hill left

his family in the care of his younger brother and joined thousands of other young Canadian men heading to the United States. As a youngster, Hill had conjured up visions of piloting a ship in the Orient, and this is what he now had in mind.

St Paul, Minnesota, a thriving city of 10,000 people, was strategically located at the head of northward navigation on the Mississippi and at the base of the Red River. The route into Fort Garry by the Red River was difficult, but still easier for Canadians going west than the overland trek over the bog, swamp and rock of northern Ontario. Elaborately undulating, the river begins its course two hundred miles south of the Canada-U.S. boundary and ends its twisting route at the point where it empties into Lake Winnipeg seventy-five miles north of the border. It was a perfect transportation corridor for settlers and fur traders who made their way along it by the famous Red River cart, steamboat and canoe. Even more vital, to the few who recognized the fact, the banks of the river, which was two hundred miles wide at some points, encompassed some of the richest farm land in the world, most of it unsettled. St Paul was a hive of activity, a marshalling and outfitting point for eager-eyed settlers and a conduit for the thriving trade in bootleg furs from Canada.

The seventeen-year-old Hill's arrival in St Paul coincided with the golden age of steamboating. The business gave rise to romantic tales of gambling, derring-do and adventure; it was also a highly profitable activity.* Hill's dreams of sailing to the Orient faded when steamboat fever gripped him. Soon after his arrival he found a position as a steamboat agent, an extremely physical job involving the complex and frustrating transfer of freight from one mode of transportation to the next.

Hill mastered the intricacies of this confusing world, an ability which he would later apply to his railroading ventures. In 1860 he began a four-year stint with the firm of Borup &

---

*There were only 85 steamboats chugging up the Mississippi as far as St Paul in 1849. Within seven years the number had increased tenfold, to 837.

Champlin, a prosperous wholesale grocer and forwarding agency. At the same time he moonlighted, bidding for contracts to feed the hundreds of horses stabled at nearby Fort Snelling and to provide wood to fuel the steamboats. Voluble and convincing, Hill rapidly built up a network of business and political contacts that served him and his partners for decades.

Hill was a terrier of a man, short and lithe, with a volatility that often masked his calculating mind. Often he undercut his carefully laid plans with outbursts of emotion, but once committed, Hill's tenacity and stubbornness in carrying out a project were among his greatest strengths. He was a stern man, whose aura of authority was enhanced by a baleful look resulting from the loss of an eye in a youthful archery accident. Although Hill was physically unattractive, with an oblong face, a big nose, receding hair and a squirrel's mouth, the passing years silvered his hair and, with the full beard he later grew, he acquired a distinguished air.

George Stephen became involved in railroading because it was a source of wealth and power; J. J. Hill had a genuine passion

St Paul steamboats in 1859

for it. In the late 1850s, when he was still a steamboat agent, he'd walk for hours along the graded but as yet trackless right of way of the Minnesota and Pacific Railroad, dreaming of what could be done. He was part of the wildly cheering throng that gathered on the levee on September 9, 1861, to greet the steamboat *Alhambra* with St Paul's first locomotive, the *William Crooks*, lashed to its foredeck.[21] Hill was also an interested onlooker when the Minnesota and Pacific Railroad faltered and was reorganized under the name St Paul and Pacific.

In January, 1864, Hill refused a post with the Northwest Packet Company, which monopolized steamboat traffic on the Mississippi south of St Paul. He was tempted, he wrote, but didn't think it fair to leave Borup & Champlin in the lurch. His sentiments were noble indeed, but the very next year he discarded them and negotiated an exclusive contract to act as the freight and passenger agent for the Northwest Company and its feeder railroad, the Milwaukee and Mississippi Railroad. The contract shut Borup & Champlin out of the business entirely. It was quite a coup, pulled off by Hill with the help of his friend William A. Wellington, Northwest's agent in Dubuque, Iowa, who provided him with a constant flow of inside information about the firm's plans. "Look out for all chances and keep us posted," Wellington wrote to Hill about one of their dealings. "Let no one know we are together. Much will depend on that. They may suspect and hint as much as they please, but if they know nothing, all will be well." Wellington's letters to Hill were marked "personal" with an urgent request that they be "burned" after reading.[22]*

As an agent, Hill had a measure of independence, but he was still controlled too much by the actions of others for his own liking. He became his own master with a bold and inspired manœuvre which capitalized on a quirk of the St Paul transportation service. The problem was created by the steamship and railroad loading areas, which were several hundred

---

*This letter never was burned. It survives in the rich James Jerome Hill Reference Library in St Paul, Minnesota.

feet apart. An absurd loading and unloading dance was enacted with every freight transfer as the cargo from the train
had to be unloaded, reloaded on a wagon, hauled over to the
steamboat docks, unloaded again and reloaded onto the boats.
It was a bonanza for local draymen but added a dollar to the
cost of every ton of freight that passed through St Paul — and
the transfer process became a logistical nightmare when a
heavy rain turned the streets into a quagmire of mud.

Hill solved the problem, neatly creating his own freight-
handling monopoly into the bargain, by building a railroad
siding and connecting it to the steamboat dock with a large
warehouse. Transferring cargo was simply a matter of hoisting
freight onto a dolly and wheeling it over to the other side of the
warehouse. Hill not only pocketed his agent's fee for the freight
but collected a transfer charge for the use of his facilities,
which also included considerable storage space.

J. J. Hill's warehouse in St Paul

HILL'S WINTER JOURNEY to Fort Garry, where he encountered Donald Smith in the blizzard, proved to be the first step towards forming his own company. Reporting back to Joseph Howe on the Riel Rebellion and the mood of Canadians at Red River, he painted a gloomy picture:

> Almost the entire English speaking population and fully one-third of the French are looking and hoping anxiously for the early assumption by Canada of the government of the country. Many of the better class of the French and a large number of the English around and north of Fort Garry contemplate moving to Saint Joseph and other points in the States unless the Canadian Government speedily acquires control of the country. . . .
>
> There is a great deal of anxiety and fear on account of the Indians and in the event of trouble with the Indians the people want Canadian and British troops to protect them or else they will leave in large numbers for the United States. . . .

But Hill, keeping an eye on his own self-interest, offered a neat solution to the dilemma:*

> If the Dominion government desire to send supplies thro' by way of Pembina in bond from Canada, we will see that they go through safely. We are now sending supplies to HBC Co., and the missions and . . . it need not even be known but that [the government's supplies] were trading goods. . . . If you think it would be of any advantage I could go to Ottawa and assist in bringing thro' any amount of goods the government might desire. . . .[23]

A few months later Hill acquired the means to carry out his promises. In August he formed a company, along with Chauncey W. Griggs, an associate of Hill in the fuel business, and Alexander Griggs (no relation), a steamboat captain, to begin a steamboat business on the Red River. Within the year they constructed their own boat, a shallow-draft, 110-foot sternwheeler. On its maiden voyage in April, 1871, the *Selkirk* was "loaded to the guards" with 100 passengers and 105 tons of

---

*Hill later enlarged his offer to include "even gunpowder," an act that was illegal under American law.

freight, with "the gallant and delighted Jim Hill himself on the Hurricane Roof."[24] Hill's enjoyment of the momentous occasion was enhanced by the knowledge that he and his partners were to clear $7,000 from that single voyage.

It was the perfect time to become a steamboat owner. Crowds of passengers were being fed into the system by the St Paul and Pacific Railroad, and the numbers were steadily increasing. Even better, the Northern Pacific Railroad, financed by Jay Cooke, a powerful American businessman who had made his name financing the Northern side during the American Civil War, was about to increase the traffic with its line from Duluth on Lake Superior to Fargo, North Dakota, on the Red River. And Hill had hardly any competition on the river apart from the Hudson's Bay Company, which was operating its own boat, the *International.*

Knowing that no amount of rate cutting would drive the HBC out of business with Donald Smith now its chief officer in Canada, Hill turned to other tactics to squeeze the Canadians out. He bribed a United States Treasury Department official into ruling that only an American firm could operate a vessel in American waters and that goods carried in bond in the United States could be carried only by a company bonded south of the border. (It seems to have escaped everyone that Hill himself was still a Canadian citizen!) Smith, though admiring Hill's strategy, retaliated by selling the *International* to Norman Kittson, the HBC's agent in St Paul, a wily former fur trader.

In the early 1840s Kittson had thumbed his nose at the powerful Hudson's Bay Company by opening a trading post at Pembina on the American side of the border. There he competed with the giant monopoly, purchasing furs from halfbreed trappers who were not under the HBC's direct control. By 1856 Kittson controlled the entire flow of furs from Canada to the United States. That year, 93,000 pelts worth $97,000 passed through St Paul. Two years earlier Kittson had moved to St Paul himself, and there he rapidly became the city's leading citizen, acquiring a grab-bag of investments in gas works, real estate and banks. In 1859, he was elected mayor of the booming junction town. At one time, a Kittson-Hill skirmish would have been a fair match. But at fifty-four, Kittson, no longer robust, had little taste for a head-to-head battle with the thirty-three year old Hill, who exuded energy, ambition and vigour from every pore. By the time Hill muscled his way into the steamboat business Kittson was dreaming of spending long, warm winter days raising racehorses in Florida.

Kittson didn't go down without a fight, however. After he acquired the *International* he and his new rival embarked on a vicious bout of rate cutting. But it wasn't long before the two agreed to cooperate, forming Kittson's Red River Transportation Company, in which Donald Smith retained a silent share.[25] They split the business between their two boats and set rates to the profit of everyone except the public.

It was a business to make fervent monopolists swoon. The Red River Transportation Company dealt mercilessly with any would-be competitors. In 1875 one foolhardy line put two boats on the river, the *Manitoba* and the *Minnesota*. Using his own two vessels and the leverage of his railroad and steamboat agency, Hill strangled the interlopers by slashing rates so deeply that their enterprise was doomed the moment it was launched. When the nuisance went away, the rates shot back up again. From 1872 to 1878 all transportation into and out of Manitoba via the United States was under the control of the Red River Transportation Company, which became a law unto itself. Although rates were somewhat lower than they had been in the past, they didn't drop nearly as much as the huge volumes of freight and passengers warranted. Winnipegers loathed the profitable monopoly. It was an attitude that was to haunt first George Stephen and then the CPR for more than a century.

CHAPTER 2

THE MINNESOTA GOLD MINE

The purchase of the St Paul and Pacific by George Stephen and the Associates turned out to be one of the sweetest business deals in history.

I n retrospect, the takeover of the St Paul and Pacific Railroad was such an obvious bonanza it's hard to imagine why investors weren't falling all over themselves to grab it. It was this American railroad, chartered to run from St Paul, Minnesota, to Emerson on the Canadian border, that brought George Stephen, Donald Smith and J. J. Hill together, providing the basis for their immense fortunes and giving them the confidence and wherewithal to tackle the construction of Canada's impossible dream — a transcontinental railroad ten times as long.*

The St Paul and Pacific, originally chartered as the Minnesota and Pacific in 1857, limped along, underfinanced, and controlled by several different ineffectual groups until Jay Cooke and William Moorhead, the powerful railroad financiers who controlled the Northern Pacific Railroad, purchased it in 1870. Cooke and Moorhead shortsightedly relegated the St Paul Road to a feeder system for the Northern Pacific. When

---

*The main line of the St Paul and Pacific was barely over two hundred miles long, though it had several uncompleted branches as part of the system.

the Northern Pacific went bankrupt in 1873, the St Paul and Pacific was left in limbo, operated by Jesse P. Farley, a court-appointed receiver in his late sixties. Farley's considerable rail-roading experience was negated by laziness and a propensity to make decisions, as a receiver, for his own personal profit.

When Donald Smith and J. J. Hill met in the middle of the blizzard in 1870, they agreed that controlling the transportation corridor from St Paul to Winnipeg was the key to exploiting the riches of the Red River Valley and Manitoba. By 1873, their steamboats had a stranglehold on the river traffic, but they knew that their lucrative monopoly would vanish overnight when the St Paul and Pacific Railroad was finally completed.

Hill made it his business to become intimately informed about the railroad. With the St Paul and Pacific's affairs in disarray, he began serious scheming and by 1876 had a clear-cut plan of action. His meticulous calculations, based on hours of on-site investigation, revealed that an investment of $5,540,180 to buy out its current bondholders and to complete the line to St Vincent would purchase a staggering $19,402,923 in assets, including $11.4 million worth of track already laid and $600,000 in townsite property on the mainline. But the St Paul and Pacific's hidden nugget was land. If the railroad was completed on time, it would earn a land grant, provided by the state of Minnesota, of more than 2.5 million acres, which in Hill's words lay "for the most part in well-settled counties and of a quality above the average of western land, worth at least the U.S. government minimum price for lands within the limit of the grant, $2.50 an acre."[1] Most of the land was worth far more than $2.50 an acre but even at that conservative selling price, the railroad's grant alone was worth $6.7 million.

Hill's figures also showed that, properly managed, the railroad could pay its own way almost immediately. The line could count on a $600,000 net profit annually and the extra freight revenue in good crop years would boost revenue to as much as

The St Paul levee, about 1870

$800,000. If he were right, the St Paul would be one of the most profitable railroads in the world.

The St Paul and Pacific plum was ripe for the picking but there were formidable obstacles. Equity in the line was held by a committee headed by Johan Carp, a Utrecht businessman representing a group of six hundred Dutch investors. Those trusting souls, encouraged by the promise of dividends that never materialized, had purchased St Paul bonds in 1871 for

$11 million.* Another financial reorganization had divided the
St Paul into two companies: the First Division, which actually
owned the completed lines, and the St Paul and Pacific, which
held its other assets. Furthermore, E. D. Litchfield, a financier,†
had a disputed claim against the common stock of the First
Division which he made sure everyone knew he intended to
pursue. Farley, the receiver, was yet another member of the cast,
who continued to spend most of his time looking after himself to
the exclusion of all others. Clouding the situation further was the
well-founded doubt that the St Paul would be able to earn the
bulk of its land grants by completing the line on time.

The pivotal figure in the chain of ownership was John S.
Kennedy, a powerful American banker and railroad financier,
who was acting as agent for the Dutch bondholders and trustee of the mortgages that secured their bonds. The Dutchmen
were trying to recoup some of their investment by foreclosing
on the St Paul's mortgages.

When Hill approached Johan Carp, Carp made it painfully
clear that he thought Hill and Smith, who wasn't present, were
minor players lacking either the stature or financial clout
necessary to carry off such an international deal. The story
could have ended right there, but Smith had been tantalizing
Hill and Kittson with passing references to a mysterious
Montreal financier who might be interested if their own negotiations failed. When Hill's plan fell apart in the face of Carp's
flat rejection, he pressed Smith to produce his man. He was
none other, of course, than Smith's cousin George Stephen.
The meeting was arranged, and Smith and Hill travelled to
Montreal to meet Stephen in May, 1877.

---

*This was an interesting example of railroad financing. Of the $11 million invested by the
Dutchmen in St Paul bonds, only $5 million actually reached the railway company. The
remainder was siphoned off in financing fees and into a fund reserved to ensure that the
bondholders were paid their interest for the first three years. The bondholders were actually
using their own money to guarantee themselves a return on their investment.

†The brother of E. B. Litchfield, who operated the line in the 1860s.

J. J. HILL, HARDLY SERENE at the best of times, arrived in Montreal vibrating with excitement and aching to hammer out terms with the man who could get them the needed millions. Hill had made the journey alone, leaving Kittson sick at home in St Paul. After a brief meeting with Hill, Smith introduced the two men and then waited in the wings to see what developed. Hill faced Stephen in his lair alone.

The St Paul entrepreneur was immediately thrown off stride when he was met not by the fast-talking promoter he expected, but by an elegantly slender, broad-browed and bearded man who spoke and behaved as if he was London's social emissary sent to civilize the colonies. His surroundings only heightened the effect. The rich, dark walls, polished floors and carved mahogany balustrades of the newly completed Bank of Montreal reflected none of the rawness of the young country. The marble-floored corridors resonated with the hollow chords of power, the sort bestowed by centuries of existence, not mere decades. Tall, moulded ceilings enclosed the subtle aura of fortunes made and in the making. Inside Stephen's dark-panelled enclave an elaborate tea was silently proffered by a butler carrying eggshell china on a tray of heavy silver. Hill was subdued and just a little intimidated.*

Stephen spoke in the calm, confident manner of a man with vast resources at his fingertips, and when he casually assured

---

*The sanctum sanctorum of the Bank of Montreal's executive offices evoked the same atmosphere even in the 1920s. Floyd Chalmers, then a young *Financial Post* reporter, recalled the day he was ushered into an interview with Sir Frederick Williams-Taylor, General Manager.

> My appointment was for around twelve o'clock. I had about half an hour with him and then, at half-past twelve, he stood up — he looked immaculate to me — and went behind a screen. He said: "Keep on talking." And he changed his striped trousers to another set of striped trousers. He came out and put on his grey gloves. He thanked me for coming in, pressed a button, and an attendant in a frog-like uniform opened the door of his office. Williams-Taylor walked as far as the inner door of the bank leading to the street. Two attendants there opened the door outside. Still another one, with a broom (because this was in early winter) swept the steps to his car, where a uniformed chauffeur was waiting to take him to the Mount Royal Club for lunch. This kind of protocol reflected the character of the banks which, at the time, didn't have much interest in the public or small businessmen — except to try and impress them. (Quoted in Peter C. Newman's *The Canadian Establishment,* Volume I, p. 107.)

The Bank of Montreal building in Montreal

his visitor that he would have no problem raising the $5 million in short-term funds during a forthcoming trip to England, Hill could only bob his head gratefully. As the heavy carved doors of the bank swung shut, Hill walked away feeling as if a great honour had been bestowed upon him.

The next day Smith confirmed Stephen's interest but mentioned that he wanted to inspect the property before making a final commitment. Hill dashed off a note to Kittson, scarcely hiding his jubilation: "Mr Smith says that both himself and Mr. Stephen are very much pleased with the look of the St. P&Pac matters as shown in our statements maps &c and that he thinks the money matters will be very easy in England, in fact I think he said it was about arranged."[2]

In September, 1877, Kittson, Smith and Hill took Stephen,

John Knuppe (a representative of the Dutch committee) and R. B. Angus (now Stephen's second-in-command at the Bank of Montreal) on a tour of the completed sections of the St Paul and Pacific. Smith and Hill knew from first-hand experience that the Red River Valley was a fertile farming area, but Stephen's idea of farmland was formed by the verdant Scottish countryside and the neat, productive farms of Quebec. The sunburnt prairie, devastated by two successive years of locusts, failed to inspire his confidence. Years later, Donald Smith recalled the trip they took, riding along the completed sections of the railroad. "All went well at first. But beyond Litchfield it was almost nothing but wild, untenanted prairie. Mr. Stephen shook his head ominously. Whence was business to come to the railroad? When would there be settlers in this barren waste?" Stephen's eloquently silent disapproval sent shivers of despair through the party. They attempted to point out something — anything — in the countryside that would spark his interest and lift his black mood. Angus, as always taking his cue from Stephen, sat mute and glum.

> At last the station of De Graff was reached. It was Sunday morning. Around a rude but good-sized structure there were crowds of people; the trails leading toward it were covered with conveyances, most of them drawn by oxen.
> "What is all this?" inquired Mr. Stephen.
> "Why" answered quickly his friends, desperately seizing on any sign of interest, "this is but an instance of what is soon to occur along the whole line of the railroad. This is a colony opened by Bishop Ireland one single year ago. Already the settlers brought in by the Bishop are counted by hundreds, and hundreds of others are coming to join them from different parts of America and Europe. This is Sunday morning, and the settlers are going to Mass."
> The certain rush of immigrants to the West was pictured to Mr. Stephen in glowing terms. He already saw enough to make the prophecy credible. From that moment he was won over to the new enterprise.[3]

At the end of September, 1877, Stephen sailed to London to get financing for the St Paul line. At this point none of the Associates had any intention of risking their own money.

Stephen approached Sir John Rose, governor of the Hudson's Bay Company and senior partner in the prestigious London financial house of Morton, Rose & Company. Rose was the logical source of capital for such an enterprise. Now a refined, sober and respectable financial man, he was also one of Sir John A. Macdonald's closest friends, who had enjoyed many lighthearted, and some drunken, capers with the Canadian prime minister in their earlier years.*

Rose had held the critical Finance portfolio in Macdonald's Confederation Cabinet, resigning in 1869 to go into business. He entered a partnership with Levi P. Morton, a London financial firm that had dealt exclusively in stocks until Rose appeared. The former Canadian MP maintained his strong Tory connections and continued to advise Macdonald as a quasi–high commissioner for Canada. He was an important "mole" inside British financial affairs, passing on to Macdonald vital financial tidbits from Whitehall and elsewhere.† Rose quickly moved his firm, renamed Morton, Rose and Associates, into banking. By the time he met with Stephen in 1877, the firm was involved through ownership, financing or director-ships with more than 10 percent of the total U.S. railroad mileage then in existence.

"What I proposed was this," said Stephen, describing his meeting with Rose. "Here is an enterprise to carry through which requires an advance — I think I named the sum of eight hundred thousand pounds. If you will advance this money to . . . us four gentlemen, . . . we will give you an equal interest with us in the final outcome."[4] Hill's mouthwatering figures, coupled with the offer of a free fifth share in the enterprise and underscored by Stephen's own conviction and prestige,

---

*During one memorable holiday they got up a little act with Rose prancing and growling like a circus bear and Sir John tripping along behind as the strolling minstrel.

†A. T. Galt became the first official high commissioner. Rose, a Scotsman and permanent resident of England, did not qualify for the position. However, lacking Galt's conceit and personal animosities, he was far more useful to Macdonald than Galt ever was.

failed to interest Rose. Or at least so Stephen claimed. "After considerable negotiation, I utterly failed. Nobody believed — or at least I failed to induce anybody to believe — that the property was good for anything."[5] The failure should have been humiliating for one who placed such store in his reputation as a money man, but Stephen was remarkably sanguine about his supposed debacle.

NOTHING WAS STRAIGHTFORWARD and simple where George Stephen was concerned. Far from turning Stephen down flat, Rose expressed the sort of mild interest one would expect from an experienced banker as an opening gambit in any serious negotiations. After all, he had only Stephen's information on which to base his deliberations. Rose duly sent an agent to St Paul to examine the road and take a look at the books. His report was somewhat lukewarm, but the London firm began a serious in-house discussion of the project. As late as June, 1878, Rose was still considering either a loan or an ownership position in the St Paul and Pacific. But he never heard from Stephen on the subject again. When the firm learned that Stephen had placed the financing with his own Bank of Montreal without informing them, Rose and his senior officers were enraged. All the more so when they discovered that Stephen was justifying his dealings with the bank by saying that Morton, Rose had turned him down flat. "An advance such as the Bank of Montreal made to Stephen and his associates would never have been made by a national bank or, if made, would not meet the approval of the Banking Department — In fact a bank that made such an advance would be put in the hands of a receiver," Rose's New York partner George Bliss fumed.[6]

Stephen never had any intention of financing the railroad through London. His cursory trip to England was window dressing to deflect criticism when he borrowed the money from the Bank of Montreal. Using his own bank offered several compelling advantages. First of all, he didn't need to bestow a "fifth share" on it to ensure maximum cooperation; normal interest rates and fees would be more than adequate. More to the point, Stephen's presidency and his and Smith's shareholdings, coupled with Angus's unwavering support, ensured that there would be no difficulties if repayment came a little slowly. What was the point of controlling a bank if you didn't use it?

Stephen's story about the origins of the Bank of Montreal financing for the St Paul and Pacific proved to be quite variable over the years. In 1888 he gave sworn testimony that before the formal agreement to purchase had been reached, no consideration had been given to obtaining a loan from the Bank of Montreal. In fact, he asked Hill and Kittson to execute a demand note for $280,000 to that bank on February 7, 1878, five weeks earlier.[7]

Though the large loan had been in the works as early as February, 1878, Stephen and Angus managed to keep the bank's shareholders in the dark until the June 2, 1879, annual meeting — a full sixteen months later. He would have kept them ignorant entirely had it not been for an impertinent question placed by John McDonald, a prominent shareholder. Stephen, having presented a self-congratulatory report, was about to adjourn when McDonald asked about a rumour he'd heard of the bank's directors' involvement in the financing of an American railroad. Stephen always gave shareholders' questions short shrift and he answered cryptically that the bank had no railroad loans that couldn't be called in at a moment's notice. Angus abruptly short-circuited further prying by stating that the bank's loans were confidential business. He warned that any further demonstration of lack of confidence such as displayed by this line of questioning might result in the withdrawal of the loans from the bank — to its and the shareholders' great misfortune.

The supposed London failure not only provided Stephen with a rationale to use the Bank of Montreal but it also gave him a powerful lever to use against the Dutch bondholders and, not incidentally, his new associates. The Dutchmen, trying

R. B. Angus in later years

to unload their wretched investment for years, were tantalized by the scent of the deal Stephen waved under their noses. As quickly as their hopes were raised they were dashed again when the London financing "fell through." Stephen believed in bargaining from strength. He knew that once the whiff of a settlement was dangled in front of the bondholders and then yanked back, they'd be far more malleable. Hill and Kittson also needed a little bringing into line.

Neither of them was anxious to put up his own money, and even Stephen's London failure hadn't changed their minds. Hill's net worth was a hefty $150,000, but in the depression of 1873–78 he would have been fortunate to realize even half that in cash. Kittson was old and, though wealthy, reluctant to gamble, even on what seemed like a sure thing. On January 2, 1878, with no financing yet in place, Kittson, Hill, Smith and Stephen had travelled to New York to meet John S. Kennedy and discuss a deal. A number of plans were tossed around, but none of them amounted to anything. As the men were leaving on January 5th, Kennedy commented that they would have to consider providing a large amount of cash on short notice themselves if anything was to be salvaged. Stephen blandly replied, with a wave of his hand in the direction of Hill and Kittson, that his colleagues were good for the money. Hill recoiled in shock and an embarrassing little contretemps ensued, broken only by their abrupt departure for the train station.

Hill slunk home to St Paul to be greeted by a chastising letter from Donald Smith, sent via Kittson. "The little episode just as Mr. Stephen and I were leaving Mr. Kennedy's office for the train on Saturday last greatly surprised and I must add not a little pained me, as I felt there must be some grave misunderstanding. . . . I regretted extremely that it should be made to appear to our friends Messrs. J. S. Kennedy and Barnes that there existed between ourselves anything other than the utmost cordiality where we have one and the same intent to serve. I . . . hope to have from you an explanation. . . ."[8] The letter may have been written by Smith and sent to Kittson, but Hill knew that it was Stephen's message and that it was intended for him.

Hill hurriedly sent a grovelling letter to Stephen, leaving no doubt as to who was in charge:

> I am especially sorry that yourself and Mr. Smith or either of you should have got the impression that I differed with you in any way, or that I thought for one moment there was any want of mutual confidence, personal cordiality, or good faith, for I beg to further assure you that I had no such feeling, and I trust that nothing that has occurred will be allowed to disturb the absolute confidence and mutual trust necessary in an affair of the kind we are endeavouring to carry out. . . .
>
> My hesitation was solely due to my desire that neither Mr. Kittson or myself should undertake to do what was totally beyond our power

J. J. Hill

— while at the same time we are ready and entirely willing at all times to risk everything we have got in the world upon our faith in the property, and will gladly join in securing to the fullest extent of our means whatever loans may be necessary to carry out our offer to the Dutch Committee. . . .[9]

From that point, Hill signed his name on whatever Stephen told him to.

STEPHEN'S ELEGANT MACHINATIONS established his ascendancy over the Associates and brought the bondholders to the verge of a favourable deal, then left them panting. But Stephen was a man who left nothing to chance. He decided to buy a little insurance in the form of the Dutchmen's own representative, John S. Kennedy. A few days after the meeting with Kennedy, Stephen invited him to a private meeting, during which he offered him the "fifth share" that Rose had supposedly turned down. The transaction has been variously camouflaged by calling it a "bonification" and the "fifth share" but in simple fact it was a bribe, nothing more, nothing less. John S. Kennedy turned out to be the best purchase of George Stephen's life.

The whereabouts of the fifth share remained a mystery for many years. The Associates, including Kennedy himself, stoutly denied, even under oath, knowing what happened to it. Stephen admitted its existence but he managed to avoid telling anyone what he had done with it.

Ironically, it was Stephen himself who let the secret slip in a boastful 1908 letter to Sir Arthur Bigge, secretary to the Prince of Wales.[10]

> When I first knew Kennedy in 1878 he considered himself a *very rich man*, having by 20 years hard work accumulated *$500,000*. He was agent for the Dutch Bondholders from whom I bought the Bankrupt St. Paul & Pacific Railway, which became the St. Paul Minn. & Manitoba Railway in 1879 & years afterwards the Gt. Northern; Kennedy was very useful to me. To reward him I gave him ⅕ interest making him equal to Hill, Kitson [sic] Smith & myself & that is how he became the Scotch millionaire.*

Kennedy was in a position of the highest trust and ethical responsibility. As trustee of the railroad's mortgages and the bondholders' U.S. representative, he had the greatest moral and legal responsibility to act in the Dutchmen's best interests.

---

*This revelation was uncovered by Heather Gilbert and published in her article, "The Unaccountable Fifth," *Minnesota History* (Spring, 1971), p. 176, but it is crystal clear from reading the Hill-Kennedy correspondence that Kennedy controlled his "fifth" from the beginning. Such depreciating, subtly self-aggrandizing and often wildly inaccurate statements are entirely typical of Stephen. Kennedy, in fact, was far richer than Stephen when they first met, having averaged net earnings from his business of between $200,000 and $300,000 annually for many years. (Kennedy to Hill, February 11, 1877, JJHP) It was as if Stephen had a compulsion to denigrate those he'd successfully bought and who were instrumental in his own success. Even the loyal R. B. Angus, who served Stephen as ably as Kennedy, was a target of Stephen's derision. Angus was, he wrote to Sir John A. Macdonald in 1885, as "facile as clay in the Potters hands" and "made of material that couldn't be trusted." (Stephen to Macdonald, January 7, 1885, NAC)

Counterbalancing these ethical imperatives was the opportunity to make huge sums of money doing what Stephen wanted.

Kennedy, then fifty years old, was a dour, austere man, fussy about his appearance and obsessive about personal cleanliness. He was another of the ubiquitous Scots who dominated the American and Canadian railroading of the time. His banking house, J. S. Kennedy and Company, was one of the most influential railroad financing firms in the United States. By the time he met George Stephen he was already practised in the creative and profitable use of positions of trust, having used his appointment as receiver to gain control of the Indianapolis, Cincinnati and Lafayette Railroad. On his death in 1909, Kennedy's estate was half again as large as that of the legendary financier J. P. Morgan. But wealth never calmed his frequently disabling headaches. His letters to Hill are punctuated by a litany of physical infirmities, "my old turns," as he called his sick spells. As he got older his nervous, hypochondriac disposition overwhelmed him. Retiring early, Kennedy spent his final years travelling from spa to spa in Europe, seeking a cure for his ailments.

With Kennedy's now highly enthusiastic cooperation, all things were suddenly possible. Stephen quickly negotiated a brilliant deal, buying out the bondholders for $5 million using the Dutchmen's own money. This neat trick was accomplished by convincing the Dutchmen — who were encouraged by Kennedy's strong recommendation and the inducement of a 10 percent discount — to exchange their old bonds for new ones in the yet-to-be-reorganized line. The new bonds would be redeemed out of the railroad's future profits, minimizing the amount of cash the Associates had to come up with. In fact, the only immediate cash outlay was $280,000 advanced by the Bank of Montreal, which went as a down payment to cover the bondholders' expenses.* The Associates' plan was to gain

---

*By the time the St Paul sale was finalized, the Bank of Montreal had lent them $750,000. According to Hill the Associates had a total of $2 million tied up in the venture, mainly in loan guarantees.

control of the St Paul and Pacific by foreclosing on the Dutchmen's bonds once the interest came due. In the interim, Farley would continue operating the railroad as receiver.

The contract was signed on March 13, 1878, in Kennedy's New York office.* The Associates' own agreement became official two weeks later. Each of the four — Kittson, Hill, Smith and Stephen — was to have a fifth share of the enterprise, with George Stephen controlling the additional fifth. Stephen was president, Smith vice-president and Hill general manager. As part of the Associates' partnership, Stephen and Smith were added to the board of Hill's and Kittson's Red River Transportation Company, which promptly began to churn out money as never before — a $75,000 net profit in one month alone.

ONCE THE DEAL WITH THE DUTCH bondholders was signed, the Associates' most pressing problem was finishing the railroad in order to get the land grant. Most of the uncompleted sections had to be built over ground that hadn't even been surveyed, much less graded. Hill used his political connections to get the deadlines staggered over three years, but the first one, January 1, 1879, was only months away. It was Hill's job, as general manager of the railroad, to build the line, though he had a lot of help from Kennedy.

If the New York banker hadn't earned his bribe during the negotiations, he more than did so during the construction phase. He provided short-term loans to tide the enterprise over rough patches and personally arranged for the Cambria

---

*The Dutch bondholders must have felt thoroughly whipsawed by Stephen's slick negotiating tactics. There is sufficient ambiguity in their parting gift — an antique silver bowl fashioned to commemorate the 1666 destruction of a sizeable portion of the British fleet by a Dutch admiral — to suggest as much. The Dutchmen likely made no distinction between the origins of a Scot and an Englishman. After Stephen retired to England he was entertaining King George V when the monarch spied the bowl and read the inscription. "Why don't you destroy the damned thing?" he grumped to his host. (Gilbert, *Awakening Continent.* Vol. I of *The Life of Lord Mount Stephen*, p. 49)

Iron Works, in which he had a substantial investment, to supply 8,650 tons of rail for payment primarily in receivers' debentures — debentures which hadn't even been authorized. He also monitored Cambria's scheduling carefully to ensure that the Associates' orders received priority over those of cash customers.

To power the road to completion, Hill called in every favour he'd earned over the years. He knew that if he got the job done at all he might be hammering the last spike as midnight tolled on January 1st. So he made sure there would be no last-minute hitches. "I have it arranged with the Governor to send a friendly engineer to inspect the road and have it accepted by the state the day it is completed," he informed Stephen.[11]

The road forged ahead and fortune glimmered in the Associates' eyes. But their worries weren't over. Litchfield, with his claim against the common stock, proved to be an enormous pest. Hill had a go at him first, but when he bluntly asked for Litchfield's selling price, the intransigent shareholder casually replied, "a million dollars." True to form, Hill lost his temper and threatened the old man with legal action. Litchfield was perfectly happy to go to court and said so. At that point Hill abandoned any pretence at negotiating and stomped out.

A master at getting things done and balancing a dozen demands at once, Hill was hopeless when the delicate touch was required. He went at negotiations like a prize fighter, always wanting to land his heavy punches immediately. If an opponent escaped, he was twice as wary and Hill never got the chance to close in again. "Hill is inclined to make messes of negotiations in which he has no special experience," observed one business colleague after watching him in action.[12]

In subtle matters Stephen reigned supreme. A virtuoso of noncommitment, he took pains to never appear desperate or even anxious to make a deal — refusing to move until his opponent's throat was perfectly positioned for the slash.

Litchfield's claim developed into the most dangerous problem the Associates faced in their takeover effort. Although the Associates thought his claim was legally shaky, they couldn't

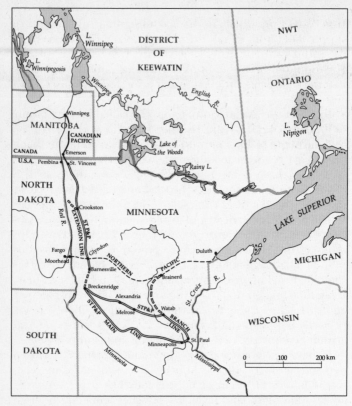

The St Paul and Pacific Railroad (later the St Paul, Minneapolis and Manitoba Railroad), 1873–1879

afford to test it in court. A lawsuit would almost certainly hogtie construction, and if they missed the deadline, the land grants would evaporate. As the weeks went by, however, Litchfield's position strengthened. With every rail laid his stock became more valuable. Worse than the prospect of a delay was the distinct possibility, one that Kennedy kept anxiously bringing up, that the Associates might not be able to take final control of the company by foreclosing on the mortgages. He feared that the railroad would begin to make money too soon, forcing it to pay the interest on its bonds — most of which were held by the Associates. In that case a court might well decide against allowing a foreclosure, reasoning that there was no need for such a drastic step if the railway could become profitable. The Associates would then be left with the bonds but not control. Litchfield rubbed the Associates' noses in their dilemma, grandly referring to "our road" and his plans for it.

Hill knew what had to be done but couldn't bring himself to do it, so he gladly abandoned the negotiations to George Stephen. Although he, too, took an immediate dislike to Litchfield after their first meeting in the summer of 1878 (referring to him thereafter as the "old rat"), Stephen masked his feelings and played down the urgency of the Associates' need to buy his stock. Frantically ramming the construction ahead, Hill grew more distraught by the day. In late 1878 he fired off a volley of letters to Stephen, echoing Kennedy's fears. "The figures under all the circumstances are to me the strongest argument in favor of settling with William Street [Litchfield's office was on William Street in New York] before he learns the situation . . . ."[13]

Stephen, letting none of this information leak out, tranquilly upped his offer to $400,000, but Litchfield stubbornly stuck to his $1 million selling price. Preferring to come at a deal sideways if he could, Stephen manœuvred to undermine Litchfield's strongest bargaining point — his belief that the Associates would eventually pay up to avoid a court battle. But Stephen had a pigeon in his pocket in the form of Frederick Billings, another St Paul railroad man working on a peripheral deal, the success of which depended on Litchfield selling. Stephen sent a letter to Billings who, as expected, took it directly to Litchfield. It read: "My friends in St. P. and N.Y. do not hesitate to say that my offer was absurdly too high. Notwithstanding all that I wrote to Mr. L from Chicago giving him to 2nd Dec. to say yes or no. If he says yes I shall be pleased. If he says no all my friends will be pleased."[14] Thanks to Stephen's little piece of disinformation, Litchfield believed he was losing his suitors. On January 17, 1879, he agreed to sell for $500,000.

On the surface it was Stephen's triumph, but the stage manager of the deal was actually Hill. He knew what had to be done to bring Litchfield around; he just kept losing his temper in the older man's presence and couldn't get the conversation past the shouting stage. Ten days before Litchfield gave in, Hill had written a detailed letter to Stephen prompting him on every move.[15]

ALTHOUGH THE LONG MONTHS prior to the final takeover of the St Paul and Pacific in the summer of 1879 seemed clouded by the constant threat of failure, in the end nothing really went wrong. The Associates won every point they went after. The only blot on the landscape was an ugly lawsuit initiated by Jesse P. Farley on June 13, 1879. The case dragged on until Farley died in 1888, periodically exposing the Associates' affairs to unwanted attention and generating gleeful headlines. Newspaper editors, if they themselves weren't bought and sold by a specific railroad, generally portrayed railway builders and promoters as the lowest forms of life, and the Associates, because their road was so profitable, were prime targets.

Farley claimed that the original idea for the takeover of the St Paul, through the stratagem of purchasing the discounted bonds from the Dutchmen, was his. In return for the cooperation he could readily provide as receiver, he claimed he had been promised a fifth share in the newly organized company. Barefacedly he owned up to having engaged in fraud and other malfeasances in return for the payoff that his alleged co-conspirators had reneged on.

Hill, Smith and Kittson vigorously denied ever making such an arrangement, although Stephen admitted that a "bonification" of some $10,000 or $20,000 might have been mentioned to Farley. The lawsuit bumped its way right up to the Supreme Court of the United States. In the end it came down to Farley's word against that of Hill, Smith, Stephen and Kennedy. The judge found in the Associates' favour. Farley's claims were dismissed, and he has been posthumously branded a lying opportunist. One wonders what the judge would have decided if he'd known that Kennedy, who testified he knew nothing of the fifth share, already had it in his pocket.

The purchase of the St Paul and Pacific by George Stephen and the Associates turned out to be one of the sweetest business deals in history. Their timing was exquisite. The effects of the depression were receding rapidly, the locusts that had been infesting the West disappeared in 1878 and traffic in immigrants and freight was booming, supplemented by carload upon carload of supplies destined for the construction of the Canadian government's railway line from Winnipeg to Pembina. The "obscure" road, renamed the St Paul, Minneapolis and Manitoba Railroad (and thereafter referred to as the Manitoba Road), hadn't even been in operation a year when the Associates were offered $1 million cash to sell out.

The Associates announced a new stock issue: $15 million worth on May 23, 1879, $2 million of which they retained to compensate themselves for their expenses. Within a short time eager investors snapped up the shares, allowing the Associates to pay off the nearly $2 million they'd borrowed to buy out the bondholders and finance construction. Smith was a little perturbed that the market might look askance at the new issue, especially since the railroad had been virtually moribund only months before. "Aren't you afraid that the capitalization will startle the public? Isn't there some danger that we will be charged with watering the stock?" he asked. "Well," shrugged Hill, "we have let the whole lake in already."[16]

The real bonanza came with the Great Bond Grab of 1883. To avoid legal entanglements, a complicated scheme was hatched, allowing the Associates — Stephen, Hill, Kennedy and Smith* — to purchase $10 million worth of bonds for only $1 million.

*Kittson had sold out to the others because of ill health in 1882.

It was a windfall of $9 million, free and clear. George Stephen and the Associates also profited hugely by purchasing numerous mines and other properties in their own names — or more often hidden in a plethora of holding companies — and then at a later date selling them to the railroad at an inflated price. It was a highly profitable practice that Stephen continued with the Canadian Pacific Railway. The technique had the added benefit of being hidden from the prying eyes of the public. One such tidy deal involved Climax Coal Co., purchased in equal shares by Stephen, Smith, Hill and Angus on January 6, 1881, for a total of $63,000. A year later, in January, 1882, though no development work whatever was done on the property, they sold to the Manitoba Road for $210,000, a profit of $36,750 each.[17]

Hill's labours increased the Manitoba Road's operating revenue dramatically but the real key to the line's early fortune was land. Every month sales of land grant allotments injected $100,000 into the company's coffers, and total sales during the critical thirteen-month start-up period were $1,305,932.64. "The average price of lands sold is about $5 per acre," crowed Hill to John S. Kennedy,[18] boasting about doubling his earlier $2.50 per acre estimate. Most of the land was sold within five years for over $13 million. Hill kept a few blocks to himself, some of which later sold for $40 an acre.

THE PURCHASE OF THE ST PAUL AND PACIFIC made George Stephen one of the richest men in the Empire, but he never seemed to appreciate the source of his wealth: J. J. Hill. Hill endured savagely exhausting sixteen-hour days bullying workers, bribing officials and forcing suppliers to lower rates as he raced to meet the construction deadline. At the same time he ran the Red River Transportation Company during two of the busiest years in its history. And at the end of each gruelling day he sat writing letters well into the next morning. They were really elaborate daily reports on the conditions of the road —

some as long as fourteen pages. Years later Hill recalled, "I often worked in my office until one in the morning. One night my wife said she would go to the office with me and bring me home at half past ten. It was a summer night and I gave her a book and a chair by the window, where she presently fell asleep. At two I waked her and took her home."[19]

The wear and tear on Hill of singlehandedly building and running the railroad was compounded by having to use Farley the receiver as an unwilling marionette. Until the Associates gained full control in the summer of 1879 he was still legally in charge of the railroad. Even the most trivial tasks had to be cleared through him. "The fact is," wrote Hill to Stephen in disgust, "Mr. Farley has so much to do that a week or so of hard work lays him up and he has to go home and rest and during his absence there is no one to take any responsibility."[20]

While Hill was slaving away in St Paul, Stephen remained safely ensconced in Montreal, far removed from the realities of everyday railroading: the battles with bureaucrats and minor politicians, the vagaries of the weather and the organization of myriad details regarding supplies and workers. On June 23, 1878, Hill, mired down in his work, wrote a long note to Stephen and Kennedy, who were relaxing at Stephen's summer house at Causapscal on the St Lawrence River. He ended with a wistful statement. "Hope both yourself and Mr Kennedy have a good time with the salmon."[21]

Late in 1880, Stephen dispatched R. B. Angus to lighten Hill's load. The fact that Angus replaced Smith as vice-president while Hill remained in a subordinate position as general manager is a clear indication of exactly where Stephen put Hill's contribution in the scale of things. It has been commonly assumed that Angus was awarded his munificent stipend of 5,500 shares in the Manitoba Road — shortly worth $1 million — as an incentive to leave his position as general manager of the Bank of Montreal. The fact that the shares were allocated in 1879, before he left for St Paul, strongly suggests they were a payoff for keeping the Bank of Montreal in line and for protecting the Associates from criticism. In the end Angus worked with Hill in St Paul for less than a year before he returned to Canada.

Once the financing was assured, Stephen needed Hill far more than Hill needed Stephen, something that never seemed to occur to either of them. It was Hill who was developing the expertise and the vision to make the enterprise work. But for all intents and purposes the letters that passed between the two give an entirely different impression. In January, 1879, Stephen let it be known to Hill via Farley (an insulting bit of circumlocution) that he was concerned about the construction costs. Far from taking umbrage at Stephen's roundabout comments, Hill replied, "I am glad you have called attention to this. . . ." Once again he patiently justified his actions to Stephen as if he were a junior clerk addressing a senior officer: "The cost of repairs . . . shows the importance of using the best ties, and a good gravel ballast put on the track as early as it can be done, and in that way capitalize this heavy outlay, besides a great saving in the area of . . . rolling stock, and the increased immunity from accidents."[22]

When the first fiscal year ended on June 30, 1880 — little more than two years after the Associates had first begun taking over the road — net earnings were $1.58 million, double Hill's earlier estimates of $700,000 or $800,000. From then on Hill's biggest problem was hiding the line's profit lest it prove an embarrassment. In 1881 net earnings rose to nearly $2 million. A year later they had more than doubled to $4.7 million on gross revenue of $9.3 million,[23] and by 1884 Hill was boasting that the line was completely debt free.[24]

In 1885, each of the Associates' one-fifth share in the Manitoba Road was worth $5 million when the stock hit $170. Even so, the line was undervalued because of Hill's tactics of pumping every available dollar — 13 million of them in five years — into upgrading the railroad. It was a tactic destined to make the Manitoba Road a fearsome competitor, as others would learn to their sorrow.

CHAPTER 3

THE RELUCTANT
RAILROADER

*It was classic George Stephen, couched in the manner
of one with no self-interest in the matter, giving
dispassionate advice to a friend.*

Financing the CPR was George Stephen's great public
achievement. It won him a knighthood and made him a
peer of the realm. But once the line was laid he began to claim
he'd been either tricked or coerced into taking charge. "It was
the success of this venture [the Manitoba Road] that led Tupper
and Pope to inveigle me into taking up the C.P.R.," Stephen
wrote to Sir Joseph Pope, in 1914, "which I was most unwilling
to do and refused doing . . . and only yielded to the pressure
which Hill and Angus [exerted on me], who were both living in
St. Paul and looking after the St. P. M. & M. They assured me
that if I would consent to head the Syndicate, they [Hill and
Angus] would do the work and build the road without bothering me in any way. I yielded and many a day during the next 6
or 7 years did I bitterly repent doing so."[1]

During their long years together Hill never persuaded
Stephen to do anything that he "was strongly opposed to." In
any case Hill, who was utterly absorbed in running the Manitoba Road, had been leery of Sir John A. Macdonald's transcontinental line from the outset. The very idea of Angus
pressuring or coercing his mentor, George Stephen, is
hilarious. A subservient letter Angus wrote to Stephen in

September, 1880, when he is supposedly forcing the latter into taking part in the CPR, clearly shows the nature of their relationship. "With regard to the Canada Pacific," wrote Angus, "if you and our friends take it up as seems now certain, I want to share with them the risk and labour if agreeable to you."[2]

Stephen had been carefully scrutinizing the ebb and flow — mostly ebb — of the Pacific railway fortunes since 1871 when Parliament had refused his application to build a railway from Fort Garry to St Vincent. His letters to Macdonald between 1877 and 1879 are sprinkled with references to railway matters. Then, in early 1880, Stephen took control of a failing line — the Credit Valley Railway, owned largely by railroad contractor George Laidlaw. With this company in his hands Stephen had positioned himself to be an important player in any cross-Canada railway plan, no matter who built it. Though almost insolvent and incomplete, the line was chartered to cover the 121 miles between Toronto and St Thomas, Ontario, near Lake Erie. At first the investment appeared simply to be the act of a good samaritan, but on closer inspection it is obvious that the Credit Valley was perfectly placed to become part of a transcontinental line. Furthermore, it was the kind of multifaceted purchase that Stephen preferred because it paid off in many ways. It gave him control, at firesale prices, of a line that was sure to be the basis of a national railway's southern Ontario feeder system — a system that the line had to develop if it was to avoid being shut out of eastern Canada by the Grand Trunk Railway, the British-financed railway with a large network of lines in Ontario and Quebec.

Secondly, Stephen earned the undying gratitude of an extremely useful man, George Laidlaw, which began to pay off in 1881 when Laidlaw helped Stephen take over the Toronto, Grey and Bruce Railway. It was a key acquisition, providing a supply route for equipment and materials destined for the eventual CPR main line along the north shore of Lake Superior.

A bonus in the whole deal was the appreciation of John A. Macdonald, a close friend of Laidlaw. Stephen unblushingly informed Macdonald of his largesse: "As a friend of Laidlaw you will be glad to hear that I have succeeded in getting him and the Credit Valley Railway out of their troubles, and putting both in an independent position. . . ."[3] The prime minister was, of course, the man that Stephen would have to deal with if he hoped to build the transcontinental line.

STEPHEN EDGED INTO THE CPR with mincing steps and verbal feints. The act was played out largely for Macdonald's benefit, a negotiating partner who could match every Stephen bluff and parry with a dozen of his own. Stephen was a world-class schemer on his own turf but Macdonald's Machiavellian plans and pork barrel politicking were something he didn't understand or appreciate. Because Stephen never fathomed Macdonald's motivations he couldn't control him. Stephen saw right to the heart of a problem but Macdonald often seemed to take the scenic route to its solution, craftily parcelling out favours, juggling priorities, delaying and dodging. If Macdonald didn't see how to resolve an issue, he procrastinated until conditions changed in his favour — a practice that earned him the nickname Old Tomorrow. Stephen, on the other hand, was accustomed to altering circumstances to suit his needs.

Not only was Stephen faced with the tangled mass of Macdonald's political considerations, but the PM's drinking binges injected a disquieting element of randomness into any negotiations. Stephen could never be sure when Macdonald became adamant or evasive on an issue whether he was doing so because of favours owed, for the good of the country or simply because he was badly hung over. George Stephen was not a pious man but when Macdonald's empurpled, beaky nose seemed a little more vein-shot than usual, he had difficulty hiding his disapproval.

Macdonald's drunkenness was indiscriminate; he celebrated both triumph and sorrow with brandy. During the months of negotiations leading up to the proclamation of Confederation on July 1, 1867, Macdonald was pickled almost continuously. "Add to all this that Macdonald has been in a constant state of partial intoxication and you may judge whether we have had a pleasant week," an exasperated Alexander Galt, minister of finance, and a key figure in the Conservative party, wrote to his wife on the eve of Confederation.[4] On at least one occasion, Macdonald was so drunk he had to be carried out of the Parliamentary lunchroom.

Stephen's rigidly correct deportment was in great contrast to Macdonald's frequently coarse behaviour.* The PM could slum with the best of them and Stephen, though an ordinary man himself, associated strictly with those in his new financial and social class. Stephen kept his passions, vices and fears well hidden. Macdonald, on the other hand, flaunted his. Richard J. Cartwright, who walked away from the Tories in 1866 when Macdonald gave the minister of finance post to Francis Hincks, primly charged the drunken prime minister with making improper advances at a state ball towards Princess Louise of Britain, wife of the governor general, the Marquis of Lorne.† He "presume[d] to take a liberty" with the princess, who was so repulsed "she was obliged to request his retirement from her presence."[5] Certainly the greatest trial for Stephen was Macdonald's penchant for disappearing, sometimes for days, at critical times. No one, not even his wife, could find him and Stephen would be left to pace and fret until he made his unapologetic return. But even in his cups, Macdonald was a brilliant manipulator of men and events.

George Stephen had every reason to approach the transcontinental railway with the greatest caution. Not only did he have Macdonald to contend with, but almost nothing to do with the scheme had gone right since 1871. That year three

---

*Macdonald's vagrant-like appearance could be quite a shock to even the most ardent supporter. "Seedy-looking old beggar, isn't he?" exclaimed a young Tory after seeing Macdonald for the first time during his triumphant 1886 cross-Canada tour. (Sir Joseph Pope, *Public Servant: The Memoirs of Sir Joseph Pope,* ed. Maurice Pope, p. 53)

†Sandra Gwyn, in her book *The Private Capital,* presents an amusing and yet pathetic glimpse of the days of Lord Lorne, a practising homosexual, and the highly sexed Princess Louise in Canada.

competing parties were vying for the right to build Canada's great road. David L. Macpherson, a partner in the railway contracting firm Macpherson, Gzowski and Company, a close friend of Macdonald and an important Tory fund raiser, headed up one group. The second group was led by C. J. Brydges, general manager of the Grand Trunk Railway. Sir Hugh Allan, head of the profitable Montreal Ocean Steamship Company (the future Allan Line), Canada's primary link with Great Britain, headed up the third. Unfortunately, each group had serious deficiencies as far as Macdonald was concerned.

On the face of it, Allan's bid was the logical choice. Widely hailed as Canada's richest man and enjoying considerable stature in England, Allan had vast business interests, including coal and textile operations and the Canadian Telegraph Company. Big-bellied and hard-eyed, he was a virulently ambitious man and not overly fastidious about issues of ethical propriety. In short, he was just the sort of man who could push to completion Macdonald's impossible promise to British Columbia: a rail connection with the east by 1881.

But Allan's group was politically impossible. At the heart of it was Jay Cooke, the prominent American financier and railroad promoter who owned, with a group of others, the Northern Pacific. Cooke intended to use the Pacific railway to give his line a link to the west coast. Also on his mind was ownership of vast tracts of western Canadian land, long rumoured to be fabulously fertile. Cooke made the mistake of giving his intentions voice. In an 1872 prospectus for Northern Pacific land grant bonds, his line was described as "an international enterprise, whose early completion will strengthen the unity and promote the prosperity of the Dominion of Canada, and render accessible the vast and fertile portion of British America which extends from Winnipeg to the Rocky Mountains."[6]

Macdonald had no intention of rendering accessible any part of Canada to Americans, let alone trying to sell a transcontinental road owned, built and operated by them, to the voters. "Take steps to make known that Dominion is about to construct Pacific Railway through British Territory," he cabled to John Rose in London after seeing the Cooke prospectus.[7] Brydges was eliminated because his Grand Trunk was the single most unpopular company in the country. Owned by the British and run by a London-based committee headed by Sir Henry Tyler, Canadians had little conviction that anything the GTR did was in their best interests. Macdonald's personal preference was Macpherson, but his crony simply didn't have the financial depth or stature to tackle the job. Old Tomorrow kept all three groups dangling, hoping to encourage an amalgamation with a suitable political blend or to flush a new bidder out of the wings.

HUGH ALLAN'S INTRIGUE over the railway contract has often been described as a departure from a hitherto unblemished career. In truth, he took to corruption with a flair and gusto that suggests some small experience. Never a particularly patient man, Allan grew increasingly irritated through 1871 with Macdonald's incessant harping about a predominantly Canadian railroad. The only way to bend Macdonald in his favour, he reasoned, was to improve the political climate a little. First he tried to buy up his foes and competitors with substantial offers of free stock in his proposed company. Macpherson, Brydges and influential politicians like Donald A. Smith were all offered $100,000 worth. He even honoured the press with an offer of $50,000 in shares — waved under the nose of George Brown, editor of the Toronto *Globe*, and its railway critic.

When that failed, Allan went right to the source of his problem, the politicians — hatching a brilliant scheme of bribery and blackmail. The key individual in Allan's plans was Sir George Etienne Cartier, leader of the Quebec wing of the Conservative party and the man who carried Quebec for Macdonald. On the surface, Cartier was an unlikely choice. A fighter in business and on the hustings, he was a solid Macdonald ally. The respect between the two men, born of mutual dependence, ran deep. Cartier was one of a handful upon whom Macdonald bestowed and inflicted his confidences and anxieties. But in 1873 Cartier was ill with a mysterious swelling in his arms and legs, a malady that appeared to sap his will as well as his ability to control the always fractious Quebec caucus.

The most astonishing aspect of the Allan affair is not that it happened, but that it was so well documented. In July, 1872, Allan actually outlined his blueprint for buying the government to General G. W. Cass, one of the "yankee confreres" Macdonald so vehemently opposed. It was nineteenth-century political hardball at its best—or worst.

Sir Hugh Allan

In essence, Allan planned to subvert Cartier's forty-five member Quebec caucus through bribes to newspaper writers, editors and publishers and by sending paid agents into the countryside to influence the inhabitants, most especially the powerful village priests. "This succeeded so well," gloated Allan, "that in a short time, I had 27 out of the 45 on whom I could rely, and the electors of the ward in this city [Montreal], which Cartier himself represents, notified him that unless the contract for the Pacific Railway was given in the interests of Lower Canada, he need not present himself for reelection. He did not believe this, but when he came here and met his constituents, he found, to his surprise, that their determination was unchangeable. He then agreed to give the contract as required. . . ."[8]

Cartier's capitulation was swift. With only token scratching at the noose so deftly placed around his neck, he set about running Allan's errands and organizing the substantial campaign "donations" necessary to bring Macdonald around to his viewpoint. "The friends of the Government will expect to be assisted with funds in the pending elections," Cartier stated baldly to Allan on July 30, 1872, "and any amount which you or your Company shall advance for that purpose would be recouped to you. A memorandum of immediate requirements is below." The memo read:

NOW WANTED

Sir John A. Macdonald	$25,000
Hon. Mr. Langevin	15,000
Sir G. E. C. [Cartier]	20,000
Sir J. A. (add.)	10,000
Hon. Mr. Langevin	100,000
Sir G.E.C.	30,000[9]*

In all, Allan spent the huge sum of $365,000 to implement his plan, which culminated in the successful re-election of the

---

*The names are duplicated presumably to separate constituency needs for money from personal payments to the men themselves. While the commission discovered that substantial amounts of Allan's money were bribes for election purposes, it was never proven that Macdonald benefited personally.

Conservatives on September 1, 1872. Six days before the election Macdonald personally cabled Allan. "I must have another $10,000. Will be the last time of calling. Do not fail me. Answer today."[10]

WHITHER ARE WE DRIFTING?

Sir John A. Macdonald always claimed he had nothing to do with the Pacific Scandal bribes.

THE ELECTION WAS A SQUEAKER, with the Tories retaining power by only two seats. In the months previous, Macdonald had been bucking and kicking against the long list of Allan's railway contract demands. He caved in on several issues but stood firm against Allan's continued association with the Americans and his desire to provide generous stock in the enterprise to his friends. Now confident of getting the contract, Allan finally realized his U.S. colleagues would have to go. The group was coming apart anyway, but when George McMullen, one of the partners, heard about the inevitable dissolution he was furious at what he took to be Allan's double cross. A vengeful man, he went to Macdonald with threats and accusations, supporting them with an appalling quantity of documented information about Allan's activities. McMullen was as adept at deception as Allan, and though he gave the Conservatives the assurance that he and Allan had come to terms, he turned his documents over to the Liberals. Armed with the evidence of skullduggery and reinforced by papers burgled from Allan's safe, the Opposition attacked. The Liberals' foppish smoothy Lucius Seth Huntingdon languidly rose on April 2, 1873, and introduced a resolution condemning the government's behaviour.

The motion was defeated, but over the next several months, as revelations about the Pacific Scandal were heaped one upon the other in a smelly pile, Macdonald's party disintegrated. One member after the next went over to the other side or chose to abstain from the final vote. In the end the government's future hinged on the decisions of one man—none other than Donald A. Smith.

Smith was an enigmatic Parliamentarian. Elected as an independent for Selkirk, Manitoba, in 1871, he had always followed the Tory line. Nonetheless, few knew where his true loyalties, concerning his country or the party, lay. On November 4, 1873, at 1:00 A.M. Donald Smith stood to speak on the Pacific Scandal. The debate on the Throne Speech had raged and thundered for six long days, inciting even the most passive to denounce their opponents in searing language. Smith, in contrast, remained irritatingly silent and calm in the storm that swelled around him. When he rose the House was hushed and expectant. Sir John A., slumped in his seat, looked like a cadaver. He had met with Smith earlier and tried to work out a last-minute deal. He feared the worst — but Smith didn't rush the execution. Instead he cruelly played with the Tories like a cat with a paralyzed mouse.

One minute they were assured of victory, the next they were plunged into despair. "His opening remarks were complimentary to Sir John and his great service to Canada," recalled George Ross, then a rookie Liberal MP, "and with that the faces of the Opposition lengthened. But Mr. Smith had not finished. With respect to the transaction between the Government and Sir Hugh Allan, he did not consider that the First Minister took the money with any corrupt motive. He felt that the leader of the Government was incapable of taking money from Sir Hugh Allan for corrupt purposes. And now we thought we were done for."[11]

At this point a crowd of eager Conservatives scuttled out, sneering derisively at the Opposition. They made their way to the Parliamentary restaurant, where they popped champagne corks and set about getting a head start on celebrations.[12] As faint bars of "Rule, Britannia" and "God Save the Queen" reached the House, Smith's face grew sad but his words more harsh. "But wait a moment," Ross continued. "He would be most willing to vote confidence in the Government (loud cheers from the Government side) could he do so conscientiously (great Opposition cheers). 'Conscientiously' — it was a bolt from the blue to the Government side of the House. To the Opposition it was a song of deliverance, and we all concluded that a Scottish conscience was a good thing to keep on hand."[13]

"For the honour of the country," Smith ended, cutting the rope, "no Government should exist that has a shadow of suspicion resting upon it, and for that reason I cannot give it my support."[14]

SMITH THEN AND LATER explained his "flop," as the Conservatives called it, as a matter of high conscience, a contention
he was forced to make time and time again. Sir Charles Tupper,
who never forgave Smith, offered the House his own interpretation in a volcanic 1876 session: "Mr. Smith was a representative of the Hudson's Bay Company and he had been
pressing his right honourable friend [Macdonald] for public
money; Sir John held back, and Mr. Smith came to the conclusion that it would be just as well to jump the fence if there
was to be a change of Government. But Mr. Smith was a canny
man; he held back and sat on the fence and watched the
course, certainly not in the interests of his country, because he
did not want to jump too soon and find he had jumped into a
ditch. But when he came to the conclusion that the Government was going out, he made the bolt, and I have no doubt that
he has had a great deal of reason since for congratulating
himself on having jumped as he did."[15]

A hot debate ensued, during which Tupper repeatedly called
Smith a "Mean Treacherous coward!" as well as a host of other
epithets the overwhelmed Hansard reporter neglected to record. After the debate he and Macdonald were so beside themselves with rage that the sergeant-at-arms had to be called in to
restrain them. Smith, unperturbed by the insults, simply strolled
past his apoplectic former colleagues.

Matters of conscience aside, the key to Smith's actions most
likely lay in the awarding of the Pacific railway contract, in
which he had a clear personal interest. Certainly no one knew
better than he the potential wealth of the northwest, and he
wasn't anxious that the lush Red River territory be entrusted to
the whims and self-interest of Hugh Allan. Macdonald had
offered Smith a chance to participate in the venture with a
position on Allan's board, but the bull-headed Allan was a
difficult man to work with, particularly if you had your own
ideas about how things should be done. Smith had turned
down the offer.

Donald Smith could never be accused of lacking in intestinal
fortitude. When a general election was called in 1873 he

unhesitatingly stood for the Selkirk seat, in support of the Liberal leader, Alexander Mackenzie. During the campaign, Smith faced numerous questions about his conduct. He stuck firmly to his conscience, which in turn stuck firmly in the craw of his opponents. "Smith!" cried Thomas Wilson, an opposing speaker tired of the endless sanctimony. "Why, fellow-citizens, who is Smith? What is Smith? Is the palladium of our destinies to be entrusted to Smith? What has Smith done that he should seek to grasp the Ark of the Covenant with one hand and with the other wrestle for the sceptre of the Almighty? Smith, why Smith isn't a name, but an occupation!"[16]

TUPPER WOULD NEVER HAVE ADMITTED it, but Macdonald might have conceded, if only to himself, that Smith's treachery came at a fortuitous moment. If the Tories had to lose power, it couldn't have come at a better time. A depression was dawning, the national railway scheme was in a shambles and the country mired in debt. Better to turn the whole mess over to someone else for awhile, let him get tarred with failure, then ride in like white knights and save the country.

Alexander Mackenzie, the former stonemason, faced a cruel dilemma when he formed the government in November, 1873.* A painfully honourable man, Mackenzie felt bound by the pact with British Columbia, yet he had been opposed to the project — at least as Macdonald conceived it — from the beginning. Two years had passed since the Tories had promised British Columbia that the railway to the west would be completed by 1881, but not a rail had been laid.

More pressing even than railway matters was the unhappy state of his own party. One historian described Mackenzie as "stout, serviceable Scotch tweed, which would wear well, stand up to hard usage, and outlast more stylish materials two to one."[17] Serviceable he may have been but inspiring he was not,

---

*Mackenzie formed the government in November because Macdonald resigned, but the election was not held until January 22, 1874.

*Alexander Mackenzie (holding the whip) takes control as Sir John A.
lags behind.*

at least not enough to attract or create more than an unim-
pressive and insipid Cabinet. Edward Blake, the former premier of Ontario, should have been a formidable weapon at
Mackenzie's side. Instead, he was one of the liabilities that
made the new PM's time in office a misery. Brilliant, emotional,
blind to his own faults and ultra-sensitive to those of others,
Blake had all the loyalty of a switchblade. He was convinced
that the job of prime minister rightly belonged to him. Unwilling to compromise, he eroded Mackenzie's leadership. When
Mackenzie offered him a portfolio, Blake refused, preferring
to have nothing rather than second best.

Nor had Mackenzie been able to persuade Luther Holton,
the veteran Quebec member and one of the few real Liberals
in the government with significant experience, to take a portfolio. Those members who did have experience were turncoats
like Richard Cartwright, his minister of finance. Five others,
including the redoubtable Smith, were given portfolios as pay-
offs for abandoning Macdonald during the Pacific Scandal.

It wasn't the soundest foundation upon which to build an untried government.

Then there were the money worries. The frugal Mackenzie chafed and fretted over the economic burden he had done nothing to create but which he was expected to relieve. The depression slashed into budgetary revenue which dropped from $24.6 million in 1874 to $22.6 million in 1875 and hovered there until 1878. Macdonald, freely handing out goodies to grease the way for the 1874 election and paying for the initial railway survey, had managed to boost government expenditure by $4 million in less than a year. Mackenzie was left with the unpopular prospect of raising taxes to eliminate the deficit.

Hampering Mackenzie still further was his own sense of propriety, or squeamishness as some saw it. Macdonald had larded the civil service with party hacks and old friends. As a result, many of the bureaucrats, the people Mackenzie relied on to implement his policies, owed their jobs and thus allegiance to Macdonald. Mackenzie abhorred the "spoils system" that Macdonald had perfected but his sense of fair play stopped him from wholesale dismissals. Surrounded by incompetence, undermined by sabotage and forever fending off the greedy, Mackenzie felt like a man under constant attack: "Friends expect to be benefited by offices they are unfit for, by contracts they are not entitled to, by advances not earned. Enemies ally themselves with friends and push their whims to the front. Some attempt to storm the office. Some dig trenches at a distance and approach in regular siege form. I feel like the besieged, lying on my arms night and day. I have offended at least 20 parliamentary friends by defence of the Citadel. A weak minister here would ruin the party in a month and the country very soon."[18]

Underlying it all was the railway bugaboo. Both Mackenzie and Blake did, in fact, support the construction of the line, but they wanted to build it in stages as the country could afford it and traffic warranted. They both thought that the most sensible proposition was for a route that ran through the United

States and then up the Red River Valley to Fort Garry. And, of course, such a plan pleased Donald Smith, who had his eye on the Red River Valley.

The Liberals had denounced the 1871 agreement with British Columbia in the strongest possible terms. But now they were in power, and the 1881 deadline was looming. In 1874 Mackenzie pushed through the Canadian Pacific Railway Act, offering a subsidy of $12,000 cash and 20,000 acres of land per main-line mile to the contractor with the most suitable bid. There wasn't a single nibble. Those capitalists who hadn't been frightened away by the whole Pacific Scandal mess were lying low until economic times improved.

Mackenzie had no choice but to take over the construction himself, adopting a cautious, piecemeal strategy aimed at appeasing British Columbia while constructing a minimum amount of track. His plan was to build as few short lines as possible, linking them up to steamboats and existing railroads — just enough to satisfy the demands of the west without incurring the wrath of his divided caucus or the electorate. He personally took on the thankless Ministry of Public Works, mainly because he had no one else he could trust with such a delicate portfolio. At the same time he reopened negotiations with British Columbia, hoping to ease the terms of Confederation.

STEPS WERE BEING TAKEN but far too small ones to satisfy the critics. "Mr. Mackenzie has been tacking about among the magnificent water stretches for two years and a half;" snorted a Toronto *Mail* editorial, ". . . yet to this day nobody knows what he purposes doing, and it is a very doubtful point whether he himself knows. If it were not for the mountain of steel rails on the Lachine canal, we should say that he did not intend to build the road at all."[19]

Precious little was accomplished under Mackenzie's stewardship, apart from the completion of the Pembina branch line, running from St Boniface to the Manitoba border, linking

Winnipeg with eastern Canada via the United States and, incidentally, with the Associates' Manitoba Road. Considering the financial conditions of the time, however, it's doubtful anyone could have done better. Only 237 miles had actually been laid, but from 1874 to 1878 $6,469,361 had been spent on construction and preparing for construction. Total railroad expenditure for the period, including surveys, was $8,812,331.* In comparison, in 1877, the total cost of running the government was $14,889,900. What Mackenzie had accomplished by appeasement and incremental progress was to keep the spark of the transcontinental railroad alive, ready to be brought to full flame when economic conditions improved and the right group came forward.

Alexander Mackenzie's beleaguered and wretchedly unsatisfying tenure came to an end on September 17, 1878. Macdonald's Conservatives rode back into power on the wings of their National Policy, a code name for a protective tariff designed to shield Canadian industries and end the rampant dumping of American overproduction at cut-rate prices that had occurred during the 1873–78 depression. On the eve of his re-election the world obligingly began to haul itself out of its bleak economic bog, but still, Old Tomorrow wasn't about to do anything hasty in the matter of the railway. The last thing that Macdonald wanted to do, even after the Pacific Scandal, was to be saddled with building the road himself. Aside from anything else, he would have no one to blame, no convenient scapegoat, should anything go wrong. His almost somnolent approach to picking up the railway promise and running with it led a few sarcastic members in the B.C. legislature to dub him "Old Never Never."

---

*The surveying, commissioned in 1871 by Sir John A. Macdonald, and carried out by Sandford Fleming (later knighted), was extremely costly to the Canadian government in dollars and cents: $3,734,000 from 1871 to 1878. But it was even more costly in human lives. By 1872 fourteen surveyors had died, half in forest fires and half by drowning. Before the surveying was completed, the carnage would hit nearly forty, not counting an unknown number of Indians who weren't considered worth including. Ironically, the bulk of Sandford Fleming's survey, with its huge cost in money and lives, was never used.

Sir Charles Tupper

By virtue of his dedicated slashing at Mackenzie's lackadaisical railway progress, Sir Charles Tupper assured himself of the Public Works portfolio and the new Ministry of Railways and Canals when it was formed. He grabbed both jobs, determined to make up for the treachery and scandal of the Pacific Railway contract fiasco. In April, 1879, in a move designed to show progress, Tupper reopened the question of the route through the Yellowhead Pass and the choice of Burrard Inlet as the western terminus. A month later he grandly announced the commencement of 125 miles of track construction in British Columbia — an empty gesture, since no route had yet been chosen. He made the extremely popular decision to reroute the main line through Winnipeg instead of Selkirk and onward to Portage-la-Prairie.

THE INCORPORATION OF THE MANITOBA ROAD, on May 23, 1879, received little attention in railway financial circles initially. The London *Times* dismissed it as "an obscure" Canadian road. But closer to home the rumours about the profits the Associates stood to make from their coup were not long in spreading. Any doubts were eliminated when the company published its first annual report in May, 1880, revealing net earnings of $1.58 million. It was the most profitable new line in railroad history. "Catch them while their pockets are full," John Henry Pope, the influential minister of agriculture and one of the strongest Conservative supporters of a transcontinental railway, advised Macdonald.[20]

Macdonald needed no prompting. When the report came out he had been in office nearly two years and still the railway burden hung, unrelieved, around his neck. Tupper was impatient to forge ahead, even if it meant making direct overtures to capitalists. But Macdonald was biding his time. All along he had been thinking about a syndicate led by George Stephen but he didn't want to play all his aces at once.

Flushed with the glories of their American gold mine, Stephen, Smith and Angus had been privately discussing the transcontinental line. Stephen saw several reasons to get involved. Hill, Stephen and Smith had reached an agreement to lease the Pembina branch from the Canadian government, but the agreement was tenuous. Once the Canadian Pacific was completed their deal ended. As Hill repeatedly pointed out, if an unfriendly group built the transcontinental and reneged on the lease, the profitable carpet of the Manitoba Road could be yanked right out from under them.

Manitobans, disgusted with the stranglehold on all traffic to Winnipeg via the Red River Transportation Company and the Manitoba Road, would have been only too delighted to give the Associates a fast exit from the province. A revitalized Northern Pacific still hovered avariciously. Its promoters would jump at the chance to get into the Red River Valley, and Manitobans were contrary enough to let them in, if only for

First locomotive in the Canadian West arriving in St Boniface, near Winnipeg, in 1877

the sake of getting rid of the Associates. Even the eastern press derided the Pembina arrangement, saying transportation had "already been too long dictated simply by regard for the interests of Mr. Donald A. Smith."[21] The Winnipeg *Times* accused Hill of dropping $1 million into the greasy palms of officials to pull off the lease agreement.

After months of pestering, Tupper persuaded Macdonald to go full steam ahead in a search for someone to build the railway from Lake Nipissing to the Pacific. The dribs and drabs of construction were getting them nowhere except into hot water with British Columbia, which was making noises again about secession. Macdonald agreed, and the Ram of Cumberland — so named for his dalliances with women — formulated a plan.

He and Macdonald were after Stephen from the start but their approach was made subtly and circuitously, in Stephen's own style. Tupper submitted a memorandum to Cabinet on June 15, 1880, detailing his position that it would take a cash subsidy of $45.5 million plus a land grant of 25 million acres to get a private group interested in building the railway.* Cabinet gave Tupper the authority to seek out the capitalists he needed, but they substantially cut down the offer to $20 million and 30 million acres.

Guided by the crafty Macdonald, Tupper continued his machinations, aided by a sudden rash of aspiring railway barons. After seven years of drought, when railroad backers were as scarce as a budget surplus, they came bounding out of the bushes. There were whispers about the Brassey firm of Great Britain, which had built the Grand Trunk. Andrew Onderdonk, the contractor on the Kamloops-to-Yale section, was said to be getting up a syndicate, and Duncan McIntyre, controlling shareholder in the Canada Central Railway, a short but important line, had put out feelers as well.

To the irritation of many party members, Macdonald treated

---

*Tupper calculated that the subsidy would be repaid within ten years through the sale of the remaining 75 million acres of the 100 million that Parliament had approved to finance the railway.

every offer and rumour with exaggerated seriousness. Even Lord Dunmore got a hearing. A jolly, optimistic chap, Dunmore found great favour at tea parties but not in political circles. Alexander Campbell, Macdonald's former law partner and a frequent drinking buddy,* was astonished that the prime minister should even consider the aristocratic lightweight. "You spoke of Lord Dunmore as if his name added weight, great weight, to the proposal made by him and Mr. Brown [of the financial firm Puleston, Brown and Company, which Dunmore represented], whereas it seemed to me just the sort of thing men of business and of means would not resort to, and tricksters and stock-riggers would — I mean to put forward a nobleman. And besides that he is, if I rightly understand it, a spendthrift and most probably a dupe of some knave or other."[22]

In the wings, but not out of the play, was Duncan McIntyre. Four days after the Cabinet meeting a confidential memorandum laying out the government's best offer of $20 million and 30 million acres was sent for his perusal. It was essentially Tupper's opening gambit to hook Stephen. He knew that McIntyre had neither the means nor the stature nor the stomach to carry out the project on his own, and he suspected him of acting on Stephen's behalf. Stephen liked to have a front man, and Smith usually played that part, but the continuing hostility of the Tory caucus towards Smith demonstrated that his cousin's visible presence was a liability.

Less than a month after the initial Cabinet meeting, McIntyre responded with a counter offer of $26.5 million and 35 million acres of land. The Cabinet wouldn't budge, and McIntyre broke off negotiations on July 5th. Four days later a letter from Stephen to Sir John A. ended the shadow boxing. It was classic George Stephen, couched in the manner of one with no self-interest in the matter, giving dispassionate advice to a friend. It alternated between sadly enumerating the failings of the other

---

*Campbell was knighted in 1884 and became leader of the Senate in 1885.

groups seeking the charter and humbly revealing his own virtues and capabilities. Threaded through the letter is the spectre of failure should Macdonald make the wrong choice — that is, not to follow Stephen's advice. It was a tactic Stephen would use many times in future dealings with the prime minister.

Private and Confidential

My dear Sir John,

Referring to your private and confidential note of the 5th. instant. . . . I quite understand the difficulties the Government have to contend with in dealing with the work of constructing the Pacific Railway: they have to be guided by considerations quite different from those that you or I would have to deal with were it a personal matter in which we were free to use our own best judgement.

I am aware it is often impossible for a Government to adopt the best course, and it is the knowledge of that fact that makes me rather hesitate to commit myself to the enormous responsibility involved in this undertaking. You will have no difficulty, I feel sure, in finding men on the other side, more or less substantial and with greater courage — mainly because they will adopt measures for their own protection which I could not avail myself of.

There are two ways by which you can get the road built and operate: one by getting up a financial organization such as Allan contemplated and such as Jay Cooke & Co. got up for the construction of the Northern Pacific Railway — with what result I need not remind you.

A scheme of this nature involves the issue of a large amount of Bonds, just as large as an attractive prospectus will float (and you have capital material to offer for a very 'taking' prospectus): the outcome of a plan of this character is that the real responsibility is transferred from the Company to the people who may be induced to buy the Bonds, while the Company or the projectors pocket a big profit at the start out of the proceeds. This, in the rough, is I fear the method any English financial organization is likely to follow. — The risk to the Government and to the country of allowing the matter to be manipulated in that way is sufficiently obvious. — It would indeed be a disastrous affair to all concerned if the English public were induced to invest in a bond issue which the road could not carry — that is one on which the interest could not be paid —.

The other plan, and the one I should have followed, had we been able to come to terms, would have been to limit the borrowing of money from the public to the smallest possible point, and if we issued a bond at all to take care it did not exceed $5,000 a mile — (Five thousand dollars) a mile — to have looked for the return of our own capital and a legitimate profit entirely from the growth of the country and the development of the property — after the work of construction had been fully accomplished. — I could not be a party to a scheme involving a large issue of Bonds on a road which no one can now be sure will earn enough to pay working expenses. — I am more willing to risk my own means in the venture than those of the English public.

It would be quite useless my going over to London; we are certain to be outbid there, and for the reasons I have given. — No English or American organization could really do the work as advantageously and at so little cost as we could, nor could they so readily develop the earning power of the property; but, while we should wait for our profit and take the risk of its coming at all, they would inevitably pocket theirs at once.

When I met Pope [the minister of agriculture] in Montreal on Saturday he told me that the Government had *decided finally* to give no more money than twenty millions, and as I could not see my way to do the work for a less cash bonus than twenty-six and a half millions, I thought it better to end the negotiations, leaving you perfectly free to make the best bargain you could on the other side.

Pope was disappointed and not very pleased with me, but I thought and still think it was the right thing to do. — Mr. Angus [R. B. Angus] has been with me all the week, and we have done little else than discuss the matter, the salmon being few and far between. We are both satisfied of our ability to construct the road without much trouble, but we are not so sure by any means about its profitable operation; but in regard to this, if we cannot operate it successfully no one else can.

We think, as I explained to you at Ottawa, that we could immediately utilise the Thunder Bay branch for our Lake traffic and in this, and other ways, earn enough to secure the payment of interest upon such indebtedness as we might incur. Our experience of settling lands in Minnesota would be a great help to us in the management of the lands granted to the Road. — We are also clear on the point that the Canada Central and the Quebec roads would have to be incorporated. Nipissing is nowhere. Montreal or Quebec must be the starting point.

Although I am off the notion of the thing now, should anything occur on the other side to induce you to think that taking all things into consideration, our proposal is better upon the whole for the country than any offer you get in England, I might, on hearing from you, renew it and possibly in doing so reduce the land grant to some extent. Here let me say that, so far as I am able to gauge public opinion, I think most people and especially the opposition (if we may judge from the utterances of the 'Globe') would prefer limiting the grant of land and increasing the cash subsidy — that is, they would prefer giving 30 millions cash and 20 million acres of land to 50 million acres of land without any cash; but as to this you can judge much better than anybody else.[23]

Yours faithfully
Geo. Stephen

The absence of Donald Smith's name in the negotiations was a necessary fiction. Macdonald loathed the man, but for the sake of political expediency, it is highly unlikely that he would have refused to deal with him. The rest of his party didn't see it that way, though. Tupper, for one, was quite prepared to burn Smith in effigy — or, preferably, in person — at any opportunity. Macdonald knew he would have a fight on his hands to push the terms of the contract through his own party, without the added inflammation of Donald Smith's involvement.

IN THE JULY 9TH LETTER are sown the seeds of Stephen's eight-year nightmare entitled "The CPR." Not only were his key advisors neutered by circumstance, but, puffed up with the success of the Manitoba Road, he underestimated the difficulty of financing and constructing the CPR. He also overestimated the magnitude of his own achievement with the St Paul and Pacific. Though he was hailed as a genius, Stephen had only provided the key financing. It was Hill who had performed minor miracles in resurrecting the shattered hulk they had taken over. Even so, as Hill repeatedly warned Stephen, only 97 miles of track over relatively simple terrain had been constructed to complete the line. In contrast, the CPR would require a minimum of 1,900 new miles of line to be laid, much of it through the Rockies and along the north shore of Lake Superior, terrain that many considered impassable.

Hill was a gritty fighter and a fast learner, but he was a relative neophyte to railroad construction. The sum total of his experience was the short time spent finishing the Manitoba Road. There he succeeded through innate cleverness and the brute physical energy he put into the job. Still, he had a lot to offer — that is, he would have if he had been available. He was already doing the work of three men in St Paul and could hardly take on the vast responsibilities of constructing the CPR. And even if he could have, he was vehemently opposed to the project, especially to the idea of the all-Canadian route. He estimated that costs of the 550-mile Lake Superior route, for a daily train, would be 50 percent higher than the amount required to run trains west of Winnipeg. And where, he constantly asked, would the traffic come from to pay for it?[24]

Curiously, in spite of all his miscalculations and oversimplifications, Stephen's belief (partly based on Hill's analysis) that the railway could be built in five years, proved to be uncannily accurate. But it was financing, Stephen's area of expertise, that got the enterprise into the most trouble. At the heart of the problem was his conviction that the CPR could be built for $45 million. In contrast, the costs of the easy five hundred miles of Intercolonial Railway, chartered in 1858 to run from Halifax to Montreal and finished in 1876, had come in $14 million overbudget, for a total of $34 million. Sir Sandford Fleming, who had at least seen the country, estimated that it would take a minimum of $100 million to complete the job.*

THE DELICATE TO AND FRO between Stephen and Macdonald and Tupper continued through the summer of 1880. By

---

*The reason for Stephen's catastrophic underestimation of the costs of the CPR is primarily his overconfidence, but another more subtle reason is the uncharacteristic disarray of his normally meticulous business affairs. During the critical summer and early fall period of 1880, when the CPR negotiations were at their height, Angus was assigned to bring some order to the mess that was the company of George Stephen and Associates. Angus discovered that Stephen's business had been "conducted rather informally, especially at Montreal." So informally that Angus could find no account books or for that matter any other useful financial information. He was forced to reconstruct the accounts using J. J. Hill's and John S. Kennedy's voluminous correspondence. (Angus to J. Kennedy Tod, July 28, 1880, JJHP)

September, any reticence, if it had ever existed, was gone and Stephen was firmly in the driver's seat, hell-bent on closing the deal.

Hill watched Stephen's seduction into the grand new venture with increasing unease. It was distressingly clear to him that Stephen was not going to go to war with Macdonald over the choice of route. He was deeply worried about the requirement in the contract that the eastern part of the line, along the shore of Lake Superior, would have to be built in order for all the land grant to be claimed. At midnight on October 19, 1880, a weary Hill sat down and composed a letter to R. B. Angus, expressing his doubts:

> As it presents itself to me I can see nothing but absolute loss of everything invested before five years unless the plan is to borrow money that can never be repaid to an account that will tide over.
>
> The only reason for going into the scheme was for the purpose of benefitting the St. P. M. & M. Ry [Manitoba Road] but now it assumes the position of a deadly enemy. I sincerely hope I am all wrong but I fear the result much more than I can tell you.[25]

To everyone but a handful of insiders it appeared that the CPR contract was the creature of Stephen, Macdonald, Tupper and Pope. But in the background, pushing, advising and nagging, was the fearful Hill. He went to Montreal in October to try to persuade Stephen of the pitfalls of Clause 4 of the contract, which made the land grants taxable. He was still arguing his point two days before the contract was signed. "Lands should not be taxable while title is in Company," he emphasized to Angus in a telegram. Stephen didn't tell Hill that in response to his advice the clause had already been changed.[26]

Macdonald and Stephen danced the minuet around the matter of the Associates' vastly conflicting interests. Macdonald knew perfectly well that they would have preferred a route that dipped into the States, thus benefiting their Manitoba Road. Stephen realized that the line would pocket substantial profits anyway because it would be serving the CPR while the transcontinental line was under construction, so he was prepared to barter away the route for something better — the monopoly clause.

Nothing less than the appearance of Beelzebub himself could have excited the horror, anger and indignation that the monopoly clause did. It gave the CPR an absolute monopoly on lines "to be constructed by the Canadian Pacific Railway, except such line as shall run South West or to the Westward of South West; nor to within fifteen miles of Latitude 49 [the international boundary]." Macdonald was dead set against these provisions, knowing that they would inflame opposition in Manitoba. But Stephen was adamant. He made it clear that if there was no monopoly clause there would be no George Stephen.

Protection of the CPR wasn't all Stephen had in mind. He needed to shelter the Manitoba Road from predators like the resurrected Northern Pacific, which was still itching to build into Winnipeg. He also wanted to mollify Hill in order to be sure of the continued financial support of Kittson and Kennedy.

Three days before the contract was signed Macdonald was still dithering about the monopoly clause. Manitoba was up in arms and even his own party was on the verge of revolt. "I was told by a member of the caucus," recalled George Ross, the rookie Liberal MP, "whose word could not be doubted, that on its first presentation, the caucus was so shocked and overwhelmed at the enormous concessions made by the Government that not a single member of the party expressed approval."[27]

THE CONTRACT WAS SIGNED on October 21, 1880, binding the Syndicate (comprised primarily of Stephen, Kennedy, Hill, Angus and Smith, whose name didn't appear) to complete the remainder of the main line, approximately 1,900 miles — within ten years. The road would run from Duncan McIntyre's Canada Central Railway terminus near Lake Nipissing via the Yellowhead Pass to Port Moody on the Burrard Inlet. One of the most important clauses from the government's point of view specified that whoever got the grants to build the railroad would subsequently "for ever efficiently maintain, work and run the Canadian Pacific Railway."*

In return, the government was to pay the Syndicate $25 million and grant it 25 million acres of land in stages as the work was completed. Not everyone was impressed by the vast amount of terrain that was thrown into the deal. "I daresay a great deal of it is very wet," sniffed George Stephen's mother when she was told. On completion of the line the government would turn over, free of charge, the Pembina branch, the already contracted sections between Red River and Lake Superior and between Lake Kamloops and Port Moody — a total of over seven hundred miles of track. In all, the assets were worth $75 million.†

The land grant, the monopoly clause and the cash subsidy received the most sensational coverage but it was several apparently minor secondary provisions that saved the railroad millions of dollars. One exempted the CPR from import duties on the massive quantities of construction materials (rails, spikes and the other hardware needed to tie the rails together). Another delayed taxes on the land grant properties (this was Hill's idea) until they were sold or for twenty years after they had been selected by the railroad. A further clause gave the railroad free additional land for stations, marshalling areas, sidings and right of way, this time tax free in perpetuity. Other clauses laid the groundwork for what would become the CPR's shipping fleet and its telegraph and telecommunications system.

A vicious and exhausting two-month Parliamentary debate to ratify the terms of the contract agreed to by Macdonald began on December 13, 1880. It was the perfect forum for the oratory bombast of Edward Blake, who had succeeded a

---

*It was a statement that was to cause considerable bad feeling in the future. Many have maintained that the CPR has reneged on its contractual obligation to provide a passenger service. But nowhere does the contract specifically mention that passenger service needs to be provided.

†Estimates of the assets turned over by the government range from $60 million to $100 million, depending on what items are included.

beaten and ailing Mackenzie as leader of the Liberal party. Blake used his fierce eloquence like a club, bludgeoning the government unmercifully. At one point he sneeringly asked if there wasn't anyone else who "could not have done this work as well as a dry goods merchant in Montreal, or a gentleman who had been engaged trapping muskrats in the North West." Blake unhesitatingly went for Macdonald's soft underbelly — Donald Smith — even though his name appeared nowhere on the contract. "I know you do not see it, but it is there for all that, you know it well," he stated in one interchange.[28] Macdonald was wretchedly uncomfortable, forced to defend a man he hated and whose name wasn't part of the deal to begin with.

Smith alternately sputtered and sulked about the omission of his name. "I have had a terrible bother with Don Smith," Stephen wrote plaintively to Sir John Rose on December 16, 1880, "because his name is not printed in the papers submitted to the House. It was not necessary to have it there and both Angus and I thought we were doing him a good turn in keeping it out. He was like a baby over the thing."[29] What Stephen neglected to mention was that he hadn't bothered to let Smith know his name would be left off the contract. Smith only learned about the omission from a newspaper reporter.

In late January, 1881, Macdonald was ready to bury the hatchet with Smith, if only to neutralize the jibes and sarcasm about his unseen presence. He agreed to put Smith on the contract because he would appear as a major shareholder anyway. Stephen approached Smith suggesting reconciliation, but this time Smith was intransigent. "The fact is that he is not anxious to make friends with you," Stephen recounted to the prime minister, "that I could see from the way he expressed himself when I told him what you said to me about his being in the Syndicate. . . ."[30]

The contract debate seethed day and night, week in and week out. It wasn't just firebrands like Edward Blake who leapt on it with vindictive glee. The young and sour-faced Wilfrid Laurier got his first big exposure in the House with the issue. He characterized the enterprise as a satanic "monster" that put its creators "in constant danger from the claws and fangs." And he taunted the government on its failure to dump the enterprise into other laps.

Continuing his theme, Laurier painted a picture of the country in the grip of an avaricious beast:

> What has seized the Government of this country that they have been compelled to accept this contract from the Syndicate? Who in the world compelled the Government to negotiate with the Syndicate? What great calamity has befallen this country that the Government should be compelled TO SURRENDER UNCONDITIONALLY to the Syndicate?
>
> . . . If this contract is to be judged in the light of modern British ideas and principles, it carries with it its death-warrant, and the only duty that remains for this House to perform is simply to reject it on the first opportunity.[31]

The firestorm of dissension came from all sides and within. Tory members from Manitoba, having had ample first-hand experience of the Associates' monopolistic practices, didn't relish having to return to their ridings and defend another one controlled by the same men and paid for by the taxpayers. Toronto members were upset that there were no Toronto residents on the Syndicate and rightly feared that the selection of Lake Nipissing as the eastern terminus of the Canadian Pacific was merely a public relations ploy to calm the waters until Montreal could be made the easternmost station.

Macdonald, Pope and Tupper held firm, overseeing the defeat of amendment after amendment (twenty-three in all) pushing through more than thirty sessions that extended past midnight. At the end of it all their yellowed, haggard faces showed the cost. After the battle was over it appeared that the angel of death had laid its wings on the three men. Macdonald was so wracked with bowel cramps he was confined to bed when the governor general signed the railway bill into law. Never a particularly healthy-looking man, Macdonald at sixty-six, with greying hair, sunken and pouched eyes and weasel's face, looked embalmed. When he staggered off to England in May to recuperate, many thought they'd seen the last of him. A few weeks before his departure Stephen wrote wishing him a speedy return to strength and vigour. But he also took the opportunity to offer Macdonald a little work to do, just in case he mended quicker than was expected. "When on the other side you will doubtless be thinking of some plan by which we can rope in the Govt into the good work of settling the far West & at the same time relieving Ireland . . . . I am not a very wise politician but I think it would be a great thing for your Govt if we succeed in roping in 'John Bull.'[32]

All three recovered, once relieved temporarily of the appalling stress of little sleep, constant attack and poor food. The diagnosis of Macdonald's condition—"catarrh of the stomach"—sounds suspiciously like too many brandies. Tupper, according to his doctor, was "strained but not sprung."[33] Pope was simply old, and the rest "delayed the call from on high."[34]

The Pacific Railway bill passed its third reading on February 15, 1881. Stephen wasted no time, incorporating the Canadian Pacific Railway Company on February 18, 1881. That same day he deposited the $1 million performance bond with the government and called his first board meeting.

CHAPTER 4

GEORGE STEPHEN'S NIGHTMARE

"If we can't sell the land we'll give it away."
— George Stephen to Sir John A. Macdonald, 1881

George Stephen entered 1881 on a cloud. Firmly in control of the greatest railway project in the Empire, there was no doubt that the carpenter's son was the richest and most influential man in Canada. His ascendancy was confirmed by the construction of his Drummond Street home, right at the core of Montreal's exclusive Square Mile. Unlike Ravenscrag, Sir Hugh Allan's miniature castle, or Donald Smith's mansion, Stephen's home didn't scream opulence from every room. It was subtle where the other two were overwhelming and oppressive, emphasizing with finesse and craftsmanship what the other two did with sweeping gestures. Smith filled every room with a dizzying array of expensive art but Stephen was content to place a single picture on a wall. He imported the finest fabrics, carpets, stained glass and wood panelling from around the world and hired two maids just to keep the exotic wood dusted and polished. His home was a gem of architecture and decorating, but once it was finished in 1883 Stephen stayed in it so infrequently that friends called it "Mrs Stephen's house."

The most gratifying aspect of Stephen's association with the great railroad scheme was his change in status. From wealthy businessman he was transformed almost overnight into a consultant on weighty issues to Her Majesty's ministers. Suddenly the future of an entire country was in his hands. His frequent journeys to London now carried the additional cachet of political importance. Although he didn't like or truly understand the political milieu, he enjoyed being influential within it. Even before the CPR contract was formally ratified, Stephen met with W. E. Forster, the secretary of state for Ireland, and the Canadian high commissioner, A. T. Galt, to ponder a variety of plans aimed at promoting emigration to Canada. With the government's $25 million subsidy assured and another $5 million from the Syndicate's purchase of Canadian Pacific stock, Stephen was almost boastful about the CPR's prospects. "We can provide the remaining $15 million from our own resources, if we deem it necessary, or expedient to do so."[1]

Stephen decided on a conservative financing strategy. "No financial fireworks," he promised Macdonald.[2] His whole plan

The conservatory in George Stephen's Drummond Street home

centred on selling the $25 million in land grant bonds*
allowed by the charter. But he intended to tap the North
American market first. On the face of it, it was a bold move.
The traditional method of large-scale financing in the colonies was to go, cap in hand, to London. In truth, Stephen knew
he had little chance of interesting the English market. Even
the risk takers were soured on railways after a raft of American
failures and the abysmal record of British investment in the
Grand Trunk Railway — nicknamed "Big Suitcase" for the
large quantity of money it had made off with.†

The millions invested in the Grand Trunk had not earned
a single penny of dividend since 1876. Stephen repeatedly
vowed to risk his own money in the venture rather than go to
England for funds. Stephen's "risk" was born of sheer necessity. He wanted to sell the CPR in Britain but he first had to
create a market elsewhere. Most of the major British financial
houses had branches in New York and some in Montreal.
Once a good market developed in North America, Stephen
intended to "make 'John Bull' buy these bonds by sending
orders to this side for them at a premium."³

At first his plan unfolded perfectly. Land sold briskly in
England: 300,000 acres at an average price of $2.59 an acre by
the spring of 1881. Capital stock in the CPR had been set at $25
million, of which $6.1 million had already been taken up, but
the Syndicate's own purchase of $5 million worth of stock had
comprised most of that sale. The Syndicate also heavily supported the land grant bonds. J. S. Kennedy and Company took
$7.5 million, and Stephen, Smith and Angus, through the

---

*Railway bonds were commonly backed by all or parts of the various assets of a railway, includ-
ing fixed assets like track, rolling stock, and treasury shares. In the case of a default, the bond-
holder would have a claim against the entire railway. The CPR's land grant bonds were backed
only by a mortgage on the as yet unsold land.

†Most railway nicknames were based on initials. Some were damning comments on the road
itself; others were affectionate. Included among dozens of monikers in North American railroad history are: Old and Weary (New York, Ontario & Western), Hell Either Way You Take It
(Houston, East & West Texas), Leave Early and Walk (Lake Erie & Western), and Bent Zigzag
and Crooked (Bellaire, Zanesville & Cincinnati).

Bank of Montreal, bought $2.5 million.[4] The rest of the bonds were to be sold by the newly created Canadian North West Land Company, which was headquartered in London and controlled by Donald Smith. In July 1881 the company gratifyingly reported that interest in the land grant bonds was beginning to stir.

EVEN THE PRESS OBLIGINGLY CONTRIBUTED to Stephen's euphoria with a ceasefire throughout that first summer. But the lull was just the eye of a hurricane, and it ended on September 1, 1881. That day the influential London weekly *Truth* published an article dismembering the railroad tie by tie, shredding its foundations, denouncing its intent and mocking its future. A superbly concocted blend of misstatements, outright lies and clever analysis, the article became the benchmark for CPR abuse. It was quoted, reprinted, paraphrased and plagiarized by newspapers and politicians all over the world.* Every word was honed to surgical sharpness and the first slash was the title, "The Canadian Dominion Bubble," a bubble being in stock market parlance of the time, the most speculative of all investments. After revealing that the Syndicate was likely to come to Britain for financing, even though it appeared to be selling its bonds only in North America, its writer launched into a devastating description of the land through which the new railway was slated to pass:

> The Canadian Pacific Railway will run, if it is ever finished, through a country frost bound for seven or eight months in the year, and will connect with the western part of the Dominion a province which embraces about as forbidding a country as any on the face of the earth.

---

*Some swore the ink used to write it was CPR blood. The author of the article was *Truth*'s editor, Henry Labouchere, whose fans hailed him as the "Voltaire of the Victorian Age." Labouchere's uncle had been the British colonial secretary in 1857. Henry had camped in the St Paul area for six weeks and claimed the honour of being hosted by Chief Hole in Heaven of the Chippewa Indians in 1853. In 1854 he was a British attaché in Washington during the testy reciprocity negotiations between Canada and the United States. His familiarity with North America — coupled with general British ignorance of the colonies — gave the article enough authenticity to make it truly devastating.

Donald Smith's home in Montreal

British Columbia, they say, has forced on the execution of this part of the contract under which they became incorporated with the Dominion, and believe that prosperity will come to them when the line is made. This is a delusion on their part. British Columbia is a barren, cold, mountain country that is not worth keeping. It would never have been inhabited at all, unless by trappers of the Hudson's Bay Company, had the "gold fever" not taken a party of mining adventurers there, and ever since that fever died down, the place has been going from bad to worse. Fifty railroads would not galvanize it into prosperity.

Nevertheless, the Canadian Government has fairly launched into this project and I have no doubt the English public will soon be asked to further it with their cash. The parade of selling bonds in New York and Montreal is the new way of doing business that "Syndicates" bankers and loan contractors have adopted in order that it may seem that they have faith in the schemes they father.

I doubt if ten millions of dollars of ready cash could be found in all of Canada for this or any other work of utility in a pinch, but the Canadians are not such idiots as to part with one dollar of their own if they can borrow from their neighbours. The Canadians spend money and we provide it. That has been the arrangement hitherto, and it has worked out splendidly — for the Canadians — too well for them to try out any other scheme with the Canadian Pacific, which they must know is never likely to pay a single red cent of interest on the money that may be sunk into it.

A friend of mine told me — and he knew what he was talking about — that he did not believe the much-touted Manitoba settlement would hold out many years. The people who have gone there cannot stand the coldness of the winters. Men and cattle are frozen to death in numbers that would rather startle the intending settler if he knew; and those who are not killed outright, are often maimed for life by frostbites. Its street nuisances kill people with malaria, or drive them mad with plagues of insect; and to keep themselves alive during the long winter they have to imitate the habits of the Esquimaux. . . the Canadian Pacific Railway has yet five and twenty million acres to sell and it is through a death-dealing region of this kind that the new railway is to run.[5]*

The gist of the *Truth* article was snatched up, and made an appearance in every prominent paper in England and the colonies. Each day a new vile clipping was deposited on Stephen's desk. Denouncing the coverage, Stephen blamed it all on the Grand Trunk "and its paid ink slingers in London."[6] It was standard practice at the time to own key papers and columnists, secretly or otherwise. (J. J. Hill would later make an art of it.) The Grand Trunk supported two anti-CPR columnists in the *Globe,* who wrote under the pseudonyms "Ishmael" and "Diogenes." The Tories controlled the Toronto *Mail,* whose columnist "Mohawk" was little better than a CPR sycophant. Stephen was always extremely sanctimonious about the practice of owning newspapers and writers but that didn't stop him from quietly financing, in late 1882, the *Canadian Gazette,* a London-based publication devoted to promoting the CPR's interests.†

In his battles with the press, whom he considered little better than vermin, Stephen was dogged by bad luck. Travelling to London in February, 1882, to promote Canadian immigration and drum up support for the flagging land grant bonds, Stephen toured the major papers faithfully, only to find that every interview he gave was either diminished or bumped from the paper altogether in favour of Jumbo mania.

---

*In *Van Horne's Road,* Omer Lavallée points out that *Truth* recanted the story in a 1936 review of J. M. Gibbon's *Steel of Empire,* in which the entire article appeared.

†Stephen's interest in the *Gazette* was so secret that Van Horne didn't learn of it until 1890 or 1891.

The London Zoo had committed the heinous and unpatriotic act of selling Jumbo the Elephant, a docile beast upon whose spiny back thousands of Britons had ridden. "The Pride of the British Heart" was sold to American circus owner P. T. Barnum, and every effort was now being made to stall Jumbo's departure. A "Save Jumbo" fund was established and, failing in their bid to keep the beast, the fund raisers were spending the money on every possible pachyderm delicacy to ease his long trip to New York. "Jumbo the big elephant recently bought by Barnum is a matter of ten times more interest to London than twenty Colonies," Stephen complained bitterly to Macdonald.[7] The irony of Jumbo's death gave him little satisfaction. On September 15, 1885, just three weeks before the pounding of the last spike, Jumbo was mowed down by a Grand Trunk locomotive.*

The Grand Trunk under Sir Henry Tyler never really believed that the CPR would get off the ground, but once it did, the railroad was determined to thwart it.† The competing railway supplemented the newspaper attacks with a massive London pamphlet campaign, and it wasn't long before "CPR" and "flop" were synonymous in the British mind. Stephen countered by ordering Alexander Begg, a florid journalist in the CPR's employ, to get up his own pamphleteering campaign. The gesture, coming on the heels of the announcement that the company had laid only 130 miles of track in its first season, made Begg's assurances about the security of the Canadian road laughable in financial circles.

---

*As Jumbo's final show in St Thomas, Ontario, was drawing to a close, thirty-one elephants were being loaded into their cars. The last two, Jumbo and a smaller clown elephant, were heading towards their car. Without warning a freight engine came charging up the hill, bearing directly down on them. The engineer frantically engaged the reverse lever but in vain. The small elephant leaped to one side, breaking a leg. Jumbo, afraid to jump, ploughed into the locomotive head on. A few hours later the wretched beast died from the trauma of having his tusks driven back into his skull.

An interesting postscript to the Jumbo story was provided by Canadian newspaperman Walter J. "Wallie" Wilkinson, whose reputation in scooping his journalistic confreres was both feared and admired. He scooped even the truth in his fanciful but touching story on Jumbo. He wrote that the dear elephant had in fact died valiantly, trying to protect the baby elephant. The story of this act of selfless courage, passed far and wide by the wire services, was greeted by many a wet eye.

†The war continued until the GTR was absorbed by Canadian National forty years later.

Jumbo the elephant

Early in 1882 the sale of land and land grant bonds had slowed like sap in winter, but Stephen wasn't perturbed. In April he confidently told Macdonald that he had vanquished the company's enemies and their attempts to portray the Northwest as an uninhabitable desert. As for the sale of land grant bonds, he glossed over the uninterested market by saying, "My strong card has been that we can build the C.P.R., if need be, without a dollar of English money; that the Company have no bonds to sell, having sold all its bonds to a syndicate who were selling them to the Canadian public much faster than was expected."[8]

The sale of land was never important in Stephen's mind, but settlers were. "If we can't sell the land we'll give it away," he assured Macdonald.[9] During his trip to England in 1882 he authorized an advertising campaign in Britain, including Ireland and Scotland, extolling the virtues of Canada and the opportunities for "rich and poor alike." His whole strategy, built on sand though it was, might have hung together but for a single fact: interest in Canadian land had died.

STEPHEN'S STRATEGY FOR BUILDING the Canadian Pacific was largely shaped by the Associates' experience in St Paul: finish the line as quickly as possible, thus physically demonstrating — through rapid progress — the viability of the company; at the same time, buy railroads and complete critical sections to provide immediate traffic and revenue. He intended to leave the costly and technically difficult Lake Superior section to the end when investors, impressed by the vigour of the CPR, would throw open their pocketbooks for the money required to build it. Stephen wasted no time purchasing the Canada Central Railway from Duncan McIntyre in March, 1881. It gave the CPR the beginning of a through line from Brockville on the St Lawrence River to Ottawa and on to Montreal. It was this act more than any other that incited the wrath of the Grand Trunk. Somehow its executive had complacently believed that the CPR intended to leave all the lucrative traffic in eastern Canada alone.

Completing the line post-haste meant cutting corners and curves with the abandon of a racing car driver. And that meant summarily abandoning, in May, 1881, Sandford Fleming's* northern route through the Yellowhead Pass. Surveyed at the cost of millions of dollars and over forty lives, Stephen cast it aside in favour of a southern route with no proven pass through the Rockies. The astonishing decision has been dissected for over a century.† Some have claimed that the Syndicate's faith in the northern growing season and the fertility of the Northwest lands was shaken. Others attributed the new route to a nefarious scheme hatched by J. J. Hill to use the Canadian Pacific as his railroad link to the west coast. There is

---

*Sandford Fleming was another of the many Scots associated with the CPR. He was instrumental in establishing standard time zones around the world, and he was a sizeable investor in the Canada-Australia telegraph cable. He was a member of the CPR board for thirty years until his death in 1915. He owned a substantial amount of stock in J. J. Hill's railroad, the Great Northern.

†The prospect of an alternative route had been raised by Duncan McIntyre in August, 1880, when he emphasized to Macdonald that the CPR should be allowed to locate its line wherever they wanted to.

probably some truth in all the explanations, but the most compelling reason for the new route was expediency. Skirting closer to the border was shorter and required far fewer costly bridges—only two in the 832 miles of line between Winnipeg and Calgary.

The key to the gamble was finding a southerly pass through the mountains. The man entrusted with that job was Major A. B. Rogers, one of the most eccentric characters in Canadian railroading. Rogers, or "The Bishop," as he was sarcastically referred to by the sharply disapproving J. H. E. Secretan,* the CPR's locating engineer, was "a 'rough and ready' engineer, or rather pathfinder. A short, sharp, snappy little chap with long Dundreary whiskers. He was a master of picturesque profanity, who continually chewed tobacco and was an artist of expectoration. He wore overalls with pockets behind, and had a plug of tobacco in one pocket and a sea biscuit in the other, which was his idea of a season's provisions for an engineer. His scientific equipment consisted of a compass and an aneroid slung around his neck."[10]

Even Rogers' eccentricities had quirks. "He was a mono-maniac on the subject of food," revealed one of the many CPR employees who fought to stay out of his survey parties, "and had a strong liking for that which cheers and also inebriates. We usually had plenty of bacon and beans and they were our *pièce de résistance* three times a day, as he believed that a variety of food, and much of it, did not conduce to physical or brain

---

*Secretan bore a grudge against Rogers. When his survey crew came stumbling out of the forest into Secretan's camp near Medicine Hat at the end of that first season, Secretan sniffed that "they were hungry and in rags, and were headed by the Major himself, the worst looking ruffian of them all." Secretan was aghast at the "half-starved . . . scarecrows" and treated them to his comforts, which were considerable. He was very put out to learn later that Rogers had complained to General Rosser, the CPR's chief engineer, that Secretan "was living like the Czar of Russia and would absolutely ruin any Railway Corporation in the world. He said I had my tents carpeted with Brussels carpet, that I live upon roast turkeys and geese and many other expensive luxuries, unheard of in the cuisines of a poor unsophisticated engineer, etc. etc." Though Secretan's camps were oases of luxury in the bush his "Brussels carpets" were actually burlap sacks sewn together and the *haute cuisine* consisted of game he shot himself. (Secretan, *Canada's Great Highway*, p. 189)

activity."[11]* Rogers' late night campfires must have been alarming auditory experiences considering his taste in food and drink.

Though distinctly unsavoury and unsanitary in appearance and habits, Rogers was far from the rube he liked to portray. He was a highly educated man with an engineering degree from Yale. Nonetheless, at fifty-two, he was a little long in the tooth for bushwhacking. But J. J. Hill had the highest confidence in "poor old Major Rogers" and hired him to find a southern pass almost immediately after the contract was signed. The risk was heightened because rails were already being laid over unsurveyed terrain, as if a suitable route had been discovered.

Rogers set out that first season from Kamloops, British Columbia, on April 29, 1881, accompanied by his nephew Albert and ten Indians recruited through the offices of the Oblate mission in Kamloops. If Rogers' tyrannical ways weren't enough to motivate his crew, the contract with the Indians stipulated that he could turn their wages over to the mission if they behaved badly. Adding a little zest to their cooperation, their chief was instructed to treat them to 100 lashes should they return in disgrace. With so much at stake, Rogers drove them unmercifully. Albert's vivid tale of the adventure is a litany of privation and danger.

> Being gaunt as greyhounds, with lungs and muscles of the best, we soon reached the timber-line, where the climbing became very difficult. We crawled along the ledges, getting a toe-hold here and a finger-hold there, keeping in the shade as much as possible and kicking toe-holes in the snow crust. When several hundred feet above

---

*Van Horne, whose own love of good food was legendary, once had occasion to question Rogers' feeding of his men.

"Look here, Major, I hear your men won't stay with you, they say you starve them," bellowed Van Horne.

"T'aint so, Van."

"Well, I'm told you feed 'em on soup made out of hot water flavoured with old ham canvas covers."

"T'aint so, Van. I didn't never have no hams!" (Secretan, *Canada's Great Highway*, p. 192)

the timber-line, we followed a narrow ledge around a point that was exposed to the sun. (Here four Indians fell over the ledge.) It was late in the evening when we reached the summit, very much exhausted.

Crawling along this ridge, we came to a small ledge protected from the wind by a great perpendicular rock. Here we decided to wait until the crust again formed on the snow and the morning light enabled us to travel. At ten o'clock, it was still twilight, on the peaks, but the valleys below were filled with the deepest gloom. We wrapped ourselves in our blankets and nibbled at our dry meat and bannock, stamping our feet in the snow to keep them from freezing, and taking turns whipping each other with our pack-straps to keep up circulation.[12]

Rogers dropped out of touch with his employers as he trekked deeper into the Rockies, and as the days and months went by they began to fret. Even Hill developed a few doubts but he kept up everyone's spirits with a barrage of "don't worry" and "I have the fullest confidence" letters to Stephen, Kennedy and Angus. Just when it seemed as if the peculiar fellow had fallen off the end of the world, he turned up on Hill's St Paul doorstep, drunk and looking even rattier than usual after eight months in the bush. It was just before Christmas, 1881, and the major's present to Hill was the news that he had found "a good and very direct line through the Kicking Horse Pass" and that he had "enough information to remove any serious doubts about . . . being able to find a pass through the Selkirk Range."[13]

An overjoyed Hill loaded Rogers into his private rail car and sent him along to Montreal. There George Stephen's splendidly liveried butler was accosted by a stinking and disreputable little man who demanded, in terms not commonly heard in that household, to see the master. Totally flummoxed, the butler risked interrupting a dinner party to inform Stephen of the man's presence. The butler was astonished when Rogers was hailed as a prodigy, then washed, coiffed, decked out in finery and delivered as the main attraction at dinner.*

---

*The Syndicate lavishly rewarded Rogers for his find with a $5,000 cheque. Van Horne met Rogers by chance in Winnipeg about a year later and in his abrupt way demanded to know

CPR men at Field, B.C.: Van Horne (extreme left) and Smith (fourth from the left); the man sixth from the left is likely Hill.

Not everyone was impressed by Rogers' achievement. Secretan pointed out, rather huffily, that nearly every pass had already been discovered by Sandford Fleming and Rogers' own pass through the Selkirks had been documented "and condemned" by Walter Moberly, "but this fact did not deter the indefatigable Major, who proceeded to discover them again."[14] Van Horne wasn't happy about trusting only the major's account, and he sent two other engineers, one of them Fleming, to examine the route again. It wasn't until August, 1882, that final confirmation of Rogers Pass was received.

The pass may have been spotted, but getting through it was another thing entirely. Between Stephen in the Rockies and Revelstoke on the western slopes of the Selkirks, the trains faced hideous grades. Rogers had confidently declared that a good route existed along the Kicking Horse River. Unfor-

---

why Rogers hadn't cashed his cheque.

"What!" roared the engineer. "Cash the check? I wouldn't take a hundred thousand dollars for it. It is framed and hangs in my brother's house in Waterville, Minnesota, where my nephews and nieces can see it. I'm not in this for the money." (Hanna, *Trains of Recollection*, p. 45)

tunately, it required a 1,400-foot tunnel through the nose of Mount Stephen itself. Special permission was granted by the government to increase the maximum allowable grade for this section from 2.2 percent per mile to 4.4 percent. The splendid alpine hotel, Glacier House, at the summit of the Rogers Pass was built because trains, even those pulled by four or five locomotives, couldn't make it up, or down, the Big Hill with a heavy dining car attached.* The car was dropped off at the foot of the ascent and the train puffed to the summit, where passengers disembarked for refreshment.

WHEN STEPHEN WROTE TO MACDONALD in April of 1882 assuring him that all was well, the CPR was close to collapse and had been for some time. Money disappeared as if by evaporation. The CPR's books and Stephen's own accounts were a tangle of conflicting and sometimes nonexistent entries. McIntyre was completely overmatched in his job of general manager and vice-president. Stephen, with no practical railroad experience, was out of touch with the daily business of the CPR, which was seething and bubbling away in a bog of ineptitude and corruption. Hill did what he could, but no man could run two fledgling railroads at the same time. Angus was so distraught over disorder in the whole enterprise that he considered resigning, and Donald Smith was still sulking because his name had been left out of the charter documents.

Orders for crucial equipment had gone astray and some invoices had been paid twice, but most had not been paid at all. The rolling stock and track-laying equipment was next to worthless, having been badly abused and poorly maintained by the government crews in their efforts to build the line.[15] To top it all off, only 130 miles of track had been laid by the time the season closed in 1881 — and that puny effort had somehow

---

*A special locomotive was designed by the Baldwin Locomotive Works in Philadelphia, just for service on the Big Hill.

swallowed up $10 million — nearly one-quarter of Stephen's estimate of construction costs for the whole railway.

The CPR's highest western officials were snout-deep in the trough. The company's Winnipeg headquarters had been transformed into a giant combination bar-room/casino and it seemed as if every drifter, land speculator and con artist in the Western world had converged on the little town. "Sealskin coats and cloaks and diamond pins were greatly in evidence. The city was all ablaze with the excitement of prospective riches. Champagne replaced Scotch and soda, and game dinners were very common. Auction sales were held daily and nightly . . . people bought recklessly. Property changed hands quickly at greatly enhanced values. Certainly a land-office was being done. The craze spread to the rural districts, and land surveyors and map artists worked overtime to fill orders. If there ever was a fool's paradise, it sure was located in Winnipeg. Men made fortunes — mostly on paper — and life was one continuous joy ride."[16]

J. J. Hill watched the CPR chaos with growing, and eventually frantic, unease. The lack of order or even a general sense of what was going on horrified him and he believed that if something wasn't done quickly the railroad would be beyond salvation. He had no respect for, or confidence in, McIntyre and lobbied hard for a replacement. The man he wanted was William Cornelius Van Horne, an American with a formidable reputation for resurrecting railroads in desperate circumstances. The more hopeless they were, so the stories went, the bigger the miracle he wrought.

WILLIAM CORNELIUS VAN HORNE AND J. J. HILL were easily the foremost railroad builders and operators in North American history. Though often described as Hill's "protégé," Van Horne was a far more experienced railroader. Only thirty-eight years old when he became the CPR's general manager, he had spent nearly twenty-five years mastering every facet of railway operation from telegraph operation to the intricacies of financing. The three years Hill had spent completing and running the Manitoba Road did not begin to compare.

Van Horne had all of Hill's shrewdness and brute energy, as well as inventiveness, daring and unassailable confidence. Hill acknowledged as much in a letter to George Stephen. "I have never met anyone who is better informed in the various departments, machinery, cars, operation, train services, construction and general policy which with untiring energy and good vigorous body should give us good results."[17] But there were also caveats. "You need a man of great mental and physical power to carry this line through. Van Horne can do it. He will take all the authority he gets and more, so define how much you want him to have."[18]

Van Horne's achievements reached such mythic proportions that his legend virtually wrote itself. Today many credit him with conceiving the idea of the CPR, finding the money, building the line and running it almost singlehandedly — all on a diet of twenty-five-hour days, cigars, poker and tough talk. Of above-average height, Van Horne had an ample girth that made him appear rather short. Even so, he was the physical incarnation of force and will. "The Van Horne regime on the C.P.R. was the most remarkable innovation that had happened to the business life of the Dominion," wrote D. B. Hanna,* who first met Van Horne in 1882. "He was astonishingly aggressive. His vocabulary had all the certainty that belongs to the Presbyterian conception of everlasting retribution, without its restraint. He laughed at other men's impossibilities, and ordered them to be done—a dynamo run by dynamite."[19]

William Cornelius Van Horne was born on February 3, 1843, at Chelsea, in Will County, Illinois. His Dutch forebears had come to the Americas in the 1630s and had prospered, becoming landowners and businessmen with large families.

---

*The first president of the National Railways, later the Canadian National Railways.

Van Horne's father, Cornelius Covenhoven Van Horne, was a lawyer who chafed at the dullness of life in that profession and cast it all aside to go west in 1832.

Cornelius wasn't much of a farmer but he supplemented the meagre amount of legal work that came his way by running a small sawmill and working his land.* William was born in Chelsea near the old Oregon Trail, to Cornelius's second wife,† Mary Minier Richards, the offspring of a South German father and a mother native to Pennsylvania but of French origin. William Van Horne was the oldest of her five children.

In 1851 the educated, sophisticated and restless Cornelius, tired of the bucolic life and his marginal existence, moved his family to Joliet, a thriving Illinois town of two thousand people. The recent arrival of the railroad brought with it settlers and prosperity. Cornelius's ambition resurfaced as he resumed his practice, and within a year he was elected Joliet's first mayor. His new status and expectations of a better life were ended by his death during the cholera epidemic of 1854. William was only eleven. His father had left them little save "a lot of accounts payable and some bad accounts receivable. He was a lawyer who seldom took fees."[20]

The death of a father, the main provider, was a devastating blow, but Van Horne's mother eked out a living for her five children by taking in sewing and selling vegetables from their garden.‡ Even so, the family was forced to move from their

---

*The nearest court house, where Cornelius travelled to conduct business, was at the state capital more than 150 miles away. Reputedly, Cornelius's acquaintances included one Abraham Lincoln who was also practising law at the time.

†The years in Chelsea were bitter ones, fraught with tragedy and hardship: his first wife and two children died, and a fire destroyed his home, barn and, worst of all, his precious library of law books. Undaunted, Cornelius borrowed enough to buy a 360-acre homestead and started all over again.

‡Van Horne's mother was a truly remarkable woman. Later in life the railway magnate steadfastly credited his mother's early patience with his success in life. When he was three, he discovered a small stone that turned out to be slate. His mother showed him how to use it to draw on blackboards, and Van Horne was entranced by the results. Once his piece of slate wore out, she encouraged him to draw, first with a sharpened piece of lead pipe and later with pencil and chalk, on the whitewashed walls of the house — creating a mural that covered virtually every square inch both inside and out.

comfortable home to a tiny cottage. "My mother was a noble woman," Van Horne remembered, "courageous and resourceful, and she managed to find bread — seldom butter — and to keep us at school until I was able to earn something — which I had to set about at fourteen."[21] The bread Van Horne remembered was mostly hominy* and that was served for virtually every meal.

Van Horne's early years were spent exploring first the Chelsea, then the Joliet, countryside. As he got older, his scavenging forays became more systematic and wide ranging and he brought home interesting pebbles, a collection which soon grew into a small mountain. One day he found a treasure with unusual markings. He dubbed it his "worm-in-the-rock" and the talisman accompanied him everywhere. When he was fourteen, while idly reading a book at the home of his best friend, Augustus Howk, he was thrilled to see a picture identifying his "worm-in-the-rock" as a fossil. The discovery transformed him from a scavenger into an impassioned collector. Accompanied by Howk, Van Horne tramped every creek, river and quarry within walking distance looking for new finds. Learning of his nephew's interest, Howk's uncle sent him a copy of Hitchcock's *Elements of Geology*.

"In all my life, I never longed for anything as I longed for that book!" recalled Van Horne in later years. "I never envied anyone as I envied that boy. I would have sold all my chances in life and thrown in my soul too to have had it. Sometimes I was allowed to peep at it if I had washed my hands."[22] The book teased Van Horne's imagination, and his lust for it was inflamed by the fact that Howk, sensing a seller's market, doled it out to him at infrequent intervals and always in return for favours. "I believe I grovelled to the boy while I courted him in every way."[23] That summer, when Howk's family travelled to New York, Van Horne purchased the use of the book in return for all the duplicate fossils in his collection.

---

*A food consisting of maize hulled and coarsely ground and then boiled to a mush-like paste in either milk or water.

4 George Stephen's Nightmare / 111

As soon as the book was in his possession, Van Horne disappeared "to a place sixteen miles off, and . . . slept there all night under a hay-stack in case the boy should change his mind."[24] Van Horne pored over the book night after night, but he felt strangely unsatisfied. He could read it and hold it in his hands but it wasn't his. There was, however, an answer. Sitting in his pocket was a munificent twenty-five-cent tip he had received for running an errand. Instead of indulging in a bag of sweets or turning the money over to his mother as he usually did, Van Horne bought a ream of paper. For the next five weeks he spent virtually every waking hour and sometimes the entire night hunched over Hitchcock's book, lovingly reproducing every single page, including the introduction, footnotes, illustrations and bibliography.

"The copying of that book did great things for me," Van Horne remembered. "It taught me how much could be accomplished by application; it improved my handwriting; it taught me the construction of English sentences; and it helped my drawing materially. And I never had to refer to the book again."[25] Copying became a trick of learning for Van Horne. In 1858 when he started as a telegrapher, he learned the basic elements of drawing and perspective by surreptitiously duplicating the railroad draftsman's texts. His work was good enough that when the draftsman discovered what he was up to, he insisted that Van Horne do all the fine lettering his job required.

Van Horne's passion for rocks lasted all his life. During his days as a railway employee in Joliet, a particularly fertile area for fossils, he continued his Sunday treks and made many important geological finds. Van Horne discovered nine previously unclassified specimens that today still bear the suffix "Van Hornei" in palæontological encyclopædias. While he was superintendent of the Chicago and Alton Railroad in 1878, he spotted a choice fossil, which had been well preserved in the pavement of an Alton street. The torture of walking by such a fine specimen and not possessing it was too much for Van Horne. One morning he slipped out and stealthily chiselled it out of the road. Railroad men who otherwise feared Van Horne's heavy tread, critical eye and quick anger knew they could divert his attention (and earn a few extra dollars) by showing him an interesting rock they had found. During his CPR days, he wouldn't hesitate to yank on the emergency cord to halt the train near a curious geological formation.

If Van Horne were a schoolboy today, he would be classified as an underachiever with an acute behaviour problem. He showed little interest in learning specific lessons, relying instead on his memory, native intelligence and voracious reading — particularly about geology — to get by. He was noteworthy only as an unredeemable prankster, whose wicked caricatures of teachers caused many loud guffaws in the playground. Though tubby, he was strong and pugnacious, willing to take on all comers, and mostly win, in schoolyard brawls. One day Van Horne's reputation as the toughest boy in school was tarnished when a visiting older boy thrashed him. But he quickly re-established his dominance by issuing a general challenge and fighting every taker until there were none left.

All through these years, the family income hovered at subsistence levels, and Van Horne had to supplement it by chopping neighbours' wood. It was a job he abhorred and would later proudly describe as the only real work he'd ever done. "Work! I never work," he was fond of saying. "I never worked since I was ten years old and split logs. I have only enjoyed."[26]

Van Horne was thirteen when he formed his first business. It consisted of a lengthy roll of wallpaper on which he painted a creditable panorama of the Crystal Palace, with London in the background. He got it all from reading his mother's treasured *Harper's Magazine*. He hired a tent and charged a penny to see the panorama, which was stretched between two rollers and turned with a hand crank. The travelogue he wrote and performed himself. Intended for his peers, the show was professional enough to attract a considerable number of adults. Realizing he was onto a good thing, he promptly raised the fee.

On a more regular basis, Van Horne delivered messages for

the Joliet telegraph operators. It was a new and glorious experience and he devised elaborate strategems to allow him to lurk in their office — running free errands, cleaning up, anything to be near his new obsession.

VAN HORNE'S CULTIVATION OF THE JOLIET telegraph operators paid off in 1857 when one of them recommended him for his first job, as a telegrapher with the Illinois Central Railroad Company, located just outside Chicago. Shortly before the job offer, his undistinguished school career had ended after the principal beat him vigorously upon discovering that he had been featured in one of Van Horne's caricatures. Van Horne wasn't long into his new job before the jester surfaced. He attached a live wire to a good-sized metal plate in the train yard and was vastly amused by the contortions of the men unlucky enough to step on it. Those who foolishly bent down and touched the plate were literally knocked off their feet. The principles of electricity were not widely known, and some poor victims, failing to recognize the cable for what it was, were shocked two and three times. Unfortunately for Van Horne, his final victim was the superintendent. Seeing little humour in being humiliated in front of his men by a precocious teenager, the man fired him on the spot.*

A few months later Van Horne found a job as a freight checker, messenger and gofer for the "Cut-Off," the forty-mile-long Michigan Central feeder line that linked Joliet with the main line. His powers of persuasion, even as a fifteen-year-old, were considerable. He talked the superintendent, who somehow got the impression that Van Horne was a fully qualified telegrapher, into installing a telegraph line and putting him in charge of it. Armed with only the rudiments of

---

*Many of his pranks were simply in bad taste. During the Civil War he concocted a bogus telegraph message, complete with authentic-sounding detail, proclaiming a great victory on the field for the North. The ensuing wild celebration was cut short when the evening papers carried no mention of the supposed battle. A party of men went looking to have a word with Van Horne, who had prudently disappeared.

telegraphics, Van Horne tackled with missionary zeal the subject he had supposedly already mastered. Shortly, he could decipher messages by merely listening to the clicks and clacks, without having to refer to the tape — a handy skill for eavesdropping. He was one of the few in the whole country able to perform this feat. It was the beginning of the Van Horne legend.

DEVOTING HIMSELF TO A SINGLE TASK was impossible for Van Horne, and his curiosity soon began to turn to every other job in the office. The timekeeper, cashier and accountant were all subjected to his intense scrutiny and irritatingly penetrating questions. Any spare time Van Horne had was spent challenging the older men to memory competitions, wagering on who could remember most exactly the numbers on long trains as they passed.

Up to this point Van Horne's inquisitiveness and energy had been largely aimless. But the visit of the general superintendent of the entire Michigan Central line, in his private car, changed all that. The man arrived to crowds of lesser beings employed on the line. The glory, stateliness and pomp of the occasion transfixed Van Horne. Years later, Van Horne was still able to describe in minute detail the trappings of the superintendent's car, the blazingly white linen on the dinner table, fresh flowers for decoration, polished silver and soft, luxuriant chairs in the parlour: "I found myself wondering if even I might not somehow become a General Superintendent and travel in a private car. The glories of it, the pride of it, the salary pertaining to it, and all that moved me deeply, and I made up my mind then and there that I would reach it." He swore that day to achieve the position and he devoured everything in his path that led him closer to his goal: "I imagined that a General Superintendent must know everything about a railway — every detail in every department — and my working hours were no longer governed by the clock. I took no holidays, but gladly took up the work of others who did, and

I worked nights and Sundays to keep it all going without neglecting my own tasks."[27]

In 1861, when the American Civil War broke out, Van Horne enlisted with the Federal Army, but before his papers were processed the assistant superintendent of the Cut-Off interceded, on the grounds that telegraphers were essential to the war effort. As the war progressed and freight revenues diminished, rumours of impending layoffs ran up and down the track. One day a message came from head office instructing his boss to cut staff. Van Horne, now the sole support of his family, went home sure that he, the youngest employee of the railroad, would be the first to go. His peril seemed even more serious because at least two others in his office were related to members of the board of directors. "That evening when the Chief sent for me I was in despair. He said, 'You know the instructions sent out. The staff here has to be much reduced, but I expect to keep you on. Now, how much of the work can you do.' I said desperately, 'I guess I can do it all.'"[28]

Van Horne and one other worker replaced nine employees. Word spread about his capabilities and in 1862 he was lured away, at a considerable increase in pay, to a position as the Joliet ticket agent of the Chicago and Alton Railroad. Competence was always in short supply, especially during the war. Van Horne had more than any two men's share and his promotions came in almost indecently quick succession. As his authority grew Van Horne discovered outlets, other than pranks, for his inventiveness. Once, seeing that butter was deteriorating as it sat waiting for shipment, he designed a crude cooler that was so successful it became a standard feature in all stations.

Van Horne grabbed every new bit of responsibility he was given and then took any that wasn't nailed down besides. He operated from the basic assumption that he was right about everything and didn't trouble to hide it. It was an insufferable attitude and the only things that saved him from the animosity and physical violence of his colleagues, most of whom were older, were his sheer competence and devilish sense of humour, which he always exercised at the expense of higher-ups. When he was still at Michigan Central, Van Horne created a satirical "life history," containing text and meticulously drawn caricatures, of a senior official who had raised his ire. The book circulated the length and breadth of the line, making a laughing stock of the unfortunate superior, but it endeared Van Horne to the rank and file. In Bloomington, Illinois, he provoked enormous delight and great respect by illustrating headquarters memos with rude cartoons of the senior trainmen who sent them.

In 1864 Van Horne was partway to his goal when he became the train dispatcher at Bloomington, a major Michigan Central station containing the company's car maintenance facilities. That same year he met his wife, Lucy Adeline Hurd, the daughter of an Illinois civil engineer involved in railroad construction. Lucy, educated at Lombard College, Galesburg, Illinois, was a great beauty, with an endearing and ethereal fragility that lasted until her death. Van Horne could not have chosen a more contrasting mate had he created one himself. He described her as "tall, slender, and dignified, with softly waving black hair, hazel eyes, and apple-blossom complexion."[29]

Lucy and William met by chance, after she'd been stranded late one night at the Joliet station without a ride home. Van Horne, twenty years old, summoned his most gallant manner and volunteered to escort her home. He was so caught up with his chivalry and his efforts not to stare that he stuffed his lit pipe — he'd started smoking to make himself look older — in his pocket, where it promptly set his suit on fire. Lucy laughed as if it were a great trick he had designed just for her. That was enough for Van Horne, who assiduously courted her until March, 1867, when they were married. Van Horne moved everyone in together: his mother-in-law, his mother, his sister and his new bride shared the Bloomington house. All lived with Van Horne until their respective deaths.

Though Van Horne spent many days and nights away from his wife he was intensely devoted to her. Lucy became infected with smallpox in 1873, then a dreaded disfiguring disease with

Lucy Van Horne

a high mortality rate. Van Horne personally nursed her at home instead of sending her to the quarantine pest-house as was commonly done. It was an exhausting regime, caring for Lucy during the day then disinfecting himself and his clothes before he returned to work late at night when there was no other staff around.

Despite their differences in manner and form, Lucy filled an essential role in Van Horne's life. Gracious where he was boastful, Lucy soothed where he ruffled, providing tranquillity and ease in a relationship that was buffeted by his excesses. His work and personality demanded continuous entertaining and she orchestrated endless dinners and weekends for all manner of guests both exalted and ordinary. Sometimes Van Horne didn't even know his guests but invited them to visit simply because they had piqued his curiosity. Others came unannounced to the door and were summoned in if they appeared sufficiently interesting. It was enough to give even the most liberal-minded chatelaine heartburn, but Lucy bore it all with grace and charm. Introducing yet another new caller to her husband in his vast study in Montreal, she would cock her head at him silently as if to say "Well, here's another one of your foundlings."

IN 1868 VAN HORNE WAS MADE SUPERINTENDENT of the Chicago and Alton's telegraph system and promoted again that year to superintendent of the entire southern division of the railroad. Two years later, he was transferred to the Chicago headquarters and put in charge of transportation for the whole railway.

Van Horne was only twenty-nine years old when he earned his coveted private car. That year he became general superintendent of the St Louis, Kansas City and Northern Railroad, a small 581-mile line. The appointment made him the youngest railroad head in the world. It was also the beginning of Van Horne's reputation as a salvage expert.* On the St Louis Road the only thing lower than revenue was the morale of the employees. The road suffered from the most common illness in the industry, skimping on equipment and overspending on inevitable repairs. Van Horne badgered the owners to purchase durable steel rails, with a far higher load capacity and lifetime than the standard iron ones. Then he incessantly repeated his dictum that a road was only as good as the number of people it could convince to use it. The morale of employees, frequently battered by his searing diatribes over some act of stupidity, actually rose when the trainmen saw the

---

*With this posting, Van Horne began to build his fortune. It was common at the time, particularly with failing railroads, to pay executives with a combination of salary and stock or stock options. A failing railroad had plenty of cheap stock available. Van Horne, never shy about betting on his own prowess, whether at poker or in business, took the limit he could negotiate in stock and then cashed in when the road began turning a profit and the share prices jumped.

extraordinary hours Van Horne was devoting to making the line pay. He was tough on his men but he also sympathized with their problems. The improved food, reading rooms and clubs he introduced at divisional points made their lives away from home a little easier.

As he resurrected the St Louis Road Van Horne looked much as he would for the rest of his life. He was a striking man with fine features and blue eyes so alive their fire even leaps out of hundred-year-old photographs. His smallish nose was perfectly chiselled, and his immaculately trimmed short beard gave an impression of a granite jaw beneath. Despite his fine-grained complexion, more that of an indolent fop than a hard-driving railroad man, no one would describe Van Horne as handsome. The hair on his high forehead had already receded clear to the middle of his pate, and his eyes were so watchful and alert they appeared lidless. His clothes, though of the best cloth and cut, invariably looked slept-in: his trousers bagged where they should have hugged and strained tight where they should have fallen smooth and loose. His figure didn't help. Even then he was politely described as being "rather heavy set" and his set got ever heavier as the years rolled on. But his bulk never suggested softness. He radiated strength and power and a barely leashed volatility that was ready to escape at any moment in Richter-scale magnitudes.

Van Horne lowered himself into chairs with all the delicacy of a free-falling bag of cement. Getting up again, he was even less refined, heaving himself to his feet with mammoth gruntings and groanings and frequently tangling his legs in the chair legs. In later years he solved the problem by sitting riverboat-gambler style, his belly shoved against the back of an armless office chair. When he wanted to get up he simply walked forward, leaving it crashing to the ground between his legs. While standing, his conversation was punctuated by expansive gesticulations and unexpected kicks aimed at the nearest piece of furniture. In motion, he was a human steam engine. "You always knew when Sir William Van Horne was approaching his office," remembered a close friend, Colonel

Allan Magee, "even when he had just got off the elevator, was still coming down the corridor, but had not yet turned the corner. The sounds were unmistakable — the heavy tread, the wheeze, the snuffle, the snort, all warnings that a portentous figure was about to loom into view."[30]

Van Horne's sheer physical presence intimidated even the most conscientious trainmen. He turned intimidation into

William Van Horne

terror with his propensity to pop in unannounced and conduct surprise inspections at the most obscure outposts. It also
seemed that he was clairvoyant and omniscient, an image he
took great pains to perpetuate. During his tenure with the
Chicago and Alton line he gave a group of trainmen a tremendous scare. Van Horne had learned that, in strict violation of
the rules, these workers were taking cushions from the passenger coach while they were on duty and creating comfortable beds for themselves in the baggage car. Van Horne sent a
wire, which he ordered to be delivered late at night to the head
of the crew. The man received it in a small waystation out in the
middle of nowhere. It contained the simple message, "Put back
those cushions."

IT WAS THE ST LOUIS TURNAROUND that earned Van Horne the
beginnings of his railroading reputation, but late that first
summer, he was the central figure in a story that travelled all
along the great lines of the United States. Van Horne was in
the midst of one of his cherished inspection trips. Travelling in
second class as he often did at that time, his ruminations were
interrupted by the rude and boisterous behaviour of four
young, exceptionally seedy-looking toughs. They were teasing
a crying infant, clutched in the arms of a worried mother.

One of the men, growing irritated by the baby's wailing,
grabbed and slapped the child, shouting, "Shut up!" which
only made him cry harder. The mother was black and she
knew better than to stand up to these men, whose contempt
for her was palpable. Panicked, she looked for some escape.
One of the bullies laughed in derision at her fear. At that
moment Van Horne, who had been watching the disturbance
with increasing anger, rocketed out of his seat and hauled the
offender into the aisle by the scruff of his neck.

"Leave that child alone!" he barked.

"Who the hell are you?" came the unrepentant snarl.

"Never mind," Van Horne responded ominously. "Be careful
how you conduct yourself or I shall throw you off the train."[31]

He was badly outnumbered, but something in his voice and the ferocity of his icy gaze made the man back down. Shrugging off Van Horne's hand, he sat down. As they pulled into the station his courage returned and he moved threateningly towards Van Horne, but his companions dragged him off the train.

The conductor, mysteriously absent until then, dashed over to Van Horne and ordered him to duck down. "Do you know who those men are?" he whispered, his voice cracking with fear. "That's Jesse and Frank James and the Younger brothers. Lie as you are or they may take it in their heads to shoot you as the train leaves." Van Horne was a little shaken, but he pretended that nothing out of the ordinary had occurred. The story of how the "super" had bested the most notorious train robbers of all time thrilled and titillated railroaders for years to come.*

WITHIN TWO YEARS VAN HORNE had turned the St Louis, Kansas City and Northern into a paying proposition for the first time. Then another poorly financed and mismanaged road beckoned — the Southern Minnesota, headquartered at La Crosse, Wisconsin. It not only offered a new challenge — it was actually in receivership at the time — but added to his authority as well. Endowed with the titles of general superintendent, president and director, he had a free hand in renovating the company's sagging fortunes.

It took Van Horne barely three years to pull the Southern Minnesota out of receivership by improving the efficiency of the line and chasing after freight, settlers and branch lines, all

---

*The bully was probably one of the Youngers, since Jesse James had a reputation of being kind to women and the poor. The James brothers' career spanned a decade from 1870 to 1881 and they stuck up Van Horne's line, the Chicago and Alton in 1879. The only train they considered off-limits was the Chicago, Burlington and Quincy, which had thoughtfully granted their mother a lifetime pass on its line. James was shot in 1882 by a member of his own gang for a bounty. Frank turned law-abiding and joined a wild west show, dying of old age in 1915.

of which were vital if a road was to avoid stagnation or takeover by rival interests. He also had his first taste of politics and he developed a lifelong distrust of politicians. The Southern Minnesota had lost its charter for an extension line because it had not completed the required construction. Van Horne went to St Paul to get it back and in the process met with members of the State Assembly. Though they granted his wishes, Van Horne's bluntness offended some of the representatives, which led one of them to comment wryly that Van Horne was a man "who knew what he knew for certain."[32]

This backhanded admiration was not reciprocated. While president of the CPR, Van Horne didn't hesitate to jump in and throw support behind political candidates, especially if he thought an opponent might damage the company's interests, but even though some of his closest friends were politicians, as a breed he never quite trusted them. He likened their work to that of an undertaker or bailbondsman — necessary, but distasteful and faintly tainted.

He may not have trusted politicians but he was never uncomfortable in their presence. Perhaps the only time Van Horne ever suffered discomfort was in the company of women, around whom he became awkward and stilted. His colourful language and racy stories choked in his throat and he dared not discuss world affairs or business because his comments were invariably tarted up with a good measure of expletives. As he grew older, particularly after his intelligent, strong-minded daughter Adeline was born, he became easier among the fairer sex. Still, an excess of gush in petticoats left him gasping. One day in Montreal a titled woman paid him a short visit. As she was shown out Van Horne turned to his friends and mopped his broad brow: "My God, it's over! That woman has nearly frightened me to death."[33]

After he restored the Southern Minnesota to health, Van Horne was offered the general superintendency of the Chicago and Alton, one of the most powerful lines in the Midwest, operating nearly 1,000 miles of track. His main fight during his short time with the C & A was with other railroads, all competing fiercely for traffic that had diminished during the depression of the mid-seventies. One way to snare customers was through their stomachs. Van Horne helped design the C & A's own dining cars to rival those of the famous Pullman company.* He also ordered that all meal portions be larger than those on the competing line. He had a personal interest in portions, finding most on-line dinners far too small for his satisfaction. To ensure he got a good feed at his destination he frequently telegraphed ahead for two, and even three, complete meals and ate them all himself, much to the astonishment of the dining car staff.

Van Horne had barely settled in when, in 1879, the Chicago, Milwaukee and St Paul Railroad lured him away into what was destined to be his last job in the United States. Suddenly he was overseeing 2,200 miles of track, much of it gained from a too-quick absorption of smaller roads. Van Horne was needed to blend it all into a harmonious whole.

As Van Horne consolidated the Milwaukee Road's vast and jumbled network, he turned his attention to expansion.† Naturally he wanted a piece of the richest railroad country on the continent, the Red River Valley. Such plans sat poorly with J. J. Hill, who had just fended off Jay Cooke of the Northern Pacific. He wasn't about to let anybody into what he considered his private preserve. Hill and Van Horne met to settle the

---

*George Mortimer Pullman began experimenting with sleeper cars after an excruciatingly uncomfortable trip from Buffalo to Westfield, New York, and many of his prototypes were given their maiden voyages on the Chicago and Alton. But Pullman's palatial and innovative car, the Pioneer, was universally derided for its size — it wouldn't fit under bridges or in stations. His big break came in 1865 with the death of President Lincoln. Lincoln's widow rode the Pioneer on one stage of the funeral trip, since it was the only car grand enough for the occasion. Bridges and stations were altered and no more was heard of its size again. The comforts he instituted in his "hotels on wheels" were not extended to his employees, however. He paid them as little as he could, and they lived in pathetic, unsanitary shacks. When he died in 1896 with a fortune of $7 million, his cars were running over 125,000 miles of track, three-quarters of the trackage in the United States.

†He also dabbled in architecture, drafting plans for station houses that were warmer, more efficient, less costly and, above all, attractive. Some of his designs were used twenty-five years later in the building of lines in the Puget Sound area.

problem. There was plenty of thrust and parry in the inter-change, but it ended indecisively. Recognizing a serious threat when it was staring him in the face, Hill knew he had to do something about William Cornelius Van Horne.

His first gambit was to offer Van Horne the position of general manager of the Manitoba Road, but when he hinted at the possibility during their meeting Van Horne had laughed so hard Hill thought he was going to have a seizure. Then a happy solution occurred to Hill. If he could convince Van Horne to take on the faltering CPR, it would eliminate him as a rival and with a little luck save the CPR at the same time.

CHAPTER 5

VAN HORNE
TO THE RESCUE

*Van Horne . . . took the CPR in his hands like a
giant whip, cracked it once to announce his presence,
cracked it again to shake loose the sloth and
corruption and cracked it a third time simply because
the first two had felt so good.*

V an Horne was a far more subtle man than was generally
supposed. He made a thorough and completely incon-
spicuous reconnaissance of the CPR with Hill before he accepted the job, which, at $15,000 a year, made him the highest-
paid general manager in North America. Then on January 1,
1882, Van Horne swooped into Winnipeg and took the CPR in
his hands like a giant whip, cracked it once to announce his
presence, cracked it again to shake loose the sloth and corruption and cracked it a third time simply because the first two
had felt so good. The railroad never knew what hit it. R. K.
Kernighan, a newspaper writer whose work appeared under
the pseudonyms "The Khan" and "the Dervish Khan," vividly
brings to life Van Horne's visit to Flat Creek, Manitoba, then
the small administrative headquarters at the western end of
track. Kernighan called his article "Massacre at Flat Krick."

. . . when Manager Van Horne strikes the town there is a shaking of
bones. He cometh in like a blizzard and he goeth out like a lantern.
He is the terror of Flat Krick. He shakes them up like an earthquake,
and they are as frightened of him as if he were the old Nick himself.
Yet Van Horne is calm and harmless looking. So is a she mule, and
so is a buzz saw. You don't know their inwardnesss till you go up and

127

get the feel of them. To see Van Horne get out of the car and go softly up the platform, you might think he was an evangelist on his way west to preach temperance to the Mounted Police.

But you are soon undeceived. If you are within hearing distance you will have more fun than you ever had in your life before. He cuffs the first official he comes to just to get his hand in and leads the next one by the ear, and pointing eastward informs him that the walking is good as far as St Paul. To see the rest hunt their holes and commence scribbling for dear life is a terror.

Van Horne wants to know. He is that kind of man. He wants to know why this was not done and why this was done. If the answers are not satisfactory there is a dark and bloody tragedy enacted right there. During each act all the characters are killed off and in the last scene the heavy villain is filled with dynamite, struck with a hammer, and by the time he has knocked a hole plumb through the sky, and the smoke has cleared away, Van Horne has discharged all the officials and hired them over again at lower figures.[1]

The Flat Creek massacre was a piece of high theatre, replayed up and down the line. The performance was almost as good as a raise in pay for morale, but not everyone was thrilled by the changes Van Horne wrought. For every appreciative trainman or onlooker there were dozens more who considered him to be about as constructive as a plague of locusts. If Van Horne had set out to alienate as many Canadians as possible, including the press, he couldn't have planned it better. Even J. J. Hill as far away as St Paul heard about the reaction. "Van Horne has made a clean sweep of the office and will only re-employ such as can show clean hands. This has already caused some bad feeling . . . and some . . . in high places, against Van Horne."[2] The job was too big and in too desperate a condition to worry about bad feelings, and Van Horne trampled unrepentant over the sentiments of those who believed the road should be built by Canadians. He imported an entire crew of men he trusted and knew. Among them was John Egan, an abrasive, unsympathetic Fenian supporter who fired people with more zeal than his boss. If the CPR wasn't loathed in Manitoba by the time Van Horne arrived, within a few short months he made sure it was.

BY THE TIME VAN HORNE SET FOOT on Canadian soil, the CPR's top officials in Winnipeg were carrying on a roaring business of land selling and information peddling. Chief among them was the railway's head engineer, General Thomas Lafayette Rosser.* A southern aristocrat who had fought in the American Civil War against his West Point classmate General George Custer, Rosser pushed derring-do into entirely new dimensions. He had achieved considerable notoriety during the war by leading his men in an insanely hopeless attack against the Federal lines, instead of surrendering with his superior Robert E. Lee at Appomattox. On another occasion he was shot in the knee and escaped capture by riding all night in agony, his useless leg hanging down limply. After the war, his fortune devastated, Rosser brought the same suicidal élan to railroading. He worked his way up through the surveying ranks until he was the chief surveyor for the Northern Pacific.

Rosser had also worked briefly for Hill on the Manitoba Road. There, as the man responsible for land purchases, he got a first-hand look at the profits to be made from speculation, and when he joined the CPR he wasted little time in selling his privileged information to railroad land gamblers. What's more, he wasn't even doing it quietly. "It looks as though everyone from Genl. Rosser down has been engaged in town-site operations. It is openly advertised that Genl. Rosser is a promoter of the town of Raeburn," Hill told Angus in disgust.[3]

On February 1, 1882, between puffs on his oversized cigar, Van Horne fired Rosser, but the object of his dismissal wasn't one to saddle up and ride out of town quietly. Instead, he went looking for hostages. It would be Van Horne's closest brush with death during the building of the transcontinental railway. One evening that summer Van Horne was dining with a companion in the Coffee Room of the Manitoba Club, a gathering

---

*Also involved but not as active as Rosser was his superior, Alpheus B. Stickney, the general superintendent of the CPR's western division. It is estimated that together they netted more than $130,000 from their speculations.

place of Winnipeg's elite. Their conversation was halted by a commotion in the doorway. General Rosser strode into the room and uttered, sotto voce, some distinctly uncomplimentary words about Van Horne. Then, turning to the general superintendent's companion, Rosser told him he was sorry to see him in the company of such a son of a bitch before wheeling about and leaving the room.

A few minutes later a club member hurried over to Van Horne and warned him that Rosser was waving a revolver around and threatening to shoot him. Nothing ever came of the threats, and the board members of the Manitoba Club, who were disposed to be lenient, merely sent the wild major-general a letter of rebuke, saying his behaviour could not "for a moment be tolerated" and if an "ample apology" was not immediately forthcoming the club would consider rescinding his membership. Rosser meekly apologized.

FROM THE MINUTE VAN HORNE CANNONBALLED into Canada, J. J. Hill began wondering if he'd made a grave error. Rather than neutralizing a potential enemy by saddling him with an enormous burden, Hill had unintentionally placed Van Horne in a position where he could do even greater damage than before. Van Horne had boasted far and wide that he would lay a total of five hundred miles of track in 1882. It was a staggering, maniacal declaration, and no one from Stephen to Secretan, the CPR's chief surveyor, believed it could be done.* To achieve his boast, Van Horne focused exclusively on the considerable problems at hand. Picayune irritants — in particular the mosquito whine of J. J. Hill's advice couched in the tones of a mentor instructing an inexperienced protégé — were ignored.

---

*The doubts of the senior officers of the CPR were well founded. Hill's laying of ninety-seven miles of track in slightly less than a year, in rather more hospitable terrain, was deemed a considerable feat. Van Horne was proposing to lay five times as much track, in far more difficult conditions.

In the spring of 1882 Van Horne galvanized Winnipeg as he readied his army of men and equipment to get a running start on the tracklaying season. Hampering him was the wave of fortune seekers — five thousand in a single week in April — clogging virtually every available means of transport. Ties, rails and provisions that should have arrived in Winnipeg months before were stranded on sidings all over the eastern United States and Canada. Unloading of supplies was going so slowly in the Winnipeg yards that every siding on the track to St Paul was jammed up with flat cars — most of which belonged to the Manitoba Road. Hill pestered Van Horne to free up some of his cars, but as the weeks sped by the situation only worsened.

Van Horne's unresponsiveness was infuriating. Hill was a major shareholder and a member of the executive committee, but Van Horne treated him as if he were a pest. Hill had eased the CPR's way with a "huge rebate" and "below-cost freight rates" not to mention the wholesale loan of equipment and men. The ingratitude was intolerable but the stalled cars were money out of Hill's pocket. That was unforgivable. One day, Hill counted 254 of his flatcars loaded with CPR-bound rails,

Construction along the main line, about 1885

tied up in St Paul. It was the last straw. "[I] am entirely unable to see how they have been held loaded until this time, as during the 20 days interruption you surely had time enough to unload the cars then on hand or five times as many."[4*] Van Horne cabled that he would attend to the rails immediately. Two days later, Hill's Winnipeg spies informed him that not a single one had been unloaded.

"You people do not get to work early enough," Hill raged at Van Horne. ". . . We have so many cases reported of their neglect that your messages [of denial] can only be accounted for on the ground that you are not well informed."[5] Hill punctuated his annoyance by threatening to send his own men up and down the line, unloading the flatcars and leaving the rails wherever they fell. Van Horne, who was on the verge of unloading the cars anyway, did the job in less than a week, a record unheard of before or since. Hill chose to interpret it as a personal victory. "Mr. Van Horne I have no doubt is a little vexed at my persistent efforts to get cars around faster," he smugly confided to Stephen, "but that will be over when I see him and in the meantime the situation is improved."[6]

Even more annoying than Hill's incessant letters and cables were his Winnipeg visits. Each time he decided "to run up to Winnipeg and survey the situation" Van Horne launched himself on an exhausting inspection tour. As a result, either Van Horne wasn't there at all, or Hill was forced to tag along at his employee's heels, as he roared through twenty-hour days. But Van Horne soon learned that leaving Hill unattended in Winnipeg was a serious mistake. On several occasions Hill gave contradictory orders to CPR contractors and on another he embarrassed Van Horne by taking the contractors' side in a dispute. On one trip Hill arbitrarily ordered a change in the route south of Qu'Appelle in present-day Saskatchewan, in order to "save considerable distance and get better alignment."[7]

---

*The twenty-day period Hill was referring to was the flooding of the Red River, which brought transportation to a standstill.

Van Horne paid him back tenfold. To compensate Hill for the lower rates, equipment loans and shipping privileges extended to the CPR, George Stephen had promised not to open the section under construction from Thunder Bay to Winnipeg until the spring of 1883 at the earliest. This would shield the Manitoba Road by ensuring that freight went through St Paul, an agreement which also benefited Stephen by virtue of his investments with Hill. If Van Horne was aware of the deal he didn't feel bound by it in the slightest. No sooner was a mile of track laid than he ordered CPR agents to beat the bushes for traffic. His action elicited howls of indignation from St Paul: "It would only be common courtesy to a connecting line to have at least given us some notice, and not leave us to get our information from the newspapers," Hill complained to John S. Kennedy. "While I am sure Mr. Stephen does not share in the feeling but on the contrary will regret its existence, there is I know a feeling . . . of ill concealed hostility [on the part of Van Horne] towards this company."[8]

Van Horne never got the running start on construction he had envisioned in early 1882. The transportation tieups, coupled with widespread spring flooding in the Red River Valley put him badly behind schedule. Barely 70 miles of track were in place by the end of June. But from then on progress was prodigious. By the end of the year, 420 miles of the main line, 28 miles of siding and 100 miles of feeder line in Manitoba had been built, bettering Van Horne's boast by 48 miles. During a forty-two day stretch in August and September, an average of 3.14 miles of track had been laid each day.[9] Secretan grumped that construction was moving so quickly grading crews passed him in the night, grading ground that hadn't yet been surveyed.

Van Horne may have pushed his men to the limit, but he provisioned them well. The general manager was sure about most things but the thing he was absolutely certain of was food. To his mind, a small amount of it was almost a greater sacrilege than none at all. After J. H. E. Secretan had produced a list of supplies for his crew for the summer of 1882, Burdock, the

Sir William Van Horne at his desk

chief purchasing agent, slashed his requirements by 30 percent, cutting out little luxuries entirely. When Van Horne got wind of the abominable act Burdock was hauled before The Presence. In a booming monotone and amid threatening gesticulations Van Horne gave him until evening to pack up and ship out a huge load of delicacies to Secretan. "You can come back at six o'clock and tell me you have shipped it, you understand, but if you have not, you need not come back at all, but just go back to wherever you came from."[10] Secretan smoked Havana cigars and drank fine whiskey until the frost appeared.

Secretan, a fastidious martinet himself when it came to precision in his chosen profession, was a sardonic observer of the man who caused him many instances of indigestion, fine grub notwithstanding. "The Czar of the CPR," as he called him, would simply issue an order, shove his pince-nez up the bridge of his nose and expect to have it carried out, whether it was possible or not. One day Van Horne was unrolling a map and scowling at it as if faced with some colossal stupidity. "Look here," he barked, jabbing his finger at a point on the Bow River in the Rockies, "some damned fool of an engineer has put in a tunnel up there, and I want you to go and *take it out*!" Secretan calmly replied that there was probably a good reason for its existence, but Van Horne shouted him down.

As he turned to leave, the beleaguered surveyor asked, "While I'm up there hadn't I better move some of those mountains back, as I think they are too close to the river." Van Horne rewarded him with the bellowing laugh that sometimes woke his houseguests up in the middle of the night. "I could see the generous proportions of his corporation shaking like jelly,"[11] Secretan recalled.

IRONICALLY, AS VAN HORNE FORGED AHEAD, driving the railroad ever nearer to completion and drawing freight and passenger revenues with him, the CPR edged closer and closer to a financial abyss. Like a controlled madman, Van Horne ordered, coaxed, lashed and cajoled his construction bosses onto greater feats each day. And as he went, so did the money: $22 million had been consumed by December 31, 1882. But tracklaying wasn't solely responsible for the rapid disappearance of funds. Stephen was gobbling up branch and feeder lines like a trencherman.*

Things might have been a little easier had it not been for the government, which was being positively languid about handing over the cash subsidy as the company completed each twenty-mile section of the line. In order to meet current expenses, the CPR was forced to take out a short-term $1.5 million loan from the Bank of Montreal, backed by some Manitoba Road shares belonging to Stephen, Smith and

---

*It is impossible to fully document the numerous railroad lines that Stephen had his hand in through ownership of debentures and common stock and by other means. Among the lines acquired at this point were the Canada Central line (purchased by assuming the remainder of its mortgage, which represented about $1.8 million) and the Montreal-Ottawa section of the Quebec, Montreal, Ottawa and Occidental Railway. This line, which had cost the Quebec government more than $14 million, was purchased with $500,000 cash and a $3.5 million promissory note. Typically, Stephen held such purchases in his own portfolio or in the hands of a strawman before vending them into the CPR.

Stephen was also surreptitiously buying up such roads as the Manitoba Southwestern, to which he already had $1 million personally committed.

Angus. Still short, Stephen arranged to sell $20 million worth of capital stock at a discounted $25 a share.* The shares, netting the CPR $4,974,475, were taken up by the Syndicate members themselves. Stephen was juggling so many personal railroad investments, he had to sell his prized Bank of Montreal stock to pay for the allotment.

All through the fall of 1882 Stephen had been planning a coup designed to extricate the CPR for good and all from its financial bog. Writing to Macdonald he confidently asserted, "Our pinch is now. After New Year we shall have plenty of funds from other sources. I think we have at last found a 'bridge to cross the stream.'"[12] Stephen's bridge turned out to be a complicated infusion of $75 million in new financing. (The company's authorized capital† had been increased from the original $25 million to $100 million.)

He announced the formation of the North American Railway Contracting Company, which would take over construction of various uncompleted portions of the main line— in particular, the treacherous section through the mountains and the line north of Lake Superior. In return the company would receive $31.9 million in cash and $45 million worth of stock (par value) from the CPR. In a secondary deal $30 million worth of stock was turned over to a number of financing houses, called The Stock Syndicate, for sale to investors. "I have been at work here night and day and have left myself only time to say goodbye," he wrote to Macdonald on the eve of his December 12th departure to holiday in London. "I start with a

---

*The par, or face, value of a security is its nominal worth. Its real worth, or market value, is what anyone will pay for it. The par value of CPR shares was $100 each, but their market value would not go above $100 a share until 1901 when the price hit $117.

There is great confusion about exactly how much private investment was actually made in the CPR, and George Stephen must bear much of the blame for his gross and repeated exaggerations. On February 11, 1888, he boasted of his part in "getting some $150 million of private capital into the C.P.R." when in fact the total par value capitalization was only $65 million. The sale of these shares realized barely $20 million for the CPR. (Stephen to George M. Grant, Montreal, February 11, 1888, NAC)

†Authorized capital is the amount of par value shares that the shareholders, subject to government regulation, have approved for sale to raise capital for the company.

light heart having added greatly to our *achieving power* since I came here as will soon be seen when we come before the public [put the shares on sale] in January. The C.P.R. will be built without a dollar of money from London."[13]

His plan was smoke and mirrors. The North American Railway Contracting Company, a shell registered in New Jersey, never constructed an inch of track, nor was any money ever paid to it. Its purpose was to project a sense of financial solidity to lure investors. The $45 million in stock remained in limbo until 1884 when it was used by the CPR to fill the gaps in another crisis.

The other $30 million in stock supposedly sold to the land syndicate was in fact only optioned* to W. L. Scott, an American financier and an associate of John S. Kennedy. Scott was also part of the North American Railway Contracting Company. The agreement allowed Scott to purchase $10 million par value stock in January, 1883, at $50 a share, $10 million par value on June 25th at $52½ a share and a final $10 million par value at $55 a share in December, 1883.[14] Scott also made a secret deal with Kennedy that the members of the CPR Syndicate would not sell any of their own shares and thus deflate the price until the $30 million worth of stock was all sold.

George Stephen conceived the plan, but the deal itself was put together by Kennedy, a much overlooked figure in the CPR's early financing arrangements. Stephen told Macdonald he had worked around the clock on the details, but when he turned it over to Kennedy on December 12th it was still a fragmented hodgepodge. The agreements "were nominally prepared in Montreal but came to us in such shape that they were of no use until they were corrected and entirely remodelled from beginning to end," Kennedy informed Hill. ". . . The labour over all these things has been immense and I

---

*An option is the right to purchase a certain amount of stock at a set date and for an agreed price. Whether the option is exercised or not is strictly at the discretion of the purchaser.

have sat up night after night till midnight correcting and remodelling them."[15] Kennedy also represented the CPR before "some of the brightest and cutest men" in New York to get swift stock market approval for the agreements, and he personally completed the transaction with W. L. Scott.

Kennedy was hoping for prices near $60 a share, but the market resisted and the stock hung consistently below $50. Of the $30 million in optioned stock, $10 million never even left the CPR treasury. The remaining $20 million worth netted the CPR less than $10 million, an unknown percentage of which was bought by Smith and Stephen themselves to bolster the market. In all, the $75 million in new financing netted barely $10 million in new money by the end of 1883.

An injection of that much money — though a huge sum then — paid for less than half of one year's construction. With an earlier start in 1883 — grading began at the end of March and the tracklaying a few weeks later — Van Horne rammed the track all the way through to the Kicking Horse Pass by November 27th, consistently bettering the previous season's record pace. During a forty-eight-consecutive-day stretch that summer, the crews averaged 3.46 miles of track each day. On July 28th they laid a phenomenal total of 6.38 miles.

WHILE STEPHEN WAS SCRAMBLING to find money, Van Horne was pushing, prodding and inspiring his crews to ever more herculean efforts. No place on the line was safe from his inspection. He frequently waded unbridged rivers, walked for miles overland and once went two days without meals to personally look at a trouble spot. If an engineer refused to drive across a shaky trestle, Van Horne shouldered him aside and drove the engine across himself. On one occasion he was strongly advised not to cross an unfinished trestle — essentially two loose planks strung across a 160-foot-deep ravine — where a few days before, several workers had fallen to a grisly death. Van Horne marched across, his corpulence jiggling as if he were operating a jackhammer, leaving his accompanying engineers to crawl behind on their hands and knees.

Van Horne seemed to materialize at work sites at the most unexpected moments, bellowing, cussing and cuffing. Progress was never made fast enough, no matter what the previous day's records. No one could keep up with him during the day but rare was the night that he didn't arm-wrestle, play poker, tell stories, drink and swear until dawn and then wash up and be on his way. The men admired Van Horne's stamina, daring and eating capacity, but what they liked best about him was the fact that he never put on airs. Once, when he'd fallen into a river and couldn't find any dry clothes to fit, he spent the rest of the day, to everyone's vast amusement, in a red flannel shirt and a pair of pants that were split down the back and held together by clothesline.

The work was burning money: another $22 million had been spent in 1883. By December 31, 1883, construction, engineering and the purchase of various subsidiary lines had

A timber trestle bridge on the CPR line during construction

swallowed up a further $58,695,377.* A year earlier Stephen had been buoyantly optimistic about the new financing. Now he was desperately scrambling for cash again.

None of Stephen's money-making schemes would have been necessary had the CPR been able to sell a reasonable portion of its land at a good price. On the face of it a fair amount was sold between 1881 and 1883. Settlers bought 794,240 acres, and corporations, including the North West Land Company (controlled by Donald Smith), purchased 2,837,400 acres. The proceeds totalled $10,378,900, but after the deduction of deferred payments and the heavy expenses incurred by advertising for land sales and immigration, the CPR netted only $6,667,000—enough to cover capital costs for just four months. The land grant bonds left them no better off. Only $10 million worth of the $25 million worth available were ever taken up by the sluggish and suspicious market.

AS THE CPR'S NEED FOR CASH became more acute, Hill and Kennedy began to notice a sharp increase in "bear raids" and short selling† in the stock of the Manitoba Road. Independent brokers were selling large blocks at the peak of the market and then, when the price fell, were buying back similar amounts at a lower price. No one seemed to know who was behind the activity, but the Manitoba shares were closely held by relatively few individuals.

Hill's suspicions quickly turned to his Associates. He repeatedly asked Smith, Stephen and Angus about the mysterious raids. They commiserated but offered no answers. Then in

---

*This sum doesn't include the cost of sundry lines that members of the Syndicate were holding privately.

†Bear raids are organized attempts, usually through strategic selling coupled with carefully placed rumours, to drive the price of a stock down. Short selling involves selling a stock one doesn't own at today's price with a future delivery date, anticipating that the price will fall. The short seller then buys the stock at the deflated price, netting the difference. At the time the CPR was raising funds, there were no restrictions on short selling, and small bands of short sellers armed with inside information or conducting so-called bear raids, could make fortunes forcing stock prices up and down to their advantage.

January, 1883, he was sitting reading a letter from Angus, who was promising to hold on to his 5,700 shares, when a cable from Kennedy arrived telling him that Donald Smith had surreptitiously dropped $300,000 worth of Manitoba stock on the market.[16] A few months later Angus sold his shares and then even George Stephen admitted he had sold some of his holdings.[17]

Hill had nothing against a little judicious working of the market. A few months later, he and Kennedy took advantage of the widespread rumours "that it is the Canadian parties that are selling out"[18] to do a little profit taking of their own. Working through nonassociated brokers they were able to unload $580,900 of their Manitoba Road stock, without anyone realizing what they were up to. What Hill did object to was the fact that he wasn't in on the deals.

IF HILL WAS IRRITATED BY THE SYNDICATE's fiddling around with Manitoba Road stock behind his back, he was infuriated by Stephen's machinations over the Manitoba Southwestern

Smith and Van Horne (middle) at Smith's summer home,
Silver Heights, Manitoba

Colonization Railway. Chartered in 1879 to build southwest of Winnipeg for thirty miles and then west again into the nearby Souris coal field, the Associates' rival Northern Pacific group seized the Southwestern in 1881. It was the centrepiece in a plan to invade the Canadian West and siphon off Red River Valley traffic. But the CPR moved in and ruthlessly squeezed them out with a competing line that ran down the west side of the Red River to within thirteen miles of the border and then headed westward again. Canadian Pacific's tactics immediately deflated the Southwestern's stock prices, and the Northern Pacific's interest in its property dried up. During 1882 Stephen began quietly buying as many shares as he could get his hands on.

Just before Stephen resigned as president of the Manitoba Road in 1882 he bought, on the Manitoba Road's behalf, his own interests in the Southwestern line for $1.25 million without consulting Hill.* Stephen mollified him somewhat by explaining that he had only "stored" the Southwestern temporarily until the CPR could afford to take it over in February, 1883. That was when he expected the new CPR financing to yield some results.

February came and Stephen showed no signs of fulfilling his promise. Hill wrote a chiding letter to Angus. "I hope you will soon be in a position to take the Southwestern off our hands as the hard winter and deep snow have cut our earnings down to an extent that we are quite hard up."[19] A month passed and he heard nothing. "The inability of the Canadian Pacific Co. to carry out its undertaking in regard to the Manitoba Southwestern has been a very great inconvenience to us, inasmuch as it ties up nearly $1,250,000," he complained to J. Kennedy Tod,[20] John S. Kennedy's nephew and a partner in J. S. Kennedy and Company.

Meanwhile, the Canadian Pacific showed signs of becoming

---

*At this point, Hill was still only the general manager of the Manitoba Road. Stephen was president and Angus, vice-president.

the deadly enemy Hill had predicted. Determined to fill every mile of track with traffic the minute it was laid, Van Horne began a campaign of rate cutting. Hill wrote numerous complaining letters to Stephen, Hill and Kennedy, as if he had been grievously wronged and would never do such a terrible thing himself. Typically, he exonerated Stephen from any blame in the matter, saying that the directors were helpless pawns in the face of Van Horne's manœuvring: "The manifest policy of the CanPac," he wrote to Kennedy in 1883, "is to do everything in their power to keep business from going or coming south over our lines, and our only plan to counteract their efforts would be to use the river from St Vincent to Winnipeg which would in my opinion lead to an unpleasant contest in which the CanPac would I think get the worst of it. . . . Mr. Van Horne who is the only one having any practical knowledge of such matters . . . is inclined to take the view that the St P. M. & M. are powerless to help themselves and must simply accept any situation that may be assigned to it by the CanPac. . . . I think Mr. Stephen would prefer a good fair arrangement between the Companies but he has to rely on someone else to tell him what that should be."[21]

Hill's presence on the CPR board and its executive committee was becoming farcical. His advice was no longer sought let alone heeded and he was in the awkward position of owning substantial stock in a railroad that competed vigorously with his own. He'd already threatened to sell his shares late in 1882, but had held onto them only as a personal favour to the Syndicate. Stephen couldn't put him off indefinitely and as Hill's agitations increased, Stephen offered to buy nearly 15,000 of his original 25,000 "at about cost" ($46 a share). Hill officially resigned from the CPR board on May 3rd for the good of "my old associates."[22]

Still, there remained the aggravating issue of the South-western. He told Willis James, a well-connected New York businessman and a new Manitoba Road board member, that he was ready to take legal action if he couldn't get satisfaction any other way. "I went carefully over the purchase of the

Southwestern today with Judge Clark our counsel and he says Mr. Stephen who gave the instructions to buy the property . . . exceeded his power and was liable to the stockholders of the Manitoba Company for the sum paid for it."[23] In spite of all the evidence, Hill steadfastly refused to blame Stephen personally for this or any of the other decidedly unfriendly acts of those months. "I think Mr. Stephen means well but has pursued a somewhat vacillating course and we must encourage him by making his load as easy as we can, at the same time we cannot afford to hold the property until they deem it is of no value and then let them leave it on our hands."[24]

Hill had applied just the right kind of pressure. The last thing in the world George Stephen wanted was to be tied up in a time-wasting and likely all too revealing lawsuit with Hill. He certainly didn't want to provide the Canadian and British newspapers with a new brush to tar the CPR. In June, 1883, Stephen sued for peace. He reaffirmed his promise to repurchase the Manitoba Southwestern and submitted his and Smith's resignations from the Manitoba Road board, which Hill promptly refused. Stephen also sent Hill signed proxies for all their voting shares which, as Stephen said, would enable Hill to "give full effect to [his] own wishes."[25] The deal had all the elements of black comedy, for, as it turned out, it was one of Hill's greatest blunders. The Southwestern had completed 52 miles of track, earning a land grant subsidy of 332,200 acres when the CPR took it over. By the time Van Horne completed the line it possessed 1.4 million acres of the best farmland in North America.

IN AUGUST HILL, HAVING SETTLED matters with Stephen, was startled to discover that Van Horne had made preferential rate agreements with the Northern Pacific, the Manitoba Road's greatest enemy. The agreements called for a mutual lowering of freight and passenger rates, none of which had been offered to Hill. "After so many promises to Mr. Kennedy and myself that a fair arrangement would be made," he moaned to

J. Kennedy Tod, "the present situation is to say the least a hard one. . . ."[26] Hill had already been to Winnipeg on several occasions hoping to bring Van Horne into line by virtue of his close connection to Stephen. If Van Horne didn't feel he owed Hill anything perhaps he could be persuaded that he owed something to Stephen, who suffered financially if the Manitoba line's revenue declined. But Van Horne wasn't impressed by the weight of Hill's associations, even if one of them was his boss. He bluntly told him that the Manitoba Road had no business seeking special deals on the CPR's home turf. "I think you were more surprised than I was at the position taken by Mr. Van Horne that virtually we had no business in Winnipeg," Hill reminded Stephen.[27]

On November 7, 1883, Hill sold his final 10,000 shares. "While this closes my connection with the C.P. enterprise, I trust that nothing will ever occur to disturb the good relations between our two companies," he wrote to Stephen. "You will understand that for yourself personally I always have the sincerest wishes for your prosperity and happiness."[28] Purchasing Hill's shares required money that Stephen could ill afford. But he had no choice. He was desperately trying to shore up the stock price to ensure that W. L. Scott exercised his options. Any large block suddenly appearing on the market would topple the already unstable share prices and then Scott wouldn't buy one share, let alone $30 million worth.

STEPHEN'S CAVALIER TREATMENT OF HILL was not born so much of malevolence as of too many months staring into the pit of ruin—the brutal fact being that Stephen had simply not raised enough money to pay the bills past, present or future. Equally harsh was the cold reality that no matter how he rejigged the company's affairs, shuffled books and created dummy façades, few investors were willing to put their faith in the CPR. In its two years of existence, the company had paid out $58,695,377 and collected only $21,318,222 from land sales and the Canadian government subsidy. The gaping

$37,377,155 void was only partly filled by the less than $20 million* invested by shareholders.[29] The CPR was dragging around $17 million in floating debt, though the executive only admitted to $7.5 million. Huge accounts payable made up a large portion of the debt and it was only the nimble work of Thomas Shaughnessy, purchasing agent, in dodging creditors that kept the CPR out of receivership. Finishing the line meant finding at least another $27 million.

When it was clear that the Stock Syndicate and the North American Railway Contracting Company were miserable failures, Stephen hatched yet another scheme to buoy the market in CPR shares. If the government would guarantee investors a 3 percent dividend to shareholders, the CPR would set aside an $8.56 million fund to ensure its payment. The CPR would also endeavour to find another 2 percent to bring the total dividend up to 5 percent.† But the guarantee was just throwing good money after bad. The CPR had already paid $2,128,000 in dividends at this point and that hadn't propped up prices or improved market interest.

The dividend guarantee, announced on November 5th, rallied the stock ten points to $68 a share, but within two weeks heavy selling had returned it to its original point. The *Wall Street Daily News* wrote a scathing editorial denunciation: "There is one stock on the list whose pretensions deserve to be thoroughly exposed. The Canadian Pacific is masquerading around as a 5 percent security. It is a dead skin, and any

---

*The par value at $100 a share of the 550,000 common shares sold was $55 million, but the only ones bought at that price were the original 50,000 shares purchased by the Syndicate at $100, which netted the CPR $4.9 million with commissions deducted. The second lot of 250,000 shares sold at $25 each to insiders and the third lot of 200,000 at less than $50 a share. The gross amount invested came to just over $23 million. After brokerage and other fees were deducted, the CPR netted less than $20 million.

†Stephen actually intended to cover $100 million worth of stock with the guarantee, but that meant a fund of $15 million, and he wasn't able to raise that much money. To pay for the guarantee, Stephen borrowed $5 million from J. S. Kennedy and Company against the $10 million in unallocated stock (stock authorized for sale by shareholders, but still in the company treasury). He borrowed the rest of the money he needed from another source, secured by a portion of Smith's, Angus's and his own remaining stock in the Manitoba Road.

Laying ties in the Fraser Valley

investor who buys the stock on the humbugging pretenses
made for it will lose every cent."[30]

Stephen began to feel like a crippled matador trapped in an
arena full of irritated bulls. Even the government, while seem-
ing supportive, was indulging in a little sabotage. A. T. Galt was

a man Stephen never liked or trusted, but since he was Canada's high commissioner to Great Britain Stephen had little choice but to deal with him during his many voyages to London. Galt, who would have liked to build the line himself, had little faith in the CPR project, and he jealously undermined Stephen to Macdonald whenever he could. Shortly before Stephen concocted the guarantee program Galt wrote to Macdonald, "One thing I am sure of, and that is that the Canadian Pacific will never be finished without coming to London for money, and that it is bumptious folly for Stephen to neglect — as he has done — every means of conciliating this market."[31]

In public Stephen exuded an "everything is possible" optimism, but among friends his gloom and frustration showed. "Geo. Stephen — for the first time — seemed depressed notwithstanding his enormous pluck . . . ," observed Macdonald in a letter to Tupper on November 22nd.[32]

Personally, he was well past the point of no return. He had most of his own assets either pledged as security for or actually invested in the CPR.* If it went down, so would he. Stephen didn't even have the luxury of selling his shares — if that much stock were put up for sale, the market for CPR shares would certainly crash. And if word ever got out that Stephen himself was selling, there wouldn't even be a "dead skin" left to pick over. He really had no choice but to see the job through. Bills were pouring in. Van Horne warned Stephen of impending revolt by contractors and crews if some cash wasn't found to pay

---

*Exactly how much Stephen and Smith ever really had at risk during the construction of the CPR is hidden in their own destroyed papers and the likewise destroyed papers of the nominees and strawmen they used to cloak their activities. The chief, in fact, the only evidence that they had everything at risk, are their own statements to the press, and Stephen's self-serving and self-aggrandizing letters to Sir John A. Macdonald.

Hill's railroad and the Associates' ancillary interests were generating fabulous sums for Stephen and Smith during this period. Part of the reason Smith was crimped for funds during construction of the CPR was his purchase of Hudson's Bay shares as part of his successful takeover of the company. Stephen's involvement with the takeover is unknown, but considering the closeness of their investments during this period, his financial involvement with Smith is almost certain.

salaries — most of which were long overdue. To pay the most pressing bills, Stephen was forced to rely on high-interest short-term loans from the ever-helpful Bank of Montreal. Then, having no place else to go, Stephen turned to the Canadian government. "Things have now reached a pass when we must either stop or find the means of going on," he wrote to Macdonald on December 15, 1883. "Our enemies here and elsewhere think they can now break us down and finish the C.P.R. forever."[33]

Macdonald, who knew a touch was coming when he saw one, shuddered at the idea of a government bailout. He was still being vilified about the original terms of the contract, and even though Stephen had arranged a face-saving show of restoring "friendly relations" between Smith and Macdonald, animosity towards the Syndicate still ran deep in the Conservative caucus. It took a lesson in political realities from John Henry Pope, then acting minister of railways, to force Macdonald to see that helping the CPR was the lesser of two evils. "The day the Canadian Pacific busts the Conservative party busts the day after," was the essence of Pope's message. Stephen told Sir John A. that without government help the CPR would surely collapse: "You may be sure I will do all I can to keep things moving, and in life, till relief arrives, but you must not blame me if I fail. . . . If I find we cannot go on, I suppose the only thing to do will be to put in a Receiver. If that has to be done, the quicker it is done the better. . . . I am getting so wearied and worn out with this business that almost any change will be a relief to me."[34]

The Railway Relief Bill debate drew all the acrimony Macdonald feared. Every niggling problem ever associated with the transcontinental railway was regurgitated and paraded before the House: the Pacific Scandal, the hydra-headed Syndicate and Stephen's unethical investments using Bank of Montreal money. Even the construction of Stephen's magnificent house was fodder for the Opposition, who called it a "palace" during the debate. Contemplating the provisions of the bill, one Liberal MP remarked, "This Company are not spoon-fed, I believe the Government feed them with a shovel."[35]

ANOTHER CASE OF

"OPEN YOUR MOUTH AND SHUT YOUR EYES!"

Spoonfeeding the CPR

The Opposition's outrage and sarcasm were no match for Macdonald's majority. The Relief Bill became law on March 6, 1884. The major clauses included an immediate cash loan of $7.5 million and an additional $15 million dollars, to be paid in instalments for a grand total of $22.5 million. It wasn't nearly enough. The bulk of the $7.5 million went immediately to satisfy the Bank of Montreal's short-term loans, now swollen to $7 million. The $15 million, along with $12 million in yet-to-be-earned subsidy money, in theory covered the $27 million Stephen needed to finish the line. But there was nothing left to pay for the company's roughly $10 million in debts. Nor was there any provision for interest payments or a budget overrun. The most expensive sections through the mountains and along the north shore of Lake Superior had yet to be built and no one had a clear idea of what they would cost.

BUOYED AT FIRST BY THE MARCH BAILOUT, Stephen was again depressed by June when the stock hovered hesitatingly in the $40 range. He doubted if it could be supported, even at that price. "I am going down to the Matapedia [fishing resort] tonight to try and get a little rest for 8 or 10 days," he wrote morosely to Macdonald, "as after the 1st July I shall have to be on guard here alone. We are so harassed to find money to keep things moving that my efficiency for work is not improving and I must make an effort during the next 10 days to get myself into condition. If I could only see myself clear to the end of the year I should feel at ease."[36] Macdonald must have sensed what was coming, for he sternly warned Stephen, "You must not look for any legislative assistance for the CPR & must 'work out your own salvation' by your own means."[37]

The stock dipped again to $39 a share, and Stephen concluded he had to rid himself of the CPR's limp London agent, Morton, Rose & Company, whose lassitude in promoting the stock was worse than no promotion at all. Sir John

Rose* was still an ally but he held little sway in his old firm, which Stephen suspected had developed a nasty case of Grand Trunk sympathy. The only other financial muscle he could approach was Baring Brothers, but at first glance this was a ridiculous notion. Baring's was the prime agent for the Grand Trunk Railway. John S. Kennedy, though no longer part of the CPR Syndicate (he left shortly after Hill's departure in 1883), again lent a helping hand. One of his employees, Alexander Baring, was a relative of the firm's principals, and Kennedy sent him to London to make inquiries on Stephen's behalf. But the trip was taken to no avail. Baring's, long regretting its Grand Trunk association, was not yet ready to get mixed up in another Canadian railway mess.

Between November, 1884, and February, 1885, Stephen tried every remedy he could conceive of, from asking the government to exchange the Manitoba Southwestern land grant for cash to issuing stock on the Ontario and Quebec Railway—guaranteed by the CPR. The newspapers hooted at the proposal. "The idea of a company which has not yet earned a single penny on its own capital guaranteeing the rate of interest on the stocks of an infant and subsidiary line is certainly, to say the least of it, an extremely novel one," chortled a *Money* editorial.[38]

As a consequence of the agreement he'd negotiated with the Canadian government in 1884, Stephen could no longer directly raise money from the sale of stocks or bonds. Nor could he pledge the assets of the road; they were already encumbered by the government. He was in a corner again. The most pressing concern was the dividend owed to share-holders. In August he'd managed to scrape together enough to pay the CPR's 2 percent, but he had no idea where he would find the money for the next one, which was due in February.

---

*A much overlooked but compelling reason for the lacklustre support Rose gave the CPR at this point was the bitter relations between himself and Donald Smith. Rose, an influential member of the Hudson's Bay Company's London Committee from 1873 to his death in 1888, was Smith's main opponent in his efforts to take the company over.

"Do not let *anyone* have a *hint* that we are in such straits," he urged Macdonald.[39] When February came there was, of course, nothing in the CPR treasury, so he and Smith used what was left of their personal fortunes as security against a $650,000 loan to supplement the dividend and a further $1 million promissory note to keep the railway operating. "What Smith and I have done and are doing individually is simply absurd on any kind of business grounds," he wrote to Macdonald. ". . . But as long as we are able to save and protect the Company against its enemies who seem bent on its destruction, we shall not grudge any risk or loss that may occur. Personal interests have become quite a secondary affair with either of us."[40]

Though he'd been given little encouragement of aid privately by Macdonald, Stephen formally presented another proposal for assistance to the government on March 18, 1885, just over a year after the initial bailout. "I don't know how Council or Parliament will take it," was Macdonald's bleak comment to Tupper. "We have blackmailing all round. How it will end God knows — but I wish I were well out of it. . . ."[41] The proposal was quickly turned down.

Stephen, a beaten man, dragged himself off to his quarters and listlessly packed his bags to return to Montreal. That evening Frank Smith, a large, jovial MP, appeared in the lobby as Stephen prepared to pay his bill. After one glance at the man's haggard, defeated countenance Smith trotted over to talk. Upon hearing of Stephen's intention to give it all up, Smith used his charm and sincerity to persuade him to stay for a few more days. By some accounts Smith purposefully kept him talking so long that Stephen missed his train.

Together with John Henry Pope and Charles Tupper, Smith was one of the strongest proponents of the railway. He was also a clever businessman with a substantial financial stake in the success of the CPR. His wholesale grocer company had been carrying the company on its books for months and Smith knew there was no hope of seeing the money if the line went under. Though resigned to failure, Stephen agreed to extend his Ottawa pilgrimage a few days and submit a new proposal. Macdonald had developed a peculiar obsession with the Franchise Bill (which proposed the establishment of a uniform federal electoral system) and he insisted that it wind its interminable way through the House before the CPR's problems could be addressed. Finally, Stephen could wait no longer and he returned to Montreal on April 15th. There, in the gloomy light of evening, he got more bad news from Van Horne: "Have no means paying wages, pay car can't be sent out, and unless we get immediate relief we must stop. Please inform Premier and Finance Minister. Do not be surprised or blame me if an immediate and most serious catastrophe happens."[42]

With strikes up and down the line, the threat of open revolt and creditors driven to their knees because of the company's debt, Old Tomorrow still showed no eagerness to tackle the CPR thorn. Stephen, never patient with politicking, could hardly believe that the relatively minor Franchise Bill could supersede one that would determine the future of the company and perhaps the country. "It is impossible for me to continue this struggle for existence any longer," he wrote despairingly to Macdonald. "The delay in dealing with the C.P.R. matter, whatever may be the necessity for it, has finished me, and rendered me utterly unfit for further work. . . ."[43]

Stephen's mood alternated between bleak depression and fury. To everyone he declared he was a "ruined man." Van Horne valiantly tried to keep his recalcitrant contractors and crew from wholesale rioting. Several nasty incidents had already broken out. Creditors completely stymied by Shaughnessy had taken to tracking Van Horne down and placing their tale of woe before him. "Go sell your boots and buy C.P.R. stock," he curtly told one of them.[44]

AFTER ALL STEPHEN'S MISCALCULATIONS, market misfortunes and plain bad judgment, the CPR was saved, not by any financial legerdemain, but by Louis Riel. On March 26, 1885, a second Métis uprising led by Riel, the Northwest Rebellion, gave Van Horne, at long last, the chance to demonstrate the CPR's value to Canada. Until then the public and politicians alike had seen the enterprise as little more than a massive and unending drain on the Treasury. Fifteen years earlier, General Wolseley's army had slogged through bush, rock and muskeg for three months to reach Winnipeg from Montreal in order to crush the first Riel Rebellion. In April, 1885, Van Horne dedicated every resource of the CPR to the astonishing transportation feat of hauling nearly 3,000 troops over the still-uncompleted line. The first contingent reached Winnipeg in only seven days. The soldiers were chilled to the marrow, but they'd arrived months earlier than Riel had expected, and the revolt was crushed by May 14th.

About the same time, Stephen applied to the Bank of Montreal for $500,000 in temporary financing to pay construction crews, who were laying down their tools all along the line. The Bank refused. John Henry Pope once again interceded at the critical time, reportedly showing Macdonald a list of prominent Conservatives and party supporters who would go bankrupt if the CPR went under. The matter was debated by the Cabinet, most of whom were more favourably disposed toward the company since the Riel business.

On May 26th Van Horne, who had taken over Stephen's Ottawa vigil, received the news from Pope that the government had agreed to back the $500,000 loan. It would be enough to tide the CPR over until a second relief bill could be introduced. Van Horne's stern face barely twitched until Pope had gone. "I think we had that much sanity left us! and then we began. We tossed up chairs to the ceiling; we tramped on desks; I believe we danced on tables. I do not fancy that any of us knows what occurred, and no one who was there can ever remember anything except loud yells of joy and the sound of things breaking!"[45] Van Horne tore off to the CPR telegraph office with a hastily scribbled note to Shaughnessy. The poor operator, startled half to death when the general manager burst into the room, nervously tapped out the first few words. "Move

The Canadian Pacific Railway in 1885

0   200   400 km

over!" bellowed Van Horne. "I'll do it!" Shaughnessy, anxiously pacing his office in Montreal, pounced upon the messenger boy, snatching the telegram out of his hands. "Delay
over," it said. "Pay creditors now. Van Horne."[46]*

The government aid proposal was presented at long last and
passed on July 11, 1885, receiving royal assent on July 20th.

---

*It was only enough to tide the CPR over, but Van Horne and Stephen knew the guarantee
was the signal that Macdonald intended to bail out the CPR. The $500,000 could only pay
some wages and the most pressing creditors; the others had to wait several more months yet.

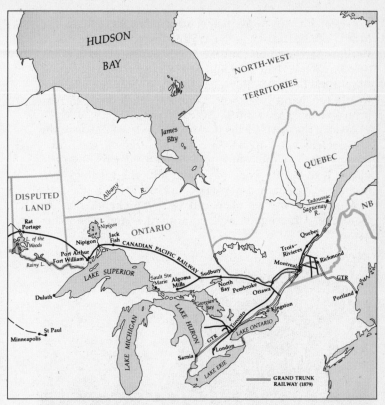

The key provision was the issuance of $35 million worth of 5 percent first mortgage bonds, secured by the assets of the road and also guaranteed by the Government of Canada. Some claim that the lengthy delay was simply Sir John A. Macdonald's way of putting pressure on Stephen and that the real deciding factor was a £40,000 necklace presented to Lady Macdonald, along with numerous other "bonifications" bestowed on government members. Stephen later admitted to spending $1 million between 1881 and 1886 to ensure government support. With the promise in hand, Stephen immediately set out for London, where he convinced a newly interested Baring's to take half of the bonds at $95 a share. The firm optioned the remainder at $91 a share. The main reason Baring's agreed to take up the bonds was an understanding that Stephen and Smith would personally purchase a sizeable proportion of them. "Between ourselves," Stephen admitted to Macdonald on July 23rd, "I doubt if much over half have been actually sold to investors."[47]

Most of the assets pledged were CPR lands at $2 an acre, the value of which was open to question, according to the British press. "Whether the company holds sufficient real estate to enable it to pay the coupon in land until the earnings shall become sufficient to disperse pay "in kind" [cash] is not made clear; nor for the life of us can we comprehend what the Dominion Government will do with the land when they get it."[48]

Sir John A. and Lady Macdonald heading west on the finished
CPR line, 1886

Though it was well known that Smith and Stephen had reached deep into their own pockets all through the harrowing construction period, not everyone was impressed by the sacrifice. "It is noticed that in one of the finest streets of Montreal, where imposing mansions rise to meet the eye, there is a row of handsome houses which are pointed at as the homes of the Canadian Pacific 'syndicate'. . . ."[49] Stephen's house was actually not among the "imposing" group, but rather set into a copse of trees on Drummond Street, very close to the heart of Montreal's business community. Beautiful though it was, his pleasure in it was soured by the insinuation that it had been built with pilfered CPR money. Any shred of joy left in his home fled when the government marched in to assess its contents as part of the aid package. One can only imagine Stephen's humiliation and anger at watching grimy underlings pawing through his possessions—but watch he did. D. C. Coleman, a later president of the CPR, recalled: "A former officer of the Company, who died three or four years ago, used to relate that he went with officers of the treasury to inventory all of Stephen's possessions. They not only counted all his cash and securities, but went to his home and valued, with expert assistance, his paintings, his statuary, his furniture, also his household linen, his china and silverware. And he liked to add: 'The old gentleman looked over the long list carefully, and without a flicker of the eyelid, signed it all away.'"[50]

The "old gentleman," then only fifty-two years old, lost at that moment any patriotic spark he had ever had.

On November 7, 1885, the last spike of the Canadian Pacific Railway was driven at Craigellachie, ensuring the company's financial future. Completed in barely five years, the railroad was hailed as one of the great construction feats of all time. Yet George Stephen, the railroad's financial architect — embittered by unrelenting newspaper attacks and drained by the pressures of the previous months — gleaned scant solace from his success.

CHAPTER 6

SHAUGHNESSY BACKSTOPS VAN HORNE'S BIG PUSH

Not only did he hold together the precarious structure that was the infant CPR, but Shaughnessy paid for it with little more than sleight of hand.

Thomas G. Shaughnessy has been submerged in history beneath the monumental bulk of the man who hired him — William Van Horne. No books have been written extolling his virtues, and even dedicated railroad buffs are hard pressed to remember exactly who he was, much less what he accomplished. Yet, during the critical 1882-to-1885 construction period, Thomas Shaughnessy was as essential to the survival of the CPR as George Stephen or William Van Horne. Stephen found money when none was to be had and Van Horne spent it, pushing the line ahead through sheer force of will. But Shaughnessy held it all together, stretching every dollar until it was paying for two jobs directly and another two on credit. He knew the location of every CPR-owned rail, fish plate, nut, bolt, whaleback, shovel, barrel of beans and keg of dynamite. He knew where every pound of supplies came from, where it was going, if it was delivered on time, whether it was being properly used and, most importantly, how much it cost — particularly if it cost even a penny too much.

Shaughnessy was as anonymous as Van Horne was illustrious. Van Horne did nothing by halves, accenting even the smallest act with the most expansive gestures. There was a bigness about him that extended beyond physical size to his ideas, his homes, his art and his zest for life. Van Horne engulfed, awed and overwhelmed; Shaughnessy enmeshed, infiltrated and controlled. If anything, Shaughnessy's ambition was greater than Van Horne's, but he was a ponderer, a plotter and a careful man, who hid his own considerable emotions and peculiarities behind a stern visage.

Thomas G. Shaughnessy arrived at the Montreal offices* of the Canadian Pacific Railway early on a cloud-shrouded morning in November, 1882 — late in the second year of construction. The night before, he had registered his family in a modest hotel that was walking distance from the offices so he wouldn't have to pay cab fare. Looking far more like an aristocrat than a recently promoted clerk, the thirty-year-old American cut a commanding figure. Slender and erect, he wore his clothes impeccably. Creases stayed where they were put, lint did not cling to his shoulders and street muck seemed to shed itself voluntarily from his shoes. His soft black tie was knotted exactly so, and he wore a sober morning coat modestly enlivened by light striped trousers. On his head was a black felt hat, and in his hand he carried a long slim cane. His narrow face, punctuated by sizeable out-thrust ears, also featured a thin, angular nose. A thick and carefully groomed moustache topping a prim Imperial beard lent an authoritative air to his still evident youth. He was not handsome. In a man of lesser character the sharpness of his features would have suggested cunning rather than astuteness and intelligence. Shaughnessy's face had many distinctive parts but his eyes demanded the most attention. Penetrating and precise, they instantly gauged the exact value and cost of everyone and everything.

The young Irish American walked alone into an impossible situation. Before he set foot inside the door he was branded as yet another of Van Horne's legion of Yankee interlopers. He

---

*Canadian Pacific construction headquarters were at Winnipeg, but supplies were all coordinated from the Montreal offices at 103 St James Street.

Thomas G. Shaughnessy, about 1882

had to cut across the authority of senior people to make drastic
economies, changes in purchasing procedure and improvements in general efficiency, yet Shaughnessy had none of the
physical or mental credentials that Van Horne used to intimi-
date his opposition. In essence, he was an administrator — a
gifted paper shuffler without a moment of first-hand experience on the line itself. Further, Van Horne had impressed

upon him that the railroad was in crisis — he had no time to win the natives over gradually.

Shaughnessy strode through the front doors of the Montreal office and calmly announced: "I am T. G. Shaughnessy and I have been hired by Mr. Van Horne as chief purchasing agent."[1] Without waiting for any general acknowledgment, he called for all ledgers, pricing lists and invoices, and within ten minutes of arriving, he was hard at work. By the time he left late that night, Shaughnessy had reviewed every CPR file and had summoned and interviewed the majority of company suppliers, manufacturers and their agents headquartered in Montreal. He told them in his brusque, clipped, almost rude manner of speaking that the good old days were over; the Shaughnessy system was now in effect.

No longer would CPR business be allocated on the basis of nepotism, bribes and friendship. Price, quality and speed of delivery were all that counted. Though he didn't mention it, he might also have pointed out that a willingness to carry CPR delinquent accounts indefinitely was another prerequisite to obtaining work from the railway. Estimates, written and adhered to, were to be the rule, not the exception, as they had been. Two office clerks, A. J. Dana and E. N. Bender, overheard his interviews with suppliers and spread the word that the Shaughnessy manifesto was now law. The new regime brought widespread changes in the way the CPR operated. Many believed that Duncan McIntyre, the first general manager and one of the original Syndicate, left the company in 1884 not because he had lost heart in the enterprise, but because Shaughnessy thwarted his practice of awarding contracts to friends.[2]

Described by contemporaries as a hard man, Shaughnessy was actually rather highly strung and temperamental. The only way to control the Irish heat in his soul was to mask it with a deadly façade of unbending competence. Hard he may have appeared, but he was also drivingly ambitious, and out of his ambition grew a loyalty to THE COMPANY that placed the institution above the mere mortals who comprised it. In his mind he deified the entity. Fealty was due and those who didn't pay would be punished, shunned or struck down.

THOMAS G. SHAUGHNESSY CAME FROM A CLAN of resilient, stalwart men. His father, also Thomas, was the son of poor Irish tenant farmers, who, like many of his generation, had fled the famine and poverty of a country caught in the awful transition between feudalism and industrialization. He joined the rush to America in 1841 and headed to Milwaukee, Wisconsin, where a well-established Irish community already existed. The city's third ward was home to America's new poor: first-generation Irish, Polish and Italian immigrants. A disproportionate number of saloons and brothels lined the ragtag streets, and the alleys resounded with the obscenities and gaieties of impoverished lives.

Milwaukee's ward system epitomized American machine politics. It was a spoils system that rewarded loyalty to the party — working to get out the vote and voting several times oneself, as well as casting ballots for the dead, lame and as yet unborn — with civic jobs. Thomas, Sr.,* registered as a Democrat, which was then the ruling party, and willingly ran precinct errands, performed the occasional strongarming and carried out election duties. Though his efforts paid off with political appointments and other plums, he wasn't just another political hack looking for an easy life on the gravy train. In 1849 he distinguished himself as an employee of the city's health department for his efforts during a dreadful cholera epidemic.

---

*Thomas, Sr., was a short man but the "picture of physical strength," as one contemporary described him. He had the same deep-set eyes, bushy moustache and determined carriage as his son. He also had an extraordinary will. When it came to carrying through a decision, his determination was as stiff as a rod of steel. While still in Ireland he pledged a temperance oath, which he honoured until his death. His other distinguishing characteristic was a prodigious memory, which he used to great advantage in horse racing, his passion. At the age of eighty-five he could still reel off the history and vital statistics of every important horse that ran at Curragh — the home of the Irish Derby — and at the Kildair, Roseborough and Tipperary race tracks. (Eagle, "Baron Thomas Shaughnessy: The Peer Who Made Milwaukee Famous," *Milwaukee History 6* (Spring 1983), p. 29)

By 1851 he was important enough to be chosen a delegate to the powerful Democratic state convention.

In 1846 Thomas, Sr., had married Mary Kennedy, a twenty-one-year-old native of county Killarney. They produced a large brood of six children, three of whom died from drowning. Thomas George, born in 1853, was the eldest. Aided by his political connections, his father was able to provide him with a better than average education for the time, sending him through the St Aloysius Jesuit Academy, and paying for several months at the private Spencerian Business College, which specialized in bookkeeping and commercial arithmetic.

In 1869, at the age of sixteen, Shaughnessy left college to take a clerical job with the Milwaukee and St Paul Railroad, commonly known as the Milwaukee Road, a powerful and expansionary line.* The man who would launch an unrelenting drive from obscurity to the very top of the CPR had a mediocre start. In his first eleven years with the company he only advanced from the position of clerk to that of bookkeeper in the supply department. Railroading was simply a sideline and income supplement to Shaughnessy's real passion — politics. Following his father's lead, he became deeply involved with Milwaukee's Democratic party. In July, 1875, he stood in a by-election and was elected to city council. During the next general election he won the full three-year term by acclamation.

Tall† and thin, the twenty-two-year-old Shaughnessy was initially the source of considerable amusement for his fellow

*The road was first formed in 1850 as the Milwaukee and Mississippi Railroad. By 1869, when Shaughnessy joined it, the line was in a commanding position, controlling virtually every through route from the Wisconsin shore of Lake Michigan to the Mississippi. In 1874 it was renamed the Chicago, Milwaukee and St Paul. It was the first railroad to install electric lights in its passenger trains and in 1887 became the first line west of Chicago to heat passenger trains with steam. In 1909, the road completed a link from Dakota to Puget Sound. Today, after three bankruptcies, it exists in a much truncated form.

†Shaughnessy's height is a matter of some dispute. He has been variously described as "tall," "short" and "stocky." In later years he certainly didn't look tall; he was almost shrunken and gnome-like.

councilmen as well as for the newspapers. The *Milwaukee Sentinel* referred to him as the "pumpkin-haired alderman" because of his red hair, and the other council members mockingly refused to seat him until he produced proof that he was of legal age. The patronizing bothered him not at all, and showing a ready grasp of the realities of ward politics and giving the first evidence of his ambition and perseverance, Shaughnessy methodically carved out his own influential niche. But he hadn't yet mastered the art of camouflage and the rawness of his aspirations was all too transparent. When he unsuccessfully ran for the Democratic nomination for clerk of the Milwaukee circuit court in 1876 — a position that had been averaging the princely sum of $11,000 annually in fees income — the *Sentinel* newspaper noted that he was "an eager candidate for the office, but the impression prevails that his vaulting ambition needs a rest."[3]

Shaughnessy was re-elected for his second full three-year term in 1879 and took on four committees, including the chairmanship of the key legislative committee which guided the city's legal and financial policies. By 1882, with a third term easily won and his subsequent election as president of the city council, he was such a force in Milwaukee politics that most conceded he would soon move on to state office. At the age of twenty-nine the pumpkin-haired alderman was a powerful politician in the city, with his sights firmly focused on becoming governor, the top office in Wisconsin politics.

MEANWHILE ANOTHER FORCE — more like a peril of nature — was converging on Thomas George Shaughnessy to jolt him rudely out of his chosen career and set him on the course of the presidency of the Canadian Pacific Railway. William Van Horne had been hired in 1879 to guide the swollen Milwaukee Road through the digestion of the numerous smaller roads it had recently purchased. Characteristically, Van Horne's arrival was a time of upheaval, with numerous firings, hirings, resignations and promotions. Obscured by his bravura was Van Horne's talent-spotting ability, even when that talent was carefully hidden.

Within months of taking over, Van Horne sized Shaughnessy up as a man doing his job competently enough but capable of doing far more. Instead of firing him Van Horne promoted him to purchasing agent of the whole line and in less than a year advanced him to head storekeeper. It was a position of great responsibility and the centre of real power in any railroad. The job required precise coordination and a kind of sixth sense in order to keep the flow of supplies running smoothly at just the right pace to meet demand. Too few supplies meant expensive delays, and too many clogged costly warehouse space. Van Horne not only promoted quickly but he rarely allowed star employees more than a deep breath before heaping further responsibility on them. In short order Shaughnessy had control of materials for the rolling stock departments, including passenger trains and all the stores necessary for tracks and bridge work. Then he took on accounts for the locomotive and car departments and payrolls for engineers, firemen and shopmen.

Shaughnessy thrived on his new-found stature and began carefully cultivating a relationship with Van Horne; not really a friendship, it was more the closeness that can grow between a professor and a particularly promising student. Shaughnessy was bright but not nearly so widely read as Van Horne, who lent him volumes from his considerable library. The two men often drank whiskey, smoked cigars and talked of fossils and geology far into the night,[4] though there is no evidence in later years that Shaughnessy had the slightest interest in the subject. He listened patiently as Van Horne told his stories and expounded his theories. It was a relationship Shaughnessy grew to despise as being patronizing.[5] Even so, he carefully nurtured the association.

Before Van Horne left the Milwaukee Road on January 1, 1882, he asked Shaughnessy to join him in Canada as the CPR's purchasing agent. But politics looked a lot more exciting than a job in a northern city with a line that most Americans believed couldn't be built at all, let alone on time. He turned down the offer but not before using it to lever a handsome raise out of his employers. Astounded by the supply and accounting mess he found in Canada, Van Horne returned twice to Milwaukee, once in February and once in October, 1882. On the second visit his monumental powers of persuasion, oiled by more than a few glasses of Milwaukee beer, finally convinced Shaughnessy that his future lay with the CPR.*

THE SUBTLE LOGISTICAL AND FINANCIAL masterpiece woven by Shaughnessy during the construction years escaped the notice of all but a precious few of his contemporaries. Van Horne could grandly order up 5,000 men to work on a section of the line, but someone had to put the advertisements in the paper, hire the workers, transport them, house them, feed them, pay them, supervise them and make sure that they had tools and materials to work with. Thomas G. Shaughnessy was that man. If he didn't do it himself, he caused it to be done and if it wasn't done to his exacting specifications, there was hell to pay. And, if his rendition of hell didn't feature Van Horne's spectacular pyrotechnics, it was just as feared. When Shaughnessy fired someone, he stayed fired.

Not only did he hold together the precarious structure that was the infant CPR, but Shaughnessy paid for it with little more than sleight of hand. He was a master of the "cheque-is-in-the-mail" school of keeping creditors at bay. At the same time he demanded immediate payment for even the smallest sum owed to the company. His were vital skills to the perpetually cash-short CPR. No detail was too small to escape his notice.

Van Horne had talked Shaughnessy into the most obnoxious and difficult job in the whole railroad. When he arrived, there was no uniform administrative system. Tendering for

---

*Another factor in Shaughnessy's decision was no doubt his recently started family. He married Elizabeth Bridget Nagle, another native of Ireland, on January 12, 1880, and their first child was born on October 28, 1880, almost exactly nine months after they were married.

bids was a joke, contracts were often let without even an original estimate, much less a competing one. Supplies came from here, there and everywhere. In one case he discovered that the supplier of saws and other hand tools had changed four times in less than six months and all of them were screaming breach of contract because their bribe had been surpassed by that of another firm. One of the companies had never made saws before but was hurriedly thrown together by a former blacksmith whose cousin, a CPR employee, assured him a bid would be accepted. "Who are these people," Shaughnessy demanded of Archer Baker, general superintendent of the eastern division, "that they think they can make such fools of us? We may have been foolish for a short time, but not for long."[6]

To do his job successfully Shaughnessy was destined at best to offend and at worst to make mortal enemies of the senior bosses. It was tough enough chipping and chiselling away at the accounts and budgets of older, experienced men like John Egan, James Ross,* I. G. Ogden, William Whyte and Archer Baker. Worse was doing it without the immediate respect he would have garnered with a solid railroad background. Many didn't like Van Horne's imperious, know-all ways, but no one doubted that he could personally do every job on the railroad from engine wiper to engineer. Shaughnessy wasn't a railroader, merely an administrator who happened to have worked on one. His only experience with dirt was on the grimy statements he sifted through as they came in from the survey and construction heads. Although his authority flowed directly from Van Horne, the general manager's appearances in the Montreal office were rare and hectic occurrences. As a result Shaughnessy made crucial decisions every day with no one to back him up. If supervisors and section heads balked at his demands, there was nowhere to pass the complaint. It was a sudden and brutal initiation, which Shaughnessy, the politician, not only survived but turned to his advantage. It wasn't

---

*James Ross was head of construction in the mountains of British Columbia (no relation to John Ross, head of engineering for the Lake Superior section).

long before most forgot that the upstart clerk was really just making up the rules as he went along. One thing Shaughnessy had learned well in his years as an alderman was that those who set the rules eventually come to rule.

Unlike Van Horne, Shaughnessy was tactically uninclined to confront transgressors personally. Instead, his suggestions and displeasure were conveyed in terse correspondence, which he felt left a more enduring and painful impression. Those letters cowed and intimidated some of the toughest men on the railroad. Most of them contained the insidious implication that the recipient was either lazy, stupid, disloyal or dishonest, and sometimes all of the above at once.

It wasn't that Shaughnessy feared confrontation, far from it. He simply believed that his letters were more damning than any momentary anger and they also left a lasting record for future reference. Shaughnessy's temper was considerable but he kept it reined, allowing it to surface only as monumental irritation. Van Horne's anger usually constituted a consummate theatrical show that few forgot but was soon over. Shaughnessy, on the other hand, was an artist in verbal surgery. His deft slashes left the recipient standing and functioning but badly scarred. When annoyed—even when sitting erectly in his office with his elbows neatly angled at his side — a coldness seeped out of him like a tangible thing. His speech, never increasing in volume, became ever more precise, concise and exact, until the words fell from his mouth like perfect cubes of ice landing on the floor at the feet of the unfortunate object of his scorn.

Though rules, regulations and policies were the holy trinity to Shaughnessy, they didn't stop him from slicing through the chain of command to make the slightest economies. He even overrode Van Horne himself on occasion. John Egan, the fierce-tempered Yankee Irishman Van Horne hired as general superintendent at Winnipeg, stepped aside for no man, including his boss, but he meekly accepted Shaughnessy's ridicule: "I should judge from the appearance of the trimmings in the sleeping car Kananaskis that your CarCleaners had been using pumice stones or bath bricks in cleaning them," wrote Shaughnessy disparagingly. "If so some of them should 'lose their heads.'" Shaughnessy went on to instruct the vastly experienced Egan, in considerable and insulting detail, just how the trimmings ought to be cleaned.[7]

Shaughnessy harassed all the section heads, in one case instructing Archer Baker to fire the man who took the mail to and from head office and the trains in order to save his $2.50 a day in salary.[8] However, William Whyte, one of the CPR's most loyal and popular employees, was his favourite target. Whyte, a Scot like Stephen and Smith, was often spoken of as the likely successor to Van Horne. He worked his way up to the position of station agent in the Scottish Railway before emigrating to Canada at the age of twenty in 1863. After hiring on as a Grand Trunk brakeman, he spent the next nineteen years with that company, advancing to the position of divisional superintendent. In 1883 Whyte became general superintendent of the Ontario and Quebec Railway, and when the line was officially absorbed by the CPR he stayed on as general superintendent of the Ontario division. In 1886 he was sent to Winnipeg to take over the western lines. Known as "smooth William" for his cleverness and unflappable temperament, Whyte was one of those railroaders who could do every job well. Next to Van Horne, he was the most respected man in the company. "Mr. Whyte's door was always on the swing," a friend recalled, "and a wiper from the roundhouse could see him just as readily as a captain of industry."[9] Interestingly, considering Shaughnessy's initial persecution, Whyte became his most trusted advisor, but only after Shaughnessy had established his ascendancy.

When Shaughnessy discovered that a ticket agent under Whyte's nominal direction had turned away a customer, mistakenly assuming that the sleeper cars were full, he couldn't simply point out the misunderstanding. Instead, Whyte's agent was "either too stupid to have anything to do with our ticket business, or he was secretly acting in the interests of the Grand Trunk and Pullman Companies."[10] Shaughnessy painstakingly scrutinized Whyte's accounts, memos and staffing requirements, heavily marking each offending section in blue and supplying indignant comment.

Whyte had a long fuse, but after many provocations he tired of the harping and the harassment of creditors, whom Shaughnessy, safely ensconced in Montreal, avoided. He gave one particularly persistent lumber contractor a pass so he could travel to head office. Shaughnessy was not amused: "For heaven's sake, don't give any of these men passes to come down here and worry us about their accounts."[11]

Not surprisingly, considering his own background, another group permanently under Shaughnessy's microscope were CPR storekeepers. He treated them as if they were some kind of devilish creation sent to test his vigilance. Upbraiding them for every real and imagined inefficiency in their departments was not enough; he also demanded that every scrap of paper and every half-bottle of ink be utilized to the maximum. He pointed out to W. K. Kelson, general storekeeper at Winnipeg, that the lifetime of pencils could be extended considerably if they weren't sharpened so much. "Run a little closer to the wind," he advised.[12]

Shaughnessy rarely asked for opinions on budget cuts, preferring to present them as a *fait accompli*. Kelson, for instance, sat down at his desk one morning only to find that during the night Shaughnessy had removed his secretary as an economy measure. He was tersely informed to use the telegraph operator, who also knew shorthand, for departmental correspondence, since "I presume," wrote Shaughnessy, "that only a very small part of his time is occupied in telegraphing."[13]

Shaughnessy took particular pleasure in combining a criticism of Whyte with an attack on a storekeeper. At the end of one hectic week in 1883 he spotted, within a lengthy column of expense entries, a debit for a rubber stamp. The Winnipeg storekeeper had ordered it to speed processing of the hundreds of invoices he dealt with each week. Shaughnessy quickly wrote to Whyte, who had *pro forma* approved the purchase, peremptorily telling him to deduct the cost from the man's pay chit, "as it is an article that is entirely unnecessary in connection with his duties as storekeeper."[14]

Next to economy measures, Shaughnessy's favourite topic was cleanliness. It was almost a fetish — he washed his hands a dozen or more times a day. In later years, his personal secretary, Tom Callory, kept a supply of clean dusting rags in his desk drawer, and whenever the boss stepped out he would rub down the entire office, taking care not to ruffle the geometric piles of paper on Shaughnessy's desk. At Fort Tipperary, the summer estate Shaughnessy built in St Andrews, New Brunswick, a squad of maids would scour the house before it was opened for the season and then Shaughnessy would conduct a white-glove inspection, touching every surface he could reach to see if there was any missed dirt. He also had a horror of bad smells, insisting that every room in his homes be thoroughly aired daily and leaving standing instructions that his private car was to be aired and cleaned every day whether he was using it or not.

Shaughnessy's personal obsession extended to the railroad and as a result the CPR had a prosperous and well-cared-for appearance even when its books were awash in red. "One of the coaches was badly spotted although only out of the shop a few weeks. I am afraid that our system of car washing is hardly perfect!" he admonished Baker.[15] He chastised Whyte because his emigrant sleeping cars were "in a filthy condition, not having been washed since they went into service."[16] But there were limits to Shaughnessy's mania for cleanliness and those limits were reached the instant they involved unnecessary expenditures. When F. R. Brown, the mechanical superintendent, ordered some rolling stock painted to make the cars look a little better, Shaughnessy shrilly denounced him for letting "your man Stevenson" commit the "almost inexcusable" act of painting the flat cars after converting them into ballast cars.[17]

Another of Shaughnessy's obsessions was the quality of the CPR's rolling stock, especially passenger cars. His endless complaints about J. Harris and Co., a well-respected car-building firm, were catalogued in point form and covered an entire page, at the end of which Shaughnessy added, ". . . these two cars are made up of the worst material and are put together and finished in the most disgraceful manner. It would seem to indicate not only gross negligence on your part but also culpable disregard of the requirements of a first class passenger car job."[18]

Even when he occasionally relented and actually complimented a supplier, as he did in July, 1884 — conceding that Barney and Smith Manufacturing Company's latest cars were a vast improvement over their previous "abominable article[s]" — he couldn't resist a criticism: "The difference in color of the trucks would look like an inexcusable blunder on the part of your painter."[19]

Interior of a CPR dining car

SHAUGHNESSY'S BADGERING OF MANUFACTURERS ensured that the CPR received only their finest products, but his incessant nitpicking served an additional purpose. As long as he could find something wrong with a job, he could legitimately refuse to settle the bill. It was a tactic Shaughnessy used so skillfully that suppliers pressing for payment continually found themselves on the defensive. In one typical letter he pointedly referred to serious irregularities in a contractor's invoices, neatly omitting mention of his own company's delinquent account. When the contractor took umbrage at the implication of dishonesty, Shaughnessy replied with an air of bewildered innocence, "It was not my intention to insinuate any lack of good faith on your part."[20] The net result was a lengthy delay as the man concentrated on defending himself rather than pressing for payment. One coal shipper soon regretted calling his account to Shaughnessy's attention. "I am satisfied that every cargo of coal received this year from yourselves and other shippers was short," he wrote, "mainly owing, no doubt, to the fact that steam barges drew upon their cargos for their own use. In this instance the shortage is so material that I have ordered it charged to your account."[21]

Shaughnessy's ploys and personal style did little to endear him to CPR employees or the army of suppliers, but they garnered for him enormous respect and not a little fear. His "my way or the highway" personality fit perfectly with the necessity of the time. Van Horne, though good with details himself, simply didn't have the time to bother with technicalities in his war to move mountains and cinch the country with a steel belt. But it was those little details that offered loopholes for scoundrels hovering on the fringes, ever ready with scams to fleece an overworked, understaffed and generally unpopular organization.

Shaughnessy spent a great deal of time ferreting out pilfering and featherbedding and when he did, retribution was swift and irrevocable. He didn't trust the railway contractors to keep their men in line because they were more interested in getting the track laid and cared little about picayune swindles.

MEN WANTED!

A number of Men will be wanted by the undersigned during the grading season this year on west end of **CANADIAN PACIFIC RAILWAY.** Wages will be

$1.50 PER DAY,
BOARD $4.50 PER WEEK,

During the Summer Months for good, able-bodied, steady men.

Apply on the work at end of track, now near Cypress Hills, about 600 miles west of Winnipeg.

LANGDON, SHEPARD & CO.,

END OF TRACK
April 20th 1883.

CONTRACTORS

Advertisement for CPR construction workers

Because there was a constant need of men, blanket advertisements for labour ran all across North America. Unfortunately, there were also times of glut and every contractor was then annoyed by the endless stream of men who travelled to their section demanding work as promised by the advertising. When none was forthcoming the company was forced to pay for their transportation and lost work days. Word spread that the CPR was paying even if it wasn't hiring and a plague of ne'er-do-wells descended on various sections of the track. It was a scam that particularly incensed Shaughnessy. "About every laborer in Lower Canada will present a claim before we get through with them, for loss of time etc.," he grumbled.[22]

The last straw came in February, 1884, when Seraphin Cloutier swore out an affidavit claiming $106 from the CPR for travelling expenses and lost wages. Shaughnessy had had enough. When his investigation revealed that Cloutier had been employed the entire time elsewhere, he decided to lay charges. "These 'scaliwags' in every portion of Canada," he angrily wrote about the Cloutier matter, "are presenting claims aggregating thousands of dollars, most of them no doubt utterly without foundation. If we succeed in sending one of them up for perjury, we are satisfied it would have a wholesome effect upon the balance."[23]

SHAUGHNESSY'S GREATEST ACHIEVEMENT was his work in keeping CPR creditors at bay during the critical 1884-to-1885 period. During that time George Stephen was desperately searching for private-sector money as the CPR edged perilously close to failure. In January, 1884, Van Horne promoted Shaughnessy to assistant to the general manager and with this extra authority in hand he performed one of the great feats of account juggling in business history. At the peak of the CPR's cash crisis Shaughnessy flawlessly manipulated a huge shortfall of between $10 and $17 million, moving it from one column to the next and shuffling accounts to cover overdrafts. His dodging and ducking of creditors was particularly impressive, as he did it when the details of the CPR's financial woes filled headlines for months on end. Shaughnessy, wearing the Emperor's clothes, represented the company as if it were the Bank of England. There was always a rational explanation for nonpayment of bills and it had nothing whatever to do with nasty words like insolvency.

By the end of the summer of 1884, the major sections left to construct were the hideously difficult and expensive route through the Rockies and the line north of Lake Superior. It had been clear to Shaughnessy and Van Horne for some time that despite the money Stephen had received from the Canadian government they would be desperately strapped for funds from the fall of 1884 until the spring of 1885, at least. But somehow the work had to continue; if there was one constant in the crisis, it was the fact that if the line wasn't completed it would be worthless.

The opening gambit of Shaughnessy's strategy was bold and diabolically simple. He knew he couldn't afford to wait until the winter to order supplies. Aside from the minor detail of not having the money to pay for them, the publicity about the

CPR's wretched financial state was escalating and might scare off suppliers. Paying in advance was impossible and that's what he might be facing if suppliers got too nervous. The only thing to do was to have equipment and materials delivered seven or eight months before they would actually be used, ensuring that everything was in place before the close of navigation in 1884. That way, work could go on throughout the winter with no fear of shortages. Shaughnessy stockpiled more than $2.5 million worth of materials and thus placed suppliers in a rather weak position to press for payment. Their primary recourse — seizing the goods and carting them off — was out of the question until the spring thaw and by that time most of the material would be used.

During the fall and winter of 1884, Shaughnessy's response to the suppliers' increasingly frantic demands for payment was simple: delay, delay and delay again. The versatility of his response is amazing, considering his single weapon. Every debt was carefully handled according to its ability to cause problems. Replies were couched as if it was eminently reasonable and normal that the creditors not be paid. "There are times with us, as with every other large concern, when large demands upon our funds make it necessary for us to postpone payment for accounts that are less pressing," he informed a small creditor writing for payment on October 23, 1884.[24] Such statements did little for businessmen who were already hard pressed to pay their own bills. After repeated failures to get even a penny out of the CPR, some of them got positively wistful on the subject of money: "Don't you think it might be possible to settle some part of this account," inquired Simon Blanchette, general manager of Farley's Fasteners, "it has been such a very long time since we have seen anything that could be called a payment."[25]

Large creditors, especially those providing essential goods like food and coal, couldn't be treated with such impunity. Shaughnessy met their initial demands for settlement with requests for a detailed invoice, whether they'd already submitted one or not.[26] When he finally acknowledged receipt of the bill, usually after it had been hand delivered to the Montreal office, he contrived to find something wrong: "the unit price is not as quoted," the delivery dates "are quite incorrect," or the product received was "in very bad condition" — anything to force the creditor to retreat.

By forcing suppliers to jump through his invoicing hoops Shaughnessy managed to postpone payment until well into the spring and summer of 1885 on the bulk of the material he'd had in hand since the previous summer. Those few who were relentless in their demands for payment were treated as if the problem was of relatively recent origin and that the matter had suddenly materialized on Shaughnessy's desk. No apology was offered for the CPR's delinquency or for the problems it might have caused and at no time did he offer to pay the account. Even powerful friends of George Stephen and Sir John A. Macdonald, like Frank Smith, were stalled.*

Before tackling a major creditor Shaughnessy had his agents determine exactly how much that individual himself owed and to whom before plotting his moves. Armed with the information, he offered a promissory note to those in the worst circumstances. (In other words, he was asking suppliers to consider the debt a loan on which the CPR would pay interest at a later date.) That suggestion usually necessitated more correspondence and more delay. He made such an offer to Frank Smith, blandly stating that not settling the debt was every bit as good as handing over cash. "Could you not make it convenient to use our note at say four months with interest at 6% from the time the account was due? This would assist us in tiding over the pressure of the next two or three months and it would probably be quite as convenient for you."[27] Others judged in more desperate straits—and hence likely to take the most unpleasant action—were offered 7 percent interest on the

---

*Frank Smith was the MP who had waylaid George Stephen in Ottawa in March, 1885, persuading him to stay a few extra days to wait for the government bailout. His wholesale company was carrying an enormous unpaid account for the CPR.

entire amount or a small cash payment on the balance, carefully calculated as the minimum necessary to keep them quiet. To soften up creditors Shaughnessy quoted line and verse of their own financial obligations, often suggesting that they substitute the CPR's promissory note for their own paper or use the note as security against a loan. Both were ridiculous suggestions, since no banker in his right mind would accept anything but money itself from the debt-plagued railroad.

By the time the first series of promissory notes came due in March, April and May of 1885 Shaughnessy, having used up every other conceivable ploy, opted for a degree of frankness. "We are exceedingly anxious that none of our paper should be presented for payment at a time when we would find it impossible to meet it and we are quite sure that all the larger holders will be willing to grant an extension of say forty-five (45) days."[28]

Shaughnessy conveyed to the creditors the sense that he was doing them a distinct favour rather than vice versa. The only whiff of the desperation he must have felt was the final line invariably appended to letters of the period. "If notes forwarded for collection before this reached you, kindly recall them by wire."

The railway contractors were tougher, and at the same time more delicate, nuts to crack. Unlike the suppliers, who were far removed from the action and helpless once their goods were delivered, the contractors held the CPR by its tender parts. If they weren't paid, or more precisely if their men weren't paid, they'd simply drop their tools and refuse to work. And if the work wasn't completed, estimates couldn't be forwarded to the government and the CPR wouldn't get its subsidy. There was no getting around it, no way to avoid an outlay of money for the workmen. The contractors could be made to wait for their share, but the labourers couldn't.

Shaughnessy matter-of-factly laid out his solution to the problem to Harry Abbott, one of the CPR's eastern construction managers: "What we want to do is this. Pay the men in full and if in your opinion some small payments on account should be made to the Contractors for supplies etc. we shall send you funds to make them. I think you will clearly understand from the above what our purpose is. If not let me know and I will make it clearer. . . . In a word, we don't want to pay any more on Contractors accounts before the completion of the work than will be absolutely necessary to keep the men satisfied and insure rapid progress."[29] Shaughnessy devised a number of clever stratagems to ensure that the money actually went to the workers and not into the contractors' pockets. In many cases he simply refused to pay the contractors' invoices until the labourers' pay was up to date. In other cases he paid the workmen directly, bypassing the indignant contractors. To camouflage his tactics he directed Abbott to send the invoices through an accounting no-man's-land, allowing the company to pay the workers while delaying the final reckoning up.

IN JUNE AND JULY, 1885, as the railroad neared completion and while George Stephen was in London trying to sell CPR mortgage bonds, the slough of promissory notes accepted by the contractors, most having been renewed two and three times, came due. Shaughnessy began minutely questioning their estimates for work conducted. Initially it was just another ruse to delay payment, but events soon took an unexpected turn. Since the beginning of construction in 1881, there had been persistent rumours of pilfering and petty frauds up and down the line. Shaughnessy did what he could to stamp out the minor abuses, but because there was no substantial evidence of major crimes he didn't mount a wholesale investigation. Then, when a cursory inspection uncovered extensive irregularities, he sensed something serious was afoot. He sent off a solemn boilerplate message: "We have made a preliminary Examination of work done by Contractors on the Lake Superior Division of this Road and are quite satisfied that grave errors have occurred involving large sums in the original measurements upon which . . . final estimates have been made. In justice to everybody concerned we believe that all this work should be carefully revised and remeasured before any further payments are made. . . ."[30]

A corps of engineers, accompanied by representatives of the contractors, began remeasurement of the rails on August 30th, and within a week it was evident that the overstatements were far more than anyone could have imagined. What had started out as just another of Shaughnessy's patent delaying tactics had exposed one of the biggest frauds in the history of Canadian railroads. In one stretch of only thirty miles the overcharge by contractors Conner & McLennan amounted to a staggering $485,567.49, or 32 percent of a total billing of $1,533,301.61.[31] The CPR had been taken for nearly half a million dollars on a paltry thirty-mile stretch of track. In all, the overcharges amounted to more than $3 million.

Shaughnessy took "these errors of which it is impossible that you could have been ignorant"[32] as a call to arms. Another round of letters, with distinctly ominous undertones, went out. In the case of Conner & McLennan, he stopped only a millimetre from calling the contractors thieves as he unilaterally subtracted $131,931.03 from their total invoice and cancelled two outstanding CPR promissory notes of $40,000 each. He then billed them for the balance owing and, to underscore his determination, pointedly sent a copy of his letter together with the bill to the contractors' lawyers, essentially daring them to do anything about it.

As results from the engineers' examinations were analyzed, a disturbing pattern emerged. Though overcharges were found along the entire line, those of the magnitude of Conner & McLennan's appeared only in the area supervised by John Ross, head of engineering for the CPR's Lake Superior section. Aside from the Rockies, it was the most imposing section of the line. Ross had nearly 15,000 men and 4,000 horses working from Lake Nipissing to Port Arthur in the summer of 1884, and the monthly pay car hauled $1.1 million to cover their wages. The miserly Major Rogers would have been appalled by the food the CPR army consumed: twelve tons of it a day and four tons of tobacco a month.

By 1884, any pretensions of building a quality line had been abandoned and Van Horne battled constantly with Ross over the need to economize. All the company could afford, Van Horne argued, was a line that held together for a few years so the trains could get over it without incident — even if they had to slow to a snail's pace over some trestles. They bickered back and forth about timber and fill versus steel and masonry on the bridges. Ross resisted cheaper substitutions, saying he would not allow his section to be the most inferior in the country. He cared little about Van Horne's assurance that the work would be upgraded once the road was operating and producing revenue.

Despite their disputes John Ross did his work well. He got the track laid and his estimates in, all more or less on time. By the end of 1884 the hardest part of his section was surveyed and graded, sixty-seven miles of rails were down and another ninety-three miles had been completed except for ballasting. Van Horne argued vehemently with Ross but in the end passed off their contretemps as a difference of opinion between professionals. Shaughnessy, with his considerably more jaundiced view of life, wasn't as impressed with Ross's competence, as he made clear in a letter written in August, 1884: "If we rely upon John Ross or his men to see that this material as well as the rails, about which I wrote you before, are shipped to the points where he requires them before the close of navigation, I fear it will not be done."[33]

As for the costs Ross was submitting, everyone expected that part of the line to be hideously expensive, so what was a few million more or less? The bog, swamp and virtually impenetrable Precambrian rock obligingly threw up enough obstacles to camouflage an army of con artists, let alone the activities of a single man. One ninety-mile section gobbled up more than $10 million, an average of $111,111 a mile. Another stretch had been blasted out of sheer rock for more than $700,000 a mile. There was so much blasting to be done that Van Horne set up three separate factories to manufacture dynamite rather than transport it from the United States. Each plant turned out about 2,000 pounds of explosive daily and by the time construction was finished the CPR had sunk $7.5 million into explosives alone. Van Horne instructed the contractors to avoid blasting whenever they could but often the alternative routing close to the shoreline proved to be worse.

At Nipigon, the excavation of a pit for a bridge support pier spanning the Black Sturgeon River was buried when the entire bank broke off forty feet above the excavation. At Red Rock, a section so rocky Van Horne intended to bypass it by building embankments in Lake Superior, the lake bottom proved so unstable that a dock collapsed and sank to the bottom when a load of rails was offloaded onto it from a ship. In November, 1883, a three-acre patch of ground at McKay's Harbour, complete with construction supplies, buildings and docks, simply slid into the water.[34]

Rock cut north of Lake Superior during construction

When the contractors weren't fighting the terrain, they were besieged by the weather. In the summer, if it wasn't windy — and it seemed to be windy no matter what the season — it was so hot and humid that sweat poured off the labouring crews, clouding their vision and enticing a fog of insects that hummed, buzzed and stung until the navvies were almost driven mad in a frenzy of slapping, wiping and cursing. The only respite from the heat came when the rains poured down with a jungle-like seriousness that filled every gully and creek to bursting and caused flash floods, mud slides and washouts. After Ross got yet another dressing down from Van Horne over his extravagant use of masonry, he sent off an account of what could happen during a Lake Superior storm. "When the contractors commenced the masonry near (Gravel Point) which I wrote you was built — they piled a lot of stone on the bench over 20 feet above the water. A storm came up that night and carried it all off. . . ."[35]

In winter, snow drifted into banks forty or fifty feet deep. To speed spring laying, the crews, buffeted by gale force winds coming off the lake that drove temperatures down to fifty degrees below zero, laid rails on top of the deep banks where the line was supposed to be. After spring thaw the crew supervisors were horrified to discover they'd missed the graded section entirely.

Ross's insistence on top-quality work and materials was a threat to the budget, but he was pushing the line ahead against considerable odds. During one day in January, 1885, with the thermometer at minus thirty-eight Fahrenheit, 5,640 yards of track were laid. So Van Horne was not inclined to aggravate him too much, and he explained away the expense as the cost of a good man. But a more sinister interpretation of Ross's perfectionism began to take shape as the remeasurements began to trickle in. Shaughnessy ordered an immediate investigation, and by November 21, 1885, he reported confidentially to Van Horne that systematic thieveries had occurred — and the trail of every one led back to John Ross: "When preparing to let contracts he appears to have gathered around him a number of relations and camp followers with whom he had been associated on other roads, & whose interests were with him paramount to all others. No system of holding competition was inaugurated, but instead, he appears to have magnified, to an enormous extent, every difficulty with which contractors would have to contend, because of the remoteness of the work and the condition of the country and fixed prices accordingly."[36]

Ross's methods of enlarging the contractors' profits were quite ingenious and, fully detailed, would constitute the definitive primer on railroad construction fraud. Almost every contractor under his supervision did an excessive amount of what was known as "days labour"—essentially overtime—which was charged to the CPR in addition to what was specified on the contract. Contractors were allowed a 15 percent profit on this extra work, a sweetener to encourage greater effort. Everybody took advantage of this provision and there was always a certain amount of padding, but in Ross's case the contractors stuffed the accounts enough to upholster the entire country.

Ross further enlarged profits by authorizing the company to pay for work clearly specified as the contractors' own responsibility. In one case, the additional charges amounted to $150,000 for the construction of roads "which were clearly the duty of the contractor to build and maintain at his own expense." Ironically, considering his constant agitation for first-class supplies, Ross allowed the contractors to substitute substandard materials "and a thousand other things which appear in the accounts . . . ," while charging Canadian Pacific the full quoted price of the specified material. In his report to Van Horne, Shaughnessy concluded that the contractual specifications were "given consideration only in so far as they could be utilized to the advantage of the Contractors. . . . It might be charitable to pronounce them incompetent, but I believe it would be truthful to say that they were almost without exception a set of arrant thieves. In two cases, at least, we have admissions from Contractors that they were allowed large sums of money to which they were not entitled, and in a dozen other cases the evidence is so palpable that it cannot be questioned."[37]

Despite calling Ross on the carpet and grilling him repeatedly — a process that had broken several of the guilty contractors — Shaughnessy was unable to elicit any kind of admission of guilt: "I am unable to say positively that Mr. Ross was compensated in any way by the Contractors for what was plainly a violation of his duty as an officer of the Company and a gross disregard for the Company's funds, but intimate as I have become with his affairs since the completion of the work, and after an honest endeavour to believe him straight, I have put him down as belonging to the worst type of Railway Contractors, without a clear conception of honesty or duty."[38]

Uncovering the construction frauds was an unexpected bonanza, allowing Shaughnessy to delay payment further for the honest and dishonest alike. But in other ways it couldn't have happened at a worse time. With Stephen in London trying to sell bonds to a skeptical public and share prices depressed on all stock markets, a scandal of this magnitude might kill the railroad. What's more, Stephen, Van Horne and Shaughnessy would be held up to ridicule as bunglers unable to monitor their own workers. The CPR decided to put a hermetic seal over the story. Shaughnessy told only the highest officials what had gone on and instructed them to stonewall the press. He quietly fired Ross and began industriously pursuing the contractors individually, ruthlessly cutting and slashing their invoices. If the cases had gone to court the CPR would no doubt have been able to prosecute many of the contractors, and Ross, even if he had not been found guilty, would have been blackballed in the industry. Only one small hint of scandal ever leaked out in a report by the *Anglo-American Times*. However, by then the bulk of the bonds had been sold and the whole business was stale news.

FOR THE REMAINDER OF HIS LIFE, Shaughnessy's proudest boast was that, though he delayed payment on millions of dollars in bills for more than a year in many cases, not a single creditor's claim advanced to a lawsuit.[39] For this he got his reward. In September, 1885, the man who three years before had been a lowly clerk in Milwaukee vaulted into the path of succession, becoming assistant vice-president to Van Horne, who was promoted to vice-president that year. Along with the title came greatly expanded responsibilities, including the 1885 assignment to go to England with Henry Beatty, the CPR's manager of Great Lakes Transportation, and negotiate a construction contract for three new CP steamships. It was a heady rush to power for Shaughnessy and affirmed his decision to abandon his political career permanently. But it was only the beginning of his relentless drive to the top of the CPR.

CHAPTER 7

CLASH OF THE TITANS

*"There are three liars on this continent. I am one—
and Jim Hill is the other two!"*

—William Van Horne

Between 1886 and 1892 — the years following the completion of the transcontinental line — William Van Horne*
romped through life with the *joie de vivre* of a young stallion
frolicking in a fragrant meadow. Problems cropped up everywhere but he thrived on them, chewing up and spitting out
setbacks like so many stale cigars. Ironically, Van Horne's main
task during that period was rebuilding the railroad that had
been supposedly completed when the last spike was ham-
mered on November 7, 1885. George Stephen, in his desperation to create a market for CPR stock, had repeatedly assured
shareholders that the CPR would be in "perfect condition"†
by 1886. In truth, the main line was little better than two
strips of metal hastily slapped down from Ontario to British

---

*Van Horne did not become president of the CPR until 1888, but he had total operational
control from 1886 onward. Stephen concerned himself only with financing and matters of
larger policy.

†In June, 1885, for instance, he told shareholders that by 1886, the main line would "be
finished and in perfect condition, thoroughly equipped, possessing every requisite facility
for doing its work economically and efficiently, and at least equal to the best of its competitors
in all respects; particularly as to curves and gradients, permanent way and rolling stock. . . ."
(Stephen speech to shareholders, June 13, 1885, CP Archives)

Upgrading the track: men and mules at Rogers Pass, about 1886

Columbia. For hundreds of miles on the prairie, "perfect condition" consisted of inferior-quality iron rails set on virtually ungraded ground with a minimum of ballast. Railway trestles were built of timber instead of iron or masonry and were often so rickety that trains were forced to inch across them. Hundreds of station houses, warehouses, loading docks and staff quarters had to be built, rebuilt or enlarged. Also needed were dozens of feeder lines essential to bring crops to the main line and settlers to CPR land.*

Never content with only one job, Van Horne simultaneously threw up hotels and lodges in the Rockies and Selkirks, began negotiating for an Atlantic steamer service, involved himself in the design and construction of Windsor Station, plunged into immigration schemes, enlarged the CPR's influence in the art world with sponsorship of artists and photographers and personally dreamed up a host of brilliant slogans to entice tourists to Canada. A natural advertising man, he came up with catchy promotional phrases like "Parisian Politeness on the CPR," "Wise Men of the East Go West on the CPR" and "Said the

---

*All this cost money. Annual expenses more than doubled between 1885 and 1890, from $4.5 million to $9.4 million, much of it sunk into upgraded rolling stock, track improvements and new structures.

Prince to the Duke: 'How high we live on the CPR.'" He even
sketched some of the posters used by the company on bill-
boards in Canada and Europe. One of the most famous slogans he used to describe the Rockies was "1001 Switzerlands
Rolled Into One," something which caused the Swiss government to threaten action if the CPR did not stop repeating it.

After Van Horne became president in 1888, CPR revenues
increased steadily, and the Grand Trunk ogre became about as
threatening as a newt, as its stock slid against the CPR's in 1890
and 1891. In early 1892 an enthusiastic market for CPR debentures kept the price in the 103 to 95 range, while those of the
GTR languished eight or more points behind. There was even
talk of an amalgamation of the two roads. Stephen reported
that GTR shareholders were "all so disappointed and disgusted
by the poor results of the working of the line which, week after
week, are reported, that they would greedily accept any proposal which seemed to them to promise better net results."[1]
Even the press became positively enchanted with its former
whipping boy. "The brilliancy of its past achievements and of
its prospects has disarmed the few enemies the Canadian
Pacific Railway ever possessed," gushed the *Financial News*,
once harshly critical.[2]

Van Horne's already considerable bravado swelled like a
dirigible and he exuded invincibility from every pore. He
never believed for an instant that anything or anybody could
ever defeat him. But in the end he was beaten, not by the
worries of a fledgling railroad or even his arch-enemy J. J. Hill,
but by the treachery of friends. The seeds of his downfall were
sown shortly after the last spike was driven, and they took root
in the form of two apparently insignificant railway lines: the
Minneapolis, St Paul and Sault Ste Marie and the Duluth,
South Shore and Atlantic, both located in the United States.

EARLY IN 1886, GEORGE STEPHEN and Donald Smith quietly began buying control of the Minneapolis, St Paul and Sault Ste
Marie Railroad. The "Soo Line," as it was most commonly

Windsor Station

known, was chartered to run from St Paul to Sault Ste Marie. It was a classic Stephen move: buy up a strategically placed railroad, hold it secretly until a critical moment and then sell it either to the CPR or to J. J. Hill at a profit — all under the guise of doing a great public service. But this time Stephen badly miscalculated and the purchase blew up in his face.*

---

*Exactly why Stephen miscalculated isn't clear, but the reason likely lies in the preoccupation of his usual partners. Hill and Van Horne were busy with their own concerns, and in any case Stephen wasn't letting them know what he was up to. Donald Smith, at the time, was deeply immersed in his takeover of the Hudson's Bay Company which culminated in his being named the chief factor.

Van Horne had examined the Soo Line and passed it up. He believed that it might be a useful acquisition one day, but the heavy capital outlay needed to finish and improve the line made it an extremely low priority when so much money was needed by the CPR just to bring it up to operating standards. * There were rumours that the Grand Trunk was interested in the Soo as a piece of its own proposed transcontinental line, but the Grand Trunk was in a worse financial position than the CPR and could hardly afford the gamble. Hill, too, had carefully eyed the Soo and had eliminated it for the same reasons that Van Horne had. Besides, if the line ever presented a threat he'd squash it flat with his low-cost freight rates and then buy it up at a bargain. So the Soo Line sat in stasis: incomplete, underfinanced, unprofitable — and unattractive.

Then, in the spring of 1886, the scheme suddenly began to show unexpected financial strength. Concerned, Hill made inquiries through his "network" and was astonished to find that the injection of capital came from, of all places, the Bank of Montreal, which had advanced $750,000. Though George Stephen had sold his Bank shares, he and Donald Smith, still the major shareholder, remained powerful voices in its affairs. Hill wasted no time demanding an explanation from his old friends, still the largest shareholders in the Manitoba Road, next to Kennedy and himself.

> I have to request that yourself and Mr. Smith as directors of the Manitoba Company, will ascertain if possible, and advise me if it is true that they are getting their money from Montreal. It would hardly seem possible that the Bank of Montreal would loan money for this enterprise on its own merits. We have no controversy with the Sault road, but when they undertake to build into territory served by our lines, it becomes this company to take whatever steps are necessary to prevent the success of their enterprise.[3]

Stephen's return cable blithely advised Hill not to put so much credence in idle gossip. "My former letter was not based

---

*Van Horne for all his aggressiveness never showed any real interest in expanding wholesale into the United States. His moves in that direction were primarily defensive.

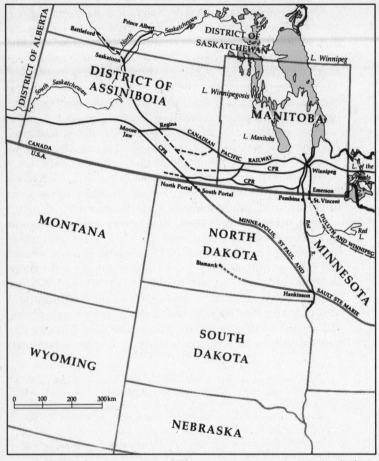

The Minneapolis, St Paul and Sault Ste Marie and the Duluth, South Shore

on any rumour . . . ," retorted Hill, "and my information as to their finances was direct. I could not have asked yourself or Mr. Smith to take any specific steps in behalf of this company except upon actual knowledge."[4] Stephen responded with an unequivocal denial. "I am quite surprised at what you tell me

and Atlantic (the Soo Lines)—and the Duluth and Winnipeg, 1897

about Washburn's extensions into your territory, and cannot imagine where the money comes from. Of one thing you may be sure that they did not get it here & that there is not the least chance of any help being got here for any such schemes. . . . No one here has a cent of interest in the Sault Line."[5]

Hill, no longer willing to tolerate Stephen's shenanigans, refused to let the matter drop, especially after he learned that Stephen and Smith were actively acquiring Soo Line shares. Shortly afterwards, Stephen and Smith began buying up the Duluth, South Shore and Atlantic Railroad as well, another tiny line chartered to run from Duluth to Sault Ste Marie. Hill had no real problem with Stephen buying the Soo Line; his attitude was that if someone had to buy it, it might as well be a friend. What he objected to was having it done behind his back, and then being treated as if he were mentally deficient when he protested.

After making it clear that he knew exactly where the Soo Line financing was coming from, Hill struck a distinctly threatening tone in his May letter to Stephen: "The only thing however that looks unfortunate is that yourself and Mr. Smith seem to be getting into a position where your investments seem to conflict."[6]* Stephen, while admitting for the first time that the money had come from the Bank of Montreal, adamantly denied any personal involvement. It was a long letter, demonstrating his habitual underestimation of Hill — a mistake Hill was soon to correct.

> As to the Sault line you still seem to be under the same delusion as to Mr. Smith & myself being in some individual way [investing] in it. The CPR Co. has not and does not mean to have any interest direct or indirect pecuniary or otherwise in this line. . . . This is the position of the Coy to which it will stand so long as I have any say in its affairs.
>
> As to Smith and myself. We neither of us, have or mean to have any personal interest in the Sault line, direct or indirect. . . . The story that the CPR Coy or that we personally had given the Bank a guarantee, is a pure and simple Canard & whatever you may hear to the contrary you may safely rest assured that the truth is exactly as I state it.

---

*Although the purchase by Stephen and Smith of the Soo and the South Shore lines was not consummated until the spring of 1888, they had essentially controlled at least the Soo Line since the Bank of Montreal financing in 1886.

> This being the fact, neither Smith nor I can see how our invest-
> ments conflict with each other. . . . If you can find out where Wash-
> burn is getting his money I wish you would let me know.[7]

Furious with Stephen's lies, Hill put the Soo Line in a vice,
slashing his own competing rates and using his considerable
influence to divert traffic away from the line. Nasty confronta-
tions between Manitoba Road and Soo Line workers erupted,
culminating in a bloody showdown that fall when twenty hefty
Manitoba Road labourers set upon three Soo trackmen near
Elbow Lake, Minnesota. Name calling and shoving escalated
into an all-out fist fight. Badly outnumbered, the Soo workers
were saved only when one hundred stalwarts arrived as rein-
forcements. The Soo contingent cornered those of their opponents who could still walk in the Elbow Lake courthouse and
threatened to set fire to it if they didn't come out. Serious
bloodshed was averted only by the arrival of the police.[8]

Hill's long letters to John S. Kennedy during this period are
full of fretting and fuming about the duplicity of Stephen and
Smith. He told Kennedy that the two of them could no longer
be trusted with sensitive information about the Manitoba
Road and began to see Stephen's and Smith's habitual absence
from the board meetings as a major aggravation. Without
their presence the always ailing Kennedy had to travel to St
Paul or, more often, Hill to New York, to make up a quorum.
Though egged on by Kennedy to make a clean break with
them, Hill was reluctant to risk a split. Then, in late September,
1886, he learned by accident that Stephen, without informing
him, was on the verge of departing for a year in England.

ON OCTOBER 5, 1886, HILL FORMALLY asked for Stephen's resignation from the board of directors of the Manitoba Road: "While
I cannot feel other than the greatest reluctance in making the
suggestion for reasons both personal and otherwise, I feel that
the work we have in hand for next year cannot go forward as it
should without a more active Board."[9] Stephen received the
letter immediately before sailing for Europe on the Cunard

steamship, the *Etruria*. It was an important psychological moment for him. He was feeling increasingly alienated by the ingrates of his adopted country. Instead of being lauded for his sacrifice in building the transcontinental road he had been branded a profiteer by the press. Even Sir John A. Macdonald avoided him or put him off whenever he tried to press settlement of the land grant issue or compensation for the Onderdonk section.* Stephen had two choices: either rededicate himself to Canada and the CPR or move over into the Hill camp. He decided by not making a decision and cabled back to Hill that he would respond when he arrived in England.

No reply ever arrived. During 1887, Kennedy pressed Hill to force the break. "We get no assistance whatever from Stephen or Smith. Can you write the former calling attention to your letter of last Autumn and remind him that you have never received his promised answer?" he pleaded.[10] Kennedy believed that Stephen and Smith would sell their shares and be out of the picture by the end of the year — but Hill knew better. He'd sent a message that Stephen couldn't fail to understand; it was time and more than time to choose sides. No response was tantamount to a decision in Hill's favour, and he was content to wait patiently for his ultimatum to bear fruit.

But just to make sure that his message didn't slip Stephen's mind, Hill continued his financial pressure on the Soo and South Shore lines, forcing them to the verge of insolvency by 1888. What superficially had seemed to be one of Stephen's brilliant manœuvres turned into a sinkhole of awesome proportions. Stephen and Smith had millions tied up in their share purchases and through guarantees of the numerous loans to the two lines — and it all looked as if it was going to be

---

*The immensely difficult 127 miles of track from Yale, British Columbia, situated at the head of navigation of the Fraser River, to Kamloops Lake is known as the Onderdonk section, after the contractor Andrew Onderdonk, who built it as part of the original government contract in 1879. (Onderdonk also built the section from Yale to Port Moody.) It became a source of bitter complaint when it was taken over by the CPR, as per the 1881 contract, in 1885. The CPR estimated that it would cost between $6 and $10 million to bring the Onderdonk section up to a reasonable safety standard and demanded that the government compensate them for this outlay. Macdonald, as was his wont, delayed. In 1891, the CPR accepted a paltry $579,225 award.

J. J. Hill and his son, Louis, at Billings, Montana, in later years

worthless. Hill could well have afforded to take the companies off Stephen's hands but once his mind was made up he stuck to a decision with monumental stubbornness.

Hill subtly threatened Stephen and Smith with far more than the loss of their seats on the Manitoba board. The extent of Stephen's and Smith's investments in the Manitoba Road was generally known. But carefully guarded secrets were the millions invested in peripheral businesses, including coal properties, operating mines in Montana, Dakota and Iowa, water power companies, raw land, hotels, rolling mills and even a bank.* Some of the investments were in their own

---

*The extent and intermingling of the Associates' nonrailroad investments is so vast and complicated that an entire book would be needed to document them fully. A March 16, 1901, letter from Hill illustrates how they managed their portfolios. The letter was written to E. T. Nichols, head of the Manitoba Road's New York office and later treasurer of the Great Northern. In it Hill mentions the "Coal and Supply companies stocks" held by the Associates, but all in Hill's name. Nowhere on the official list of shareholders does either Angus or Stephen appear, though their investment in this area totalled $406,000. Under the same circumstances they held 100,000 shares with a par value of $100,000 in the capital stock of Webster County Coal & Land Company.

names but the bulk of them were sheltered behind Hill's and Stephen's go-betweens, such as Hamilton Brown or John Sterling of Sherman & Sterling, a powerful New York law firm. So complex was the labyrinth of dealings that sometimes even Hill and Stephen lost track.*

RELATIONS BETWEEN THE TWO ASSOCIATES improved slowly until the end of the decade, each ignoring the unpleasantness of 1886. Then on July 16, 1888, Stephen wrote Hill a warm eight-page letter containing what can only be called an unconditional offer of peace. He finally admitted that he and Smith, as Hill well knew, indeed had control of the Soo Line and had just assumed ownership of the Duluth, South Shore and Atlantic Railroad† "entirely for the protection of the Canadian business of the CPR & not in the least with the object of adding to the extent of one cent to our own means." Sprinkled throughout the letter are profuse and entirely uncharacteristic statements of Stephen's and Smith's great affection for Hill and his railroad.

> Both Smith and myself would like nothing better than to work with you in every possible way for the mutual benefit of all our interests, and while on this subject let me say what I dare say you are not aware of that we each of us have a greater pecuniary interest, in one way & another, in the St. P. M. & M. than we have in the C.P.R. but if it were otherwise we would still take the greatest pleasure in doing anything we could to secure and increase its prosperity. . . .
>
> I often feel, if it were not for the sake of others whom I may have induced to put their money into the C.P.R. that I would like to shake the dust of Canada off my feet and turn my back on the country forever.[11]

---

*In one case $300,000 worth of stock languished in a safe for years until Sterling stumbled across the certificates and gaily informed Hill of his discovery: "You will be glad to know that, having looked at my books, I find that there are still 1,000 shares of Northern Pacific Common, registered in my name, and 2,000 shares registered in the name of Clark, Dodge & Co. [one of Hill's shells] the whole 3,000 shares being owned by Lord Mount Stephen and the Certificates being in the vault here." (Sterling to Hill, August 7, 1901, JJHP)

†Once the two lines were owned by the CPR they became known as the Soo Lines.

Just in case Hill didn't get the message, Stephen sent an even clearer statement three weeks later, prompted by criticisms in the Toronto press and a decision by the Manitoba legislature to charter yet another line to compete with the CPR. "This is the reward we (you & I) get for first giving them [Canadians] their first 2 railway connections [the Manitoba Road and the CPR] with the outside world & next for what the CPR has done to make them a country," railed Stephen. "It is disgusting to be treated this way by the very people we have made. But it seems to be the way of the world. I am thoroughly disgusted with the whole business & for the thousandth time bitterly repent that I ever had anything to do with them or their country."[12]

Stephen's anti-Canadian diatribes have often been dismissed as fits of pique. On the contrary, his feelings during this period were well thought out and eloquently expressed in similar letters to Sir John A. Macdonald and Principal George M. Grant of Queen's University, a man he barely knew.

> . . . scarcely a day passes that I do not see in newspapers from all parts of the country from Vancouver to Halifax, including that "slimy" sheet the *Witness*, the most violent attacks on the company for its "brutal" greed and which is "drawing the life blood out of the country" . . .
>   Why in the face of these facts should I waste my life in promoting the interest of people who believe me to be a public robber?
>   . . . but my interest in Canada is at an end, and I am longing for the time when I can shake its dust from my feet, I have had enough of it, I am not saying this in irritation of a temporary character. . . .[13]

Three days later, on August 7, 1888, George Stephen officially announced his resignation as president of the CPR. His last act as president was to purchase the Soo Lines from himself for the CPR. "I cannot refrain from congratulating the Shareholders upon the arrangements recently completed by Sir Donald Smith and myself," he wrote to CPR shareholders, "which will have the effect of securing to the C.P.R. the permanent friendship of the two new and important American lines extending from Sault Ste Marie to Minneapolis and St Paul, on the one hand, and to Duluth on the other, and reaching a traffic the importance of which it would be difficult to over-estimate."[14]

It was an eerie reprise of 1882 when Stephen resigned from the Manitoba Road board at the same time he announced the company had purchased the Manitoba Southwestern, which he and Smith owned. But this time it was the CPR and William Van Horne who were left holding the bag, not J. J. Hill. Not only did the CPR take over Stephen's and Smith's holdings, but the deal unconditionally guaranteed the debts of both lines, completely freeing the two cousins from any further responsibility.

Most believed that Stephen, as he claimed, had "retired" to England because of ill health and exhaustion. Then and since he was widely described as a "broken man," heart sore with disappointment and a sense of failure over the CPR. Disgusted he was, broken and exhausted, not at all, for he threw himself into J. J. Hill's affairs with a will. Though Stephen resided in England thereafter, he would be intimately involved with Hill's business empire for the next twenty years.

Early in 1889, Stephen, Smith* and Hill bought up 12,500 Manitoba Road shares to tighten their control.[15] It was the first step in a complicated reorganization, masterminded by Hill and Stephen, and made official on September 12, 1889, which transformed the St Paul, Minneapolis and Manitoba Railroad into the Great Northern Railroad, a company determined to push its track to the Pacific coast and challenge the supremacy of the CPR and the Northern Pacific in the west. Smith and Stephen became board members of the new company and Stephen even wrote boastfully to Hill that he was recommending that friends buy its stock instead of investing in the CPR. He also persuaded an influential London broker, Thomas Skinner, to become the Great Northern's London agent — which Skinner did without relinquishing his seat on the CPR board.[16]

---

*At the same time, Stephen retained his chairmanship of the CPR's board. He and Smith were still the major shareholders in the CPR and, along with Angus and Van Horne, comprised the company's powerful executive committee.

If Stephen had any real intention of retiring to titled splendour in England, comforted and buffered by his fortune, Hill soon ended it by dangling a bait in front of him he couldn't refuse — the Northern Pacific Railroad. The prospect of seizing control of that meddlesome, financially unstable but asset-rich line which had caused the CPR and the Manitoba Road so much grief, was a seductive lure. "I am 10 years your senior," Stephen wrote, "& not the man I was 10 years ago but I would gladly put myself to some considerable inconvenience to capture and control the N.P."[17] Even if the line eluded them, he was still fired by the chance to build a cross-country line on American soil: "If we decide that a control of the N.P. is out of reach then I suppose we ought to go vigorously and promptly to work on a new line,"[18] he wrote in June, 1889. From then on, Stephen was irrevocably in Hill's camp, and though he shrouded his subsequent actions with much high-minded talk, they were all directed at preserving and protecting those interests.

IF WILLIAM VAN HORNE FELT the sands of avarice shifting beneath his feet when he assumed the CPR presidency in 1888, he gave no sign. Though he was clearly unhappy with Stephen's last-minute purchase of the Soo Lines, he was unaware of the true extent of his old friend's financial involvement with Hill and continued to use Stephen as his sounding board and the company's direct connection to the British financial markets. Van Horne wrote to Stephen in England sometimes two or three times a week, asking his advice on the most confidential matters of company policy and strategy. When, in late 1889, Stephen announced his intention of resigning from the CPR chairmanship, Van Horne even wrote to Macdonald, a man he disliked, begging him to intercede. "Sir George is in an unreasoning mood — has made himself believe that he has in some way sacrificed or betrayed the interests of the Company, and I don't know what all . . . if there is anything you can do without injury to the country, that will help us to hold him, I hope and pray that you will do it."[19]*

Stephen's desire to leave the company wasn't entirely because of his investments with Hill and his disgruntlement with Canada — Van Horne himself was part of the problem. He was just too independent, opinionated, pigheaded and direct. But worse, in Stephen's eyes, was the fact that Van Horne let his competitive nature and his inability to resist a challenge push him far beyond the limits of prudence. Nowhere was this more evident than in the preposterous Battle of Fort Whyte, a conflagration that ignited when Premier Greenway of Manitoba leased a partly completed line to the Northern Pacific and also granted it a charter to build from Winnipeg to the border, right in the heart of CPR territory.†

At one point the extended line — called the Northern Pacific and Manitoba Railway — violated a section of the General Railway Act and laid its track up to the CPR line, installed a diamond connection to cross it and continued on its way, leaving a guard of twenty constables behind as protection.‡ Van Horne let loose with howls of indignation and ordered William Whyte, western superintendent, to stop the incursion.

Whyte knew exactly what Van Horne wanted. In the middle of the night he blocked the line with an ancient engine, soon dubbed the "Fort." "We are here to protect the company's interests, and if necessary we will tie up the whole western system and bring in every man to hold the 'Fort,'"[20] Whyte told the press. To emphasize the CPR's determination, he took personal command of the situation, housing a squad of twenty special constables and two tame magistrates in a nearby private car. Further, he called up 250 of the toughest men

---

*In the end, Stephen did not resign from the chairmanship until 1892.

†Joseph Martin, the Liberal attorney general and also the commissioner of railways, was instrumental in granting the charter. The Northern Pacific added a little sweetener to its application by making Martin vice-president of the new Manitoba line. He was also a major shareholder.

‡The Act required a hearing before the railway committee before another company's line was crossed.

available from the Winnipeg repair and refitting shops. The offending diamond was ripped out, paraded about the grounds by a CPR crew and mounted as a trophy back in the Winnipeg yard. A legion of Northern Pacific workers soon gathered, and for five days the two battalions traded insults, ceasing only briefly when a cluster of provincial Cabinet ministers, accompanied by a bevy of reporters, paid a visit.

The Battle of Fort Whyte ended as abruptly as it began when the courts rejected Van Horne's application for an injunction. The diamond reinstalled, the army was reassigned and Van Horne turned his attention elsewhere. The Battle provided great fodder for railway yarns but it was a public relations blunder on the part of Van Horne that cost the CPR whatever remained of the meagre support it had in Manitoba. George Stephen would rather have bitten off his tongue than give his enemies that kind of ammunition.

THE SOO LINES HUNG ABOUT Van Horne's fleshy neck like a steel albatross. Not only did they fail to pay operating expenses — thanks in part to the indefatigable Hill's diversion of traffic — but they gobbled up precious CPR revenue to finance upgrading and expansion. Van Horne made his displeasure clear and Stephen, in order to mollify him, began pressuring — or at least claiming to Van Horne that he was pressuring — J. J. Hill into taking them over.[21]

Conventional thinking accepts Stephen's later contention that Hill had in fact reneged on a promise to buy the Soo Lines, but it is unlikely to the extreme that Hill ever made a genuine offer. He'd made it absolutely clear, through his actions, that he wouldn't be Stephen's dupe as he'd been with the Manitoba Southwestern, and he was bound and determined not to rescue Stephen from his folly.

In March of 1890, Hill did make a sly offer to take over the Soo in return for a "traffic contract of binding and perfectly equitable and effective character between Great Northern and Canadian Pacific."[22] It was an offer that no railroader in his right mind would accept. Essentially Hill was asking Van Horne to divvy up all transcontinental traffic three years before the Great Northern was in a position to compete for it.* He assured Van Horne that their two lines would thus be interlocked in an idyllic atmosphere of friendship and mutual profitability. To this Van Horne snorted a derisive "Hah!" and reported to Stephen that Hill was "concealing his poison in friendly words. . . ."[23]

Indeed, as construction of the Great Northern proceeded through Montana, Idaho and Washington towards the Pacific, Hill shot up branch lines toward the British Columbia border, reaching for the incredibly rich coal fields in the Crowsnest Pass area.† "Look at these . . . like hungry hounds ready to jump in!"[24] Van Horne thundered at engineer Randolph Bruce, stabbing his finger at a map of the province which showed the encroaching lines. Hill masked his invasion of the West through subsidiaries but Van Horne wasn't fooled. When the New Westminster Southern linked New Westminster with the international border, he knew Hill was attempting to siphon off CPR traffic between Vancouver and Seattle. "I am annoyed and disgusted at his shuffling, his evasion, and his meaningless fine talk," Van Horne wrote to Stephen.‡ "He is not building a line down the Sound to New Westminster because he loves us."[25]

Throughout his battle with Hill Van Horne was hobbled by Stephen, who continuously counselled tolerance, conciliation and caution, obscuring his own interests by deriding Hill in virtually every letter he wrote to the CPR president as "childish," "shamefaced" and "ridiculous." Stephen continued to

---

*The Great Northern's last spike wasn't driven until January, 1893.

†Crowsnest coal was of extremely high quality, easy to mine and located where grades were far less than in other coal-mining areas of the mountains.

‡In 1891 George Stephen was made a British peer, entitled to be called Lord Mount Stephen, after the mountain in the Selkirks which bears his name. Donald Smith was made a peer in 1897, taking the title Lord Strathcona and Mount Royal, later Lord Strathcona of Mount Royal. William Van Horne became a Knight Bachelor in 1894.

affirm his loyalty to the CPR: "I hardly need say to you that my relations to the Great Northern can never by any possibility become or be made the same in character as my relations to the Canadian Pacific Railway, which have always been and always will be quite apart from all pecuniary interest in either company."[26]

Intellectually, Van Horne understood that Stephen was walking a gossamer-thin line between the two competing railroads, but as Hill had done years before, he absolved him from any blame even when the facts were incontrovertible. "Neither Lord Mount Stephen nor Sir Donald Smith would knowingly do anything to injure the Canadian Pacific in the slightest degree," he wrote to Skinner in 1892, "but they naturally have a great affection for the Great Northern and are glad to believe good rather than ill of it and they are too far away from Mr. Hill to keep any check upon him even if they knew his feelings and intentions, which I am convinced they do not."[27]

Van Horne's apologies for Stephen reveal his greatest flaw, at least as a businessman. Once he counted someone as a friend, almost nothing could be done to shake his conviction. Van Horne's unwillingness to see Stephen for what he was also demonstrates the almost unnatural hold Stephen exerted on those he came in contact with.

ONCE IT BECAME CLEAR TO VAN HORNE that Stephen could not or would not convince Hill to take over the Soo Lines, he set about turning them into a paying proposition. He did it by purchasing a little railroad called the Duluth and Winnipeg, on the surface every bit as insignificant as the Soo Lines had been.* J. J. Hill had monitored the Duluth and Winnipeg since it was first chartered and financed by local Duluth citizens in

---

*In 1893 he also completed, at considerable expense, a new line from Hankinson, North Dakota, to Moose Jaw, Saskatchewan. Linking up with the Soo Line, it gave the CPR a shorter route to the Pacific from Chicago and St Paul.

1878. He recognized that the line, in the right hands — his — could be even more valuable than the Manitoba Road.

With the construction of only sixty-five miles of track, the Duluth and Winnipeg would control huge chunks of the Mesabi Range in northern Minnesota. It owned 18,420 acres outright and leased another 14,320 acres of the richest land in the area — so rich that in Hill's own words, the iron ore was lying around in such abundance it could be scooped up "without any more mining than is done with a standard shovel to load it."[28] It was the beginning of the steel industry's golden era, and high-quality iron ore was already becoming a premier commodity. Thanks to the recently developed open-hearth process North Americans were producing steel to rival that of the Germans, but at a considerably lower price.

Acting through intermediaries, Hill began buying up the railroad's debt — estimating that the line could be had for about $2 million. "The property will come into our hands in such a way that it will be worth fully $3,000,000 or $4,000,000 more than it cost," he gloated.[29] His strategy was similar to the one that he used with Stephen and Smith to take over the St Paul and Pacific: buy up the debt and then foreclose when the notes come due. But just as Hill was slipping in the back way, Van Horne kicked in the front door, buying control directly from the shareholders and beginning negotiations to settle the debt. Van Horne had outmanœuvred Hill and, heaping insult upon injury, he purchased the line in January, 1893, for an initial investment of only $1,316,924.

The Duluth and Winnipeg, irrespective of its mineral wealth, was a brilliant tactical acquisition. Together with the Duluth, South Shore and Atlantic line, the Duluth and Winnipeg gave the CPR its own route into St Paul, which bypassed Hill completely. Van Horne also saw that the D & W could be the start of an alternative all-American route to the west coast. Best of all, the purchase gave Van Horne the perfect weapon to bludgeon Hill. Had he been able to hang onto it, Van Horne would likely have destroyed the Great

Mahoning Mine in the Mesabi Range

Northern and turned the CPR into one of the richest and most powerful corporations in the world.

The idea of laying the boots to his rival was just the sort of coup that set Van Horne trumpeting like a bull elephant: "We need not fear Hill or anybody else; we can boss him and the N.P. alike," he crowed.[30] Van Horne enjoyed his early laughter but Hill was to have the last and best guffaw. Van Horne was a master of confrontation, whether battling mudslides and avalanches or crooked contractors; his blows were swift and sure. But the fight with Hill for supremacy was not an evenly matched war. Van Horne was handicapped from the start by the CPR executive committee (Stephen, Smith and Angus, besides himself), which he carried around like an ill-fitting and overloaded backpack. Moreover, virtually the entire board was in the control of Stephen and Smith.

At first Stephen claimed to be pleased by Van Horne's purchase. "I feel sure you have done a very wise thing in securing the control of the Duluth and Winnipeg and the Mineral Range lines. Their importance to the D.S.S. & A [the

Duluth, South Shore and Atlantic] . . . is very great."[31]* Hill bombarded Stephen with a barrage of cables and lashed out at the CPR like a wounded animal. Using his newly completed transcontinental line, he embarked upon a frenzy of rate cutting that made Van Horne comment wryly, "Hill seems to be like a boy with a new pair of boots & bound to splash into the first mud-puddle so that he may have an excuse for show-ing their red tops."[32] The rates cut deeply into the CPR's reve-nues, however. Hill's passenger fares from St Paul to the coast were $25 for second class and $35 for first. The equivalent journey on the CPR cost $35 and $60. Hill also boycotted the Soo Lines and, even more provocative, began to interfere with CPR schedules. He stalled trains at the border so that when they arrived in Winnipeg, passengers were too late to catch the connecting CPR train west and were forced to wait twenty hours for the next one. Several times Hill arbitrarily refused to honour CPR through tickets, leaving infuriated passengers stranded. Van Horne appealed for mediation, but Stephen, who could have stopped Hill, begged off: "So far away as I am it is quite impossible for me to interfere with any advantage to either . . . ," he wrote to the beleaguered CPR president.[33]

Hill escalated his attack on his rival, planting newspaper stories in New York and England, even bribing members of the Interstate Commerce Commission to come up with tariff rul-ings that were damaging to the company.[34] At every opportu-nity in his letters to Van Horne, Stephen continued to portray Hill as a ridiculous figure: "It is extraordinary that he should have so little control over his temper as to permit himself to indulge in such childish language."[35] This is the same man to whom he had said a few years earlier, "My inclination is always to accept your views, largely because they are your views."[36]

The rivalry between Hill and Van Horne reached legendary proportions and talk of it filled idle hours for trainmen across

---

*The Mineral Range lines were a group of small feeder branches to various mining camps that Van Horne purchased at the same time.

North America. Both men had their supporters, who vigorously championed each one by accusing the other of treachery and deceit. "There are three liars on this continent," Van Horne proclaimed cheerfully when the stories reached him. "I am one — and Jim Hill is the other two!"[37]

IN MARCH, 1893, HILL came to Montreal to talk things over with Van Horne, but negotiating with Hill was like trying to catch a shadow, and Stephen "commiserated" with Van Horne after receiving a report of the meeting.

> If you had not "forced the fidgeting" he would without doubt have gone back to St. Paul without mentioning the one thing that induced him to go to Montreal. In this respect he is the most "shame faced" grown man I ever met, more like a very shy boy of 10 or 12 years than a full grown man of 50.
>
> In dealing with him it is necessary to keep his odd ways in mind & to treat him rather as a spoilt child brimful of ridiculous suspicions of everybody he comes in contact with.[38]

Hill was stalling because he knew that the deck was stacked in his favour.

Stephen's continued vilification of Hill obscured his barely perceptible withdrawal of support from the D & W. "From what you say as to the character of the country traversed by the line, it looks very much as if it were worthless from a money-earning point of view. I had no idea how utterly bad it is in that respect."[39] Giving the first indication that he knew something serious was amiss, Van Horne wrote pointedly to London: "Mr. Hill is gambling on the belief that there are enough of our C.P.R. friends interested in the Great Northern to 'choke off' any extension of the Duluth and Winnipeg."[40]

As he inched away from the Duluth and Winnipeg, Stephen found it increasingly difficult to raise money for the CPR. A case in point was the Crowsnest Pass area. In 1890 Stephen had stressed the need to control the region at any cost to keep Hill out of British Columbia. Then, when Van Horne approached him in early 1893 with a plan to raise funds for an extension of the line into the Kootenays, Stephen mysteriously found money difficult to come by. "The only thing that occurs to me to say in regard to that is that the prospects ahead of the silver mining industry are anything but bright. . . . I expect to see a great fall in the price of silver . . . and I understand that a great many of the silver mines on the Great Northern and Northern Pacific have already shut down. . . ."[41] Hill's interest in the Crowsnest had not slackened at all because as Stephen well knew, he was after coal not silver.

Van Horne's pleasure in lassoing the D & W was further soured by the severe worldwide depression which began in the middle of 1893, and hit railroads particularly hard. Accompanying the financial unrest were floods, locust plagues, wheat diseases and low prices for grain. Van Horne was forced to reduce all officers' salaries by 20 percent. To make matters worse, the Duluth and Winnipeg line was proving to be in worse shape than Van Horne had initially thought, forcing him to redirect as much money as he dared into rehabilitating the railroad. Criticisms flew from every quarter, even from the CPR board itself, and Van Horne imparted his irritation with his fairweather friends to Stephen: "Our expenses were less in our most extravagant year than have been those of any of the other lines." Van Horne was so steamed up that he wrote Stephen a second letter in the afternoon: "I do not believe that any important railway in the United States can possibly get down to our figures."[42]

In June, 1894, Stephen insisted that Van Horne meet with Hill once more in Montreal to sort out the Duluth and Winnipeg matter. That meeting was as futile as all the others. In a letter to George Stephen, Van Horne described how it ended: "I reminded him then that we had only an hour left for the discussion of the Duluth and Winnipeg matter, and we started out fairly well on that question for a few minutes . . . he soon wandered away from the subject . . . we did not get back to the D. & W. until he had to start for his train. Then he said he would think it over, and if I would try to think out some scheme, we could discuss it at St. Paul on my way back from the

Pacific Coast. I promised to do so; and then, taking me affectionately by the arm, he said: 'Van, it is a very nice thing that
although we may disagree about business matters, our personal relations are so pleasant. We would do anything for each
other.' (The skunk.)"[43]*

As Hill was patting "Van's" arm he was preparing to plunge
the knife. He wanted the D & W and was prepared to do anything to get it. But Van Horne was a remarkably innovative
and resilient opponent. Hill hit him with every weapon in
his armory and, like a punching bag, Van Horne returned
stronger than before. Nothing seemed to stop him, not rate
wars, depression, rumours, rebellion in the CPR board or even
Stephen's subtle duplicity.

With every day that Van Horne held onto the Duluth and
Winnipeg, the situation became more dangerous to Hill and
Stephen. For the first time, the Great Northern faced ruin. If
Van Horne managed to carry out his plan of extending the
D & W, he would be in a position to strangle Hill. The D & W
would be perfectly placed to drive all the way to the Pacific
coast, giving the CPR a second transcontinental line, and a
shorter, more competitive one than Hill's Great Northern.
Realizing the risk they were facing and having tried every
other weapon to no avail, Hill and Stephen set out to discredit
Van Horne.

J. J. HILL WAS A SABOTEUR par excellence. He instigated a new
rumour campaign, playing up the desperate condition of
the D & W and planting false stories about Van Horne personally owning a vast amount of property in the region the line
served.[44] While sowing seeds of doubt among investors about
Van Horne's character and leadership, Hill increased the financial pressure on the Duluth and Winnipeg. In March,

*From his meeting with Van Horne, Hill went directly to meet with Stephen at his fishing
resort to talk about the renewed possibility of picking up their old rival, the Northern Pacific,
for a bargain price.

1894, immediately after meeting Stephen in London, Hill announced that he'd arranged financing for a new line running from Fosston, Saskatchewan, to Duluth, in direct competition with the D & W. "The right of way into Duluth has been secured and work will be begun early in the spring. The move will compel the Canadian Pacific to extend the Duluth & Winnipeg to the West," reported the Associated Press.[45]

The timing of Hill's announcement was brilliant. Van Horne had comprehensive plans to extend the Duluth and Winnipeg but Hill was forcing him to do it at the worst possible time. Railroad financing, already depressed by the recessionary times, was flattened by the news that the Northern Pacific was once again insolvent. Railroad securities were spurned in every financial centre and Stephen was finding it impossible to raise any money for the CPR. Undaunted, Van Horne decided to find the money himself. He boldly organized a plan to sell D & W construction bonds in the Minnesota and North Dakota towns that would be served by the sixty-five-mile extension. But each time Van Horne visited a town to drum up support for the bonds, Hill's agents ensured defeat "by spending a large sum in cash," as Hill later gloated to J. P. Morgan.[46]

While Hill sabotaged Van Horne's Duluth and Winnipeg fund raising, Stephen harped about the sorry state of CPR expenditures, unfavourably comparing them to those of Hill's Great Northern. Curiously, the newspapers on both sides of the Atlantic did the same, with the *Statist* calling the company's outlook "decidedly black."[47] CPR share prices slid from 76 to 63 in less than two months. Van Horne was sure recovery was around the corner but Stephen remained far more pessimistic and he recommended that the CPR's 1894 dividend be reduced from 5 percent to 2½. Gaspard Farrer, a London financier and the CPR's representative in Baring Brothers, obligingly compiled figures showing that Hill's gross earnings per train miles were 37 percent higher than the CPR's and that net earnings were 21 percent higher.[48]

Van Horne, fed up with doom and gloom, and finally realizing that Stephen wasn't holding the CPR's interests as close to his heart as he claimed, diplomatically told him to mind his own business: "Difficulties and dangers always look greater to everybody at a distance and I think I have noticed or thought I noticed a good many times in the history of the company that where you were full of belief here you were more or less of a pessimist in London . . . . I believe it to be impossible for anybody in London to make a correct diagnosis of the conditions in Canada, however familiar he may have been with the country two years ago."[49]

That fall, just as harvesting began, a devastating flood in British Columbia's Fraser River Valley carried away both the crops and huge sections of track, blocking traffic to the coast entirely. Van Horne rushed to the scene as quickly as possible. After surveying the swamp, bog and tangle of rails left behind, he cursed, "Hell! This means all the money in the treasury gone!" An engineer by the name of Macnab assured him, "Well, sir, we'll run the road whatever comes."[50]*

As if Van Horne didn't have enough problems, Hill was busy enmeshing him in a spider's web of lawsuits, which endlessly delayed the CPR's taking full possession of the Duluth and Winnipeg. Van Horne had anticipated that the takeover would be finalized by the fall of 1894, but Hill's agents ensured that didn't happen. The minute a suit by minority shareholders was settled, construction bondholders began agitating, and Hill was behind it all. Stephen, of course, was in the wings, urging a moderate and conciliatory response whenever Hill mugged Van Horne.

The immense financial pressure coupled with pinpricks of doubt about the loyalty of his friends and associates began to erode Van Horne's superhuman vitality, and during the summer of 1894 he fell ill for the first time in his life. He shrugged off the attack of bronchitis fairly quickly but used the illness to explain a holiday to Europe in December, 1894. In fact, Van

---

*When Van Horne died twenty years later the man fondly remarked, "Salary or no salary the boys would have stood by the Old Man! He had a great hold on us." (Vaughan, *Life and Work of Sir William Van Horne*, p. 237)

Horne's trip was intended to heal what he perceived as a growing rift with George Stephen. It didn't work, as Stephen made unequivocally clear to Van Horne's loyal lieutenant, Thomas Shaughnessy.

> It is quite evident that Sir William, either from failing health or from allowing other things to occupy his mind, is no longer able to give the affairs of the Company his undivided attention. His want of grasp and knowledge of the true position of the Company was, painfully, twice shown at our conference on Tuesday last, and can only be explained on the assumption that he had never given his mind to the matter. . . . His actions gave me the impression that he felt like a man who knew he was in a mess and had not the usual courage to look his position in the face. His apparent indifference and inability to realize the gravity of the position I can account for in no other way.
>
> From what I have thus said you will see that all my confidence in the ability of Sir William to save the Company has gone, and that it is to you alone that I look, if disaster is to be avoided.
>
> It is no use now dwelling on the errors of judgment that have been committed and the recklessness with which great capital has been spent and wasted in foolish and improbable schemes. . . . It is very painful to me to have to say this to you, but it is better that I should tell you unreservedly what is in my mind in view of the heavy responsibility which circumstances have imposed on you.[51]

If the London newspapers, ever quick to flay the CPR, noticed Van Horne faltering in any way, they gave no hint. "We had an opportunity of meeting him casually at the office of a mutual friend on Monday," the *Statist* reported, "and in a short interview (Sir William can say more in a few minutes than some people can in an hour) many interesting facts were discussed."[52]

THE WONDER OF HILL'S AND STEPHEN'S assault on Van Horne was not that they finally defeated him — but that he held out so long. Van Horne was like a corpulent Gulliver tethered to the ground. Each time the final strands were applied, he'd work a hand free and swat away the pests. But the Lilliputians were everywhere, and behind each was either Stephen or Hill or both. Gaspard Farrer was first and last George Stephen's man. Thomas Skinner, a long-time London CPR director and the recipient of many of Van Horne's confidences during this period, wouldn't sneeze without first consulting Stephen. He owed his lucrative 1889 appointment as London agent of the Manitoba Road directly to Stephen. New York lawyer John Sterling, who was Van Horne's advisor in all Duluth and Winnipeg matters was also George Stephen's lawyer and New York fixer.* So close were Sterling and Farrer to Stephen that they were the executors of his will. Even Thomas Shaughnessy, Van Horne's vice-president, acted questionably during this period, no doubt because of genuine fears, induced by Stephen, for the future of the CPR. Privately, he considered the Duluth and Winnipeg "a blunder of the worst possible description."[53] Unknown to Van Horne, Shaughnessy carried on "a voluminous correspondence"† with Stephen, who in turn sent extracts of Shaughnessy's letters to Hill.

If Van Horne had any doubt that Stephen was conducting a plot to paralyse the CPR and advance the interests of the Great Northern, they were dispelled by public reaction to the February, 1895, announcement that the CPR dividend would not be paid — for the first time in its history.‡ Shareholders pilloried Van Horne at the meeting where the announcement was made. A number of them called for his resignation, and one even claimed "that he could get scores of men for 1,000 dols a year who would manage the C.P.R. as competently as Mr. Van

---

*Stephen and Sterling were close friends in spite of the latter's numerous idiosyncracies. Various fears governed his life. He was afraid of crossing bodies of water and was terrified of the Atlantic. When fishing with Stephen or Hill at Stephen's fishing resort, Sterling only felt safe enough to sleep when he was securely locked in a large cage. On one occasion a prankster stole the key, which was in the butler's keeping, and it took several hours the following morning for the frenzied Sterling to be released.

In spite of or because of his fears, Sterling was a schemer of Stephen's calibre.

†Only one letter from that voluminous correspondence has been preserved.

‡The dividend was paid for the second half of 1895 at only 1.5 percent.

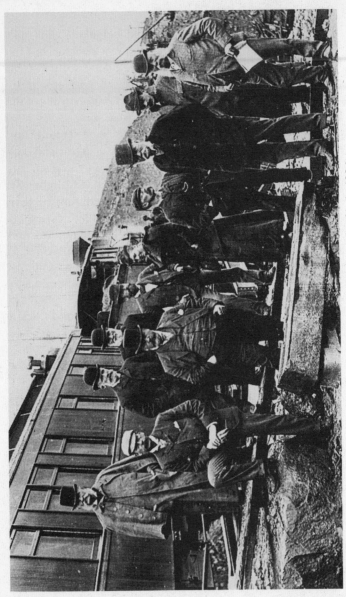

Van Horne and CPR officials in British Columbia in 1894

Horne for perhaps 50,000 dols."[54] George Stephen was conspicuously absent from the meeting* but Donald Smith attended. It was a scene reminiscent of the Pacific Scandal, as everyone knew that Donald Smith's would be the deciding voice. Smith sat passively through the bitter attacks on Van Horne, rising only at the last minute to state his sympathy for the dissenters, but even so he was going to hang onto his shares. Accordingly, no vote was held to oust Van Horne, but Smith had pointedly failed to endorse him. The next day CPR shares dropped to 44 in a single day.

One month later on May 10, 1895, J. J. Hill and George Stephen, in the library of Stephen's London house, St James Place, signed a tentative agreement that would result in the takeover of the Northern Pacific Railroad by Hill's Great Northern — a coup Hill and Stephen had been plotting since 1889. "You never saw two more excited men than Lord M.S. and Hill last week,"[55] Gaspard Farrer gleefully reported to John Sterling. Also present at the meeting was Thomas Skinner. For some months, Stephen and Smith as well as Hill had been quietly buying heavily discounted Northern Pacific shares.

With the signing of this first "London Agreement," it became a matter of life and death to stop Van Horne from using the Duluth and Winnipeg as the basis of a competing American transcontinental line. Almost immediately, rumours circulated in London and New York that CPR company directors were selling short and organizing bear raids on the stock. Share prices fell to an all-time low of $35 and Stephen began advising shareholders, many of whom were members of the royalty, to sell.

There was no justification for the drop. In fact, the CPR outperformed most of the other railways on the continent. The short selling, coupled with Stephen's advice, was a direct attack

---

*That same month in London Stephen hosted an all-male dinner in Hill's honour which was attended by twenty-two of the most important people in the city.

on Van Horne's leadership. Shareholders blamed Van Horne, not the market, for the declining share prices, making it impossible for him to raise money for any project, let alone an extension of the Duluth and Winnipeg. An endless stream of sellers appeared in every brokerage house in England. The man fingered by the Philadelphia *Daily Stockholder* and the Dow, Jones Company as leading the attacks on CPR stock was Thomas Skinner. Van Horne's friend R. M. Horne Payne had direct evidence of the treachery:

> One morning, on arrival at my office, I found two ladies who had invested in a few C.P.R. shares at my advice waiting in different rooms to ask me whether they had not better sell at once in consequence of advice they had received from Mountstephen. After reassuring them, I went across to Skinner's office to enquire what it all meant.
>
> On my aproaching the subject Skinner became very excited, and in effect said the C.P.R. was in a critical condition, and could not avoid bankruptcy, and that the accounts rendered by Sir William were misleading and dishonest, especially in the matter of a certain Reserve Fund. He applied the epithet of 'old blackguard' to Sir William.
>
> A heated altercation ensued, and although I have been forced to meet him on business from time to time, I have never spoken in a friendly way to Skinner from that day to this.[56]

CPR shares dipped even lower, to $33, but in the last half of 1895 they began to rally, just as Van Horne had predicted. Stephen then announced that he had sold his shares so as not to be accused of profiteering after advising friends to sell. In fact, though his name disappeared from the list of shareholders, Stephen hadn't sold out at all. An 1898 letter from Smith to Hill clearly proves that Stephen still had his shares, though he claimed to have gotten rid of every one.[57*]

The announcement of Stephen's sale of his CPR shares should have been the knock-out blow, but Hill and Stephen were astonished to see Van Horne rise from the mat once again. Not a block of CPR stock came available without Van

---

*Further confirmation exists in a letter from Stephen to Hill on August 23, 1897. (JJHP)

Horne buying a piece or all of it. He wrote to friends, associates and former shareholders, extolling the future of the CPR, pushing aside the gloomy predictions of naysayers who believed the depression would drag on into the twentieth century. He enlisted Dutch financier Adolph Boissevain, a long-time friend and early CPR shareholder, to head a small syndicate of buyers. By 1896 Van Horne was the largest single shareholder of the company, and his supporters controlled large amounts of stock. But it wasn't quite enough.

Throughout 1896 Van Horne continued to be optimistic about the D & W, but he still appeared sadly unaware of the full extent of the perfidy around him. "The D & W is the best property we have & this year will demonstrate that. It is moreover our *only* weapon against the Great Northern and Northern Pacific," he confided to Stephen's man Skinner on April 17, 1896.[58] Then in August the bottom fell out of the price of iron, the ore which supplied a large portion of the D & W's freight revenue. Litigation, encouraged by Hill, over settlement of the line's debt continued and Van Horne moaned that the expenses "have piled up shockingly." Even at this point he might have been able to hang onto the road, for the depression was lifting and crops for the 1896 season were excellent. But the CPR directors, led by Skinner, Stephen, Shaughnessy and Smith made it clear that if he didn't sell the Duluth and Winnipeg, they would summarily fire him, a shattering experience for the Terror of Flat Krick. For the first time in his life, Van Horne had reached the limits of his gargantuan self-confidence and superhuman perseverance, and he just gave up.

Who should be waiting in the wings ready — as a favour to his old friend Van — to take the Duluth and Winnipeg off his hands, but J. J. Hill. Van Horne would have fallen on his sword before turning his weapon over to his adversary, so R. B. Angus and Thomas Shaughnessy did the dirty work, travelling to New York to complete negotiations. In return for a traffic-sharing agreement to aid the Soo Lines, which Hill never kept, and exactly as much money as the CPR had put into the Duluth and Winnipeg four-and-a-half years earlier, Hill bought the line on April 17, 1897. "You will be glad to hear D. and W. matter settled satisfaction everybody,"[59] Van Horne cabled sarcastically to Stephen. "When it was consummated [the Duluth and Winnipeg sale]," Shaughnessy later claimed, "I do not think there was anybody more pleased than Mr. Van Horne," but J. J. Hill knew better. He feared all through 1897 that Van Horne would at the last minute try to keep the line. Hill never pretended to be acting in anything but his own railroad's interest: "We took up the matter of purchase of the Duluth & Winnipeg from the Canadian Pacific," he revealed to J. P. Morgan in 1898, "and with the aid of Lords Mount Stephen and Strathcona, we succeeded in buying the Duluth & Winnipeg line . . . and saved both the Northern Pacific and Great Northern from the competition of the Canadian Pacific."[60]

Hill and Van Horne were the only ones who realized what the real take was in the Great Train Robbery. In 1906, J. P. Morgan, who controlled U.S. Steel Corporation, bought the mineral rights to the property in return for an unprecedented and tough royalty arrangement that Hill estimated would bring the Great Northern nearly $1 billion in the future. The royalties eventually amounted to billions of dollars and untold millions in freight revenue.[61]*

Van Horne loved a fight, even a dirty one. But Stephen had betrayed him, confiscating his weapons while secretly arming the enemy. The loss of the Duluth and Winnipeg had such a profound effect on Van Horne that it would take the construction of another impossible railroad to scour the bitterness from his soul.

---

*The royalty figures weren't only for the Duluth and Winnipeg lands. Between 1892 and 1906, Hill had purchased substantial lands, which he in turn rolled into the Great Northern. In 1897 and 1898, for instance, he purchased, for $4 million, a vast tract adjoining the land they already owned from two lumbermen, A. W. Wright and C. H. Davis, who had assiduously logged off the area and were now ready to retire. The purchase also included a small logging railroad that conveniently fit into the Great Northern's feeder system. Nevertheless, the bulk of the lands, and the richest, came from the Duluth and Winnipeg purchase.

CHAPTER 8

THE LAST OF THE TITANS

*Without an epic challenge Van Horne was like a
giant electric motor whirring away without a load.*

V an Horne's reign over the Canadian Pacific Railway effectively ended April 17, 1897, when R. B. Angus and
Thomas Shaughnessy turned over the Duluth and Winnipeg
to J. J. Hill. He wouldn't resign for two more years and his
power didn't diminish, but the fire within him was gone. The
company and its concerns were no longer his lifeblood.
Rumours about his resignation constantly circulated and one
diligent Montreal *Gazette* reporter was assigned to tackle him
on the subject. He went to Windsor Station in Montreal and
announced he intended to sit there until he had an answer.
Van Horne's secretary conferred with the president, who sat
down to write out a response, which said "as plainly as words
could, that Sir William Van Horne intended to resign. True,
incorporated in it were a few ifs, ands and perhapses; but
reading it from top to bottom it meant resignation, nothing
more and nothing less."

The next morning CPR stock dropped $10 a share on the
strength of the story. But the reporter was horrified to discover that Van Horne denied the whole thing, calling him "an
undistilled liar of the first water who was capable of beating
his grandmother to death and blaming it on the C.P.R."

Embarrassed and ashamed, especially since he had thrown away the evidence, the reporter avoided Windsor Station for months until his unsympathetic editor assigned him to another interview with Van Horne. When he arrived, Van Horne's secretary gleefully related the standing orders that he "was to be thrown down the stairs or the elevator shaft, the President was not particular which."[1]

One year later, on June 15, 1899, Van Horne resigned from the presidency, retaining his position as chairman of the board. There was no lack of potential diversions to occupy his restless mind. From art, architecture, agriculture, animal husbandry and geology to his vast investments,* he had enough to keep a dozen men busy. "I had about six or seven particular interests to which I always thought I would devote myself when my time was my own," he reflected years later.[2] One of those interests was travel. Shortly after relinquishing his position to Shaughnessy, Van Horne set off on a cross-Canada tour. By the end of the first day a pile of masticated cigar butts was stacked like a pyramid in his ashtray and Van Horne was thoroughly bored. The image of the human dynamo sitting passively in his private car, forcing himself to watch mile after mile of flat prairie in self-induced torture is laughable. Even the Rockies, his "1001 Switzerlands Rolled Into One," failed to hold his attention, so he headed south to San Francisco, one of the liveliest cities in the world. "I thought I should enjoy a week or two in that city," he sighed. "I got there on a Saturday afternoon. By the evening I had been over most of the city. By the next morning, I had seen all there was to see. I was tired of the place in less than a day, and tired of playing the retired gentleman."[3]

Next, Van Horne tried to lose himself in the beauty of Monterey. "I went out on the veranda and sat down, and smoked a big cigar. Then I got up, walked about the veranda,

---

*Van Horne owned all or part of more than twenty-five companies, as well as serving on the boards of an additional twenty.

and looked at the scenery. It was very fine. Then I sat down again and smoked another cigar. Then up again; another walk about the veranda, and more scenery. It was still very fine." When the second cigar was finished, he heaved himself to his feet, stalked off to his car and made record time returning to Montreal. It was the end of his retirement.

For a few months Van Horne immersed himself in his dizzying list of hobbies and investments, but neither his beloved paintings nor the building of his summer home in St Andrews, New Brunswick, satisfied him for long. Without an epic challenge Van Horne was like a giant electric motor whirring away without a load. His business affairs still required his attention, but he went about that work with only half a heart. One day in 1900 he was sitting numbly listening to an after-dinner speech at a New York banquet, surreptitiously glancing at his watch, wondering if he was going to catch the final train to Montreal. Then an elegant gentleman, with long, flowing whiskers, stood up to speak. His name was Gonzalo de Quesada, Cuban minister to Washington.*

Quesada passionately described the beauties and potential riches of his island, which had just been liberated from Spain by the United States. During the speech, he chanced to mention that there was as yet no national railroad in this Caribbean wonderland. After completing his address Quesada left immediately to return to Washington. As his train pulled out of the station, he was astonished to see a huge, bearded figure race along the platform and throw himself aboard. The man, huffing and puffing like a red-lining steam boiler, purposefully made his way through the cars before heavily seating himself beside the Cuban. Within minutes the two were old pals. "Well, Quesada," Van Horne, bellowed, slapping him on the back and spilling his drink, "if only half the things you

---

*Gonzalo de Quesada y Arostegui was a writer, statesman and close friend of Jose Marti, a martyr of Cuban independence from Spain. Van Horne was determined that he become president of Cuba, but Quesada died in Germany in 1915 before that dream was realized.

have told me about Cuba are true, I will build a railroad through your country."[4]

THE WAR HAD DECIMATED CUBA, shredding its industrial base, tearing up plantations, destroying roads and creating severe unemployment. Spain had ruled Cuba for centuries, and when the Spanish administrators left, a bureaucratic void remained, making it extremely difficult to get anything done. The country, 750 miles long and 100 miles at its widest point, had only 1,135 miles of railroad, 965 miles of which were light-duty trackage owned by the sugar cane companies. There was no cross-country line linking Havana with Camagüey, the most important interior city, or with Santiago de Cuba, the largest eastern seaport. The eastern provinces, the centre of Cuba's prosperity and covering three-quarters of the country, were served by only 100 miles of railroad. But changing the situation would be extremely difficult because of the Foraker Act, brought in while Cuba was under an American military governor and designed to protect the country from land speculators and carpetbaggers like those who had descended on Winnipeg in 1881. Until the Cuban republic was established, no licences, concessions or franchises could be granted to foreigners, and the ban included both chartering a railroad and running it across state-owned property.

Van Horne embarked upon his Cuban adventure with the fervour of a man striving for vindication. The looting of the Duluth and Winnipeg Railroad by Stephen had sent a poison dart deeply into his soul where it festered, spoiling his otherwise robust enjoyment of life. He needed some mammoth adventure to exorcise the hurt and humiliation.*

In the construction of the trans-Cuban railway Van Horne

---

*Van Horne may have taken some solace in the fact that his faith in the CPR's recovery was quickly vindicated. In 1896 he was the largest shareholder and he purchased most of his stock at between $45 and $55 a share. His investment doubled by 1899 and tripled by 1902 when share prices hit $145. The dividend income alone made him a very wealthy man.

Van Horne's Cuban railway

broke every business rule, but he made it work. Although it
didn't present a physical challenge to rival the construction of
the CPR, the political and cultural obstacles made it every bit as
impossible a task. Building a major railroad without government subsidy was unusual, doing it without a land grant was
virtually unprecedented and without a charter — that was just
plain crazy. Van Horne accomplished all three at once.

Once he made up his mind Van Horne moved with extraordinary speed, and in April, 1900, less than a month after
meeting Quesada, he incorporated The Cuba Railroad Company in New Jersey. Initial capitalization was set at $8 million,
divided into 160 shares at $50,000 each. Still mindful of the
problems he had faced from interfering CPR board and executive committee members, he spread control widely among a
number of well-heeled investors and pointedly didn't invite
George Stephen to participate, though he did sell four shares
worth $200,000 to J. J. Hill.

There was no way to get a charter, but no law prevented Van
Horne from buying up land and building a railroad on it, just
as plantation owners did. Through agents, he purchased every
available scrap of territory. At times he bought narrow strips
only wide enough for the right of way. At other times he was
forced to acquire entire plantations, in one case, a 30,000-acre
tract. Cubans were so excited about his plan that some of them
simply turned their land over to him for free. Still, he had no
right-of-way to cross public property or other railroads.

The Terror of Flat Krick, whose gale-force entry into
Winnipeg in 1881 had left that city reverberating right into the
next century, tiptoed into Cuba with the grace and finesse of a
prima ballerina. It was a subtle and controlled side of him that
few had seen and even fewer would have believed he possessed.
Sensing the antipathy of the locals to outsiders he hired influential Cubans to work as advance men to explain the intent of
the railway and generally smooth the way. During the grading
and construction stage he hired labourers from nearby towns.
For the North Americans he was forced to use, he had two
simple and inflexible rules. When you meet a Cuban never let

him be the first to take off his hat, and when a Cuban bows to you always bow at least twice in response.* When dealing with the indigenous Cubans, who were partial to the United States and not to Great Britain, Van Horne emphasized his American citizenship. With the Spanish Cubans, who distrusted the States, he made sure they knew he was Sir William, a British knight.

When his agents ran into resistance in acquiring land, Van Horne appeared with a well-laden table, expensive gifts and limitless wine to coax the recalcitrant few into submission. Only one group resisted his charms — the officials of Camagüey. Despite his British knighthood the city's influential Spanish Cubans linked him to the U.S. government. After long hours of negotiation, Van Horne had acquired property on both sides of the city but nothing to give him a route through Camagüey itself. Even after it was announced that the city would house a major terminal containing a hotel and the repair depot for the entire line, the locals didn't budge. It was a critical point; the railroad would be next to useless if it couldn't join up with the strategically located city.

The sensible thing would have been to retreat and wait for more sympathetic officials to take power, but Van Horne went blithely ahead with construction as if he had everything he needed. When the railway was finished up to the edge of the city, he laid on a sumptuous feast and invited all of Camagüey to attend. The only people who arrived were Van Horne, a few railroad officers, the city's mayor, Barraras, with his brother-in-law and daughter Nina Adelina, and a handful of barefooted boys. Van Horne carried on as if the occasion was unfolding as intended, making one brilliant improvisation when he asked the mayor's niece to do the sod turning. On his return to Montreal he had an elaborate and impressive parchment

---

*Van Horne's careful treatment of the Cubans was in part sheer necessity; without a charter or other legal basis, local opposition to the railroad would be devastating. It is clear, however, that Van Horne genuinely respected Cubans just as he did American and Canadian Indians — a rare attitude at the time.

printed thanking the girl for participating in the historic event. He also purchased a gold watch and had it similarly inscribed. Then he returned to Cuba and, taking care of other business first, left his visit to Camagüey to the very end. The entourage that departed from Havana was an impressive group including the dignified R. B. Angus and Sir Edward Clouston, both investors touring the line. Van Horne told no one what he was up to.

They arrived at the home of the mayor's brother-in-law unannounced, bearing two elaborately wrapped packages. After introductions, Van Horne politely asked to see the little girl who had so generously helped him. The unexpected visit threw the household into a disarray made even more chaotic when it was discovered that little Nina was nowhere to be found. Word of the strange visit spread through the whole city and by the time the freshly scrubbed Nina, clad in her Sunday finery, was produced, a crowd numbering in the hundreds had gathered outside the house.

Van Horne suggested they all go out to the courtyard where the light was better and, not incidentally, where the entire ceremony was visible to the crowd. Assuming his most portentous manner, Van Horne kissed the little girl, made an elaborate speech, which was translated by a railroad official, and then presented the two parcels "as a slight token of the appreciation of the President and Board of Directors of the Cuban Railway for her gracious act in turning the first sod of the railway." Every gesture in his little theatre was accompanied by much jostling for position and punctuated by oohs and ahs from the crowd. When he drew the curtain down by shaking hands with the mother and father and once more kissing the little girl, many wept joyfully. To emphasize the importance of the ceremony Van Horne immediately left Cuba, as if the only reason for his trip was to present his gifts to the little girl.

If the crowd was amazed, Van Horne's associates were baffled. "That was pretty nice of you to give that gold watch to the little girl," remarked engineer Miller A. Smith quizzically. "I didn't give the gold watch to the little girl," Van Horne responded. "I gave it to the whole city and province of Camagüey." A few weeks later Smith figured it out. "I understand now what you meant when you said you had given the watch to the whole city of Camagüey. Why the people there can talk of nothing else. You've won them over. Come on back to Camagüey. You can get anything you want from them. There will be no more difficulty in running the line through the city."[5]

With a route finally in hand and the railroad already popular throughout the country, Van Horne began to soften up the military governor for the legal blessing needed to cross state- and plantation-owned railways. His leverage was employment. As the line neared various public lands and intersecting roads, Van Horne ostentatiously ordered all work stopped and laid off trackmen, sadly telling them that without the necessary permission the project was stymied. In case the Cubans were slow getting the point, Van Horne's agents circulated "spontaneous" petitions supporting the railroad and signed by thousands in every area of the line.

The military governor, General Wood, was in an unenviable position. The law expressly forbade granting a railroad franchise, yet his desk was covered with petitions and the population was getting surlier and more resentful by the day. Van Horne waited until several towns were near revolt before paying a visit to the man he had so skilfully set up. Full of heavy sighs and sorrowful platitudes about the terrible situation, Van Horne uncharacteristically volunteered no solutions. Finally, after many expressions of confidence in the governor's ability to solve the problem, Van Horne was asked what he would do. Sir William shook his head in bafflement and confessed he had no idea but promised to give the matter his full attention over the next few days. He then hurried over to the office of General Wood's Cuban aide, an influential man Van Horne had taken great pains to cultivate, and told him, "The Governor will doubtless send for you to advise him as to whether anything can be done to permit me to line up my railway. I thought it best not to suggest to him what he might do. But if he asks you, please advise him that he could easily solve the situation by granting a revocable permit. Once I get that I'm mighty certain it will never be revoked."[6]

Even as the two of them plotted, a message arrived from General Wood summoning the aide. Van Horne aimed a swipe at the nearest chair and bellowed in glee. He knew he'd won. A few days later, adopting his best funereal expression, he called on the governor to announce his inability to solve the problem. Wood cheerfully brushed his apologies aside and told him that he had the answer. Feigning acute distress upon hearing of the "revocable permit," Van Horne agreed to make the best of a bad situation only after hours of pleading and coaxing from the governor.

Over the next year, Van Horne shuttled back and forth between New York, Montreal, New Brunswick and Havana. On every trip to Cuba he insisted on inspecting every inch of progress. He adored his comforts but never more so than after he had chucked them aside to ride out with the men. In Cuba, transportation was by mule and one evening, preparing to dismount and make camp, Van Horne snared his waistcoat on the pommel of his mule's saddle. He hit the ground with a crash that sounded as if he would never rise again. "My God, Sir William, are you hurt?" anxiously inquired Miller A. Smith. "No," snapped the still-recumbent monolith, "that's the way I always get off."[7] Construction was completed on December 1, 1902, revolutionizing communication and travel; the trip which had once taken ten days was reduced to twenty-four hours.

Van Horne did not live long enough to profit fully from his Cuban labour and investment, though just before he died shares privately changed hands at $250,000 each, five times their initial cost. Nonetheless his impact was substantial. In a little more than ten years he brought over $30 million of new investment into the country through construction and development. The completion of the road was a remarkable achievement, in many ways rivalling his CPR feats. Van Horne was frequently displeased with the policies of the fledgling

Cuban regime, but the Cuban railway itself gave him immense satisfaction and exorcised the bitter memories of his final CPR years. He grew to love the country and was completing a winter home in Camagüey when he died.

JUST AS NORTH AMERICAN RAILROADING was irrevocably changed by the mere fact of Van Horne's existence, so too the Canadian art world bears the deep impression of his influence. Van Horne's forays into art were no Sunday outings, they were assaults. Not content to concentrate on just one thing, he enveloped his passion entirely, amassing the largest and most significant Canadian collection of his day and becoming an artist and prominent patron as well. Almost singlehandedly he started a school of Canadian painting devoted to northwestern landscapes, and here his patronage went far beyond mere encouragement. Artists who met with his approval were showered with first-class CPR tickets, hotel accommodation and meals and even had cabooses turned over to them for use as studios. One artist was given unlimited train-stopping privileges so he wouldn't miss a significant view. In return, Van Horne told his protégés what to paint, how to paint it and if he didn't like what was produced, sent the artist back to try again.

Members of the Royal Canadian Academy, a group of artists officially charged with the fearsome task of interpreting Canada, were often the recipients of his largesse. Although Van Horne's patronage was an artist's dream, it had its costs. His support of artists like Lucius O'Brien and John Arthur Fraser was so extensive he virtually ran their careers at certain points. Between 1883 and 1889 Fraser's life was dominated by the CPR. His first journey to the west was financed by the company and Van Horne ensured that two major pieces from that trip were purchased by himself and R. B. Angus. Van Horne then commissioned him to illustrate a CPR guidebook in 1885, chose the scenes to be used and arranged for the photographs to be sent to Fraser.

Fraser accepted Van Horne's suggestions with remarkably good temper but at times it seemed as if the railroader was actually guiding the artist's hand as he worked. "The black and white sketch will hardly answer our purpose," was his reaction to Fraser's preliminary study of Mount Stephen. The mountain wasn't imposing enough to suit Van Horne, so he ordered him to make it more so. "I made last night a rough sketch in lamp-black which will illustrate my idea. . . . I have taken a great deal of license but I do not think that any one going to the spot without picture in hand to compare will ever accuse us of exaggeration."[8] Van Horne's involvement in the picture was so extensive that Fraser unhappily admitted he should have signed the work with both names. "I have merely interpreted your idea for the engraver."[9] Fraser attempted two more drawings of Mount Stephen and Mount Sir Donald, the dominant peak at the summit of Rogers Pass. He was so certain of Van Horne's displeasure that he refused to sign them, leaving that decision to his mentor: "If you think it would be better for them to carry my name please sign them for me."[10]*

It wasn't just painters who shrank in relation to Van Horne. The man he hired to decorate Windsor Station in 1887 was Edward Colonna, a young German designer Van Horne discovered when he was working on parlour and sleeping cars for the Barney and Smith Manufacturing Company in Dayton, Ohio.† Colonna adorned the interior and designed a magnificent mantlepiece for the ladies' waiting room—a combination of tile, brass, columns and arches that rose out of a mosaic floor and soared toward the decorated ceiling. The tile floor, furnishings and fittings were all hailed as magnificent by critics and travellers. It was one of Colonna's first jobs in Canada, and

---

*Van Horne eventually purchased six large Fraser watercolours for his private collection.

†It is believed that Van Horne persuaded Samuel Bing, the celebrated Paris art dealer specializing in oriental art, to hire Colonna. Bing is credited with beginning the *art nouveau* movement, Colonna's work being a major force within the movement.

he was infuriated to find that the press gave the bulk of the credit to Van Horne.*

"Fatality seems to have decreed that everything I have done in the way of embellishing and decorating, or planning and designing, is attributed to you. . . . While I do not mind in the least the transfer of glory, I do mind the result as shown by the fact that I get nothing to do, depending on what work you may happen to have for me."[11] His ego was not too bruised to accept many more commissions from the CPR and to design some sections of Van Horne's own home on Sherbrooke Street.

Van Horne didn't just collect art; he consumed it. In 1892 he took one look at John Hammond's oil paintings of the Rockies and promptly bought every one available, seventeen in total. A year later he had them all exhibited at the 1893 Chicago World's Columbian Exposition even though other Royal Canadian Academy members were restricted to a maximum of three pieces at the show.

Many of the Canadian painters Van Horne favoured were virtual nonentities before their work found a spot in his gallery. He also purchased paintings by many artists on the brink of fame, becoming the first major collector of Impressionists and Post-Impressionists in North America, and bought works by artists such as El Greco well before they were fashionable. The Hudson River School of American Painters, including artists like Ryder (Albert Pinkham), was part of his collection fifty years before it came into vogue.

By 1899 Van Horne's collection included works by Monticelli, Delacroix, Manet, Daumier, Corot, Ribot, Rousseau, Monet, Pissarro, Cezanne and Toulouse-Lautrec. Eventually he had paintings from most of the major schools of

---

*Van Horne also chose the site, which happened to be on a former privy pit. Until proper drains were installed, the workmen and residents nearby were assaulted by the unholy stench that emanated from the digging. The site was interesting from an historical as well as an olfactory point of view. It was there that the St Jean Baptiste Society had been formed in 1834. On that day in June a young law student, George Etienne Cartier, sang his composition, "O Canada, mon pays, mes amours," for the first time. Cartier, of course, became one of the Fathers of Confederation, and was later disgraced in the Pacific Scandal of 1873.

art. Some of his favourites were his Dutch canvases by Vermeer, Rembrandt, Hals and Cuyp and British works by Hogarth, Constable, Turner, Reynolds and Gainsborough.*

Van Horne was a wealthy man by any standards, but his pocketbook could not compete with those of J. J. Hill, Henry Vanderbilt and others who were snapping up many of the better-known artists. Van Horne compensated by searching out the lesser lights and vaulting them into prominence. If he couldn't afford three Rembrandts, he went after a single, outstanding work. He kept abreast of current prices by instructing CPR employees in Europe to attend art sales and wire him the latest results. Like a skilled handicapper he also memorized the history and output of hundreds of the famous and not-so-famous and used his formidable knowledge to negotiate enviable deals.

Most serious collectors of the day used art experts to make their acquisitions, a practice Van Horne disdained. A terrifying presence in any crowd, he was like a purgative in the effete confines of the art world. Roger Fry, an eminent British critic, enjoyed the shaking up that a Van Horne encounter inevitably produced: "He took his chances in society as he had taken them in the backwoods of Canada, with a genial and unpretentious simplicity of manner. He did not care to hide behind the entrenchments of etiquette and formality with which most of the newly rich protect their sensitiveness to criticism."[12]

As notable as his paintings were, Van Horne's collection of Japanese pottery was even more extensive. He referred to the beautiful creations as "pots" and sometimes handled them like worry beads. It was a source of private amusement to business associates to see the huge and seemingly clumsy Van Horne,

*Years later Murray Ballantyne, a prominent Montreal historian and collector, took the assistant curator of the London National Gallery on a tour of Van Horne's house. "He was astonished," gleefully recalled Ballantyne, who'd given the man no hint of what was inside. "His mouth fell open. When he saw the El Greco *Holy Family*, he said, 'Who is this man! We don't have as fine a painting in the National Gallery.'" (Collard, "Portrait of a Collector," Montreal *Gazette*, December 2, 1972)

the poker-playing, chair-kicking tyrant, fondling the exquisite and delicate works or standing for minutes at a stretch, enraptured by a favourite piece.

Van Horne loved to flaunt his knowledge, and art provided him with the ideal arena. Once, after offering to guess the origin of any work brought to him, B. Matsuki, a dealer in Japanese art, turned up with a number of pieces to show him. Spreading them out on Van Horne's massive billiard table, Matsuki placed a lovely tea bowl in the centre and issued a challenge: "Sir William, there is a mark on the foot of that bowl, and if without looking at the mark or feeling it, you will tell me who made the bowl, I will give it to you." Van Horne stalked the subject from all angles, pondered his own collection, circled once again and then turned the conversation to other topics entirely. Without warning he said, "Matsuki, I don't see who could have made that bowl except the second Rokubei." The dealer acknowledged the victory and gave Van Horne the bowl.[13]

VAN HORNE'S HOUSE, "BIG AND BULGY LIKE MYSELF," was stolid and unprepossessing from the outside. He bought it in 1890, and with the help of the long-suffering Edward Colonna, completely redesigned it. Guests walking toward the lumpy, gloomy façade were astonished by what lay within. Lord Strathcona's home was like a museum — impressive, overwhelming and grand — but it lacked the character of its owner. It was less a home than the headquarters of a wealthy international corporation, a place to entertain and impress. Stephen's was exquisite and exotic, but no amount of rare tropical wood, Italian marble or oriental rugs could inject a touch of humanity into its pristine opulence. In comparison Van Horne's house looked, smelled and felt alive. During his life, and for many years afterwards, rich and poor alike could tour the art gallery merely by calling at the door, expressing interest and leaving a card on the mantle.

The picture gallery was 110 feet long, with German silver

candelabra stretching its length. Upstairs Van Horne's studio was two storeys high and littered with boxes of paints, reams of paper and a host of easels. This was his own aerie where, according to artist Percy Woodcock, he would attack the canvases, sometimes several at once. During one stretch he painted every night for three months, averaging nearly a painting a day. "Van Horne would like to paint by telegraph," one artist wryly observed after watching him turn out a picture in two hours. "I never believed in taking long over anything, or in making great preparations for work," Van Horne once explained to a writer, "and when I hear of studios and north lights and the impossibility of working with this thing or with that, I always feel either that a man who talks thus is a humbug or he does not know his job."[14] After dinner he often invited friends up to the studio, where they'd be regaled with tales of the art and railway worlds until dawn when the weary guests would drag themselves home to sleep. Van Horne, having consumed a dozen cigars and a quart of whiskey, would finish another painting, eat a mammoth breakfast, wash up and head off to another of his sixteen-hour work days.

His skill with a brush was arguable; some critics dismiss him as only "a competent painter," while others contend he was extremely gifted. Most, however, are attracted to the warm vitality of his work. He loved to play with the effects of colour — layered, swirling, reflective, realistic and ethereal. One of his best, *Autumn Woods and Fields,* a 32"-by-50" oil on canvas, brings the glow of fading nature right into the room. Because Van Horne usually painted at night his paintings often had an unworldly feel, caused by the distortions of artificial light. Friends were frequently amazed by the work he produced indoors without the benefit of photographs or preliminary sketches. "Yes, but I know what a birch tree looks like. Why should I sit outside in the cold to do it?"[15] he said simply. His strength was composition, which is not surprising, since he was a skilled draftsman, even as a young man. Each piece was boldly inscribed with his initials, WCVH. A few were signed backwards, enroh nav.

Drawing room in Van Horne's Montreal home

One of Van Horne's favourite jokes was to pass off one of his own compositions as a classic, particularly to an expert. Often in Montreal or later at his summer home, he would blandly ask a visitor what he thought of the beautiful new master he'd bought. After much learned discourse about the interplay between texture and colour, Van Horne revealed that he had just painted it himself. His humour was often cruel and embarrassing, but if the victim was able to swallow the humiliation and join in Van Horne's uninhibited laughter, he would be a friend for life.*

Not every piece in Van Horne's collection was a work of art but everything he bought, he liked. Sometimes it was a

---

*In his last years Van Horne turned his hand to writing. At one point he wrote several essays which he successfully passed off to friends as newly uncovered sections from Nietzsche's master work, *Also Sprach Zarathustra*. Van Horne also liked to foist off low-grade cigars on guests, in place of the expensive Havanas he preferred. He was always astonished at how few of his acquaintances could or would tell the difference. He once hired a young man who had the temerity to ask, after one puff, if he'd gotten his cigars from the stable boy.

particular shade of blue that caught his eye, sometimes it was
because a piece of fruit, another of his passions, was especially
appealing. At one point, Van Horne was in New York on CPR
business and, as was his habit, he took the opportunity to drop
in at a gallery where he fell in love with Donatello's fifteenth-
century bust of Niccola Pisano. Finding that the piece was
already sold, Van Horne gave his agents standing orders to
buy it if it ever came on the market again. Years later, when Van
Horne was beset by financial woes, the treachery of Stephen
and bouts of rheumatism and bronchitis, a telegram arrived
with the news that the Donatello was finally available.

"Hurry," was his cabled response.

"Niccola did not come a moment too soon," recalled Van
Horne. "I was ill, very ill, so low in spirit that I thought of
turning my face quietly to the wall." When the bust arrived,
breaking all railroad speed records, it was immediately un-
crated and placed beside his sickbed. "I threw my arm around
his neck, laid my cheek against his, and slept like a baby."[16]

When Van Horne died in 1915 Lady Van Horne kept everything intact and continued his open-door tradition until her
death in 1929. His beloved daughter, Adeline, inherited one-
quarter of the collection, which she donated in its entirety to
the Montreal Museum of Fine Arts in 1944. The remainder,
including his papers, went to his grandson Billy.

WHEN VAN HORNE FELL IN LOVE, he fell hard. He had always
derided the summer homes owned by men of power as a mark
of their fortunes and influence and scathingly dismissed
such retreats as "gone-aways." Then he saw Minister's Island.
Hugged into the protective crook of land that forms New
Brunswick's Passamaquoddy Bay, Minister's Island exists in a
salubrious microclimate. There the lilacs bloom three weeks
longer, the lilies arrive three weeks earlier and the mist that
caresses the cliffs and sandy shoulders of the island's shoreline
set it apart from earthly things. Nearly five hundred acres, the

island was first settled in 1788 by a Loyalist Episcopal minister.
St Andrews, the adjacent town, was the refined and elegant
summering ground of Eastern Canada's titled, newly rich and
once rich, including Sir Charles Tupper who had a magnificent summer home there. Although many claimed to be attracted to its hay-fever-free environment, the seductiveness of
seaside high society was equally appealing. Van Horne enjoyed
the town but saw no reason to join the tight cluster of estates
encircling St Andrews. His island was, in comparison, far removed from the mainstream and the home he built was equally
unusual in every way.

Covenhoven, designed by Edward Maxwell with a large
measure of Van Horne thrown in, sprawled across the southern tip of the island, overlooking the Bay of Fundy. Access to it
was restricted to a sand bar, which could be crossed twice a day
at low tide. The rest of the time it was completely buried by the
Bay of Fundy's massive tides. Every one of Covenhoven's thirty-
seven rooms, nineteen bedrooms and eleven bathrooms was
indelibly stamped with Van Horne's innovation and quirky
humour. In every possible spot he stuck windows: small ones,
big ones and odd-shaped ones. The risers in the massive main
staircase were of glass, and skylights pulled light into every
corner from sunrise to sunset. Above many of the doors he
displayed his meticulous sailing ship models and elsewhere
the pieces of art were stacked one above the other, some pieces
hanging just below the twelve-foot ceilings.

Van Horne held court in the billiard room, which was dominated by a squat, oversized table, perched on legs that looked
like the thighs of a giant. It took ten men and six horses an
entire week to haul the thing from St Andrews a few miles away.
Van Horne often challenged guests to games of billiards,
grandly offering to play with his butler as a handicap but
neglecting to mention, as the bets were being placed, that the
man was a former professional player.

The dining room, where he also spent a great deal of time,
was guarded by a winged mythological creature done in
mosaic over a gargantuan mantle. As the pièce de résistance,

Van Horne brought two large mahogany trees he personally selected in Cuba, had them elaborately carved with a swirl of grapes and vine leaves and washed with a coating of gold leaf. Standing massively on either side of the tiled hearth they gleamed softly in the glow of candlelight.*

By 1905 there were twenty-two buildings on the island and, next to the billiard room, the liveliest place was the barn. Over 150 feet long and 81 feet wide, it was an exclusive resort for a host of fortunate pedigreed animals. Their immaculate hooves rested on two-by-six-inch tongue-and-groove planks; vents and windows gave them fresh air; and a change of scenery and the best feed was stored in two immense silos fitted with an elevator and an ingenious dumbwaiter designed by Van Horne. Even the mating apparatus was constructed to provide maximum comfort during the necessary event.

There was nothing guests couldn't find at Covenhoven. Barely had they settled in before they were tantalized with delicacies like smoked salmon cheeks, succulent Little Neck clams, oysters — in which Van Horne often hid a large pearl — pomegranates, Cuban bananas and black Russian caviar. Once, when an unseasonable summer gale kept Covenhoven guests happily imprisoned for an extra three days, one gentleman collapsed onto a chair at the station, patted his distended belly and groaned, "Thank God the storm let up! I was beginning to hear the angels sing. Van was determined to feed us all to death."[17]

Van Horne was a gracious host, but he ran his guests much as he did his other affairs — and he always knew what was best. On sunny days he shepherded them down the long, sloping lawn, past the bowling green, past the tennis courts, past the croquet lawn and into the bath house. The round stone structure was perched on the edge of a cliff overlooking the smooth

---

*Some enterprising soul in subsequent years found the "yellow paint" unpleasant and painted the carvings head to foot in white.

rocks and the bay below. Servants daily scrubbed seaweed off the rocks so bathers could sit comfortably in the sun. During his first summer at Covenhoven, Van Horne ventured down every morning for a swim, flopping blissfully about like a pale walrus.

Always an irrepressible prankster, Van Horne's entertainment was often at the expense of his guests. When the weather was fine he shooed them out for a bracing constitutional before dinner was served. As soon as the door was shut he would race over to his studio and in the space of an hour produce a fine rendering of some scene from memory. When his visitors returned he would have framed and hung the painting, far enough away from them not to smell the fresh paint. After bragging about his latest acquisition the bets began, guests wagering items of clothing or other possessions, attempting to guess the artist. "Hah!" Van Horne exclaimed, gathering up the booty, "You're all wrong. I painted it myself this very afternoon." One frequent visitor moaned after a weekend of all-night poker, billiard games and guess-the-picture competitions, "I'm damn glad I'm not staying any longer else I'd be driving home in my birthday suit."[18]

Van Horne was a master of card tricks, but his favourite parlour activity was "mind reading." At one party, Donald Smith and George Stephen tried to put him on the spot by asking him to guess what Stephen was drawing at the far end of the room. "I didn't know what the devil to do," Van Horne recalled later, "and as I sat with pencil and paper before me my mind was a perfect blank. Then I began to think and think hard. I suddenly remembered Lady Stephen telling me a few years before that her husband could only draw one thing — a salmon. I cast a sly glance over to the other end of the room, and saw his hand moving quickly in small circles. The scales! So I drew the salmon as quickly as I could. And, by jinks, it was right!"[19]

BENEATH THE BLUSTER AND OPTIMISM of Van Horne's life lurked bitter frustration with his only son, Benny. Spoiled by wealth and defeated by the impossible task of emulating his father, Benny was as weak as Van Horne was strong. He established his reputation as a ne'er-do-well early in his life and about the only thing he did well was drink, sometimes three quarts of whiskey in a single day. He was a violent drunk and in his rages threw chairs, tables and anything else that wasn't nailed down. Van Horne soon tired of the damage and had chairs specially constructed out of dense Cuban mahogany. Ugly and ungainly, they weighed so much that just moving one was difficult. Tossing it against the wall was out of the question. Benny's dissipation and sodden outbursts disgusted Van Horne, who had little compassion and less tolerance for self-pity or lack of self-control. Eventually he built Benny a log cabin as far from the house as possible. There his son spent many days, emerging only to send the gardener off in search of more alcohol.

Benny's only other occupation was spending the generous allowance Van Horne provided on sleek, fast cars, which he piled up with astonishing frequency. Bank managers discreetly kept Van Horne informed about Benny's overdrafts. "On January 4 your son . . . was in our establishment and we cashed a draft for $12,000 drawn upon yourself for him. Payment on this draft was refused, the bank informing us that 'the drawer had no authority to draw,'"[20] wrote Robert Thorne of Montgomery Ward & Co., requesting that Van Horne make good the amount. He always did, but the gulf between father and son grew irrevocably wide.

The tragedy of Van Horne's daughter, Adeline, was the fact that she wasn't a man. Unconventional though he was, Van Horne never dreamt of introducing her into his business affairs. If he had, the empire he established would likely still exist. Addie inherited all of Van Horne's brains and, unfortunately, his physique. The extra poundage that added to Van Horne's image of force and power made his daughter grotesque, and gave her great difficulties with cars and other forms of transportation. When the tide was high and she had stayed late in St Andrews, two workers were dispatched to wait for her and row her back — one could not possibly have accomplished the job. One evening, fascinated by the play of light on the water, she leaned over the edge of the boat and rippled the water with her hand. Before the sweating oarsmen could shout a warning, the dory keeled over and sent Addie splashing into the bay. No amount of heaving could get her back in again. Finally, they were forced to tie a rope around her and tow her home, hauling her onto the shore like a beached whale.

Like her father, Adeline was at once shy and overbearing, but those who still remember her found her always kind. She wasn't particularly fond of social niceties, though she assiduously attended fêtes, garden parties and openings, particularly to support the St Andrews townspeople and friends. She arrived at one tea party with her pet pekinese. It was an incongruous sight, the great hulking woman and the tiny, fat, snuffling dog. Spying a chair, she plopped herself down and discovered a box of fancy chocolate at her elbow — chocolates given as a gift to her hostess. Without a moment's hesitation she shovelled the sweets one after the other into the grateful peke's mouth. When they were gone, the two of them left.

Adeline was as devoted to her father as Benny was resentful.

Benny Van Horne's cartoon showing Addie getting into her Model T, specially designed with extra-wide doors

When Van Horne died Adeline kept as a memorial a single vacant chair at the dining room table in the house on Sherbrooke Street, even when the house was full of guests. On the plate lay an orchid which was replaced every day. The flowers weren't always easy to find, even if your name was Van Horne, and the day finally arrived when not one orchid could be found in the city of Montreal. She solved the problem as her father would have, largely and irrevocably, ordering the architectural firm of E. & W. S. Maxwell to design a conservatory just to house the exotic blooms. As long as she lived Sir William's place never went unadorned again.

The only characteristics Benny shared with his father were an artistic streak and a rather cruel sense of humour. When the mood struck he could pen devastatingly funny cartoons of subjects that took his fancy, and Addie was often depicted in his biting caricatures with a massive bosom and buttocks that rose like a tide behind her. In one series he outlined the trials of Addie's chauffeur when she decided to buy a car. He was poking fun at the Model T that her father had specially built with extra-wide doors because she eventually got so large no ordinary car door could accommodate her bulk.

Benny married Edith Molson of the Montreal Molson family, and despite his drunkenness the pair managed to produce a son, Billy. Having virtually written his son off as a successor, Van Horne lavished his affection and ambition on the boy. Though slightly more resilient than his father, Billy wilted under the ferocity of Van Horne's devotion. Several rooms at Covenhoven were set aside for him alone: a nursery, a bedroom, a bathroom and one large room containing nothing but an elaborate train. In the nursery Van Horne painted a rollicking, light-hearted frieze of Dutch families working and playing. Below it he printed "For Master William Cornelius Covenhoven Van Horne in Commemoration of his Third Birthday 29th July Nineteen Hundred and Ten by his Loving Grandfather Sir William Van Horne."

During his long trips to Cuba Van Horne wrote daily to Billy, covering postcards with big loopy drawings depicting

Billy Van Horne

himself as an elephant. He spent hours talking to the child about business and financial strategies and took him to galleries and artists' studios. If Van Horne couldn't find a toy he wanted for Billy, he had it made or built it himself. One lovely piece comprises a fire station where bells ring, trucks drive out and firemen slide down poles.

Van Horne could not change the destinies of his son and grandson, nor was he able to alter his own. He was a virtual stranger to sickness except for the rheumatism that plagued him periodically. Even that he fought and kicked against. Throughout 1914, when the affliction was at its worst, he tried every quack remedy known to man, including poultices made from the nuts of Cape Jessamine, green coconut milk and fish tails. He even hobbled around for weeks with a potato in his pocket to ward off the evil.

At his best Van Horne was a terrible patient. When he was bed ridden, he spent his confinement furiously dictating dozens of letters to friends and business associates. His doctor restricted him to three cigars a day, so he had boxes of new ones specially made. Each was like a giant sausage, a foot in length and an inch and a half in diameter. Every time he lit one up he chortled in triumph at both defeating and following the instructions.

By the end of 1914 he had not quite recovered "dancing form"[21] but could at least walk without crutches. "When I think of all I could do, I should like to live for five hundred years," he bemoaned to a friend. Seventy-two was all he was granted. On August 22, 1915, his doctor diagnosed a stomach abscess and sent him to Montreal for the operation. On September 10th Benny cabled to Shaughnessy in St Andrews. "Regret tell you physicians give up all hope Sir William. Quite unconscious. Slowly sinking. End matter of a day or so." The next day Van Horne was dead. On September 15th amid the pomp and circumstance that he so disliked, Van Horne's body was borne away to be buried beside his mother's in Joliet, Illinois.

WHILE VAN HORNE exorcised the CPR from his soul in Cuba, Lord Mount Stephen comfortably settled into life as a wealthy English peer. In 1892, he had taken a seven-year lease on Brocket Hall in Hertfordshire about twenty miles north of London, and that is where he lived until his death in 1923. Sir Stafford Northcote, his son-in-law, had tried to interest him in Wimpole, a far grander house, later bought by Sir Rudyard Kipling's daughter. But when he saw Brocket Hall, even though the grounds were sadly neglected, the stables rat-ridden and the house shabby, Mount Stephen was captivated. With its four storeys, ivy-covered walls, fireplaces and expansive park-like grounds, Brocket Hall was the quintessential English manor house.*

---

*Brocket Hall had once been the seat of Lord Melbourne, Queen Victoria's prime minister. Melbourne's wife, Lady Caroline, was an extremely risqué character for her time. "The whole of her life was composed of a series of episodes in which love, or what passed for it, played a leading part." Lord Byron was among her intimates. Once after a quarrel with him, she attempted to jump out of a window and, failing in that, stabbed herself with a supper knife. (*Aberdeen Free Press*, December 1, 1921). It was from Brocket Hall that Lord Palmerston, a later Victorian prime minister penned a famous letter to Queen Victoria, in which he informed her that Melbourne "was in the melancholy occupation of watching the gradual extinction of his life." (*Daily Telegraph*, December 1, 1921)

Mount Stephen felt very much at home there, but it was his loyal consort, Lady Mount Stephen, who was most enamoured of their new residence. Her time as chatelaine was brief; she died in April, 1896. The loss of his fishing companion and confidante was a terrible blow to this most secretive of men. For a brief time he pathetically tried to recreate his life as it had been, even "taking an interest in the garden here — which was Lady Mount Stephen's favourite interest."[22] His friends were so concerned about his depression that they talked of finding some committee at the House of Lords to keep him occupied, and Northcote and his adopted daughter, Alice,* moved to Stephen's London residence, St James Place, to look after him and take care of social duties.

"You know how dependent he is in some respects," Northcote explained to Hill in May, 1896.[23] After surprisingly few months, Stephen rallied, thanks in part to the work involved in helping J. J. Hill take over the Northern Pacific and the Duluth and Winnipeg. Even so, it was a full year before he could bring himself to mention his wife's death to his partner. Writing to Hill to thank him for a picture of Anne Charlotte, he added, "I can't tell you how much Alice & I have been touched by your lovely remembrance of her, who we miss more & more as time goes on. It is very pleasant to know how much she thought of you & her great confidence in you & what she always called, 'that blessed old railway [the Manitoba Road],' to which she knew, that we & so many others owed so

---

*Exactly where Stephen obtained his adopted daughter Alice is another intriguing mystery in the life of the infinitely mysterious George Stephen. The official version was that Alice's mother, who was a friend of the Stephen family, died during a visit to Canada. George and his wife, Anne Charlotte, then agreed to look after her teenaged daughter. When the time came to send the sixteen-year-old Alice home — or so the story goes — she elected to remain, and the Stephens adopted her.

Perhaps because the story seemed so thin, another version was later floated, that Alice was the daughter of an American clergyman whom Anne Charlotte had befriended and rescued from penury. A radically different explanation was offered to the Stephens' closest friends. According to that version, Alice was the result of a union between Mrs Stephen's charwoman, who died at childbirth, and an alcoholic tradesman. (Gilbert, *The End of the Road*. Vol. II of *The Life of Lord Mount Stephen*, p. 6)

much. Poor dear soul she had no confidence in or regard for any other railway. As to the CPR she hated it because she thought it would in the end kill me."[24]

At the age of sixty-seven Mount Stephen was still a tall, striking man and, as one of the richest men in the Empire, he suddenly found himself the most eligible bachelor as well. An avalanche of consoling letters, the majority from single women, flooded his desk. Luncheon invitations soon followed, many of which he accepted, to the astonishment of his friends. It wasn't long before wagers were being laid on the possible successor to his wife. Gossip had it that Miss Ellen Willmott, an authority on roses, was the front runner, but Lady Somers, older than Mount Stephen, was given an outside chance because of her aggressive pursuit.

A year after Lady Mount Stephen's death, the Duchess of Teck, while recovering from an operation, paid a visit to Brocket Hall. During the Duchess's visit, Stephen fell in love with and proposed to the unlikeliest member of the entourage, Miss Gian Tufnell. A thirty-four-year-old lady-in-waiting and companion to the duchess, Gian was disparaged as dowdy and dismissed as an old maid. She was the daughter of George Tufnell, a royal naval officer and a childhood friend of the Duchess's daughter, Princess May, who later became Queen Mary. They were married in November, 1897, and six weeks before the event Gaspard Farrer wrote to Hill, "The Boss is beaming with happiness & so far as I can judge has every reason to be so."[25]

Alice, who had been serving as her adopted father's hostess, was far from pleased with the new wife. The two maintained superficially friendly relations but never became close, and eventually Mount Stephen settled a huge sum on Alice because he sensed a deep hostility between them. The calm graciousness of the former Lady Mount Stephen was replaced by a gaiety and festivity that suggests the dull portrayals of Gian were sour grapes on the part of unsuccessful suitors. But Stephen's cronies found the influx of blue bloods a little tedious. "A little Royalty goes a long way with me," groused

Garnet Wolseley* after one weekend, "and I had that little yesterday . . . ."[26]

It was a happy marriage, with one sore spot. Mount Stephen's Scottish thrift was not diminished by wealth — he still turned his ties to double their lifespan. He was therefore aghast at Gian's joyfully extravagant spending. Queen Mary and Lady Mount Stephen shared one passion: bargain hunting, of a royal sort. The two would descend on local sale rooms and buy anything that caught their eye, from a tapestry to a Queen Anne vase. Mount Stephen dismissed their finds as expensive rubbish and Gian finally took to smuggling her purchases in the back door while her penny-pinching husband was occupied elsewhere. The relationship between the new Lady Mount Stephen and Queen Mary deepened over the years, and Gian was later described as "the most intimate friend the Queen possesses among peeresses." Queen Mary would often motor out to Brocket Hall without ladies-in-waiting, to drop in, sometimes unexpectedly, on Gian and "Dear George" for Sunday tea.

By the early 1900s the Lords Mount Stephen and Strathcona were firmly but quietly placed among the very richest men in the entire world. Strathcona's net worth was at least $40. million, while his cousin's hovered around $25 million. At the time England's annual per capita income was $165 and savings averaged only $15. Strathcona's holdings conservatively earned between $3 million and $5 million annually and Stephen's, between $1.5 and $2 million. In comparison, the Queen of England's revenue from her vast estates was only $1.95 million in 1904.

In his later years Mount Stephen lost none of his acuity, although he became decidedly curmudgeonly, refusing to hook up a telephone and railing against the sorry state of newspapers — but woe betide the delivery boy who was late

---

*Wolseley was commander of the 1870 task force that quelled the Red River Rebellion and had been a close friend of George Stephen since the 1860s.

with the morning edition. He closely watched world affairs, particularly those affecting his investments. It was a time when biographies were popular and many of his contemporaries were so immortalized. Mount Stephen carefully read all the books, cackling at the mistakes — though he always disdained to correct them. Nor would he cooperate with biographers, even those with the official blessing of the subject's family. Beckles Willson, a well-known writer living in Nova Scotia, was determined to produce the definitive work on Lord Strathcona, partly, he claimed, to improve upon his 1902 book, "which I have since had reason deeply to regret."[27] Mount Stephen had refused to help with the first effort and he had no intention of helping with the second in 1914.

After numerous entreaties from Willson, Van Horne agreed to try to persuade Mount Stephen to lend his assistance: "Will you kindly tell him," came the peevish response from England, "that it is quite impossible for me to review . . . his proposed new work about Lord Strathcona." In the letter, Mount Stephen passed off his cousin's connection with the CPR as a minor part of "ancient history and of little or no consequence to anyone."[28] That same year a controversial exposé of Lord Strathcona was written by W. T. R. Preston, a former Canadian Liberal party organizer and Canadian commissioner of emigration to Great Britain. Strathcona's friends rallied round and condemned the biography as vicious scandal mongering. Van Horne attacked it as vile, and Shaughnessy called it "a re-hash of the lying statements made by extreme Grits in and out of Parliament in the early eighties."[29] When Van Horne tried to enlist Mount Stephen's support in suppressing it, he claimed to have merely "glanced" at the book and blamed Strathcona for its existence:

> I am afraid the old man is himself responsible for much of the rubbish of which the book is full. He always had a great fancy for public applause & liked to be in the eye of the public whenever he could get the opportunity. You remember how happy he was when I invited him to go out with you to drive the last spike.
>
> I do not remember if I ever told you how affronted he was to find on

his arrival from England in 1888 that I had resigned & had asked you to take my place. I told him that it never occurred to me that he wanted the post . . . .[30]

To his death, George Stephen was baffled by his cousin Donald Smith. Where Stephen's declining years were spent in the pleasant twilight of a man at the pinnacle of worldly achievements, Smith, who far surpassed his cousin in accomplishments, forever strove on as if he were still the young man from Labrador. In 1896 at the age of seventy-six, he lobbied hard to be named the Canadian high commissioner to England, succeeding Sir Charles Tupper. He held the position, without pay, for eighteen more years.

Donald Smith seemed invincible, continuing to work as if he would last forever. (On his ninety-third birthday, to the amazement of reporters, he put in his habitual twelve-hour day.) But on November 12, 1913, time dealt Smith a blow from which he never recovered, the death of Lady Strathcona. She had been

Lord Strathcona at Government House, Edmonton, 1909, with missionary Father Lacombe

as vital to him as his limbs, and every day of his life that they were apart he cabled or wrote to her. Barely two months later Donald Smith died of heart failure.*

Stephen's main occupation in his declining years was his charities. In his will, he settled the immense sum of £750,000, which, after death duties, amounted to around £500,000, on the King Edward Hospital in London even though he had already bestowed more than that on the institution during his lifetime. Stephen had very clear ideas as to how he wanted his money spent, and that was on the poor. Nor did he forget his old stamping grounds. He built and endowed the Stephen Hospital in Dufftown and provided sufficient stock — about £40,000 worth from his American railroad portfolio — to add £100 annually to the income of each of the parish ministers of Dufftown and its surrounding district. And then he quietly sponsored a memorial to his old mathematics teacher, John Macpherson.

As with many of their business investments, the charities of Lords Mount Stephen and Strathcona followed lockstep one behind the other. The two of them were major benefactors of McGill University in Montreal, and they endowed the Royal Victoria Hospital in the same city with $1 million to honour Queen Victoria's Jubilee in 1887. In later years Stephen took exception to the hospital's policy of catering to the wealthy, and in his will reduced his final bequest to a token sum of $10,000.†

---

*Donald Smith's estate totalled £4,651,000. Though an astronomical sum, it is still less than his net worth of a few years earlier, and suggests that Smith dispersed the greater portion of his estate just as George Stephen had. This theory gains credence when one realizes that the executor of both wills was Sterling, the man who set up Stephen's trusts.

†Though one of the most generous men of his time, Stephen could also be mean. On September 3, 1897, a Quebec City Council meeting resolved to ask him to donate a 25,000-square-foot dilapidated parcel of land he owned. The plan was to turn the land, valued at about $15,000, into a public garden and to erect a drinking fountain "or other useful and ornamental memorial" to preserve Stephen's name. No reply was received from Stephen. Amid rumours that the land was in the process of being sold to a syndicate which intended to erect buildings on it, Wilfrid Laurier wrote to John Turnbull, Stephen's agent in Montreal. Turnbull relayed the answer: "About the Symes property I am sorry I cannot make the City of Quebec a gift of it, I want to sell it and to get all the money for it that can be obtained." (John Turnbull to Wilfrid Laurier, March 16, 1898, LP)

Stephen, ever the crafty financier, even found a way to beat death. He was outraged at the "simply confiscatory" English death duties with which "he had a little experience . . . when Lady Boss died,"[31] and he had asked his lawyer John Sterling to find a way around them. The result was an astounding trust deed, set up in 1898, that provided £550,000, or $2,800,000, for the support, through annuities, of thirty-five of his more removed relatives. By 1906, the amount of money under administration had grown to $6,088,257.05.[32] During that period he settled another $15 million of stock on his nearest relatives, including Alice and, of course, Lady Mount Stephen, leaving only 31,394 Great Northern shares, worth $5.5 million, in his private portfolio.[33] As a result, Stephen's estate amounted to £1,414,319 8s 3d, still a huge sum for the times, but paltry compared to his net worth a few years earlier.

Lord Mount Stephen died on December 27, 1921. Ninety years old, he slipped quietly from life. In his final years the light dimmed gradually, accompanied by none of the "kicking" against the end that saw Van Horne on his way. An oddly sentimental instruction in his will directed that his body be borne from Brocket Hall to the churchyard on a Canadian buckboard drawn by two horses. His death was treated as the passing of a head of state. Lengthy newspaper stories, headlined with "Maker of Modern Canada" and "From Herd-Boy to Peer" lamented the loss throughout the Empire.* George Stephen's life was one of great accomplishment, he counted the most powerful among his friends, and royalty were his companions. But no one, with the exception of his first wife, really knew him. All had their own piece of the complicated puzzle that was George Stephen, and each piece was precisely the size and shape he intended. There is a particularly poignant irony in the words his devoted Gian wrote to Queen Mary after his death: "He died just as he had lived, just simply. . . ."[34]

---

*In the end Strathcona got a measure of revenge on his cousin George, who never really understood or appreciated him. In a number of stories Stephen was described as a "co-worker of Lord Strathcona's" and in other stories, Strathcona, who didn't meet his cousin until years later, was given credit for enticing Stephen to Canada and thus being responsible for the making of his fortune.

CHAPTER 9

THE GOLDEN ERA OF THE SYSTEMS MAN

*He worshipped the system as much as
any Mikado ever did his ancestry.*

O fficially, Thomas Shaughnessy's CPR presidency began
in 1899 when Sir William Van Horne resigned. In reality, it started in the mid-1890s as J. J. Hill's purchase of the
Duluth and Winnipeg soured Van Horne's taste for the job.
Any doubt of Shaughnessy's ascension was banished by the
support of Stephen, who found in Shaughnessy more of a
kindred spirit. Van Horne motivated and controlled through
the often terrifying force of his physical presence, his overwhelming competence and the fire of his unshakable opinions. Shaughnessy manipulated, buttressing his authority with
rules, policies and negotiating finesse. Stephen had little taste
for Van Horne's impetuosity and risk taking, but he could put
his faith in Shaughnessy's predictability and dependability.

Stephen and Shaughnessy were dedicated anglophiles who
revelled in the pomp and ceremony of the English aristocracy.
Van Horne, on the other hand, was informality personified in
his dress, his manner and his openness to strangers. He was
so uneasy with the idea of "Sir William" that he refused the
honour of knighthood in 1890 and again in 1891, using the
specious reasoning that a title would somehow inhibit his
relations with Americans. The morning in 1894 when his

Thomas Shaughnessy at his desk in 1904

knighthood was finally announced, Van Horne's elderly office attendant,* with whom he'd traded light-hearted banter for years, greeted him with a servile bow and "Good Morning, Sir William." Flummoxed for one of the few times in his life, Van Horne muttered, "Oh, Hell!", beat a hasty retreat and was not seen for the remainder of the day.

As vice-president, Shaughnessy was the perfect counterbalance to Van Horne. Though a master of details himself, Van Horne found endless wrestling with picayune matters uninteresting and uninspiring. Shaughnessy thrived on minutiae, eagerly grasping every job Van Horne tired of. His achievements have become less notable with the passage of time because they were performed in the unromantic realms

---

*A cross between a valet and a janitor, office attendants kept desks tidy, waste baskets empty and spittoons cleaned. They also ran errands.

of administration and expansion, rather than in the great and glorious arenas of conception and construction. Shaughnessy was largely responsible for transforming a young, chaotic railroad company — one that closely resembled a ransacked house after a wild party — into a multifaceted empire that ran like clockwork. Endowed with none of Van Horne's superhuman talents nor Stephen's gift for Machiavellian scheming, he wrought his miracles with pen, paper and policy.

During the construction period Shaughnessy established himself as a powerful force within the CPR. As vice-president he thrust the tentacles of his authority into every nook and cranny of administration and operation, even into areas that would normally have been delegated to subordinates. Van Horne, who trusted Shaughnessy implicitly, would typically create a project, see it through and then leave it to his vice-president to operate. The construction of the Château Frontenac in Quebec City is a case in point.

When the hotel opened during the winter of 1893, Shaughnessy scrutinized its affairs like a pathologist suspiciously dissecting a diseased corpse. The unfortunate recipient of his attention was the hotel's manager, H. E. Dunning. After a few weeks the browbeaten Dunning began to wonder why he had even been put in charge. Shaughnessy's long memo was typical of dozens he showered on the manager.

Referring to your letter of yesterday enclosing copies of your first bills of fare. The bills would indicate lack of supervision. If the man who makes them out doesn't know how to spell in French, he had better use English. For instance, your dinner bill is headed "potatoes". I presume you intended "Potages." Further down, instead of Rotis, you've got "Rots," and so on. There are no less than twelve errors in spelling in that single bill of fare. This must be corrected immediately, or your bills of fare will be a source of amusement for your guests.

I don't think that your long bill of fare for luncheon is necessary. Why use any bill of fare at all for that meal? It is not done in the best hotels on this continent and in Europe.

In your letter of yesterday you tell me the receipts from board on Monday were twelve ($12.00) dollars. If you had thirty-five people there, as I gather from your telegram, the receipts from board would appear to be small.[1]

Dunning also earned a rebuke for his choice of dessert. "Coconut pie, ague pudding and delicacies of that description which I notice appear on your bill of fare frequently are abominations, and if I were in your place, I would not offer them."[2]

Shaughnessy spent Christmas Day, 1893, with his family but headed for the office early the next morning to make up for the lost time. He typed his own letters in the absence of secretary James Oborne, who was allowed two full days' holiday. At the end of December Shaughnessy took one of his feared "run ups," as he called them, to personally "see to" the situation at the Frontenac. Those little jaunts — which he always warned employees about well in advance, thus allowing time for apprehension to build — slapped a clammy hand over the hearts of the diligent and loafer alike.

WITH HIS DISTINCTLY JAUNDICED view of mankind, Shaughnessy believed that the propensity for evil was heavily etched in man's soul and that only constant vigilance kept it in check. He preferred to envision every conceivable breach of the rules and draw up preventative regulations rather than reward or encourage appropriate behaviour. "[Shaughnessy] never seemed to realize the quality of the steed he was riding," observed D. C. Coleman, who became CPR president in 1947. "He sometimes appeared to feel that railway officers responded best to rough treatment."[3] Nothing incensed Shaughnessy more than a transgression he'd failed to anticipate and in those cases he relentlessly pursued the culprit.

Unused train supplies were tacitly regarded by all as the property of the crew. Everything from leftovers in the dining cars to abandoned cargo and the contents of emergency provision boxes,* stored in the baggage cars for passengers during

---

*A typical emergency box contained: cheese, one 2-pound box; biscuits, 2 boxes; tea, ¾ caddy; sugar, 1 box; corned beef, 24 cans; lamb tongue, 24 cans; bologna sausage, 2; condensed milk, 10 cans; stock soup, 12 cans; sardines, 4 tins; salt, 1 bag; tea boiler, 1; charcoal, ½ bushel (Lavallée, *Van Horne's Road*, p. 236). The boxes were vital during those helter-skelter early days of substandard equipment when trains could be stranded for days by snowslides, mudslides, derailments and breakdowns.

unexpected delays, were divvied up according to rank. When inventories came up short, the superintendent simply wrote off the difference as spoilage and requisitioned new supplies. It wasn't considered stealing; merely one of the unspoken perquisites of the job — that is, until Shaughnessy began comparing the inventory lists with the emergency-delay log and found that the bulk of the shortages occurred when no delays had been reported.

Every tactic from surprise inspections to the installation of heavy-duty locks* failed to stop the pilfering. On January 11, 1896, Shaughnessy instructed William Whyte to institute an elaborate system of checks and counterchecks. Each emergency box was to be sealed, and written receipts were required from the baggagemen at both ends of a run to ensure that they remained intact. If a genuine emergency occurred, the baggageman had to file a lengthy report detailing the reason the box was opened and exactly what provisions were used. The conductor had to countersign the report and send it immediately to Whyte's office for investigation. The men took the new security precautions as a challenge, emptying the boxes faster than ever.

Citing an experiment on the Northern Pacific line in the United States, Whyte humbly suggested that a little extra pay might ease the problem. Shaughnessy vehemently disagreed. "I do not see that there is anything for it but to keep checking them from time to time, and to fire them unceremoniously when you catch them stealing. I have very little faith in the project of the Northern Pacific to endeavour to prevent dishonesty by increasing the compensation. A man who will steal at $100 a month will do so if paid $200 or $300, or any amount."[4]

Shaughnessy hired solid, loyal, hard-working men. He tolerated none of the quirks and idiosyncracies that cropped up

---

*The keys were held by the first-class sleeping car porter because Shaughnessy suspected that the baggagemen and the conductors were the ringleaders.

distressingly often in Van Horne's employees. So closely tuned to Shaughnessy were his lieutenants that some began to sound and act like him. After a few years serving as secretary to the vice-president, James Oborne's letters were virtually indistinguishable in phrasing and content from those written by his superior. He even affected carrying a walking stick identical to Shaughnessy's and for a while tried unsuccessfully to cultivate a bushy Imperial.

No matter how dedicated an employee was, Shaughnessy never for a moment let him forget who was in charge. If there was ever an opportunity to emphasize his position Shaughnessy took it, not with loud ostentation but with quiet firmness. As he abhorred being kept waiting, he ordered the single Windsor Station elevator kept ready and vacant for him every morning and evening. Standing orders specified that no employee was to ride up with him. Though Shaughnessy only sporadically ate lunch at the Windsor Station restaurant he insisted on having a large corner table reserved day and night, whether he was in Montreal or not, and not even a vice-president dared disturb him unless invited.

Neither an art patron like Van Horne nor a grand benefactor to charities like Stephen, Shaughnessy appeared detached from everything in life but the CPR. Only his family and a few close friends were allowed to see his softer side. His grandson Thomas Shaughnessy remembers toddling into his forbidding grandfather's arms and being flung high in the air. Subordinates would have been shocked to hear his uninhibited laughter and the joy he took in the child. Shaughnessy also had compassion, though he allowed it to show only if it could be done by the book. When the Reverend John Campbell asked George Stephen to assist a woman who had been "rendered absolutely destitute" after her boarding house was completely destroyed by fire, Stephen responded by donating a box of clothes to the woman and asking Shaughnessy, then only assistant to Van Horne, to arrange for them to be sent to her. Personal requests from the company's head were difficult to ignore but Shaughnessy decided "that we cannot deviate from our rule to charge freight on everything."[5] Instead of letting the donation travel free of charge, he had the bill — which probably cost the company far more in paperwork and his own time than it was worth — sent to head office, where he paid it himself.

Shaughnessy's behaviour codes were designed to save employees from themselves. Transgressors were given the opportunity to explain the reason for the infraction, and then fired. Occasionally he relented, but always using some artifice to make it appear that he wasn't bending any rule. In 1905 a young clerk who was also an amateur boxer staged an illicit lunch hour fight in a vacant Windsor Station room and had the misfortune to be caught in the act by vice-president David McNicoll, who fired the lad on the spot. The boy's mother appealed directly to Shaughnessy, pleading that he was a good Catholic boy and her only means of support. But Shaughnessy couldn't simply rescind McNicoll's order. "Well, my lad, you have only yourself to blame," he admonished the youngster, who squirmed in embarrassment and disgrace. "It was a breach of good order in the office, and Mr. McNicoll was right in disciplining you. You are a clerk in his department, and I cannot ask him to take you back. The only thing I can do is to take you into my own office. Report to me tomorrow."[6]

SHAUGHNESSY'S PERSISTENCE IN UNCOVERING and then pursuing CPR wrongdoers reveals the skill of a first-class sleuth. Though far from a romantic, he stood fascinated on the sidelines while one of his own captains singlehandedly solved an international mystery. The villain in the case was the infamous "Dr" Crippen, an English patent medicine huckster who murdered his wife, a music hall performer, dissected her and buried the remains in his cellar. With half of England and Scotland Yard looking for him, he vanished with his lover, twenty-year-old Ethel Le Neve.

On July 20, 1909, the CPR ship *Montrose* sailed from Antwerp in Belgium. Two days later the captain, H. G.

Kendall, sent a wireless cable that electrified the CPR officers in Liverpool. "Have strong suspicions that Crippen London cellar murderer and accomplice are amongst saloon passengers. Moustache taken off growing beard. Accomplice dressed as boy. Voice manner and build undoubtedly a girl. Both travelling as Mr and Master Robinson."[7] The message was relayed to Montreal, and when the chief telegrapher received it he interrupted Shaughnessy's supper with the news. For the next eight days the president waited impatiently for every new development in the "Crippen business."

Kendall skulked around the ship gathering clues. He discovered that the "boy" held his pants up with safety pins and when seated crossed his legs like a woman. He noticed they never conversed with the other passengers and late one night he caught them holding hands. Using subterfuge Kendall was able to read the man's hat label and even managed to measure the length of their shoes. He relayed all of these little tidbits to Inspector Dew of Scotland Yard and Shaughnessy kept a pile of the decoded cables on his desk. As the *Montrose* neared Canadian waters Kendall suggested that if a policeman disguised as a pilot boarded the ship near Quebec, he could easily apprehend the criminal, "Thanks will speak you later operation here will make arrangements here meantime suggest suspect kept under direct observation . . . complements [sic] Dew,"[8] wired back the Inspector.

Crippen's arrest was accomplished without a hitch and headlines around the world paraded the case. Kendall was treated as a hero and the British Parliament awarded him a purse of £250. Winston S. Churchill, Home Secretary, signed the cheque. From the CPR he received a tersely awkward sentence relayed to him via Shaughnessy's secretary: "The President wishes to congratulate you for your bravery in assisting the apprehension of Dr. Crippen."[9]*

---

*It was the first use of the fledgling Marconi wireless in the capture of a criminal. At the time only sixty ships in the world were outfitted with the radio; within eighteen months six

SHAUGHNESSY'S NINETEEN YEARS AS CPR PRESIDENT, from 1899 to 1918, were as full of fortune as Van Horne's and George Stephen's were dogged by misfortune. It seemed as if all the gods of railway prosperity were cooperating. The company's profitability was staggering. When Van Horne was fending off the sabotage of Hill and Stephen, share prices sank to a low of $33. From there they leapt to $85 in 1897 and to $240 in 1911. Then in 1912, shares topped $276. During that magical time of growth and prosperity, dividends doubled from 5 percent to 10 percent, and the company paid out $208 million in dividends to shareholders. So prosperous was the company at its peak that one financial writer declared CPR stock was so strong that shares of the Grand Trunk had shrunk to "little Trunks" in comparison.

When Shaughnessy took over he controlled 7,000 miles of track; by 1913 he had pushed that figure to 11,366. There were 20,000 freight cars in 1901 and over 88,000 in 1914. Freight revenue jumped from $37 million in 1902 to $139 million in 1913, and though the CPR's capital expenditures totalled $336 million in those years, he paid for most of it by issuing $240 million worth of new stock, adding very little to the company's debt.

Ironically, the CPR's prosperity and ensuing growth during Shaughnessy's presidency have given him the image of a visionary. In fact, his policies, from shipping to hotels and financing, followed trails well blazed by his two predecessors. "Had there been a spark of genius in him he would have extinguished it for the sake of betterments to the most conventional Colossus in Canada," a journalist of the time

---

hundred of them were installed.

Kendall never cashed the cheque, but framed and hung it in his cabin; the original telegraph messages were auctioned in London for £1,600. The story had a strange epilogue. When Crippen was arrested, he purportedly cursed Kendall. Four years later, as the *Empress of Ireland* was going past the very spot where the curse had been uttered, it sank, with Kendall at the helm. (Kendall survived the wreck and lived past the age of ninety.) Then in 1914 the *Montrose* also sank in a gale. The last man to be removed from the ailing ship was no relation of the notorious criminal, but his name was William Crippen.

commented wryly.[10] Financing the CPR's expansion through share issues was possible only because prices were so high and investors waited in line to snap up stock as it came available. Van Horne would have done the same thing if there had been a buoyant market in the black days of 1894. Even the expansion during Shaughnessy's era is misleading. Aside from the obvious need to double track in the prime grain belts to cope with bumper crops, the bulk of the CPR's expansion came as a defensive reaction to competitors.

Shaughnessy's greatness lay not in conceiving grand plans, but in executing and managing an idea, and he was a virtuoso negotiator. Behind an unwavering image of straightforwardness and rectitude, he circled, feinted and lured, deftly turning opponents' strengths into weaknesses. Nowhere was his skill more evident than in the stalking of an Atlantic shipping service. The CPR's Pacific service* was well underway and enormously successful by 1901, but the long, tedious dance of getting control over the Atlantic showed no sign of ending. Shaughnessy wanted to absorb a shipping line already in existence, thus guaranteeing immediate revenue and minimal initial capital expenditure. He identified two takeover targets: the Elder Dempster (Beaver) Line† and the Allan Line, both of which had complacently refused to upgrade their ships to compete with those sailing out of New York. Having expended relatively little on improvements, the two lines were enormously profitable, but would be highly vulnerable if a faster Canadian competitor suddenly appeared.

---

*The *Empresses of India, Japan* and *China* were launched in 1891 with the advertising slogan, "Round the World in 80 days — $600." Van Horne designed the red and white checkered flag that flew from their decks so that it would be recognizable even when it was hanging loose. A reporter suggested it stood for "three of a kind" and Van Horne snorted that for the CPR only a straight flush would do. (Musk, *Canadian Pacific: Shipping Line,* p. 16)

†The British Elder Dempster Company purchased the Montreal-based Beaver Line in 1898 and ran its ships out of Liverpool. The Allan Line, set up by the father of Hugh Allan (of Pacific Scandal fame), had offices in Montreal and Glasgow.

SHAUGHNESSY'S FIRST SALVO, AIMED at the weaker Beaver Line, was fired during the CPR's annual general meeting in October, 1902, when he announced that the company would offer to carry the British mails across the Atlantic for a subsidy of £265,000 a year, casually mentioning at the same time that the service would involve twenty-knot steamers.* The suggestion sent a ripple of fear through the shipping corridors of Montreal and Liverpool. On their best day the Beaver ships averaged only thirteen knots. Faced with a twenty-knot competitor, the line would be lucky to sell out for scrap. In the manner of one bestowing a favour, Shaughnessy wrote to the two lines, offering to buy them out. His tactic stampeded Sir Alfred Jones, president of the Beaver Line. "I think we should tell the CPR that if they are determined to secure boats, we would sell ours," he wrote to Henry Allan, the Allan Line's controlling partner in Glasgow. "Why not do the same?"[11] Allan desperately tried to make light of Shaughnessy's threat, cautioning Jones that the CPR president didn't really want to buy them out, but only wanted to prevent the Beaver and Allan lines from joining and shutting him out of the Atlantic trade.

Allan knew that Shaughnessy was far too tough and resolute an opponent for the flaccid Jones, and he ended his letter pessimistically: "However, I take it from your letter that you mean to allow him to humbug you, and to cause you to delay taking any action to secure the Mail Service. In these circumstances we shall, of course, proceed to negotiate henceforward for our own account."[12] Shaughnessy didn't toy with his prey once it was helpless. By February, 1903, it was common knowledge that the CPR had struck a deal with Jones. Rumours and criticism flew around the Empire that the CPR was out to monopolize the Atlantic.

Within days of buying out Jones, Shaughnessy launched an

---

*The mail service was in the hands of the Cunard Line, based in New York but largely financed by British investors, much as the Grand Trunk was.

extensive advertising campaign designed to draw, not the leisured elite, but the commoners, the emigrants he hoped would take a CPR ship into Montreal, then board a CPR train to the west and there settle down and farm some CPR land with CPR-introduced wheat, which they would transport to CPR elevators for shipping via CPR grain cars. The first company ship to sail the Atlantic was the SS *Montrose* on April 21, 1903 — the same ship on which Dr Crippen was arrested six years later.

Shaughnessy didn't find Henry Allan's grip on his company quite so easy to shake loose. Seemingly content with the one line, Shaughnessy made no move to acquire his rival. Then in 1907 Lord Strathcona made a curious announcement that he intended to organize a twenty-four-knot service under the auspices of the CPR, despite the fact that Shaughnessy's twenty-knot goal had yet to be reached. Strathcona had no intention of getting into the shipping business but, as intended, his proposal shook Allan's confidence.

Sensitive about the potential outcry over another CPR monopoly, Shaughnessy let no one but a handful of senior officers know about the negotiations between him and Allan, who, when faced with Strathcona's supposed new service, capitulated with surprising alacrity. The deal was consummated in July, 1909, with the CPR buying control of the Allan Line for £1,609,000. One condition of the agreement was an extraordinary understanding to keep the change of ownership secret. In fact, for years it was widely believed that the Allan Line had been purchased by the Grand Trunk.[13] The transaction was officially announced only in 1915 when the CPR applied to the parliamentary Railway Commission for permission to treat its shipping interests as an entity apart from the railway. By then the news was of little consequence in comparison to reports about the war.

Shaughnessy made his acquisitions at the lowest conceivable price while wringing extraordinary concessions from the other side of the table. Invariably, he made opponents believe he was doing them a great favour, rather than vice versa. In

January, 1901, Shaughnessy purchased the aging fleet of the Canadian Pacific Navigation Company, to provide a link between Vancouver and Victoria. Having purchased the shipping line, the construction of a CPR hotel in Victoria was a foregone conclusion, but Shaughnessy made the citizens believe otherwise, forcing them to beg for what he intended to give them anyway. Without a large hotel in Victoria to draw tourists, the fleet's value would be halved.

On his first visit to Victoria, in February, 1901, Shaughnessy knocked the city's leaders off balance by stating unequivocally that "the company has no intention of building a tourist hotel in Victoria."[14] The president wasn't seen in the city until the following year during his annual cross-country inspection tour. Once again, he feigned little interest in a new hotel. It wasn't until May, 1903, that he reluctantly agreed to meet with Victoria's negotiating committee who by then were getting desperate. After examining the concessions that the committee had drawn up for each possible site Shaughnessy sighed, "Such an undertaking is a continual source of trouble." After a considerable dismayed silence he relented, crisply stating he would construct a hotel if the committee offered *all* its concessions, regardless of the site, *and* if free water for twenty years were thrown in. "Well, that is my proposition, if you care to accept it all right, but if not, you can make one, but bear in mind that the company is not anxious to go into the hotel business."[15] Of course, he got everything he asked for and the Empress, designed by Francis Rattenbury, became one of the CPR's most imposing and profitable hotels.

ASIDE FROM FREIGHT, TOURISTS AND SETTLERS were the lifeblood of the Shaughnessy era. The hotels and ships were finally bringing a steady stream of travellers to Canada and keeping them there, thanks to dependable train schedules and the comforts of travel in modern sleeping cars. But it was always easier to secure tourist traffic than to attract settlers and ensure that they stayed put once they had their land. The biggest problem was competing with the United States. Before it was taken over by Hill, the Northern Pacific alone had over 1,000 immigration agents scattered throughout Europe, and most of them worked on commission. Canada seemed cursed with receiving endless hordes of remittance men, few of whom were suitable for life on the frontier. "Between you and me," Shaughnessy confided to E. B. Osler, MP, shortly after becoming president, "I hardly think the people in England should send these blue-blooded young fellows out to Canada without providing means for their support until they become established at any rate."[16]

As an ambassador for emigration Shaughnessy was hopeless. His stern, austere manner was all very well in dealing with subordinates, but interviews with him seldom resulted in the enthusiastic articles needed to entice the common man and woman to Canada: "His [Shaughnessy's] talks to the press must be curt and comprehensive — or else elliptical. He had no exuding vivacity. When I talked to him or listened to him — he was cold and exact. He left the chair only to walk erectly to the window. He deviated not a syllable from the subject in hand — The System. He worshipped that: as much as any Mikado ever did his ancestry."[17]

Shaughnessy shrewdly offset his promotional deficiencies by hiring George Ham — the only officer he allowed to operate outside the CPR's behavioural straightjacket. Shaughnessy shuddered inwardly every time he saw Ham. A tall, walrus-faced and permanently rumpled man, a friend described him as "a large body of superfine humanity entirely surrounded by the Canadian Pacific Railway."[18] Ham had the priceless knack of being able to sell both Canada and the CPR just by being himself. Always ready with a quip or a helping hand, the gregarious Ham was one of the most popular men in the country. Shaughnessy, whose own schedule had as little variation as a railroad timetable, was appalled by Ham's helter-skelter ways. "You could pick him out because he is the only one that never appears to be working," a friend recalled. "If he is there at all, he is either just coming in or going out. If you are

The sign reads: WE'RE SAILING WEST. WE'RE SAILING WEST. TO PRAIRIE LANDS SUNKISSED AND BLEST — THE CROFTER'S TRAIL TO HAPPINESS.

British emigrants leaving for the Canadian Prairies

coming in, he is going out — or across. If you are going out, he'll go out with you — or across."[19]

Ham, a clever man packaged in an ill-fitting clown suit, made people laugh in spite of themselves. "The pockets of the waistcoat are always bagged under the pressure of cigars carried there against every emergency, and the trousers are mostly of the regulation length, though he once complained of a pair being a little tight under the arms."[20] He drank lots, smoked more and ate like a starving soldier. The torture of his life was the ill health of his later years. Describing it to a friend, he said that first the doctors cut out his appendix, then the thyroid cartilage and, worst of all, the booze. "You must have a great constitution," remarked another friend. Ham retorted with a grim smile, "Yes, a great constitution, but no by-laws."[21]*

Even when he was incensed, Ham's words carried more humour than rancour. Upon hearing of an injustice to a friend, Ham said of the offender: "The only thing to do is to give him hell and the devil," and then he left for the train station. At the first stop he wired, "Cut out 'hell,'" at the second, "Cut out 'the devil,'" and at the third, "On consideration, cut out the whole business."[22]

Shaughnessy's forbearance with Ham paid handsome dividends, and the unconventional promoter generated reams of favourable publicity for everything from the CPR's tourist trade to the freight rates and immigration. But occasionally his promotions backfired outrageously. He suggested that the company sponsor Rudyard Kipling on a cross-country trip, and saw to his every need, from the best of first-class rooms to unlimited drink. In return, Kipling wrote a series of funny and often poetic articles on Canada, unfortunately stressing the isolation, the cold and the peculiarities of Canadians, one of

---

*So popular was Ham that politicians would fight to sit next to him at functions. During one press gallery dinner he was seated near newspaper publisher John Willison and Liberal MP Joseph-Israel Tarte. The two were arguing about provincial politics and Tarte was losing. Ham leaned over and, sotto voce, advised him, "Deal in glittering generalities."

George Ham

whom was supposedly skilled in training avalanches to jump over train tracks. Worst of all he immortalized the country in a poem called "Our Lady of the Snows." Kipling's frozen portrayal so disturbed both the country and the CPR that a plan to build an ice-palace to stage an annual winter carnival at Winnipeg was dropped. "Not a cent for ice-palace; but five hundred dollars for a Christmas shirt-sleeve parade at Winnipeg"[23] was Shaughnessy's response when asked for a contribution.

Shaughnessy and the CPR spent millions of dollars trying to expunge the image of Canada as a frigid wasteland. But for every upbeat article or paid advertisement, another appeared characterizing emigration to the Northwest as a death-defying adventure from which only the fortunate returned alive. One such was the true 1906 chronicle of Emigrant No. 1 called "What Roughing It in Canada Really Means."[24]*

Emigrant No. 1 arrived in Winnipeg in April to find three inches of snow on the ground, freezing temperatures and no work. The land agent "duped" him into leaving almost immediately for a point seven hundred miles west, where there was also no work and where he was forced to sleep on "two dirty horse-blankets on a leaky hay mattress, which . . . smelt horribly." He found the inhabitants equally unappealing. "Canadians are silent, brooding people — even the little children thinking more of getting money than anything else. . . ." Emigrant No. 1 complained that there were "only three meals a day in Canada," and that the workday began at 4:30 A.M. and didn't end until after supper, leaving no time to repair or wash clothes, which were generally thrown away when they got too filthy to put on again. "Canadians on farms never seem to wash. No baths anywhere, even in hotels," he observed disgustedly. He reported that his landlady wiped utensils on her baby's clothes before handing them to her boarder and even took the spoon "straight out of the child's mouth into your cup. The man would pick his teeth at the table with a hairpin from his wife's head."[25]

SHAUGHNESSY HAD BEEN PRESIDENT for less than a year when his good friend, Governor General Lord Minto,† proposed him for a knighthood. The two men shared an old-fashioned conservatism and a rather low tolerance for the foibles of human nature, despite the fact that Minto carried on a six-year affair with the young and glamorous Lola Powell during his tenure in Ottawa. Minto had assured Shaughnessy that he had "taken care of the matter,"[26] but he hadn't reckoned on the

---

*The article, published in the British magazine *World's Work* was compiled from the letters of two emigrants to their friends and families.

†The fourth Earl of Minto was christened Gilbert John Elliott-Murray-Kynynmound. He was named governor general in 1898.

CPR advertisement for British settlers, 1918

opposition of Clifford Sifton, federal minister of the interior. Minto believed that Sifton was corrupt and immoral, and in the privacy of Rideau Hall he was simply referred to as "the villain."[27] Relations between the two men were chilly from the start, but when Sifton's newspaper, the Manitoba *Free Press*, dismissed Minto as a "second or third rate man,"[28] Minto retaliated by denouncing Sifton's administration of the Yukon as "criminal" on the eve of the federal election.

Sifton opposed Shaughnessy's knighthood on the grounds that only the Cabinet should bestow such titles, but the real reason was the animosity between him and Shaughnessy. Even though Sifton was one of the few westerners who didn't attack the CPR monopoly in the late 1880s and afterward, he was angry at Shaughnessy for not throwing his support behind the Liberals in the 1900 election. Sifton was also a whole-hearted admirer of William Van Horne,* the kind of direct, no-nonsense man he appreciated. Shaughnessy, on the other hand, he considered constipated, hidebound and devious. In the end Sifton's opposition came to nothing, and the CPR systems man became a Knight Bachelor in October, 1901.

DURING THE SHAUGHNESSY YEARS the CPR's incredible profit-ability inevitably attracted poachers. Foremost among them were two Canadian lines, the Grand Trunk and the Canadian Northern, and, of course, Van Horne's old nemesis, J. J. Hill's Great Northern. The Canadian Northern was the creation of a strange duo, William Mackenzie and Donald Mann. Though utterly dissimilar in shape and personality, the two men had the zeal of mid-nineteenth-century railway hucksters without the corruption that usually went with it. They could have sold ice to the Arctic if they'd put their minds to it.

Mackenzie and Mann were difficult opponents for Shaughnessy. Because he neither understood nor empathized

---

*It was Van Horne who had recommended Sifton to Wilfrid Laurier for the position of minister of the interior.

with their motives, he was unable to anticipate their plans or manipulate them, usually his strength in dealing with an opponent. Both were deeply religious and tackled railway building with the fervour of fire-and-brimstone preachers. In contrast with the shady promoters of earlier times, they were driven by a genuine passion for railroading, and Mackenzie, though acknowledged to be a financial magician, could not be swayed by talk of mere profit and loss. Sour-faced and humourless, his ferret-like features burned with a dream of another cross-Canada line.

Mann, large and lumbering, was an outdoorsman who loved the broad prairie and thickly treed wilderness slopes, but behind his bovine exterior lurked an acute opportunist, who accurately assessed that railroad builders would be most welcome in Manitoba. Moving to Winnipeg in the mid-1890s, Mann was soon perceived as the man who could give Manitoba its own route to the European grain markets through Hudson Bay. When he formed the Canadian Northern with Mackenzie in 1899, Prairie farmers saw their chance to be freed from the CPR stranglehold at last.

Shaughnessy underestimated the pair right from the start. They were disorganized, trumpeted their virtues too loudly and were far too haphazard in their financial planning. What he failed to anticipate was how completely Manitobans — always antagonistic to the CPR — would take Mackenzie and Mann to their bosoms. During construction the two men hired locals, not an endless stream of Yankees, and if a man wanted to work for a single day and then draw his pay, that was fine. When a town had some heavy work to be done, Mackenzie and Mann cheerfully lent a team of horses. They once bought 3,000 bushels of wheat seed and gave it away to the people of Dauphin. They even held picnics in villages near their lines and entertained them with whatever talent existed in the ranks of their workmen. Where the CPR always seemed to jangle the nerves of Manitobans, Mackenzie and Mann seemed able to turn any catastrophe to their advantage. When one of their locomotives accidentally killed a heifer, they didn't haggle over compensation as Shaughnessy would have done, but dressed the meat, tanned the hide and handed the farmer the profit from the sale.

By 1900 Mackenzie and Mann, to Shaughnessy's intense irritation, were heroes of the province. The legislature could not grant them enough, whether it was charters, licences or land grants. That year rumours circulated that J. J. Hill was planning to sell the Northern Pacific and Manitoba Railway, the line that had provoked the infamous Battle of Fort Whyte. Shaughnessy never for a moment believed Mackenzie and Mann would get it. After all, the 313 miles of Northern Pacific line sat right in the middle of what the CPR considered to be its territory. But J. J. Hill was still no friend of the CPR and he had a card or two up his sleeve. When Donald Mann had approached him about selling the line, he answered, "No railway ever sells branch lines to another railway," but in later conversation, he coyly insinuated that a railway just might sell to a government.[29] It would be a simple matter then for the province to lease the line to some company — and the CPR wasn't likely to be a favourite.

Shaughnessy was furious when the Manitoba government, under the ardent anti-CPR premier Rodmond P. Roblin, bid for the line. Unaware of Hill's statement to Mann, he appealed to Northern Pacific president C. S. Mellen to hang onto the line, and even asked Hill to intercede. But Roblin had been too long a farmer to agree to any deal that gave the CPR more power in Manitoba. Besides, he wanted control over his very own railway, an idea that struck Shaughnessy as absurd. "If the Government of Manitoba be determined to establish a Government Railway system, the sooner they try the experiment, and have their experience, the better. I am still unwilling to believe, however, that they will finally decide to adopt such an insane policy."[30] Roblin teased the CPR, allowing Shaughnessy to make an offer to lease the line from the government, which included a $550,000 "bonus" from the provincial treasury and a schedule of rate reductions. With that in hand he wrung enormous concessions from Mackenzie and Mann who, not stopping to wonder if they could make a profit, promised to drop passenger fares and let the government set freight rates within Manitoba and along the proposed section into Port Arthur.

After announcing the lease of the line to Canadian Northern, Roblin also mentioned that his government would provide a subsidy for Mackenzie and Mann to build toward the Lakehead on the north shore of Superior. "It is unnecessary for me to say that I am disgusted with the result, but I suppose there is nothing for me but to grin and bear it," Shaughnessy wrote confidentially to CPR director W. D. Matthews.[31] But he had no intention of either grinning or bearing it. He planted stories and rumours about the shakiness of the Canadian Northern and the unhealthy nature of the deal itself, arranging for the information to be leaked just as the bill approving the agreement went before the provincial Parliament, then instructing his paid writers and lobbyists to "drop into the background" so the CPR hand would remain unseen.

Shaughnessy was unsuccessful in his efforts, but he consoled himself with the conviction that the Canadian Northern would never get sufficient backing to expand into Ontario as well as build to the Pacific and extend its Manitoba network. He was wrong on all counts. In 1902 the Canadian Northern rolled into Port Arthur; by 1904 the company had built 614 miles of track in Manitoba (332 miles in CPR territory); and the same year Mackenzie and Mann announced they would reach Edmonton by Christmas, 1905.

Added to the Mackenzie and Mann aggravation was the Grand Trunk's determination to have its own line to the west coast. The new Grand Trunk Pacific was to end at a sparsely populated point in northern British Columbia, frequented mostly by seals and migrating birds. General Manager Charles Melville Hays explained the peculiar choice: "Having reached the Pacific Coast the company will undertake to establish a line of steamships to run to China, Japan and the Orient."[32] What became Prince Rupert was precisely the spot chosen by Sandford Fleming in 1877 as the terminus of the CPR. Barren it

Prince Rupert during construction of the Grand Trunk Pacific Railway

might have been, but it put the grain belt five hundred miles closer to the Far East, giving the Grand Trunk a chance to compete for sea traffic with its own fleet of ships.* Compared to the haphazard planning of Canadian Northern construction, the Grand Trunk Pacific tracklaying ran like a military exercise. In 1905 a CPR spy reported on progress of the two lines: "The Canadian Northern has lots of traffic and no railway. The Grand Trunk has a good railway and no traffic. God help us if they ever get together."[33]

Shaughnessy had little patience with and less faith in Mackenzie and Mann's "jerk water" line or in the grandiose schemes of Hays. He dismissed all three as "pap-fed infants,"[34] but he could hardly ignore the maze of lines erupting in the west. The Canadian Northern already controlled 5,000 miles

---

*Hays realized his plans would cause considerable consternation among the battered and bruised company shareholders but he also knew how soothing favourable stories in the press were to anxious investors. Prince Rupert was originally called Kaien Island, hardly an imposing name for a city destined to be the "Venice" of Canada. Hays announced a competition to rename it, limiting entries to ten letters and three syllables, and requiring it to be evocative of British Columbia. The winning suggestion, submitted by the niece of Manitoba's lieutenant-governor, satisfied only one of the rules, but the name stuck, and the competition kept the Grand Trunk in the press for some time.

of track, and the rash pair Mackenzie and Mann had proclaimed their intention to build and seize 2,600 more. In 1903 Shaughnessy marshalled a counterattack of steel, building and gobbling up lines with a calm ferocity that added nearly 6,000 miles to the CPR's trackage in eight years and cost close to $37 million. Fifty-one new towns sprang up virtually overnight in Manitoba, Saskatchewan and Alberta. By 1908 the railway map of the West looked as if a giant spider had run amok on the vast prairie. It was an insane race, as Mackenzie and Mann* flung rails across Saskatchewan with dizzying abandon. At one point no fewer than six lines paralleled each other, sprouting feeder branches like so many unshorn whiskers.

But the Grand Trunk Pacific and the Canadian Northern were doomed. In the end, there just wasn't enough revenue to support all the lines. Logically, the two CPR rivals should have amalgamated to produce a single transcontinental route. If they had, the lines might still be in private hands today. But William Mackenzie's blind zeal prevented that. One night, while he and a guest were enjoying the twilight from his private car, the *Atikokan,* the guest asked why he didn't sell out to the Grand Trunk and pocket his millions. Mackenzie answered simply, "I like building railroads."[35] On January 1, 1914, Canadian Northern's transcontinental service was open for business. Three years later, all but bankrupt, it collapsed into the arms of the government, becoming the first major section of the Canadian National Railways.

WHILE SHAUGHNESSY WAS SNAPPING UP LINES, erecting hotels and racing to outbuild the Canadian Northern and Grand Trunk Pacific, the ogre to the south, J. J. Hill, was far from sleeping. When Shaughnessy extended the Soo Lines into Chicago, giving the CPR an American route from eastern

---

*Mackenzie and Mann were knighted in 1911 at the height of the speculative boom that saw land prices jump fourfold over one weekend and turned everyone from housewife to navvy into a stock market gambler.

Canada to Winnipeg and allowing it to bypass the Great Northern entirely, Hill retaliated by ramming lines up to and across the international border wherever the slightest opening appeared. War was inevitable.

This time there was no George Stephen handicapping one in favour of the other. Hill was determined to counter the CPR's influence south and west of Lake Superior by snatching domination of British Columbia from Shaughnessy's hands. He already had a strong foothold with the Crow's Nest Pass Coal Company,* but also had interests in three smelters in the province, which shipped huge quantities of ore via the Great Northern, both from British Columbia and from Washington state. Shaughnessy retaliated by pouring money into the CPR's B.C. smelter Consolidated Mining and Smelting (later Cominco) in an attempt to divert some of the ore. Hill built a line to Vancouver from New Westminster, and Shaughnessy constructed one from Vancouver into Spokane. It was a swift, decisive game of run and block, run and block, with Hill darting up one alley after another and Shaughnessy throwing obstacles in his path.

Whenever Hill wanted to put a burr in Shaughnessy's starched undershorts, he trotted up to Winnipeg, where there was always a welcoming platform, and made a speech. In 1905 he announced that within sixty days, he intended to start his own Canadian transcontinental line, forgetting entirely the solemn assurances he had given Shaughnessy a few years earlier that he had no intention of invading Canada. Hill's plan was colossal and slightly demented in light of the fact that the Grand Trunk Pacific and the Canadian Northern were already hell-bent on the same goal. He grandly spoke of building 4,000 miles of new track, including twelve branch lines running into gold fields, oil fields and coal deposits at a total cost

---

*Hill purchased the company shortly after the Crow's Nest Pass Agreement of 1897 forced the CPR to turn over extensive coal lands to it in return for a subsidy to build the Crowsnest Pass line.

of $100 million. Hill piously stated that his line would be built without a penny of subsidy.

Newspapers treated Hill's statement as a formal declaration of war. The British press loved a railway fight almost as much as a boxing match, and several important papers, including the *Financial Times* of London and the *Bullionist,* assigned reporters full time to cover the duel. Large maps appeared in editions topped by banner headlines proclaiming variations of "A Railway Duel That All Canada Is Watching." Hill took the early upper hand by punching four lines across the border into British Columbia by mid-1906. Sixteen others were poised at or near the forty-ninth parallel.

Frustrated that Hill's challenge was not being met, Sir William Van Horne, still CPR chairman, loomed into view, fists and tongue cocked. "Tell Mr. Hill to go ahead," he dared, belligerence bristling from every pore, "and tell him that for every mile of track he builds in Canada we will build two in the United States."[36] Shaughnessy was horrified by the chairman's unasked-for frontal attack and quickly undercut Van Horne by stating that the reporter had either misquoted Sir William or misunderstood what he had said. Hostilities there were, but he wanted to fight them in his own way, quietly and indirectly.

The war ended in July, 1907, when Shaughnessy announced the result of a fast and furious cut-and-paste operation, designed to amputate Hill at the neck. Shaughnessy had bought, leased and negotiated running rights in a jigsaw puzzle of lines, creating for the CPR a brand-new route that hopped back and forth across the border from St Paul to the Pacific Ocean.* Not only was it an attractive alternative to Hill's Great Northern, but it was actually several miles shorter. At Spokane the new CPR line joined with the Oregon Railroad and Navigation

---

*Once Hill folded his campaign for a cross-Canada line, Shaughnessy allowed many of the running rights and leases to expire.

Company, which presented the possibility of tapping the lucrative San Francisco market. "For the present it certainly looks as if the C.P.R. has said 'check' to J. J. Hill in the big game on the railway chessboard," commented one newspaper with finality. ". . . It is getting to be an axiom in railway circles that he must be an early riser who catches the C.P.R. napping."[37] It was an ingenious coup, and ironically, precisely what Van Horne had in mind when he bought the Duluth and Winnipeg in 1893.

It was the final confrontation in an epic war that had lasted twenty-four years. Old and familiar adversaries, the CPR and J. J. Hill retreated to their respective corners, laying to rest the longest and, at times, bitterest international conflict in the history of railroading. Interestingly, despite years of animosity, he and his old foe Van Horne had always respected each other. "When I damn you or him for your numerous sins, as, unhappily, you give me frequent occasion to do, I beg to assure you that you are damned in a strictly official sense," Van Horne had written to Hill's general manager Allen Manvel more than two decades before.[38] That sentiment remained unchanged.

So massive was Hill's empire that it took him years to arrange succession in the three major lines he controlled, the Great Northern, the Northern Pacific and the Chicago, Burlington and Quincy. In 1912 he finally relinquished control of the Great Northern, his "great adventure," to his son Louis. The twilight was as unappealing to him as it was to his restless old foe, Van Horne, and Hill promptly bought two banks with the aim of creating a new and better credit system for the country's beleaguered and always debt-ridden farmers. It was his rapidly growing banking influence that put Hill in the centre of a 1915 loan to the Allies, breaking the U.S. neutrality. He collected paintings, some of them recommended by Van Horne, made speeches and played the role of railroading's grand old man, parcelling out sage advice to the managers of his far-flung enterprise. Then on May 29, 1916, after days of racking pain from untreated hæmorrhoids, J. J. Hill died. The Canadian farm boy had helped shape the destiny of America and in the process amassed a fortune of $50 million, making him one of the richest men in the world.

BY 1910 SHAUGHNESSY WAS AT THE PINNACLE of his career. Widely believed to be the most powerful man in the country, he conferred with heads of state around the world and travelled frequently to Ottawa to discuss important and confidential matters with the government. "In his general appearance," wrote one newspaperman, "Sir Thomas was the incarnation of prosperous big business. In nearly twenty years' reporting around the Canadian Pacific depot, and later about the Royal Alexandra Hotel, I met no Eastern banker, railway executive, manufacturer, statesman, or other who seemed to personify and embody what is known as the business power of the East as he did."[39]

Other reporters drew a less flattering but even more invincible portrait:

> It was unofficially believed that the head of CPR was somehow over-lord to governments. Shaughnessy, the impenetrable, the aloof, was more sacrosanct than the premier of Canada. He was not the agent of a democracy but an emperor. He had a counterpart in Japan. The Orientalism which Van Horne infused into the system even while he laughed it out of court, was solemnly accepted by the man who came after. But it was the Orientalism of efficiency.
>
> Shaughnessy was its symbol. Away from it he was of little consequence. . . . Within it he was mighty. He felt himself the apex of a thing that knew no provincial boundaries. . . . He was the great human rubber stamp. He had extra power. He lived on fiats and papal bulls. Men learned to tremble at his nod. . . . And as governments came up and capsized in the storms of public sentiment, the great system went on, in its sullen but splendid way a sort of solar system in which parties and governments gravitated.[40]

As Shaughnessy's power mounted, his image softened and mellowed. Once knife-sharp and clear-cut, it became smoother, almost as if he'd consciously gone over himself with a large eraser, buffing corners and easing angles. Even the harsh and forbidding physical features cooperated. An ailment that was to leave him almost blind drooped the outside edges of his eyes, removing their menacing glare and giving him a genial, grandfatherly air. The great, grey sprout of whiskers above and below his lips lent a friendly-old-man feeling to his face which he seemed to encourage by smiling more frequently than before.

Writers began to sprinkle their articles with adjectives like "kindly," "generous" and "warm-hearted." "He is the best of masters, because he never forgets a good servant," gushed writer William Blakemore. "He is a kindly man, indeed in this respect he resembles many others whose apparent brusqueness is but a cloke [sic] for geniality. The number of those who could tell of his benefactions could not be counted by the hundred, perhaps not by the thousand."[41]*

There was only one shadow darkening the glow of Shaughnessy's achievements, but it was one of immense size and persistence. William Van Horne came to the Canadian Pacific a legend, and left it a hero of Homeric dimensions. In 1910, eleven years after he had resigned, prominent statesmen and business leaders still wrote to him as if he were the president. Though Shaughnessy was treated with deference and respect in England, Van Horne was lionized, particularly by the press, who saluted him as an adventurer. Even after he stepped down as chairman in 1910 Van Horne was seen as the company's spokesman.

Shaughnessy professed great admiration for Van Horne,

---

*But not everyone forgot the man who walked through the CPR's doors in 1882. D. C. Coleman, later a president himself, felt compelled to correct the sentimental revisions of Shaughnessy's image in a 1936 speech to the Montreal Officers' Luncheon Club.

I know that here in our family circle you would not ask me to indulge in unmixed eulogy. Lord Shaughnessy had some peculiarities which might be described as faults. Occasionally he rebuked them in scolding terms in the presence of subordinates and their friends, forgetting that a wound so administered is one which heals slowly. That was not due to any unkindness of heart, because he was capable of great tenderness, but to a vehement nature and to a high-spirited temperament. An Irishman is one who for ever mourns over the irretrievable past, yearns for the unattainable future, but despises the impossible present. That is not exactly true of Lord Shaughnessy who had a very logical mind, but he so often looked for the impossible in himself, and in others. (Coleman, "Lord Shaughnessy, K.C.V.O." Address to Officers' Luncheon Club, Montreal, March 18, 1936)

though occasionally he let slip his irritation at being undercut by the monumental figure. Magnanimously allowing that "too much cannot be said in appreciation of the marvellous construction work that Mr. Van Horne accomplished between the time that he became general manager and the completion of the line in 1886," Shaughnessy portrayed Van Horne's work as that of an admirable and energetic — if none too bright — plough-horse, accomplishing prodigious physical feats. He derided Van Horne's "spirit of boyish self-adulation, boastfulness and extravaganza . . . and I fear that no one who knew him would charge him with diplomacy . . . it is to be regretted that he took so much to himself and failed to give due credit to the Managers of Construction and the men engaged in the operation of completed mileage, who contributed so much to his success, and without whose active cooperation he would have been helpless." Shaughnessy also attacked his business acumen: "His associates in all these enterprises, as well as in the larger railway projects, would be inclined to say that success only came after Van Horne relinquished active participation in the business management."[42]

So intensely did Shaughnessy hold his grudge against Van Horne that he elicited a promise from D. C. Coleman, vice-president of western lines, to redress the balance at some point in his life.[43]

The vehemence of Shaughnessy's opinions about Van Horne would have shocked many colleagues. Tough and inscrutable, he rarely let the passionate side of his nature show. His private life was another thing entirely. It wasn't so much that he was a different man away from the office, but fuller and more rounded. For diversions he liked his solitaire and visits to the symphony. As he grew older and wealthier, his one indulgence was the sport his father adored, horse racing. He joined the Montreal Jockey Club shortly after it was formed and imported a highly touted mare named "Silk Hose." The unfortunate beast became a laughing stock during its brief career. After one particularly inauspicious race, with Silk Hose running at least thirty lengths in the rear, Charles M. Hays, president of the Grand Trunk Railway, slyly remarked, "That's a fast mare you have, Shaughnessy."

"Yes," snapped back Shaughnessy, "she's about as fast as a Grand Trunk train."[44]

SHAUGHNESSY WAS DEVOTED to two things in life, the CPR and his family. He didn't have the same kind of rigid attitude toward his children that Van Horne did, and when his youngest son, Fred, decided to try his hand at working for the company, Shaughnessy agreed. But Fred soon learned he had a tough slog ahead of him. "It's awful to be the president's son," he complained to George Ham. "Of course, I don't mind obeying the rules and regulations of the company and I work the same hours as anybody else, but hang it all, it's a constant complaint that I am favored because I am the president's son, when perhaps, I am favored less than the others. Why, father wouldn't allow it. I am going to quit."[45] And he did.

The tragedy of Shaughnessy's life was the loss of that same son, Fred, who died in France in 1916. "How rapidly the heartbroken father had aged, and how sympathetically he grasped my hand, and with tear-dimmed eyes recalled memories of the dear boy,"[46] George Ham wrote.

Shaughnessy's oldest son, William, became a lawyer and eventually a King's Counsel. He, too, discovered that his connection to Canada's most influential man was not a guarantee of either wealth, power, respect or happiness. On June 26, 1918, he wrote a sad letter from the Front to his wife:

My dearest Chicklets:

So far the position I occupy and my connection with a great railroad have not been exactly advantageous, the whole effort having been to squash me and my ambitions and keep them squashed.[47]

Shaughnessy was instrumental throughout the war, coordinating transportation and turning over the company's shops for the manufacture of tanks and other weapons. The conscription debate is also indelibly stamped with his soundly reasoned arguments against the legislation.

Lord Shaughnessy with his wife, Elizabeth, and daughter, Marguerite

The culmination of Shaughnessy's life ambitions came with his appointment to the peerage in 1916. On the day he was to take his seat in the House of Lords, he worked his normal hours, sitting as erectly as ever at a temporary desk in the CPR's Charing Cross office. Promptly at 3:30 P.M. he left to meet Lord Northcliffe and Lord MacDonnell, his sponsors, for the induction ceremonies. By 5:30 he was back at his desk.

As the war drew to a close, Shaughnessy, burdened by the loss of his son and by his eye ailment, turned over the presidency of the CPR to a young and eager successor, Edward Beatty, retaining the position of chairman. Inside, Shaughnessy was grief-stricken and frustrated by his infirmity but outwardly he appeared to go on as before. He shocked an audience during a Montreal speech by confessing he was unable to see them and Lord Mount Stephen was appalled to discover he was virtually blind. Nonetheless, Shaughnessy put in as many hours at his Montreal desk as he could and kept to his regular habit of half a bottle of icy champagne at lunch. He became deeply involved in Irish affairs and in 1920, rumours placed him as a possible governor general of Ireland. He denied the suggestion but worked hard to prevent the establishment of an "absolutely insane" Irish republic.[48] Every summer he and Lady Shaughnessy moved their household to Fort Tipperary in St Andrews, where they continued to entertain frequently in the Fort's cavernous rooms.

Shaughnessy died as he had lived the greater part of his life, in the service of the CPR. On Saturday, December 8, 1923, the seventy-year-old chairman put in a full day at Windsor Station and commented to a fellow officer how well he felt before he went home. The next day he had a heart attack while eating dinner, and on December 10, 1923, he died. It was probably the only time in over forty years that the CPR did not get at least a full day's work out of him.

Thomas Shaughnessy had accomplished all and more than any man could ask: a magnificent enterprise spanning the globe, a peerage and the respect of the Empire's most prominent men. Yet even on his deathbed, the company loomed larger than the man himself. "Maintain the property," were his last words, spoken, not to his wife or child, but to his successor, Edward Beatty.[49]

CHAPTER 10

THE YOUNGEST BARON

*"He told me that some day, if I worked hard, I might amount to something, which was news to me —
I had never heard it before."*

— Edward Beatty, remembering
one of his schoolteachers

I n 1912 Edward Beatty, only thirty-five years old, sat firmly in the cat bird seat. As chief counsel of the CPR, he was the third most powerful man in the company and one of the favourites to succeed Sir Thomas Shaughnessy. The presidency had been Beatty's goal from the beginning, and he relentlessly drove himself upward, achieving in only eleven years what many talented and experienced executives had failed to accomplish in a lifetime. But Beatty, on the verge of achieving his dream, fell victim to the wracking doubts and corrosive uncertainties always lurking behind his supremely confident façade, and he considered abandoning his quest. W. N. Tilley, the principal of one of Canada's most eminent law firms, had offered him a partnership in Toronto, and Beatty was about to accept.

Late one evening, when the executive wing had emptied out, Shaughnessy uncharacteristically walked to Beatty's door and beckoned him into his own nearby office. There the president poured two stiff scotches from his hidden liquor cabinet and launched into one of his much-feared interrogations. Somehow Shaughnessy had caught the scent of Beatty's intentions, and after a series of rapid-fire questions, forced him to admit his plans.

Beneath Shaughnessy's carefully cultivated rubber-stamp image lay a sensitive judge of character. Ever since Beatty walked into Windsor Station, he had been watching and assessing the handsome young man now sitting in front of him like an alarm clock wound half again too much. Instead of appealing to Beatty's company loyalty or complimenting him on his success, Shaughnessy narrowed his eyes and stared penetratingly at him. "What's the matter? Don't you want to become president some day?" he demanded in the tone of one who had unexpectedly uncovered a serious character flaw. Puffing out his considerable chest and jutting his jaw, Beatty rose to the lure, "Goddamit I do!"

Six years later, six days after his forty-first birthday, Edward

Edward Beatty

Wentworth Beatty became the company's youngest and first Canadian-born president. His twenty-five-year tenure — the longest in the company's history* — was radically different from the almost unbroken prosperity of the Shaughnessy years. Beatty's reign began and ended with world wars, and in between he had to cope with dramatic economic swings and the ominous spectre of a new and powerful competitor. J. J. Hill was gone, but the Canadian National Railway Co. more than took his place. Also confronting Beatty was the juggernaut of government regulation, hitherto merely an irritating whine in the ear of the CPR overlord.

To most, Edward Beatty appeared to be a man blessed. Independently wealthy† and with a movie star's good looks, he quickly became one of the best known and most influential figures of his generation. He dominated not only railroading but academe too, ruling McGill University as chancellor for twenty-three years. Throughout his life he gave away millions to various charities and causes, including handouts to a legion of hard-luck cases and just about every dreamer in the country with a crack-pot scheme to peddle. Yet, for all the trappings of success, there lingered in the man a sense of bleak unhappiness, still palpable in his letters and public statements, though they are half a century old.

To intimates he was Eddie or Ned, a boisterous, fun-loving companion with the mud of a rugby match not long gone from his clothes. But to colleagues and subordinates he was a dictator with little time for banter. He concealed his uncertainty and self-doubt beneath a cloak of power and arrogance. Though charismatic, Beatty loathed public appearances. He could be disarming in small groups, but frequently spoiled first impressions with awkward and rude statements. A stunningly handsome man and easily the most eligible Canadian

---

*Beatty became president in 1918 and chairman in 1924. He held the dual posts until 1942 and retained the chairmanship until his death the following year.

†Beatty was the last CPR president to have a substantial holding in the company, thanks to an estate of several million dollars in investments and property willed to him by his father.

bachelor of his time, he never married, and doubts about his sexuality exist to this day.

Competitiveness pushed him quickly to the top, but he had difficulty controlling it. Normally a shrewdly cautious man, he couldn't resist challenges to his authority, nor was he capable of changing course when defeat stared him in the face. Beatty's destructive determination led him into battle — really a fight to the death — with Sir Henry Thornton, head of the Canadian National Railways. Theirs became a highly pub-licized business feud that drove both companies to the brink of ruin.

MUCH OF EDWARD BEATTY'S CONTRADICTORY CHARACTER can be traced back to a childhood spent in the shadow of a domi-neering and inflexible father. Henry Beatty, a harsh and un-compromising Scot born in 1824 and raised in Cootehill, County Cavan, Ireland, projected unrelenting severity — from his thick bull neck, glaring eyes and square jaw to his close-cropped hair and Kaiser moustache.[1] The Beattys were tenaciously ambitious men, but Henry's aspirations developed slowly. His two brothers, William and James, emigrated first, settling in southern Ontario. Although he didn't appear to have any particular medical qualifications, William set up as a physician while speculating in land and acquiring sawmills. Eventually, he came to own virtually all of what is now Parry Sound, Ontario.[2] The second brother, James, assisted William with his sizeable investments. Together they formed the Northern Navigation Company, which put the first major fleet of wooden-hulled, sail-powered freighters on the Great Lakes.

In 1834 they sent for their ten-year-old brother, Henry, who arrived to the comfortable life William and James had created in a remarkably short time. Once he left school, Henry kicked around with no particular goal, eventually drifting to St Paul, where he found work as a hardware store clerk — and, incidentally, met the young J. J. Hill. In 1861, thirty-seven-year-old Henry was finally galvanized by the throng heading for the California gold fields. He worked a few claims before realizing that a surer route to fortune lay in supplying other prospectors with equipment, so he opened a hardware store. Still restless, he gave that up in 1863 to join the great trek north to the Yale gold fields in British Columbia, and this time his Tinker claim* in Williams Creek hit pay dirt. Unlike many of the gold-besotted men who made fortunes then lost them by not knowing when to quit, Henry packed it in quickly, returning triumphantly to Ontario with $40,000 in his pocket.

By then William and James had purchased a shipping line and used it to form the North-West Transportation Company (known as the Beatty Line) which soon became the foremost carrier on Lake Superior. Henry, now settled in Thorold, Ontario, and respectably wealthy in his own right, became the operating partner, quickly making a number of innovations, including converting the line from wooden to iron hulls. Henry had a surprising flair for salesmanship, making friends in key places and garnering contracts that had long been the preserve of other lines. When Mackenzie undertook to build part of the Pacific railway, he awarded Beatty a hefty contract — and the work didn't dry up when Macdonald came back into power in 1878.

After George Stephen formed the CPR syndicate and committed the company to the route along the north shore of Lake Superior, his most pressing concern was the assurance of a secure supply and passenger service from the railhead at Algoma Mills to Port Arthur's Landing. The Beatty Line provided it. So crucial was it that Van Horne easily convinced the board to buy out the Beatty interests in 1882 and make Henry manager of Great Lakes Transportation.† Stephen offered him a full partnership in the CPR syndicate but Beatty

---

*This is the only evidence that Henry had a sense of humour. In Scotland and the north of Ireland "tinker" described gypsies, itinerant beggars and clumsy oafs.

†Beatty's first duty was to go to Scotland to supervise the finishing of the half-completed 2,300-ton steel passenger and cargo steamers, the *Athabasca*, the *Alberta* and the *Algoma*. They landed in Montreal in October, where they were cut in half to allow them to pass through the St Lawrence canals, then towed to Buffalo and rejoined.

demurred, possibly influenced by Hill's misgivings. However, when shares were sold to insiders at the discounted price of $25, he snapped up a thousand of them. Henry retired from CPR service in 1894 but kept his hand in as the company's marine underwriter.

Henry had married Harriet M. Powell, a relative of the storied Massey family, in 1869. Their first child died at three months and the next, Gordon, was a delicate boy who could neither hear nor speak. The official family line attributed Gordon's disabilities to a childhood fever, but family friends believed he was retarded. Obsessively private, the Beattys kept him cloistered and the secret so well hidden that most had no idea he even existed. Gordon died in 1923, but even during his lifetime official CPR biographies omitted Gordon's name from Edward's family tree. Henry, called Harry, was third born, Mary came next and on October 16, 1877, Edward himself, affectionately called Ned by his brother and sister. Though the three of them were attractive, personable, intelligent and rich, none of them ever married. A persistent rumour attributed this odd circumstance to a pact they had made to remain childless out of fear that Gordon's retardation was hereditary.

VICTORIAN IDEAS OF CHILD RAISING were often oppressively rigid, but Henry's unbending discipline was in a class by itself. He showered more warmth on his ships than he did on his offspring. Family dinners were dreary affairs with Henry carving the roast at one end of a long table in frosty silence, while at the other end his wife and children sat clustered in a hushed group. As soon as he finished, Henry folded his napkin precisely, nodded briefly to his family and strode from the room to smoke his pipe and drink his evening brandy in the solitude of his study.[3] It was only when the family heard the sound of the study door shutting that conversation began. In sharp contrast to her husband, Harriet was the essence of light and charm. Her joyful, compassionate nature offset Henry's frigid demeanour, and the children were totally devoted to her. Harry visited her nearly every weekend of her life and Edward, though he rarely wrote, made special trips to Toronto to see her even if he could stay only a few hours.

Henry Beatty laid down inflexible rules to govern the behaviour of the three young Beattys. Certain places and people were strictly off limits and they weren't allowed out after dark, even chaperoned. He forbade Mary to date young men, and any daring enough to call were quickly set to flight by Henry's stony visage. After his death, on the rare occasions Mary talked about her father, she called him Mr Beatty, in tones of fear and reverence, rather than love and respect. In one of the few comments he ever made about his father, Edward said: "[He] was a North of Irelander, and we all know that the North of Irelander is simply a glorified edition of a Scotsman, and they have many of the characteristics of the Scotch. We know that Scotsmen take their religion, their liquor and their education seriously, and of all the peoples in the world they have made the most consistent use of all three."[4]

Whatever may be said of the other two "Scotsman's characteristics," Henry did take education seriously. In fact, it was the only area in which he exercised a liberal attitude to his children. So adamant was Henry that the three receive good schooling that he moved the entire family to Toronto to give them all a broader choice. His liberalism didn't stop with boys because Mary became one of the first women to graduate from the University of Toronto.

For his sons, Henry decreed two professions: medicine and law. Harry, being the oldest, picked first, choosing medicine. He took his training at the University of Toronto and was preparing to settle into a comfortable practice when his father ordered him to England and paid for several years of postgraduate work there and in Europe. Henry was the kind of father who could easily have bred apathetic children with little initiative. Surprisingly, Harry thrived and prospered in medicine, becoming one of the most respected surgeons in Toronto. Only once did Edward allude to their prescribed careers: "My elder brother was to study law and I was to be a doctor. Then he decided to take up medicine, and I said: 'All right, I'll study law'. . . . I might have made a darned poor doctor."[5]

Of the three children Edward was the only one to show the slightest sign of rebellion against the old tartar, and it emerged in the form of an extremely uneven school career. Bouncing from one institution to another, his high school résumé includes stopovers at all the fashionable Ontario schools, including Upper Canada College, the Model School, Harbord Collegiate and Parkdale Collegiate Institute.[6] One school expelled him because his general behaviour and marks were so poor. Years later in a rare fit of eloquence about his early life, Beatty described those days: "If anyone were ever sufficiently interested to visit the halls of learning that I attended in my youth, and there to look up the records of a young fellow of the Gay Nineties known to his intimates as 'Banty Beatty' he would find nothing scrawled across the pages to make him think young Beatty was an asset to his classrooms. On the contrary. There exists, as a matter of fact, a letter from the learned principal of a prep school I attended, suggesting to my father that my personality and activities could be employed to better advantage in some other school. The firm, uncompromising characters of the principal's handwriting, in point of fact, deliberately urged my removal from his sight. And I was duly removed, to the pain of my parent. I was sent to another school, where my record was not known, for which I was very thankful. I there fell into the hands of a teacher who was one of the best teachers for boys I have ever met, though he had a very violent temper. . . . The first words of encouragement I ever received came from that man. He told me that some day, if I worked hard, I might amount to something, which was news to me — I had never heard it before."[7]

THROUGHOUT HIS LIFE BEATTY disparaged book learning as a required ingredient of success, pointing to his own failure in academe as proof. But he wasn't altogether the lazy young roustabout: he won the Governor General's Medal twice at the Model School and served as vice-president of the literary society at Harbord Collegiate. The latter is ironic, considering his later dislike of "fancy writing." In 1927 Beatty categorically told a reporter: "I never read novels," with the emphasis of a man denying some vile habit. "I can do only a certain amount of reading, and therefore I hunt for things that are useful to me."[8]

Though he'd shown flashes of academic potential in high school, Beatty only managed to "get by" at the University of Toronto. "My professors must have regarded me as amongst the Hopeless Cases, from the academic view at least. Somehow or other, I did manage to make my exit by the front door when graduation time came, but I was well down the line."[9] Beatty only scraped through because the joyous elixir of freedom and the boisterous camaraderie of his fellows intoxicated him. Diligent study paled beside hijinks like pulling trolley poles off their electric wires, eluding the police during the ensuing chases and learning "any number of excellent songs which were yelled by raucous young voices whenever opportunity offered."[10]

Distinguished by an almost overwhelming physicality and an aggressive, four-square stance, Beatty always seemed to have his fists clenched, even when they were shoved deep into his pockets. All the Beattys were tightly wound, but Edward's spring seemed the most tautly coiled. An average, though enthusiastic, athlete, he first tried his hand at varsity baseball but found it unsatisfying. It did introduce him to his first real friend, however: Richard Greer, a young man of rather different social circumstances. Greer had learned the sport playing with patched, fraying balls and makeshift bats on dirt lots in east Toronto, and he paid for his education with savings from many odd jobs.

Baseball didn't offer the all-encompassing camaraderie or the gladiator-like outlet that Beatty craved. But rugby football did. "Advanced football as it was played . . . consisted chiefly in

Banty Beatty in his football-playing days

being rugged enough to take a varied assortment of punishments for sixty minutes and to batter holes with one's head and shoulders in something that resembled, say, a stone wall built of human beings. . . . It was a lot of fun." The sport* epitomized team play, and Beatty gloried in the close-knit unity it encouraged, the supreme maleness of it, the post-game socializing, the pranks and the willingness to submerge oneself for the side. "If I could, I would play football. And if I were not first team timber — here lies the genius of the university spirit — I would deem it a high honour to act as a tackling dummy for the men on the team and gladly allow them to romp over my recumbent form every afternoon in practice."[11]

---

*Rugby football was similar to rugby as played today, with fifteen men to a side.

Beatty was ideal rugby material: powerful and short with strong thighs and well-muscled, almost oversized shoulders, he was quick, fearless and determined. Working his way up the ranks to a regular position on the varsity seconds squad, he played one year in the Dominion final. Known as "Banty", Beatty, he was a fierce tackler, unyielding competitor and something of a cheerleader. "Oh, you fearful idiots!" was his favourite exhortation, and when things were going poorly for the side Beatty was the first to leap up and shout, "Into the fray, lads!" with renewed vigour and optimism. He seemed destined for the first team and would likely have made it except for the presence of John Wilberforce Hobbs, an amiable, fun-loving and rotund contemporary, who had a lock on the quarterback position. Hobbs, who retained his round, boyish face and happy-go-lucky manner until he died, became Beatty's closest friend.

Beatty adored his university years, remembering them as an idyllic period — the happiest of his life. There is a haunting wistfulness, a bitter edge of sadness, in his oddly lyrical reminiscences of young, fetterless joy. "My memories of college days are tender recollections of men and teachers, games and classes, sports and fun, ivy-clad halls and the bite of an autumn breeze across the campus. . . . For these vagrant fancies of memory are phases, happy mind pictures that float to the ceiling in blue clouds of tobacco smoke, the moments one recalls when other hours grow dim in the mind's eye. They are the little pranks and escapades that one talks and laughs over with one's friends of those days, just as soldier-men, getting together, thumb the pages of harmless foolishness and skip the tales of derring-do. . . . Yes, I'm glad I went to college. I wouldn't have missed it for worlds. I wish I were there this fall."[12]

Beatty remained faithful to that little coterie of sport friends and his intimate circle didn't grow much beyond them. He never turned any of them down when they approached him for favours, loans or an investment in an occasionally outlandish scheme. One friend, whom he addressed only as Freddy,

had plans to become Toronto's ice-cream king. Beatty obligingly invested $1,000 in 1921, and when that project fell
through, anted up another $1,000 to help him purchase an
"amusement boat" for tourist excursions on the lake. Unfortunately, a summer storm capsized the vessel and Freddy
retreated for a safer position in his father-in-law's shoemaking
business.[13] Beatty wrote off the loan.

When Beatty died with an estate of over $1 million, the
money his friends owed him ranged from the $375 he had lent
a university roommate, A. L. Caron, sixteen years earlier to
$67,599.29 for John Hobbs. The original loan of $39,000 had
been made on January 5, 1928, fifteen years before. Not a
penny of principal had been paid, and interest to the tune of
$28,599.29 had accumulated. But none of it was ever collected,
as Beatty forgave all loans in his will. During his life he frequently paid his own lawyers to settle legal matters for his
buddies and he would go to considerable lengths to do them
favours. When John Hobbs declared bankruptcy in the
mid-1930s, Beatty approached creditors on his behalf and
organized his debts so the banks wouldn't seize his house. But
his generosity did not extend to CPR business. During Hobbs's
bankruptcy Beatty invited him to New York for an important
railroad function and the two shared a suite of rooms at the
Waldorf-Astoria Hotel. Upon his return, the president billed
his friend for $32.18 for his share of the room, breakfast and
valet service because the trip was on the company's tab.

AFTER BEATTY GRADUATED from the University of Toronto in
1898, he enrolled at Osgoode Hall, the country's most prestigious law school. But even at this point, he had no burning
ambition for any particular career. The final decision between
business and law was made, according to Beatty, "with the toss
of a coin!"[14] He did try at least one other profession, journalism, and newspaperman Hector Charlesworth recalled meeting Beatty when he "was 'subbing' for a reporter in Toronto."[15]
The flirtation with journalism was short-lived, however, and

Edward's father still had a strong influence on him, so after law school, Beatty chose to article with the powerful Toronto firm of McCarthy, Osler, Hoskin, and Creelman. Long associated with the CPR, Osler was also Henry Beatty's personal lawyer, and they had many joint investments.*

In June, 1901, Beatty was called to the Ontario Bar. That same year CPR hired Creelman as general solicitor and he asked his young assistant to move to Montreal for a year to help him set up the firm's business there. The salary was $50 a month and Beatty was to be paid by the firm, not the railway. Through a mix-up Beatty's name was added to the CPR's wage rolls, a fact that irritated him because he didn't want to work for a big, staid corporation, especially at only $50 a month. Creelman convinced him to stay and assured him that the salary would improve. To his surprise, Beatty discovered that he actually enjoyed the work.

Friends were astonished at the transformation of the sheltered, fun-loving and carefree Eddie. Beatty lived at a Mrs Cassidy's boarding house on Sherbrooke Street West, among a group of young blades, the same kind of men he'd revelled with at university. But after dinner, while his pals departed for drinks or played cards by the fire, Beatty stayed in his room, poring over his work, checking his briefs and making sure he was ready for any conceivable question his superiors might ask.

---

*The Oslers were among the most prominent and powerful of Ontario families. Britton Bath Osler was "internationally recognized as the peer of any pleader in the world." (Charlesworth, *Candid Chronicles*, p. 214) In his first major case, he represented the Crown in pressing for an indictment of Louis Riel in 1885. His most notorious case — and a sensation in the international media — was the successful prosecution of Reginald Birchall in 1890, an Oxford graduate who devised a novel way of raising money: luring naïve young Britishers to Canada with grand talk of a glorious farming career, then killing them and pocketing their money.

Sir William Osler, a well-known physician and professor at Johns Hopkins University, was the victim of one of the most famous cases of "fake journalism." The story, of unknown origin, stated that Sir William believed all men and women should commit suicide at the age of sixty. The story was reprinted far and wide, and try as he might, Osler, who had a considerable number of relatives in their nineties, was never able to correct the impression it left. The oldest brother, Featherstone Osler, became chief justice of Ontario.

Another young CPR lawyer, E. P. Flintoft, who later became the company's general solicitor, dreaded Beatty's late-night work habits. The telephone, still a rarity, was mounted in the unheated hall of the boarding house where he was living. When it rang he had to leave his warm quarters to stand at the phone, shivering miserably and answering Beatty's persistent questions about some legal matter. During his first few years with the CPR, Beatty occasionally crossed paths with yet another young CPR lawyer, who was fast with quips and tough, unkind remarks about those he disliked or distrusted. Beatty enjoyed this abrasive, transparently ambitious man and dubbed him R. Buckshot Bennett. When he became prime minister in 1930, R. B. Bennett was one of Beatty's few close political friends.*

At Windsor Station Beatty shared his office with Miss Kate Treleaven, Creelman's secretary and the unconquerable guardian of his door. He disliked her on sight and privately vowed to fire "that woman" at the first opportunity.[16] Four years later, in 1905, when he was appointed assistant solicitor, Beatty finally had his chance, but by then Treleaven was guarding his door, as she would for the next thirty-eight years.

Beatty's appetite for work grew ferociously and his promotions came in rapid succession,† all the more remarkable, since it was a time when young men were advised to avoid the CPR as

---

*Bennett was one of the many CPR officers to run afoul of Bob Edwards, publisher of the deliciously scandalous and frequently fabricated articles in the Calgary *Eyeopener*. The *Eyeopener* was a legendary publication that had mastered the art of the concocted story, so beloved at the time. For some slight, Bennett, as CPR's western solicitor, ordered that the *Eyeopener* be banned from all company trains and stations, which were important sources of revenue for a small-circulation newspaper. Edwards retaliated by running a series of increasingly gory CPR train wreck stories — all of them sheer invention. Edwards struck his final blow by running a picture of Bennett underneath the headline, "Another CPR Train Wreck." Shortly afterwards, the *Eyeopener* was once again sold on the CPR.

†Beatty was named general solicitor in 1910 and chief counsel in 1914. In January, 1916, he was made a vice-president and elected to the board, and the following October he obtained a position on the powerful executive committee. Not long afterwards, on October 10, 1918, he became president.

a company where advancements were slow. But more important even than the stream of titles that followed him through
his seventeen years in the legal department was the fact that he
caught the attention of gimlet-eyed Thomas Shaughnessy.

George Bury, a talented man of vaulting ambition who had
been with the CPR since 1883, believed he was heir to the
crown, especially after Shaughnessy made him vice-president
and general manager of the entire company in 1914 — then,
and now, the last stop before the presidency. But Shaughnessy

Kate Treleaven

had sized up Bury as far back as 1890, and found him wanting. "If you see Bury on your return trip I think it would be well to give him a word or two of caution," he wrote to Van Horne. "The circumstances as reported to me of a fight that he had with one of his brakemen a few days ago are not to his credit, and are not calculated to raise him into the esteem of his men. I learn that he has acted rather hastily too, and without consultation, in suspending the rule relating to no other train following an express between stations, even though, as he explains, it was necessary for the despatch of business, he should not have done it without advising his General Superintendent. I feel that in his anxiety to make a record, he has slopped over a little."[17]

Shaughnessy liked hard-working men, but Bury's ambitions were just a little too raw for him. Beatty, on the other hand, had all Bury's qualities without visibly lusting after the presidency. In 1918, when Shaughnessy announced he had chosen the forty-one-year-old Beatty to become president, Bury was beside himself. He had spent four years in the key position of vice-president and general manager and it was an embarrassment and an insult to be passed over. What's more, he had recently turned down a lucrative offer of a position as general manager of the Chicago, Rock Island and Pacific Railroad.*

When Bury received the news of Beatty's promotion, he stormed out of his office, slamming the door so ferociously that the glass shattered and the sound reverberated up and down the entire executive wing of Windsor Station. Proud and vain, he resigned immediately, citing ill health as the reason. Rumour had it that Shaughnessy approved a large retirement bonus, though the former vice-president had at least ten years of service left. Of course, the fifty-two-year-old Bury wasn't sick; he just resented losing the job and had no intention of

---

*The Chicago, Rock Island and Pacific was held up twice by the Jesse James gang, in 1873 and 1881. But management didn't hold the grudge for long. When James was shot and killed in 1882, the line hooked up a special train to transport his body and the funeral party to Nebraska for the burial.

The CPR boardroom, about 1915.
Shaughnessy is seated third from left.
George Bury and Edward Beatty are to his right.

serving under a younger and less seasoned man. He was knighted in 1919 for his war work and eventually retired to Vancouver, where he spent many days hunkered down in a favourite chair in the Vancouver Club, drinking and cursing the CPR for its latest stupidity. For the first five years of Beatty's presidency, Bury plagued him with long, sharply worded letters of advice concerning everything from the latest promotion to budget matters. During the dark days of 1921 and 1922 he harped endlessly on profits, and Beatty's "reckless" expenditures in refitting the CPR's war-torn shipping line.

CLOSE OBSERVERS WEREN'T AT ALL SURPRISED at Beatty's appointment; he clearly had Shaughnessy in his corner. But the newspapers played up Beatty's youth, and railroaders gaped at the thought of a relatively inexperienced lawyer controlling one of the largest railways in the world. A colleague, musing on the appointment, described Beatty as "a man who just the other day was a boy, and who still regards life as a game of Rugby."[18]

A month after Beatty moved into Lord Shaughnessy's office, World War I came to an end. Unofficially, Beatty had been quietly running the company for at least a year as Shaughnessy carried out his war duties, almost blind and burdened with the loss of his son. It was an extraordinarily difficult time for a new, young president to take over. The country was in disarray, and uncertainty about the future pervaded every level of the economy. In the four years following armistice, prosperity, inflation, recession and unemployment overtook each other in quick succession. Furthermore, Beatty enjoyed none of the public stature Shaughnessy had attained during the war. From the viewpoint of both industry and the public, Beatty wasn't even a railroader, just a lawyer with a recently acquired reputation for shrewd bargaining in Ottawa.

There were some desperate days ahead for Beatty, but the initial postwar buoyancy sheltered his first eighteen months, and CPR receipts increased as every spare car and ship was dedicated to transporting food and equipment to a decimated Europe, where more than 10 million soldiers had died. Gross rail revenues actually rose to $216.6 million in 1920, from $157.5 million in 1918. But Beatty well knew that the positive results were only temporary. As the revenues increased, so did operating expenses, jumping a staggering 50 percent, from $120 million to $183.4 million in two years.

The main reason for the increase was the McAdoo Award, ratified by the United States in 1918. The year before, President Woodrow Wilson had appointed his son-in-law William G. McAdoo, a prominent financier, construction engineer and politician, to the post of director general of railroads. His job was to coordinate, for the war effort, the country's $18 billion worth of rail lines, 532 in all, consisting of 366,000 miles of track. One thing he did was to authorize large pay increases to all American rail workers to compensate them for higher consumer prices after the war.[19]

McAdoo's Award could hardly be ignored in Canada, where railroad wages had already fallen far behind those in the United States. General wages in Canada had risen 47 percent between 1913 and 1917, while the CPR had boosted rates only marginally in 1916, steadfastly maintaining that without a corresponding freight-rate increase any further pay hike was impossible. Workers were becoming restive, and it wasn't long before a decision was forced on CPR management. When the details of McAdoo's decision were announced, the Canadian government pledged to follow suit. Besides, the CPR had massive holdings in the United States, particularly in the Soo Lines, and Canadian railway unions weren't about to let the company pay its workers less than those employed by the same company south of the border. Beatty had no choice. Overnight, the average 58 percent wage increase pushed costs from $2,717 a mile to $5,372, adding an additional $20 million to the company's payroll. It was depressing news for those preparing to rejoice over the CPR's $177 million gross earnings in 1919, the highest ever recorded.

Like every other railway man in the country, Beatty had expected enforced wage increases but believed that the McAdoo Award was far too high. His colleagues, including D. B. Hanna, president of the Canadian National Railways, wanted to launch a protest immediately, but Beatty's own agenda was more complicated and less immediate. He wanted to let the government and public stagger a while under the huge debt of the national railway system.

FORMED IN SEPTEMBER, 1917, when the Canadian government took over the reeling Mackenzie and Mann network, the Canadian National Railways ballooned in January, 1920, with the bitter and controversial takeover of the Grand Trunk. Consisting of 221 different railway lines, it resembled a boa constrictor after a large meal — bloated, barely ambulatory and protruding in every direction.

Debt-ridden and vilified by Grand Trunk shareholders, the

CNR was inefficient and costly to operate. Worse even than its financial affairs was morale. Labourers and executives alike were forced to work with a grab-bag of new colleagues — many of whom had been bitter competitors in previous years. In 1921 when President D. B. Hanna took the directors on a cross-country tour to meet employees, the reception was cool in many quarters. But nowhere was the atmosphere more hostile than in the Maritimes. In Moncton they found the Intercolonial Railway offices "as chilly indoors as out" and observed that the East viewed them all as western pirates. "Plainly, we were not as welcome as the flowers in May. The archangel Gabriel could not have become popular down by the sea if he had undertaken the job of co-ordinating the services of the railways which the Dominion of Canada now possessed."[20]

The new wage increases were a crippling burden to the CNR, already struggling just to stay alive. They also hurt the CPR, but that company could at least bear them for the short term. "We are becoming bound a little too tightly to American conditions," Beatty explained to journalist Charles Bishop, "but obviously this is not the time to make the break. The only way in which public support to opposition to further wage demands can be secured, is by their feeling the burden of it themselves."[21] Pointing to the spectre of strikes throughout the country, Beatty discouraged the industry from interfering with the new wages. The CPR was in good shape compared to other roads and Beatty was content to wait.

Fortunately, Canadian Pacific was superbly positioned to cope with a balance sheet that leaped and dipped like a roller coaster. Thanks to Shaughnessy's almost fanatical insistence on keeping equipment, track and structures at the highest level of performance, Beatty could cut costs by reducing maintenance levels without appreciably hurting performance or the long-term durability of the railway. Debt load was relatively small, and the company had long followed a rainy-day policy of tucking away a portion of surplus earnings for bad times.*

AS THE SERIOUSNESS OF THE ECONOMIC problems became clear in late 1920, Beatty began a vigorous program of delaying, and even eliminating, routine repairs on all parts of the line. To supplement the reduced costs resulting from extended maintenance schedules, he pressured CPR subsidiaries to increase earnings and make "daily economies." "I think you will have to make up your own mind that these continual drafts on this Company for capital will have to come to an end. In the last few years, the Consolidated Company has raised an enormous amount of money by the issue of bonds, loans from this Company and overdrafts, and notwithstanding this, its cash position is no better to-day than it was some time ago," he chastised J. J. Warren, president of Consolidated Mining and Smelting Company.[22] Shades of Banty Beatty showed through as he urged senior managers to "pull together," "draw in our horns," "ensure the company's prestige" and "honour our debt to shareholders."

Beatty's expenditure cuts affected all company operations except shipping, as the president astutely recognized this to be an area of potential growth, relatively untouched by government regulation.† Although the CPR was already in a commanding competitive position on the Atlantic and Pacific, fourteen ships had been lost during the war, and Beatty could not retain his dominance in international trade without replacements. But he had little hope of strong rail revenues for several years and was reluctant to call too frequently upon the

---

*Shaughnessy began this policy largely in reaction to what he viewed as Van Horne's bungling during the depression of the mid-nineties. He believed that if Van Horne had not spent so much money on "non-essentials" like the Soo Lines and the Duluth and Winnipeg, the CPR would have been able to pay its dividend in 1895.

†Government interference was a source of great grief to the CPR. In 1921, at the height of the recession, the Board of Railway Commissioners twice reduced rail rates.

company treasury for funds to replenish the fleet. To make matters worse, the cost of building an ocean-going vessel had more than doubled in the last ten years, and government compensation for the ships lost did not begin to pay for their replacement.

Beatty solved the problem neatly by purchasing and refitting four German liners from the Reparations Committee for a fraction of their value and using them as the basis of a new passenger service. One of them, the *Kaiserin Auguste Victoria*, had been the flagship of the Hamburg Amerika Line and the largest ship in the world when it was launched in 1906. Rarewood panelling and plush, oriental carpets, along with damask, silk and velvet upholstery, lent an aura of royal opulence to the ship. After refitting, advertisements claimed the renamed *Empress of Scotland* boasted more "private facilities" (toilets) than anything afloat. In all, Beatty spent $50 million acquiring eight passenger liners and two freighters between 1919 and 1922.*

New equipment demanded new business, and Beatty, who despised complacency, lectured his various department heads constantly on the subject, as if ruination were just around the corner. "I am still not satisfied that our soliciting agents are sufficiently aggressive after business. . . . I am convinced we

---

*During the war 52 CPR ships had been used as armed merchant cruisers, troop transports and freighters by the British Admiralty. Of that 52, 12 were sunk by mines, torpedoes and shelling, and 2 others were lost through marine accident. Five were converted into mock battleships in one of the most amusing stories of the war. Winston Churchill, Britain's First Lord of the Admiralty, dreamed up the idea of disguising merchant ships as battleships and having them accompany convoys to confuse the Germans and give them a false notion of British strength.

The five ships were meticulously converted. All cargo hoists and derricks were removed and replaced by an imposing wood and canvas superstructure, complete with threatening-looking wooden twelve-inch guns. There were nice touches, such as six huge anchors replacing the two original smaller ones and twin rows of portholes along the side where none had previously existed.

The special squadron was completed for duty in May, 1915. Unfortunately, the dummy battleships, which had a top speed of only eight knots, couldn't keep up with real battleships, which routinely steamed in the twenty-knot range. What's more, the plywood superstructure had a tendency to buckle and cave in the wind. The squadron was essentially useless, and by September, 1915, had been cast aside.

are losing competitive traffic which we should not lose and that the reports of your Division officers in this respect are not accurate," he pointedly observed to his general manager, W. R. MacInnes.[23] Beatty's tough missives left no doubt as to the seriousness of his opinions, but they lacked the rapier edge of similar Shaughnessy communications, which tended to wound rather than simply instruct.

BEATTY WAS OFTEN ACCUSED of having little interest in the worries of the common worker, but in a number of small ways he showed that he felt something for their plight, particularly during the trying period of postwar inflation. He instituted a suggestion box and offered small rewards for any idea that would cut costs. To improve morale, he also ordered staff quarters to be spruced up in hotels and stations, but oddly, on his beloved ships, he turned down a request for softer mattresses to replace the ancient pre-war ones on the grounds that "we are not in the business to make our crews comfortable."[24]

The compassion he felt for working men and women rarely reached their ears or hearts but if any were treated to a personal interview, they never forgot the warmth of his broad smile — he almost never laughed — which softened even a dressing down. Grant Hall, a vice-president during Beatty's reign, was fond of telling a story about the president's attitude to chopping expenses during his first few years on the job. Hall had been instructed to formulate cost-cutting recommendations and he responded by bringing in a list of men who could be fired without affecting the efficiency of repair work. With the list in his hand, Beatty walked over to his window and took a long look at the vicious Montreal blizzard buffeting passersby on the street below. "This is a helluva day to let men out, Grant," he said. "Let's forget it."[25]

But that was as close as any of Beatty's employees got to his softer side. Only rarely did cracks ever show in the stern and impenetrable façade he erected around himself. Aloofness surrounded him "like an aura, indefinable, unobtrusive, but always there," observed one of the few writers to comment on what everyone felt. "On the railway platform, in the hotel lounge, even when he is relaxed in his room, the atmosphere never leaves him. It says, 'thus far and no farther shalt thou go.'"[26]

With close friends, however, the president dropped his guard sufficiently to let loose the Banty Beatty of varsity days. He collected his friends' weaknesses and chided them for their follies, sometimes throughout their entire lives, but always with an endearing, gentle humour. When William Allison, a professor in Toronto, ventured into a mine for the sake of an article he was writing, he was struck by a falling rock and confined to bed for several days. Beatty heard of the incident and wrote, "I am glad, however, that the cause of some of your physical disabilities (exclusive of your mental troubles, which, I presume, are permanent) is removed. A shoemaker should stick to his last, and a clergyman, a professor and a writer should be fully enough occupied without going into the gravel pit business."[27]

Beatty maintained an unapproachable and remote manner to protect his insecure and lonely side, and one of the tools he used to guard his privacy was Kate Treleaven. Face to face, Beatty had little defence against the sad-eyed, bereft or unfortunate. In contrast, Treleaven positively revelled in icily dismissing potential interlopers. CPR oldtimers still describe the formidable woman as a cranky, fire-breathing dragon. In fact, she was quite attractive as a young woman, and when she let something resembling a smile cross her habitually grim countenance, she could be quite appealing. One octogenarian, who was an office boy at the time, claims that the only time he ever saw Treleaven smile was in 1933, when Beatty's rival, Sir Henry Thornton, former president of the CNR, died.

Treleaven was so daunting even vice-presidents hesitated before requesting an interview. After an initial searching screening, she ushered the supplicant into a small meeting room adjacent to Beatty's office and gestured to a chair at one end of a large, absolutely clear table. Treleaven reminded the individual that he or she had fifteen minutes precisely, stating when the appointment would begin and end to the minute. (Beatty divided his office hours into quarter-hour intervals.) To emphasize the point, she indicated a large, ticking clock mounted directly opposite. At the appointed time, nearly to the second, Beatty would burst through the doorway, utter a gruff hello in his deep voice and sit at the far end of the table. Without the slightest pleasantry, discussion of the business at hand began, and at the end of the interview Treleaven ostentatiously opened the door and stood, pointedly holding it open, until the interviewee left.

Treleaven worshipped Beatty with the kind of ardour born only of unrequited love. And though their relationship was clearly platonic, a touching symbiosis existed between them. Treleaven doted on Beatty, organizing his life from office to home, even decorating the Pine Avenue house he purchased in 1922. Austere and practical, she allowed not a shred of frivolity from attic to cellar, and by the time she was finished with it, the place looked more like an officer's quarters in a military barracks than a home. In return for her devotion, Beatty tolerated her idiosyncrasies, permitting her, for instance, to bring her tatty, undersized Scottie to work. Each morning, with the dog tucked beneath her arm (no one ever saw the animal walk on its own), she boarded the trolley near her home on Percival Avenue, arriving in front of Windsor Station at precisely 8:42. During the day the dog reposed beneath her desk and she left twice to permit the creature to relieve itself (no one ever saw this either). One morning a new conductor had the effrontery to forbid her to travel with a dog. Furious, Treleaven marched off to phone Beatty, and the next day she boarded the trolley as usual. The conductor was never seen on that run again.

Beatty's treatment of Kate Treleaven was unique in the company and she garnered not a little resentment for being able to deviate from the rigid rules originally laid down by Shaughnessy. Staff were permitted several visits to the bathroom every day, but the times were staggered among the departments to avoid line-ups and loss of work time. Casual use of typewriters and telephones, even after hours, was strictly forbidden. Treleaven, however, went to the ladies room whenever she pleased and treated the typewriters and telephones as if they were her own personal property.

BY 1921 BEATTY WAS HIP DEEP in his first major economic crisis. That year saw the highest number of commercial failures since 1915 and the absorption of the Merchant Bank of Canada by the Bank of Montreal. Canada's net debt of $2.3 billion was ten times the pre-war figure, and the general manager of the Bank of Montreal placed the blame squarely in the lap of railways and railway policy. "We must pay the penalty of having mortgaged our future in the building of superfluous railways...,"[28] he gloomily warned, pointing to the crippling debts rung up by Grand Trunk and Canadian Northern during the construction frenzy between 1900 and 1913. For all the depressing economic news, Beatty managed to hang onto the CPR's profits. The 1922 annual report, which could have been disastrous, allowed for the payment of the company's regular dividend and all the fixed charges, and even permitted an increase in the rainy-day surplus from $4.4 million to $4.8 million.

As Beatty pushed cautiously forward, he could feel the new government railway system breathing hotly down his neck. Extremely competitive, and incensed at government meddling in an area in which he felt it patently did not belong, Beatty despised the national railroad as much for what it represented as for the trouble it gave the CPR. No sooner had Shaughnessy handed over the crown than Beatty began his twenty-five-year campaign against the system. "Next to the war itself there is no question so important in its effect upon the earning power and prosperity of Canadians as the question of further government ownership of railways," he told a *Financier* reporter, adding his memorable comment, "Nationalise in haste, repent at leisure."[29]

While Hanna ran the national railway, relations between the

two roads were relatively free of direct conflict, largely because neither Hanna nor the CNR presented a real threat to either Beatty or the CPR. Astutely assessing his difficult position, Hanna, a highly experienced railroad man, concentrated on digesting the mass of new lines and building up his company's freight business in areas it already controlled, rather than competing for either passengers or freight on the CPR's own turf. Moreover, he was frankly worshipful of the younger man. "One's pride in President Beatty," he enthused in his 1924 memoirs, "as a man who adorns his profession, and dignifies every phase of Canadian achievement he touches is the gratification of a competitor as well as the appreciation of a colleague . . . his countrymen will have abundant cause to honour him without waiting for his absence to direct attention to the value of his presence."[30]*

Beatty treated his far more experienced colleague in a friendly but patronizing manner, often assuming a condescending tone in their numerous discussions, and dismissing any half-hearted effort Hanna made to compete with the CPR as a travesty of good business. According to Beatty, the CNR's attempts to compete were so unsuccessful that Hanna was reduced to pressuring potential customers in order to procure their freight. "We are being met with very unfair methods of competition by the National Railways," he complained to Sir John Eaton, head of the great merchandising empire. "They are prepared to make purchases for their railroad in consideration of agreements to ship exclusively via the National Railways. In other words, they purchase their goods on condition that they will get most of the traffic which the seller has to give. They are also urging that because the National Railways are owned by the people, the business interests should ship via their lines in order to decrease their deficits and therefore lessen the taxes to be paid by the individual citizen . . . this is not competition but an appeal to sentiment."[31]

---

*Interestingly, Hanna mentioned not a word about his own successor, Henry Thornton.

Beatty fought back by lighting a fire of pride in the CPR ranks, his aim being to defeat sentimental appeals by the CNR with superior service. He organized a secret service to investigate the freight accounts of the government's line. "I would like you to have a most careful canvas made from one end of the System to the other,"[32] he instructed vice-president W. R. MacInnes.

Hanna had no taste for the public spotlight and he was quite content to run his road and let Beatty be the primary spokesman for the industry. If he had remained as president, Beatty might well have been able to push him in directions of expansion and traffic that actually served the CPR. But Hanna quickly got into hot water with William Lyon Mackenzie King when he complied with a government directive and fired, in September, 1921, three workers who had campaigned for the newly elected prime minister. Mackenzie King forced Hanna to re-hire them and further harassed him with a long, searching investigation of his accounts. When Hanna cancelled a meeting at Windsor Station in November because he had to attend an out-of-town funeral, Beatty wrote, "I am very sorry indeed that you were not able to be in Montreal today and I sincerely trust that it was not your own funeral that you were attending."[33]

Hanna knew the end was nigh when he sent out a notice in the spring of 1922 forbidding railroad employees to run for political office and King immediately telegraphed a Manitoba worker to ignore the dictum. "We carried on until October, when the execution was publicly performed, and one life, at least, was appreciably lengthened,"[34] he said, not entirely in sorrow.

With Hanna gone, the search for a successor began. Many prominent names were bandied about and Sir Joseph Flavelle, chairman of the CNR board, sent out tentative feelers to the best-known railroaders in the United States. It was a difficult position to fill: the man had to be a businessman to take care of the massive debt, a competitor to ensure the line got its share of business, a diplomat to deal with the company's many bosses in the government and someone with a high enough profile to earn him industry respect and public support. Sir Henry Worth Thornton proved to be such a man. Hired in October, 1922, the big, bluff and glib American was the antithesis of Beatty, and Flavelle considered the acquisition a coup: "He is very simple and unassuming, speaks little of himself but stresses the value of team-play. Nor does he attempt to create a favourable opinion of what he may do in the future by finding fault with the present system. . . . He is an excellent mixer and has quite won the hearts of all who have met him. If he is as good in action as on dress-parade the Government has made a wise choice."[35]

BORN IN 1871 IN INDIANA, Thornton graduated from university in Pennsylvania and began his impressive railroad career in 1894 with the Pennsylvania Railroad. By 1901, he'd risen to the position of divisional superintendent and was hired away as assistant to the president of the Long Island Rail Road, which was developing into the first of the great New York commuter lines. Thornton showed a flair for short-haul passenger transportation, making the LIRR the first line in the world to convert to steel cars. It was also the first to make practical use of electricity to haul trains when it electrified a line in Brooklyn.

Impressed by Thornton's work at the LIRR, Britain's Great Eastern Railway, the largest short-haul commuter system in the world, offered him the job of general manager in 1914. It was absolutely unprecedented, a Yank running an English line, especially one who viewed the rank and file as human beings. Shortly after taking over the Great Eastern, Thornton greeted a delegation of workers' representatives who arrived unannounced at a board meeting. The directors were in a tizzy at the appearance of the motley collection, led by the feisty J. H. (Jimmy) Thomas, national secretary of the powerful British Union of Railwaymen. Their consternation turned to horror when Thornton, addressing the group as "gentlemen,"

asked them to be seated and listened at length to their griev-
ances. Acts such as that went a long way to easing labour
troubles and turning him into a near-mythical figure in union
circles.

E. A. Weir, director of European publicity for the CNR, loved
to tell a story about the magic of Thornton's name. After a

Sir Henry Thornton

dinner party in London, Weir had fallen asleep on a commuter train, missing the stop in Rickmansworth where he
lived. When he woke up, after midnight, he found himself
stranded at the end of the line, miles from anywhere. The train
crew offered no solace to the toff in the dinner suit other than
suggesting he walk the eight miles home or sleep on the
platform until morning. In desperation, Weir claimed that he
was a personal friend of Sir Henry Thornton. "The spon-
taneity of these men, the expression on their faces and in their
voices somehow told me that I would not have to sleep on the
platform."[36] Suddenly all things were possible. A deadheading
engine was flagged down, and the friend of "Sir 'Enery of the
Great Eastern" was welcome, against all rules, to ride in the cab
with the engineer.

Only five months after arriving in England, Thornton was
invited to act as a transportation advisor in the British War
Office. In no time he was seconded altogether and eventually sent to France as inspector general of transportation for
the British Expeditionary Force. For services to the realm,
Thornton received a knighthood in 1919. When he left for
Canada, the British railway unions mourned the loss. "Sir
Henry proved to be one of the best railway general managers
England has ever known," Jimmy Thomas noted sadly. "During his stay he has broken down class barriers and hatreds, and
he leaves behind him a record of fair play and fair dealing that
other general managers will be compelled to live up to in days
to come."[37] The English press honoured him with headlines
like "England to Lose Superman" and comments that he was
"a right sort of bloke."[38]

WITH SMALL, CLOSE-SET EYES, a bulbous nose, thin lips and a
tendency to jowls, Thornton was positively homely compared
to Edward Beatty. But he was amusing, impeccably polite,
interesting and eminently quotable. Beatty was a practised but
extremely uncomfortable speaker, who shone only when he
got emotional about a subject, and that happened rarely. In

the first few years he struggled desperately to avoid public appearances. "I would much prefer that, so far as that particular trip is concerned, it should be of the speechless variety," Beatty wrote to the secretary of the St Catharines Board of Trade, whom he intended to visit in 1920. He offered to shake hands and cut ribbons so long as he could avoid "anything in the nature of a formal address."[39]

Beatty's attitude toward speeches seems odd in that he gave more of them than any other CPR president. To the president of the Canadian Club he confessed, "While I appreciate very deeply the honour of your invitation, I am none the less oppressed by the conviction that I would scarcely be an acceptable speaker."[40] He seldom told those requesting a speech that he didn't have the time. Instead he took pains to point out his inadequacies on the platform: "It would be impossible for me to gratify their surprising ambition to be afflicted with a speech from me," he explained to a school chum who asked him to talk at a fund-raising dinner for one of his old schools.[41]*

Mackenzie King's choice of Thornton with his magnificent war record and hail-fellow-well-met personality generated reams of favourable publicity for the national road. Engaging and intelligent, he easily slipped into government circles, and his rapport with workers was a shot of adrenalin for the company's sagging morale. He and Beatty first met at the December 5, 1922, Montreal Board of Trade dinner organized to honour Thornton's appointment. Unfortunately, Beatty used the occasion to blurt out one of the inappropriate remarks that

---

*When it came to his favourite causes, however, he couldn't avoid speechmaking, and on a few occasions he had reason to regret anew the whole business. "Having been indiscreet enough to deliver an address to the boys of the Shawbridge Farm and Training School some time ago, I have been inundated with requests from boys and their parents for advice in individual cases," he moaned to a sports-writing acquaintance, William Hewitt. In this instance he received a letter asking for his opinions on professional baseball as a career. "I hope I am not bothering you too much but my own knowledge of professional ball-playing is gleaned from observations from the grand stands and the occasional reading of current literature which must, of course, be untrue or it would not be interesting." (Beatty to W. A. Hewitt, August 16, 1922, BL.)

punctuated his public life. Welcoming Thornton, he began, "When you, President, were good enough to suggest for me the honor of proposing the health of Sir Henry Thornton, I not unnaturally concluded that this pleasure was being afforded to me because, as representing probably the largest ratepayer in Canada, I represented the largest stockholder in the system over which Sir Henry will preside. . . ."[42]

At first Beatty was inclined to be charitable to the new president, describing him as a "man of experience and I am informed, with a very attractive personality."[43] But within a year, as Thornton's name and face appeared everywhere, increasing the visibility and raising the status of Canadian National, Beatty's magnanimity turned to rancour. "The National Railways have adopted a very extensive system of propaganda through newspaper publicity," he complained to W. R. MacInnes. "Their officials, through personal entertainment and in every other way, are daily keeping that System in the public eye. No officer of the company, no matter how high his rank, should miss an opportunity to let it be known that our position as a transportation unit in Canada is still first and not second — an idea which the National officials are combatting with every means in their power."[44]

Thornton understood the power of the press and took the trouble to cultivate journalists, drinking and socializing with them, always ready with an amusing comment or a frank opinion, no matter the time of day or night. In contrast, Beatty rarely met with the press, insisting that questions be submitted to Treleaven before he would dictate the answers, "for the obvious reason that greater accuracy would thereby be secured and my own language used instead of that of the reporter, many of whom I [have] found on other occasions made brief notes with rather inaccurate results."[45] Reporters on deadline were forced to wait hours and sometimes days to receive the turgid, boilerplate replies to their questions. Increasingly, the media turned to Thornton, not just for comment on his own railway, but also for statements about national railway issues, hitherto the preserve of Edward Beatty.

If Beatty was too complacent about his competitor at first, it was because the beast Thornton had inherited was an economic impossibility. Consisting of 221 different railway companies, 22,110 miles of track and 99,169 employees, its 1922 earnings of $234,059,025 barely covered its operating expenses, which totalled $231,172,303. Only a pittance of less than $3 million was left to service the company's inherited debt of $1,311,488,025. Thornton had to increase revenue by an astronomical 25 percent, with no increase in expenses, just to pay interest on the debt. And that revenue could come only at the expense of the CPR, particularly in passenger traffic. To make matters worse, Thornton, though decisive and innovative in his strategies, was saddled with an ineffectual board of political has-beens and corporate also-rans, none of whom had the faintest idea of how to operate a railroad.

Thornton recognized that while no short-term economic solution to the CNR's problems existed, a political one did, and he set about winning over the Canadian people to the idea of a national road. At every opportunity he emphasized that the CNR was *the* Canadian Road, owned and operated by the people. He approached customers with nationalistic sentiments, urging them to use their own line. Beneath Thornton's appeal lay the insinuation that the CPR wasn't Canadian. The CNR president rarely forsook an opportunity to address a crowd, any crowd, and he always wore his union medallion, which had been presented to him by the British Union of Railwaymen. Demonstrating a flair for publicity, he organized what today would be called "photo opportunities" whenever he went on inspection tours. His assistants would be asked to track down the oldest yardman in the company, for instance, and stories headlined "CN's oldest worker meets its newest!" would speed across the wire-service lines. He made knowledgeable small talk with workers everywhere and never flinched at shaking even the greasiest hand. Thornton's actions were part commitment and part calculation, as revealed by a 1924 letter to Martha Watriss, later his second wife:

Last night, after dinner, I visited all the Montreal yards as I never get a chance to see the men who work at night. I took about three hours and visited all offices and engine houses. I found everything in good shape and the men on the alert. It was rather a shock to them as railway presidents have been rare visitors, but they obviously were delighted to see me. I understand that it is all over the road by now and that it is exciting a good deal of comment and good feeling. So perhaps it was an evening well-spent.[46]

TWO YEARS AFTER THORNTON'S ARRIVAL, the gloves came off. Beatty characterized Canadian National's publicity efforts as "flashy stunts," "intense propaganda," "continuous glorification of themselves and their officials" and "self-adulation and vain boastings."[47] "We are, however, holding up our end . . . in spite of super publicity, slogans, radio, dog-teams, much boasting and mob appeals," he wrote optimistically to a Bank of Montreal official. "I am innocent enough to believe that we have not found the right solution yet and that Canada cannot go on much longer bearing this particular 'White Man's burden.'"[48]

Every time Beatty turned around, Thornton was there. He couldn't even escape him at home. In late 1926 Thornton moved across from Beatty's house on Pine Avenue. In the summer Beatty liked to sit outside with a drink, enjoying the warm air and evening calm while he smoked his pipe and ruminated over important matters. Thornton put an end to that. Summer and winter Beatty could hear and watch the stream of Thornton's visitors come and go. The noisy parties drove him back inside, and even when he retired to his study for several hours of work, the revelry from across the street filtered through the window and under the door.

Beatty slighted Thornton in every way possible, including occasionally omitting his title from correspondence. Once, when he derisively dismissed Thornton as nothing more than a "showman," the CNR president fired back, "Beatty says I am a showman: I'll show him a three-ring circus."[49] With those words the battle escalated into an epic corporate struggle fuelled by a bitter personal animosity. In the daily skirmishes Beatty had the advantage of controlling an organized, efficient railway system with uniform standards. Thornton's monster was still a disparate collection of once-independent roads weighed down by dozens of hopelessly unprofitable branch lines the government would not let him abandon. On the other hand, Thornton had access to the public purse and little compunction about spending it. Trying to combat his rival's popularity and seemingly limitless funds, Beatty authorized money and personnel "to let the public know, directly if necessary, that the Canadian Pacific is still the greatest and most aggressive transportation Company in the world."[50]

During the peak years of the Beatty-Thornton war — between 1926 and 1931 — Beatty added $133 million to the company's funded debt in addition to the money raised through the sale of common and preferred stock. Fixed charges rocketed by 50 percent to $22 million annually. As each railway announced an expansion or improvement, the other quickly topped it. Until 1928 virtually all CPR mileage existed in regions where the company had land grants. But in 1928 Beatty proclaimed he would construct 1,200 miles of new branch lines north and east of Prince Albert, formerly regarded as CNR territory and where the CPR had no land whatsoever. Thornton retaliated by building an additional 700 miles of track in the same area. When Charles Dunning, the minister of railways, urged them to plan their development more rationally, Beatty shrugged off his caution. "I decline to acknowledge the right of the Canadian National to claim any part of Canada as a special preserve and I intend to proceed with my programme."[51]*

Shortly after Thornton became president, he and Beatty agreed to cooperate in the erection of a hotel in Halifax. But

---

*Of the $138 million the two men collectively spent on track expansion between 1923 and 1931, over half went into Saskatchewan.

Canadian National had neither station nor terminal in the maritime city, so Thornton concluded it would be more efficient if he built a combined $2.5 million hotel-station, as existed in many European centres. Beatty took umbrage, claiming Thornton had double-crossed him, forcing the CPR to spend an unplanned $350,000 in order to complete the Lord Nelson Hotel. He publicly accused Thornton of wasting money on a ridiculous project but neglected to mention that he had made terms for sharing the CPR terminal in Halifax so expensive that Thornton had little choice but to build his own.

When Beatty announced that the CPR intended to construct "the most magnificent hotel on the continent" in Toronto, Thornton threw together plans for hostelries in Saskatchewan, Vancouver and Edmonton. Beatty trumped his rival with the Royal York, which eventually cost $16.5 million, and with 1,156 rooms, ranked as the largest hotel in the Empire. It opened in June, 1929, just months before the great stock market crash.* Hotels weren't profitable for either company. By 1926 the CPR had over $70 million invested in them but saw only $1.1 million in profit during the boom years between 1926 and 1929, not nearly enough to pay the interest on the borrowing. Although the Royal York's first year was heavily booked, it was a cavernously empty mausoleum for most of the Depression.†

As his next move in the ongoing battle, Beatty inaugurated the first all-sleeping-car train on the continent, running between Montreal and Vancouver. Thornton responded with

---

*The opening ceremonies included four balls and a lunch with 1,800 guests. Commemorative gold pencils, beauty compacts and cuff links were given to those who attended. *MacLean's Magazine* devoted most of an entire issue to the hotel, which it described as a self-contained city containing the most modern accoutrements including ultra-quiet flush toilets ("no waiting") and radios in every room. Kate Treleaven took over the decorating, selecting most of the utilitarian No-Mar furniture from her cousin's plant, Malcom & Hill Ltd., in Kitchener. Even today, what pieces remain are politely referred to by Royal York staff as "sturdy."

†Even during the worst years, management agreed not to lay off staff, allowing them to work just for tips. Some of the tips were delivered in an unusual way. At the height of the Depression a millionaire contractor threw dollar bills from a balcony into the lobby below.

huge outlays for newer and more luxurious diners and parlour cars. Beatty responded with the *Mountaineer*, another all-sleeping-car train that ran between Vancouver and Chicago. The final and most disastrous competition came over B.C. coastal service. Thornton sank $6.5 million into three steamers to ply the Vancouver–Prince Rupert route, all of them larger, faster and grander than the CPR's *Princess* vessels. But the CNR service, initiated in 1930, didn't last the year.

Throughout the feud, Beatty always had the upper hand. In most cases he was able to expand or improve upon what already existed, whereas Thornton constantly had to break new ground for the CNR. Some of his decisions, like the B.C. coastal service, would have been disasters anyway with neither sufficient passengers nor freight to support them. But the twin barbs of the Depression and the 1930 election of a new government skewered Thornton as mortally as a stake through his heart.

He had performed miracles transforming Canadian National's 221 disparate lines into a smoothly functioning network, and in 1929 he had been hailed as a saviour when he had produced the company's first operating surplus of $58 million. But no one could make the system really pay. The Depression, which swallowed up the country in 1929, starkly illuminated the CNR's huge debt, and the very same year, Thornton lost his protector when R. B. Bennett's Conservatives trounced Mackenzie King 137 seats to 91.

With an overwhelming majority in hand, Bennett set about slashing bloated government spending like an avenging angel. Thornton and the CNR proved ideal targets. During the next two years Bennett set the butcher's dogs on Thornton, dismantling him professionally and personally as well. For Beatty, the fight was over.

CHAPTER 11

THE MAN WHO WED
THE CPR

"There is no life in the CPR *without Beatty and no life
in Beatty without the* CPR.*"*

— The Financial Times

R. B. (Buckshot) Bennett needed a good sacrificial offering to begin his campaign against waste, and Henry
Thornton willingly lay down and stretched his neck for the
chop. Brusque, bullish and heavy-handed, Bennett had never
liked the popular, socially adept and charming Thornton
from the outset. If the prime minister's conscience pricked
him over his choice of victim, Thornton's free-spending reputation and the shocking publicity over his expensive divorce
offered ample justification.* Then there was the CNR's deficit.
From $13.4 million in 1929 it exploded to $60.8 million in
1931. It didn't matter that Canadian National actually fared
better in earnings in 1931 than the CPR; the huge figure stood
out like a giant boil on the backside of Bennett's fledgling
government.

Thornton's first hint that trouble was brewing came in an

---

*Beatty helped create Thornton's reputation as a spendthrift by castigating him in endless
speeches and public comments for treating Canadians' tax dollars as if they belonged to him
personally. The image was somewhat unfair. After the 1929 stock market crash Thornton was
one of the first businessmen in Canada to institute a vigorous cost-cutting program, slashing
salaries 10 percent without raising the unions' ire, and abandoning a series of unprofitable
branch lines.

331

embarrassing disagreement over his Pine Avenue home, which he had been renting since 1926. Because it was the residence of a prominent public official with many ceremonial duties to perform, Mackenzie King had agreed that the government should purchase and decorate it.

But in the middle of the arrangements, the Conservatives were elected and the Thorntons received the distressing news that the new minister of railways and canals, Dr R. J. Manion, refused to honour the agreement. "We therefore were placed in the impossible position of having contracted to buy a house which we could not pay for ourselves and which the Company could not assume without an Order-in-Council which the Government would not sanction," Thornton's second wife later revealed. "It was at this time that Sir Henry became convinced of a concerted plot to ruin his personal reputation."[1]*

Over the next eighteen months the Railway Committee of the House of Commons set upon Thornton like a pack of wolves trailing a wounded buck. Insinuations of graft, personal gain, hidden salaries and gross extravagances fuelled the headlines. The inquisitors dragged out even the smallest expenditure — like the bill for stuffing a moose head — and paraded it around as if it were a treasonous act. As Thornton edged closer and closer to the abyss, he seemed to lose all heart for the battle. Instead of denouncing his oppressors, he replied lamely to their questions and never once attempted to expose the plot for what it was. And no one came to his defence. His most powerful protector, Mackenzie King, was preoccupied with a campaign contribution scandal and was in no position to come to Thornton's aid. A royal commission

---

*Thornton wasn't the only one to come to that conclusion. J. W. Dafoe, the powerful editor of the *Manitoba Free Press*, told Thornton he believed the whole exercise was concocted at the behest of Bennett and his friend Beatty: "[The CPR's] fixed purpose right along was to bide their time until their political power made it possible for them to put a crimp in the Canadian National and 'get' you. Ultimately they succeeded." (J. W. Dafoe to Henry Thornton, March 13, 1933, DP)

under Justice Lyman Duff declared that a "red thread of extravagance" ran through Thornton's management.

Questioners zeroed in on company expenses, which totalled $2 million in 1930, ignoring Thornton's protest that the figure covered 3,500 people, some of whom travelled a great deal on railway business. They also brought up $100,000 for club dues paid by the CNR on behalf of company officials and laid out the details of Thornton's costly office in New York. His entertainment expenses, which amounted to $3,000 in 1931, received the most coverage, though the commission ignored the fact that Thornton had fêted many titled and important people at the request of the government. His salary of $75,000 was also held up as an abomination, though Beatty's was larger, at $100,000.

On July 19, 1932, months before Justice Duff officially tabled his findings, Manion announced that Thornton, believing he had lost the confidence of the Canadian people, had resigned. Though he never denied the statement publicly, Thornton later wrote his version: "I resigned because I was asked to do so by the Minister of Railways speaking for the Government. . . . I had in some curious way excited the hostility of the Govt. & did not bear its good will nor support. Under such conditions I was no good to anyone."[2]* With his reputation ruined, his health shattered and his personal finances approaching bankruptcy, Thornton bowed out of his once glorious career. He made a few attempts to seek work and undertook consulting for a British financial group interested in investing in Cuba. Throughout the fall and winter of 1932/33 his robust frame withered and shrank, and the smart

*Jimmy Thomas of the British Union of Railwaymen managed to get a little revenge for his old friend Thornton. In 1932 he was part of a three-man British delegation sent to Canada to discuss trade and tariffs. Before the conference even started, Thomas declared, "These 'ere Dominions don't only want to milk the Old Cow dry; they want to bite off 'er teats as well." The conference never quite recovered from his acid comment. Years later when asked for the reason for his behaviour, Thomas made it clear that he was actually expressing a general bitterness towards Canada. "Look at what they did to Thornton," he replied. (Stevens, *History of the Canadian National Railways*, p. 359)

suits he favoured hung like bags from his shoulders. On March 14th, the day a letter arrived at his home inviting him to a Canadian National dinner in his honour, Thornton died of previously undiagnosed cancer.

AFTER HENRY THORNTON'S DISGRACE, Edward Beatty became once again the pre-eminent Canadian business and railway figure — but it was a pyrrhic victory. His battle with the CNR had weakened the company, leaving it more vulnerable than it had been when Beatty became president. And conditions were not bound to improve very soon. As the long, grim decade of the thirties stretched on, shipbuilding, hotel construction and branch expansion weighed heavily on the CPR's shrinking profits. Shaughnessy's rainy-day surplus should have buffered the company for years, but Beatty had depleted the fund to finance expansion and improvements.

The CPR wasn't the only company to suffer grievously from the apparently endless deluge of economic misfortune that followed the October, 1929, stock market crash. Less than a month later, three of Canada's largest brokerage houses declared themselves insolvent and filed for bankruptcy. Major industrial stocks like Canada Cement, Abitibi and Dominion Bridge lost nearly 100 percent of their share value between 1929 and 1932. Canadian unemployment soared from 116,000 to a staggering 721,000 in the same period, and the country's gross national product plummeted from $6.1 billion to less than $4 billion. But for the CPR the most telling statistic was farm income, which reacted more severely than any other sector of the economy. From $609 million in 1926 it fell to $104 million by 1932 as small and large farmers alike were speared by the twin evils of low grain prices and the poorest harvests in Canadian history. As crops dwindled, so did CPR revenues, hitting their lowest level since the company was formed. Beatty quickly suspended dividends on ordinary shares in 1932, an act that had almost cost William Van Horne his job in 1895. The following year he was forced to cut dividends on preferred shares and also had to ask the government for a loan guarantee in order to borrow money to pay the interest on the company's bonds.

But even the ravages of the Depression became a tool in Beatty's hands. Using the CNR's deflated condition and Thornton's decline as a platform, he resurrected his dream of absorbing the CNR. Knowing that the CPR would never be allowed to take over its rival directly, he took a more circuitous route to the same goal. Beatty suggested to Bennett that the CPR's rail business be separated from its non-rail interests and joined with the Canadian National's operations. The government would then assume control of the whole rail system, guaranteeing shareholders dividends in perpetuity — a distinct advantage for the CPR, which had little prospect of paying dividends for some years to come. The most important part of the proposal, from Beatty's point of view, was that management of the new company would rest entirely in the hands of the CPR. He held up the embarrassing quagmire of CNR management and accounts to underscore the point that only his company could effectively run the system.

Beatty as the carpenter in Lewis Carroll's "The Walrus and the Carpenter," ready to devour the CNR

Put the whole thing in "safe sane hands" — my hands — Beatty urged the prime minister, hinting that both railways would collapse if his plan were not implemented. So intent was he on his proposal that he made dozens of trips to Ottawa between 1931 and 1934 to see key political figures and promote his idea. Normally, if Beatty wanted to see an MP or Cabinet minister, he sent for them and they scurried down to Montreal. When the press asked him what was in the scheme for the CPR, he replied earnestly, "What is good for Canadians is good for the CPR."

But Henry Thornton believed Beatty really meant, "What is good for the CPR is good for Canada." Though shorn of his crown, Thornton still regarded the throne as his and warned anyone who would listen that Beatty's frequent appearances in Ottawa and his altruistic statements hid cunning intentions. "Unquestionably there is a definite plot on the boards to turn the Canadian National over to the Canadian Pacific," he wrote to *Manitoba Free Press* editor John W. Dafoe in 1933. "It remains for those who value freedom to prevent such an occurrence."[3] A few weeks later Thornton was in Ottawa, and after lunching with his nemesis, came away even more convinced that Beatty had a hidden agenda. "There's something 'phoney' about this whole railway business," he concluded. "The C.P.R. are not doing all this for a cause already lost; they must think they see a way to re-open the question."[4] But no one paid the slightest attention to Thornton anymore.

BY THE MID-1930s THE CPR and Edward Beatty were so inextricably intertwined that one British paper declared: "There is no life in the CPR without Beatty and no life in Beatty without the CPR."[5] Scarcely an article appeared that failed to use some variation of the phrase "wedded to the CPR" to illustrate his devotion and not incidentally to explain his perpetual bachelorhood. But Beatty did have other loves, most notably his parallel and almost as demanding career as chancellor of

McGill University* in Montreal. His association with that institution began in 1919 when he joined the board of governors, a year after becoming the CPR's president. In 1920 former prime minister Robert Borden stepped down as chancellor, and Beatty, though only forty-one and the least experienced board member, succeeded him. The only problem with the prestigious appointment was that Beatty already held the chancellorship of Queen's University in Kingston, Ontario. It doesn't seem to have occurred to him that accepting the same post at McGill might create an awkward conflict, for he showed no indication that he was prepared to resign from either position.

Beatty's relationship with academe was every bit as perplexing and contradictory as so many of his social interactions. To begin with, he disliked academics and rarely passed up an opportunity to cast aspersions on the profession. "My admiration for the professors is unstinted when they are alone," he once explained to a friend. "When they are together, however, I am inclined to endorse your description of them as queer. . . . Having been brought up in the refined atmosphere of railway labour negotiations, it came as a distinct shock to have to deal with the [professor] members of the McGill senate."[6]

Beatty also loathed the pomp and circumstance that went along with the university's top job. When the principal of Queen's wrote to him politely detailing the advance plans for his inauguration as chancellor, Beatty responded with an astonishingly rude and off-hand letter, informing him that he wouldn't be able to stay for the whole thing. "I presume that the installation ceremonies will be formal and brief and that the dinner will be so arranged as to permit the fifty-seven varieties of rhetoricians, who you will have as guests, to deliver

---

*All the previous CPR presidents had served McGill in some capacity, but Beatty was the first and last to hold a position of such power.

themselves of numerous syllogisms which no one will remember . . . I observe that the program states that academic dress should be worn but that it is not essential. I have none, nor am I even the possessor of a K.C. gown, not having thought it necessary to go to the expense when K.C. patents were inflicted on me some years ago. If there is any appropriate dress, apart from the natural habiliments which anyone would wear, I shall be glad if you will let me know what it is. Perhaps the janitor has a Chancellor's gown stored away somewhere."[7]

Queen's viewed McGill's selection of Beatty as blatant poaching and a series of angry letters followed the appointment, stopping only when Beatty, unrepentant, abruptly resigned from Queen's, much to the annoyance of that university's governors. The same year Beatty became chancellor of McGill, the board hired Sir Arthur Currie as the new principal. Initially he and Beatty worked well together, with Currie effectively setting the direction for the university and Beatty relegated to a supporting role. But when Currie became ill in 1928 and was forced to take a year's leave of absence, Beatty moved in, naming his own man, Charles F. Martin, dean of medicine, as acting principal. Through Martin and other key appointments Beatty insinuated himself into McGill's day-to-day operations, something previous chancellors had left to the principal and his staff.

Beatty did all his work in Windsor Station, and on many days his McGill correspondence outnumbered his letters on CPR business. In fact, he became so attached to his wider responsibilities that when Currie returned in 1929, Beatty refused to fade into the background. Friction developed as Currie let it be known that he found Beatty's actions disloyal; Beatty tartly responded that he would be delighted if one of his own vice-presidents acted with the same initiative.

The uneasy peace between the two was broken by the October, 1929, stock market crash, which shattered the world but strengthened Beatty's hand immeasurably. McGill's revenue, largely dependent on investment income, dropped catastrophically from more than $700,000 in 1927 to only

Beatty as McGill University chancellor, with Principal Arthur Morgan

$437,000 in 1933 and then to $392,000 in 1934. The value of a prominent businessman as chancellor suddenly increased, and Beatty took a grip on McGill that he didn't relinquish until his death in 1943, governing the university as if it were a fiefdom, and taking a proprietary approach to its students and all their activities.

Beatty cemented his control over McGill when Currie died in November, 1933. In an astonishing move, he decided not to hire a replacement and happily added the principal's day-to-day duties to his own already onerous workload. Not until 1935 did he name a new principal, Arthur Eustace Morgan, and even then, Beatty still made all the major decisions. On one occasion he decided that Dr W. D. (Woodie) Woodhead, a well-liked professor of classics, was just the man to fill a vacancy as dean of the arts faculty. The position had been offered to Woodhead informally, who categorically refused to give up his teaching in order to become an administrator. Beatty summoned him to Windsor Station and after a short interview the professor emerged "shamefaced and hangdogged" to announce that he was McGill's new dean of arts. "Sir Edward was in a very forceful mood today," he explained limply.[8]

Beatty avoided having to deal with professors by holding nearly all essential McGill meetings in Windsor Station, thus keeping the centre of power off campus. Three or four times a year he summoned the board of governors to the long, dark CPR boardroom table, where he treated the distinguished intellectuals and business leaders as if they were company employees, and lowly ones at that. Precisely at the appointed hour Beatty marched into the room, two or three pipes in hand, depending on how long he intended the meeting to last. After a curt greeting, he plunked himself down at the end of the table and without another pleasantry called the meeting to order. The governors scattered to their seats like quail breaking cover. As he took up the business of the day, Beatty brooked no interference or quibbling in his headlong rush to finish — rare was the meeting that lasted longer than an hour.

In the late 1930s J. W. McConnell,* an influential Montreal businessman, tried to interrupt a McGill board meeting with the surprise announcement that he'd just convinced the Quebec government to increase its annual operating grant to

---

*McConnell founded a great corporate and philanthropic empire which still thrives today.

McGill by the huge amount of $50,000. Best of all, he had the cheque right in his pocket. Beatty cut McConnell off in mid-sentence, informing him that the matter belonged in new business and would simply have to wait until the end of the meeting. McConnell simmered in his chair until called upon to tell his news an hour later.

BEATTY WAS RESPONSIBLE for many good works during his time as chancellor, the most notable of which was keeping the university solvent. But in the subterranean coffee houses surrounding McGill, Edward Beatty is usually remembered as the man who routed the socialists out of the university and uncer-emoniously dumped the venerated Stephen Leacock. Concerned that "silly idealism" would infect lesser minds, Beatty cauterized its influence whenever it cropped up at McGill. After a large rally in downtown Montreal, he wrote to Sir Charles Gordon, president of the Bank of Montreal: "It would appear that a great many of the Professors of the University are in sympathy with what we regard as advanced socialist theories. This is probably due to ignorance, because there is no one as ignorant of practical matters as our Academic colleagues."[9]

Beatty's concerns about socialism matured into an obsession. In January, 1933, *The Alarm Clock*, a student-run socialist newspaper, made its debut, featuring mild criticisms and satires of the established order. Within days he banned the fledgling publication from campus and another, slightly more pointed student paper, *The Black Sheep*, suffered the same fate.

Beatty kept up his vigilant defence of capitalism until 1939 when he dealt the "propagandists" a fatal blow. Lewis Douglas, a prominent American academic and businessman with Canadian roots, hand-picked by Beatty to become McGill's principal in January, 1938, worked with the chancellor to devise a clever plan to rid the university of socialists for once and for all. They removed tenure from the junior staff, who were considered to be more inclined towards socialism. With their security gone, the younger professors found their idealism fading. At the same time, Douglas and Beatty drew up a promotion list of carefully screened professors who subscribed to the correct political views. In a number of cases, prominent socialists like Eugene Forsey found that their appointments were simply not renewed. To neutralize the influence of leftist professors with too much tenure or stature to be eliminated, they simply imported equally prominent academics who were strong proponents of capitalism. Over a number of years the strategy completely exorcised the socialist presence at McGill, particularly in the social sciences. "The Douglas-Beatty strategy proved remarkably enduring," concluded Stanley B. Frost, McGill's official chronicler. "The effect was that the thrust of social science research in the university was dissipated, and never again achieved the same sense of a unified purpose."[10]

Beatty's manœuvring at McGill left no doubt in anyone's mind about his political views. But, as in so many other areas of his life, he could not always be counted on to act according to his beliefs. In the middle of Beatty's campaign at McGill, one of Canada's best-known socialists, David Lewis, applied for a coveted Rhodes Scholarship. In 1932, Lewis, only twenty-three years old, was already an outspoken political activist. The man he had to face to claim the prize was Edward Beatty, chairman of the selection committee. Ruling the committee with his usual iron fist, Beatty held all the meetings at Windsor Station. Lewis, summoned for his interview — really a forty-five-minute inquisition more than anything else — found his political inclinations were the primary target. "At one point," he recalled, "Sir Edward Beatty turned to me and, with a quizzical sparkle in his eyes, asked, 'Lewis, if you become the first socialist prime minister of Canada, what would be the first thing you would do?' I could not suppress a defiant glint in my eyes as I answered with emphasis. 'Nationalize the CPR, sir.'"[11]

If Beatty was nonplussed, he hid it superbly behind the cold, blank gaze that seemed to burrow right into the young man's heart, and Lewis left the meeting sure that his cheeky responses had eliminated him from the running. To his surprise, he received an invitation to a second interview a few days later. Distinctly hostile, the committee grilled him, trying to force Lewis to admit he was a communist sympathizer. One questioner demanded to know his opinion of the Russian Revolution.

> It was obvious that if I said that the important thing was to free the Russian People from Czarist oppression, without a long speech about the evils of Bolshevism, my inquisitor would have the answer he wanted. And the occasion did not lend itself to a lecture on capitalism, socialism, and communism. So I answered in equally soft tones, "I am in some difficulty, Sir, because the question is so broad. The Russian revolution had political, economic, cultural, religious and moral aspects; which of them would you like me to comment on?"
>
> Whereupon the questioner slammed the table in front of him and said angrily, "I asked a civil question and I expect a civil answer."
>
> I was somewhat taken aback, but before I could stammer anything, Sir Edward said, with the firm authority of a chairman, "I think Lewis's answer was entirely civil; your question was very broad." And that was that. I have never felt as grateful to anyone as I did Beatty at that moment.[12]

Surrounded by sycophants, Beatty was attracted to honesty, straightforwardness and strength of character. His intercession told the committee what their decision was to be, and that same day, David Lewis became a Rhodes Scholar.

Just as contradictory as his championing of David Lewis was Beatty's treatment of his old friend Stephen Leacock, Canada's most renowned humourist and an influential professor of economics at McGill for thirty-five years. In 1925 Leacock's wife Beatrix developed inoperable cancer. Leacock, having heard about a highly experimental lead treatment for the disease in Liverpool, England, made plans to take his wife there. Beatty discovered Leacock's intentions and ordered the creation of a special sterile hospital suite on a CPR ship. He also provided quarters for Leacock, his wife's nurse and mother — all at his own expense.[13] The mission was doomed from the start, however, as Beatrix Leacock died a few days after arriving in England.

In sharp contrast to his act of great kindness is Beatty's role in the purge of Stephen Leacock and the rest of the "Senility

Gang," as Leacock called them, from McGill. Principal Morgan was the front man, but Beatty stage-managed the whole affair. In one stroke he eliminated thirteen of the most distinguished and influential faculty members.* By enforcing a previously ignored policy of compulsory retirement at age sixty-five, Beatty got rid of powerful figures like Leacock and assumed even tighter control over the faculty.

Leacock received the news in the summer of 1935 that his retirement would begin the following May. Stunned and hurt, he fought his dismissal until finally, having exhausted every other option, he appealed directly to his friend Beatty, whom he'd often publicly and privately extolled as a humanitarian and who, he well knew, made the real decisions at McGill. Beatty's totally unsympathetic response left Leacock embittered — the CPR president even had the gall to intimate that he was doing his friend a favour: "You have many years during which your influence will be increased in some way by the fact that you are no longer an active member of the staff. For yourself, I am afraid that I have no sympathy. You have had a full life and achieved fame. Beyond that I do not see what reward any man can obtain."[14]

AS BEATTY AGED, HIS ALOOFNESS became irascibility, and the contradictory facets of his personality polarized more and more. His opinions were stronger, his antisocialist views expressed more stridently, and his judgments of the men under him harsher and less tolerant.

In his first years as CPR president, Beatty allowed himself to be dragged off to concerts, endless functions, the occasional opera and, once in a while, a play (which he particularly loathed) to satisfy a visiting dignitary or the requirements of

---

*Among the faculty members forced out were such luminaries as Frank Dawson Adams, McGill's vice-principal, a geologist with a worldwide reputation and acting principal at the time of Morgan's appointment, and Dr Charles F. Martin, dean of McGill's medical school and the first Canadian to be head of the American Medical Association. Ironically, Dr Martin was the man that Beatty made acting principal in 1928.

some important event. By the mid-1930s he had dropped all pretence of enjoying cultural pastimes. When a prominent businessman tried to interest him in a fund-raising campaign for a major art gallery, Beatty brushed him aside, saying, "Never been in the damned place." When an academic asked him to speak to the Royal Society of Canada he snapped, "What the hell is the Canadian Royal Society?"[15]*

In 1935 King George V proffered a knighthood on Beatty. During the ceremonies Beatty appeared as abashed and sheepishly delighted as a rough-and-tumble boy would in receiving an award for embroidery. Back in Canada speaking invitations poured in. The RSPCA, the Girl Scouts, the Sons of England, the Young Dramatists Society, the Canadian Order for the Preservation of Native Tongues and the Alpine Club of Canada all pestered him for special engagements. At first he wrote personal no-thank-you notes, but after twenty-two he sent out a form letter. One function he did attend was a Montreal Board of Trade dinner. After a short speech congratulating Beatty on his knighthood, the board president introduced a Canadian soprano, just returned from a triumphant European tour, who was to sing in his honour. Halfway through the aria Beatty hauled himself to his feet and retreated to the lobby, where he sat smoking a cigar, until "the noise," as he called it, abated.

At the CPR, Beatty became ever more distant, speaking less, yet demanding more. Many mornings he even hurried past Kate Treleaven and his clerk Walter Pigeon without a glance or a word to either. When he strode down the CPR's marble corridors, his footsteps echoed hollowly in the silence. Sometimes he broke the hush by choosing a door at random and suddenly flinging it open to see if all within were dutifully working. But occasionally he showed flashes of remarkable tolerance for the most flagrant transgressions, especially

---

*It is impossible that Beatty, one of the most prominent Canadians in university circles, would not have known about the Royal Society of Canada, which endowed the recipients of its achievement awards with the kind of cachet beloved in academe.

those that reminded the president of himself as a carefree, irresponsible lad. One Saturday afternoon in 1937, a group of junior CPR employees was lazing around on the floor of the alcove directly in front of Beatty's office, betting on a game of pitch penny. None of them had any inkling that Beatty was inside working, and had been for hours. Suddenly the office door swung open and there, staring down into their horrified faces, was The Eminence. In the dry-throated seconds that followed, each man felt his career slipping away. Without a word Beatty carefully donned his gloves, grasped his walking stick and marched out of the room, stepping over one of the loafers as he went. Barely had the terrified group drawn a strangled breath when Beatty, having forgotten his hat, reappeared. Walking briskly to his office, he retrieved it and left, stepping over the same offender again, this time uttering a gruff "Good day, gentlemen" as he went on his way.

The rank and file rarely saw Beatty, let alone talked to him, but those who did remembered it for the rest of their lives. One night late in 1938, the president was waiting at the Pointe Claire station for the train to Toronto when he noticed a ticket agent cursing over an incomprehensible query from the accounting department at head office. Beatty appeared in the agent's cubicle and the young man frantically babbled apologies for his bad language. Ignoring the blather, Beatty gestured toward the letter, and having read it, sat down to help the clerk answer the question. The train rolled in, full of passengers, but Beatty kept it waiting for an hour until he'd sorted out the problem.

SO TAUTLY WAS THE COIL of Beatty's personality wound that he could relax in only three places: at sea, especially on board his favourite ship, the *Empress of Britain*, at his home in Pointe Claire (now a suburb of Montreal) and during long summer days at Bark Lake, his retreat in the Laurentians. During sea voyages he worked late into the night but also spent hours just roaming around the ship, chatting easily with the astonished crew and quizzing them about their jobs. In Pointe Claire Beatty's home was near one owned by Marguerite Shaughnessy, daughter of Lord Shaughnessy. When their summer visits coincided, which they frequently did, the two played endless games of gin rummy on a table set up beneath an oak tree on Marguerite's front lawn.

But it was only at Bark Lake that Beatty dropped his rigid façade of control and let the burden of his responsibilities slide from his shoulders. His cabin was a comfortable, though crude, structure surrounded by the wilderness of the Laurentians. Travelling in his private railway car to St Jovite near the lake, he always exchanged his three-piece suit for a shabby assortment of old clothes before leaving the train. He never shaved or changed — just spent days languidly hanging around, hiking through the deep woods with no apparent destination or aimlessly paddling his canoe. Through his bodyguard, who doubled as cook and valet in the field, and Seaforth Duff MacNab, an old friend and early resident of Bark Lake, Beatty let it be known that he didn't want to speak or be spoken to, an edict scrupulously honoured by local inhabitants.

C. L. Reeve, another pioneer resident of Bark Lake, recalled seeing Beatty, one of the most powerful men in Canada, idly sitting on the boat landing one day. Out of the blue, "a very pompous stranger" arrived laden with baggage. "Seeing this unshaven man doing nothing, he called him to give a hand, which Beatty did. When the job was done the stranger handed Beatty a tip, which he pocketed and went back to his seat."[16]

Bark Lake also allowed the CPR president to retreat to the glorious, carefree days of Banty Beatty and submerge himself in silly games and childish pranks — like glueing his bodyguard's coat and hat to the peg where he hung them. A friendly codger who brought groceries up to the cabin complained one day that the eggs were so ancient they were ready to hatch. The next morning he woke up to find a basket of twelve chicks on his doorstep, deposited there the night before by Beatty.

Beatty in backwoods clothes

The only people Beatty invited to Bark Lake were his college chums and lifelong friends John Hobbs and Fred

Meredith. When he arrived with them in tow, the three disappeared and the locals wouldn't see them for days. Rarely rising before noon, they spent their afternoons filling the fresh lake air with cigar and pipe smoke, damning the gods and arguing over matters that hadn't seemed important for thirty years. Fishing, or what passed for it, drinking Scotch and playing poker occupied their time. The games stretched into the midnight hours until one of them had won everything the others owned — homes, cars, pipes and the clothes off their backs. The next morning everything was symbolically returned and they started all over again.

AS THE DEPRESSED, DROUGHT-RIDDEN THIRTIES ground on towards another world war, Beatty's escapes to the lake became less and less frequent. The CPR president was still determined to merge the two Canadian railroads, and he threw himself into one final campaign. Setting up a special corps of forty stenographers, Beatty dictated hundreds of letters and sent them to politicians and prominent businessmen across the country. The man who had once used the flimsiest of excuses to avoid speaking engagements eagerly seized opportunities to propagandize amalgamation, if only to supplant others "who speak before service and other clubs whose views, as expressed, are not embarrassed by any particular knowledge of the facts."[17]

To S. J. Hungerford, president of the CNR, he wrote long letters — really lectures — on how best to serve the Canadian public and protect them from unnecessary loss. In one missive Beatty deliberately used the word "constituency" to remind his rival that the CNR was a political beast. He berated C. D. Howe, minister of transport, for hiding Canadian National deficits in a welter of confusing figures and fought hard to convince the minister that government liabilities relating to the railway should be allowed to stand naked and exposed for all to see. Only then could he drive home the enormity of the railway deficit. But in the midst of his war of words even Beatty began to lose hope. On Christmas Eve, 1936, he bemoaned to Professor W. T. Jackman, a political scientist at the University of Toronto, that "a powerful combination of ignorance and cowardice"[18] kept the railway status quo firmly in place.

Ironically, as the Depression showed the first signs of lifting, Beatty saw his chance to assume control of CN slipping away. "One of the difficulties we meet is that every improvement in commercial conditions is regarded as a step towards a final solution of the railway problem," he observed bleakly to Jackman again. "My fear is that if the improvement goes on and railway revenues respond to it, our people will become even more apathetic than they were in the past. . . . Economic waste is economic waste whether a country can meet its bills with it or fails to do so, and it is hard to understand why this simple mathematical fact cannot be more fully appreciated."[19]

As Beatty continued to ruminate glumly about the future of Canadian railways, he buried his frustrations beneath a massive pyramid of work and responsibility. Always active in education and charity, after 1935 he began darting from one crusade to another in a near-frenzy. If he believed in a cause, he immediately jumped in and seized control. Shortly after the Society for Mental Hygiene was formed, its directors asked Beatty for a donation. On Monday he wrote out a cheque for $2,500 and by Friday had taken over the entire fund-raising campaign. Sending out a volley of letters on CPR stationery, he didn't ask for support from prominent Canadians; he demanded it.

On one occasion he sent two letters to Vincent Massey, a cousin on his mother's side. When no donation arrived, Beatty notified him that he was signed up for $2,000 and would he please pay up, which Massey did. While raising money for a Montreal arena, he informed Charles Gordon, president of the Bank of Montreal and a member of the committee, that he had written to Herbert Molson and J. W. McConnell, convincing them to ante up $2,000, and was chasing after Sir Herbert Holt, then widely believed to be Canada's richest man, who had "apparently escaped again."[20]

Beatty was as generous with his own money as he asked other prominent businessmen to be with theirs. Though his salary of $100,000 a year made him the highest-paid Canadian employee, he seemed determined to spend as much of it as he could.* In a typical month in 1936 he gave more than half of it away: $1,000 to the YMCA, $15 to the Women's Temperance League, $1,500 to a McGill scholarship fund, $500 to a pension plan for artists, $35 to a benefit for railway pensioners, $750 each to three different hospitals and a $10 bill to T. Shallow, a young man down on his luck who requested his help.

As president of the Canadian Boy Scouts' Association, Beatty filled its coffers so well that in 1931 the founder of the worldwide organization, Lord Baden-Powell, awarded him scouting's highest honour — a Silver Wolf. Beatty took intense pleasure in this particular cause because he saw in it all the uninhibited purity of youth: "The Boy Scout Movement starts with the faith that boys are merely men not yet made conscious, overcautious or narrow-minded by their experience of a world which is only too artificial."[21]

As devoted as Beatty was to the clean-living scouts, it was the plight of wayward boys that really capitivated him. The primary focus of his interest was the Shawbridge Boys' Farm and Training School outside Montreal, which he first visited in 1922. In typical fashion, he became president of the school within a year, immediately installing a special railway siding so his private car could roll right up to the door. Unlike most of the other people in Beatty's life, the Shawbridge boys easily penetrated the protective field of aloofness that surrounded him. Tough or waif-like, hard-eyed or sickly, belligerent or shivering with nerves, he embraced them all. Whenever Beatty came calling, school directors and house parents invariably

---

*Beatty's monthly paycheque of $8,333.33 left him one cent short of the full $100,000. When he noticed this omission he requested that the extra penny be added to his December cheque.

At the Shawbridge Boys' Farm and Training School

put on a big show, staging demonstrations of the boys' progress and skills and dragging him away on inspections of the parade ground, hospital, classrooms, workshops and playing fields. But if he could, Beatty avoided the fanfare and slipped in unannounced, to the horror of everyone except the boys. He cherished these candid moments and could often be found with his sleeves rolled up helping with the chores. Once he was late for a meeting with the school principal because he got waylaid teaching a tall, gangly youth the finer points of tackling.

BY 1939 BEATTY'S SIXTY-TWO YEARS had deeply eroded his once magnificent face and body. In his prime he weighed 140 pounds, but now, no matter how hard he exercised, he couldn't stay under 165. Sleep came fitfully; often he didn't go to bed before 2 A.M. and in the morning the struggle to rise before nine became increasingly difficult. He played handball and squash as regularly as he could with his old college sparring partner, Pug Rennie, a former pro boxer who also doubled as his masseur. Beatty tried golf from time to time but could only be coaxed into joining a foursome if the players were all friends who would not be upset at his impatience, paint-peeling language and displays of temper. "Golf takes too much time for what one can get out of it," he once stated, denying that he ever indulged in the game, "and anyway it is a game in which constant repression is necessary. I like a game where I can get my head down and let go."[22]

Shortly after England declared war on Germany in September, 1939, the British government asked Beatty to coordinate Canadian shipping and rail transportation for the war effort. A huge task, it involved moving thousands of troops and hundreds of tons of cargo by sea, rail and air from Canada to Europe. Beatty placed himself on call twenty-four hours a day, breaking off CPR meetings to dash to Ottawa, and frequently eating his meals on the run as he shuttled back and forth. His evenings were filled with long phone calls that often lasted past midnight and his paperwork increased so much that he tripled his secretarial staff.

A month after accepting the job, Beatty complained of a persistent sore throat, fatigue and dizziness. On New Year's Day, 1940, his worried physician, Dr Raymond Brow, admitted him to Montreal's Royal Victoria Hospital. It appeared to be a simple case of tonsillitis and, writing to Hobbs from his hospital bed, Beatty confided: "I am feeling so well that I am ashamed to be in hospital, but there are certain mechanical things that must be adjusted."[23] Despite the removal of his tonsils, Beatty's health continued to deteriorate. Finally, tests revealed he had diabetes. After two months in hospital, he emerged an old man — pallid, haggard and humiliatingly frail. Reluctantly, he agreed to go to Atlantic City with Hobbs and his wife for a few weeks of sea air, accompanied by Ethel Smerdon, an attractive, bubbly young nurse, who was not the least bit awed by her famous charge. Beatty was so weak she had to push him everywhere in a wheelchair and the only form of excitement he could stand was losing endless card games to her.

Beatty grew very close to Smerdon, whom he called "Useless," tossing jokes and gentle insults her way as if she were one of his college buddies. Never a nature lover, he came to appreciate flowers and birds during their long walks and desultory conversation. After he had known her only a matter of weeks, he trusted her implicitly, allowing her to write his nightly letter to Kathleen Madill — a longtime friend of his who lived in Toronto.

THOUGH BEATTY NEVER MARRIED, a small circle of women surrounded him throughout his entire life. Many today believe that Beatty was homosexual, and occasionally he received accusatory or propositioning letters. He does appear to have preferred the company of men to that of women, being deeply attached to his chums from varsity days and unfailing in his generosity towards male friends who were in financial trouble. Although Beatty exuded an air of almost overpowering masculinity, he also had a vulnerable and tender side which he revealed mostly to his male friends.

Whatever his sexual tendencies, he formed, over the years, some fascinating, lingering attachments to women. Usually brusque, awkward and rude around members of the opposite sex, he met most of his women friends through his sister. One of the first was Katy Maclaren, a tall, slender and attractive friend of Mary who graduated from Jarvis Collegiate in Toronto with her. After the two were seen together at several Montreal functions, stories circulated of impending marriage, but Katy moved to New York after graduation and eventually to Paris, where she lived with her older sister, a physician. But the pair must have stayed in communication with each other. When Katy returned to Canada shortly before Edward's death, she made a special trip to see him.

For a short period, during his early days with the CPR, Beatty squired Norah Wilkinson, the English niece of David

McNicoll, a former CPR vice-president. Again, talk of matrimony surfaced and escalated, but Norah returned to England, where she eventually died unwed. More prominent was Beatty's friend the Honourable Marguerite Shaughnessy, daughter of Lord Shaughnessy, who divided her time between St Andrews, Montreal and her home in Pointe Claire. Everything about Marguerite suggested strength of character — "she was really more like a man than a woman," recalls her nephew Thomas. Like all the Shaughnessy women, she was thickset and sturdy, far from the twenties and thirties wispy ideal of womanhood. What attracted Beatty to Marguerite was her incisive and logical mind. Around her, the only woman he ever treated as a peer, he could swear and speak candidly.

Beatty's most intriguing female friend was Kathleen Madill, a distant relation and several years his senior. They met in early life at a family gathering and over the years had ample opportunity to get to know each other, as their families often summered together at the Muskoka Lakes. When Beatty moved to Montreal he kept in regular contact with her, writing long, detailed letters and seeing her during his Toronto visits to his sister, Mary, and his mother. Even in his last years he laboriously penned a nightly letter to "Katy" as he called her, and insisted that his male secretary, John Shearer, post it as soon as it was finished, often quizzing him upon his return to make sure the job was done.*

Oddly, none of Beatty's women ever married. Treleaven, Madill, Wilkinson, Shaughnessy, even his nurse Ethel Smerdon, remained single. They all had one other thing in common: strength of character and forthrightness. The same honesty that he appreciated in business colleagues he also valued in his female friends, and he felt it was a trait lacking in

---

*Not a scrap of Beatty's private correspondence remains. He kept his personal papers carefully sequestered and willed them all to his sister Mary, who may have destroyed them, since none of them has ever surfaced. John Shearer, Beatty's male secretary in his final months, believes that Beatty gave secret instructions to Miss Treleaven to burn certain of his papers on his death.

many women. Beatty loathed gossip and flattery and frequently said women were unfortunately inclined to both.

When Beatty returned to Montreal from his Atlantic City vacation with Hobbs, he immediately threw himself into his war duties. As he busily organized the Atlantic air service to ferry bombers to England,* worried friends urged him to slow down, and several directors cautiously suggested he turn over some responsibilities to someone else — an idea Beatty dismissed out of hand. He had been sitting at the top of his pyramid for so long that relinquishing even a portion of his power was tantamount to admitting the end was near. Then, in the fall of 1940, the pride of Beatty's heart, the *Empress of Britain*, was torpedoed and sunk off the coast of Ireland, and forty-five crew members died. The morning he got the news Beatty sat slumped and immobile at his desk for so long that Treleaven, who never disturbed him unless called for, was forced to ask three or four times if he was all right.

On the evening of March 17, 1941, Ethel Smerdon was chatting with some friends at a Red Cross meeting when Beatty's chauffeur pulled up and the driver dashed in with a message from Dr Brow: "Come quickly, 1266 Pine, Sir Edward ill." Arriving at Beatty's home a few minutes later, she discovered several doctors anxiously huddled around his prostrate form. He had suffered a massive stroke while working in his study and, though conscious, could neither move nor speak. His still handsome face was cruelly contorted and his lips frozen in a ghastly grimace. The physicians wanted to take Beatty to the hospital, but Smerdon begged to be permitted to nurse him at home.

---

*The agreement between the CPR and the British government, which lasted until 1941, gave Beatty responsibility for the Transatlantic Air Ferry Service. Planes delivered to St Hubert Airport in Montreal were taken over by CP Air Services (a department that had been set up in 1940 especially for the war), and flown to Britain or Europe. This had never been attempted before, but Beatty assured British officials it could be done. In July, 1941, the Royal Air Force Ferry Command took over the job.

DURING THE NEXT FEW MONTHS, Beatty struggled with the torture of learning to walk and speak again. At first only Smerdon could understand his unintelligible grunts. Treleaven seconded a young typist, John Shearer, to help him with his correspondence, and when Beatty could hold a pen, Shearer often had to retype letters several times, because Beatty's attempted signature deteriorated into an illegible scrawl. When he was finally able to speak again, his first words were a request to get Katy Madill on the phone, and though Smerdon had to intervene and translate a few times, he eventually spent hours talking to her, often insisting on repeating words over and over to get them right.

Once Beatty could walk without assistance he set off immediately for Windsor Station. Smerdon called ahead to Treleaven, who saw to it that employees were barred from the elevator and the executive wing corridors. Beatty wanted no one to see his stroke-induced, shuffling gait and the twisted leer on his face remaining from the stroke. By Christmas he had recovered remarkably, enough to take a trip to western Canada with his sister, John Hobbs and Ethel Smerdon. When he returned, however, the directors and his doctor convinced him to hand over the presidency to D. C. Coleman, who had been vice-president of the company since 1934 and fully expected to retire in that position. But McGill was another matter, and Beatty flatly refused to step down as chancellor.

As he painstakingly fought his way back to health, a palace coup at McGill undermined his dominance. Shortly before his first illness, Beatty had hired Dr Cyril James as principal of McGill. James vividly recalled Beatty's qualified interest in him. "You already know that Lewis Douglas wants to go back to Washington," Beatty told him. "In normal circumstances, McGill would search for a really distinguished successor in Canada and the United Kingdom, but at present all such people are being absorbed into the war effort. The Board of Governors would therefore like you to take the job."[24]

During Beatty's convalescence, James obligingly shuttled

Beatty with Edward, Prince of Wales

between McGill and 1266 Pine Avenue, carrying out the chancellor's orders. But in 1941 a group of governors, fed up with Beatty's dictatorial reign, met secretly at the Mount Royal Club to plot a coup. "The general feeling at those meetings," recalled James, "was that Beatty had exercised too much power as chancellor and that the Board of Governors as a whole should have a larger say in the running of the University." They decided to institute monthly meetings instead of quarterly ones as Beatty preferred and to convene them at the university instead of at Windsor Station. Beatty, then sick, bedridden and paralyzed, could barely speak, but still no one volunteered to beard the lion. The task fell to James. "If Beatty had been his old self," he admitted after breaking the news, "I should have been shot down in flames."[25]

The final blow to Beatty's once strong and bull-like body came with a gall bladder attack. The operation went extremely well, and all thought he would bounce back yet again. Then, at 11:05 P.M. on March 23, 1943, Edward Beatty died with his brother Harry by his side. Despite the war, his funeral was a showy national event attended by thousands, who lined the bleak, rain-swept streets of Montreal, craning to get a glimpse of the mahogany and brass coffin resting in a bed of purple velvet and flowers.

To most, Beatty's death was a tragedy, though not a surprise, but Kate Treleaven reacted as if he had never been sick. He had been her protector and she, his, and she fully intended to keep working as if he were still in the president's chair. But with Beatty gone, no one saw any reason to keep Treleaven, who was universally unloved within the company. Already seventy-two, the "old horror" was well past the mandatory retirement age. Shortly after the funeral she arrived at her office to find a clerk packing her belongings in a box and a crew in Beatty's office renovating it for Coleman. For the first time, the woman who'd humbled CPR vice-presidents for decades was defeated. She collapsed into a chair, wailing, "They couldn't wait, they couldn't wait." The company gave Treleaven a six-month leave of absence and then quietly retired her altogether. Four years later, almost to the day, she, too, died.

CHAPTER 12

CRISIS, CONFUSION AND CRUMP

"When people talk to me about the lonely cry of the steam whistle in the middle of the night on the Prairie, I say bullshit!"

— Buck Crump

Beatty believed in absolute rule, and when he died he cast the company adrift with no hand at the helm to guide it through the difficult war and postwar years. Stephen, Van Horne, Shaughnessy and Beatty, could all stare the devil in the eye and, on a good day, make him blink. But in 1943 the CPR had no one to carry on the tradition. The only potential successor was William Neal, who had only one year of experience in head office. That left D'Alton Cory Coleman — and he hadn't expected to become president, let alone chairman. Though an extremely capable railroader who had given over forty years of flawless service to the company, Coleman simply had no fire in his belly for the company's top posts. Besides, he was nearly sixty-four when Beatty died. But there was no one else, so Coleman reluctantly put aside his retirement plans.

It was a terrible time to be an interim president and Coleman didn't look anything like a saviour. With delicate features, a high forehead topped by sparse, slicked-down hair and a small, slender body, he resembled a college professor far more than a railroader. His quiet voice, learned vocabulary and meticulous manners cemented the impression. The successive ravages of overexpansion caused by Beatty's battle with

Thornton, the Depression and World War II had left the company in a shambles. During the war the Canadian government had prevailed upon the CPR to move men and transport weapons and food to the Allied forces. The company performed prodigious feats in carrying out its obligations — but at tremendous cost. Nearly every piece of equipment and every mile of track had been worn to the bone. Although the company's profits rose substantially between 1939 and 1943, new equipment wasn't available at any price, since most North American heavy-equipment manufacturing plants had been seconded for war production. Beatty had slashed routine maintenance to a minimum, as many of the CPR's own repair and fabrication shops were retooled to build armaments.

More serious, in the long run, than the deterioration of equipment was the erosion of competence caused by the loss of employees during the war. From 75,000 in 1928, the number of employees had shrunk to 48,689 by 1939. Of that total, 20,742, or nearly 45 percent, enlisted in the Canadian or British forces. With the demands of a war-time economy, the company's personnel requirements shot up to 70,775, and the retired, sick, underage and previously unemployable were pressed into service to fill the gaping manpower holes. Fortunately, thousands of women stepped into difficult, dirty jobs, and worked with an aplomb that suggested generations of experience.

D. C. Coleman, the man reluctantly facing all these problems, had joined the CPR as a twenty-year-old clerk in 1899, at the beginning of the Shaughnessy era, and his timing couldn't have been better. His methodical, almost plodding, meticulousness and attention to detail fit perfectly into Shaughnessy's system, and he advanced rapidly. His scholarly air and large, inquiring eyes, staring out from behind rimless spectacles, gave him an appearance of wisdom far beyond his years. Even as a young clerk, his intellectual manner, coupled with an inherent shyness, led others to think he was "above himself" or "superior." He spoke little, and when he did, his words were curt and to the point. Rarely engaging in small talk or banter with subordinates, he left most of his employees with the impression that he was cold, distant and relentlessly serious.*

As Coleman moved steadily through the ranks, he gained a reputation as a man who could get the job done with a minimum of fuss and who didn't need to be mollycoddled while he

D. C. Coleman

*Coleman wasn't completely cerebral, however. In spite of his almost frail appearance, the quiet executive was an avid sports fan. No one in the company ever heard him raise his voice or saw him become obviously excited, but his son, Jim, who later became a prominent sports writer recalled one time when he saw his father let go. It happened during a hockey game between the CPR and the CNR. "The CP team scored four goals in two minutes and My Old Man jumped up and lifted his hat and cane in the air and shouted 'Hurray' — and sat down again, quickly. Just like that!" (*Toronto Star*, June 16, 1951)

Jim Coleman often went along on his father's business trips. "Somehow we'd arrive in Detroit just in time to see the Tigers play the Philadelphia Athletics," he recalls fondly. "When we reached St. Louis, who should be playing but Babe Ruth and the New York Yankees?" If his father couldn't attend, he'd send young Jim to the game with the sleeping-car conductor.

did it. In 1918, after only nineteen years with the CPR, Coleman became vice-president of western lines in Winnipeg, the number three position in the company. During the next sixteen years he oversaw the CPR's huge Prairie expansion, and during the Depression he kept the system going as massive layoffs turned many departments into skeletons. Nicknamed "big little man," Coleman had no tolerance for ineptitude, but he never indulged in a Van Horne style tirade or a scathing and sarcastic criticism à la Shaughnessy. Those who displeased him were scolded, not beaten or belittled. When one employee made a mess of things after he had been entrusted with providing for visiting dignitaries in the vice-president's absence, Coleman simply telegrammed: "You have embarrassed me very much."[1]

In 1934 Beatty brought Coleman to Montreal as vice-president of the company and made him a director and executive committee member. He was the perfect right-hand man for Beatty, who continued to make all the major decisions without consultation but cared less and less for details. Coleman happily took responsibility for putting Beatty's plans into action and for the thousands of picayune details the president couldn't be bothered with. At times it seemed as if Coleman was little more than Beatty's office boy. Even after Beatty first became ill in 1939, he refused to loosen his grip, giving Coleman few opportunities to exercise his judgment in matters of law, administration or policy.

As president of the CPR, Coleman was an aloof and distant figure, using his assistant Sandy Lyle as a buffer much as Beatty had used Kate Treleaven. Lyle acted as the president's conduit to the rest of the company and at times even stood in for him at press interviews. Inevitably, Lyle became openly disliked, particularly at the lower levels of management, for his overbearing protectiveness of Coleman and his sharp tongue — which he exercised frequently whenever he came across anything that might merit the president's displeasure. Coleman was rarely seen outside his office and almost never on the line. On the few occasions when Coleman did grant interviews, the

questions were invariably twice as long as his cautious, reserved answers. Soon reporters turned to Coleman's second in
command, W. M. Neal, who appreciated the value of an appropriately flattering article.

AS COLEMAN SAW IT, HE HAD two jobs: to keep the CPR on an
even keel during his term and to groom his successor, company vice-president William Neal, a man he'd singled out way
back in 1934 as a contender for the top position. Neal, a true
man's man, had also been a great favourite of Beatty, who
preferred his robust company over that of any other ranking
officer on inspection trips. Beatty even invited Neal to accompany him when passing through divisions not under his ju-
risdiction — something that didn't sit well with the other
superintendents and general managers. Not only was Neal a
good travelling partner, but his insomnia guaranteed Beatty a
companion at all hours of the night. On one of those trips in
the early thirties, during a stop on an isolated section of track,
Beatty was alarmed to find that Neal was missing. He dispatched several officers to search for him and after a frantic
half hour Beatty was hugely amused to learn that Neal was
swimming stark naked in a nearby mist-shrouded lake.
   Coleman knew he only had a few years as head of the
company and he had to prepare Neal quickly. Immediately
after becoming president in 1942 he pulled Neal out of Winnipeg, where he'd been vice-president of western lines since
1934, and brought him to Montreal as senior vice-president.
Ideally, Neal would have been made president on Beatty's
death in 1943, with Coleman presiding as chairman. But he
had only one year of head office experience at that point.
While vice-presidents had tremendous power and responsibility, a vast chasm gaped between the number one and
number two jobs. Neal had to develop political savvy and learn
the delicate art of subtly bending the board to his will. He
needed to acquire negotiating skills while refining his sense of
superiority over the company's rival, the CNR. Finally, and

most important, he had to develop the steel backbone neces-sary to make monumental decisions affecting thousands of people and the economy of entire towns — sometimes whole provinces.

Regal, imperious, darkly handsome and well-spoken, Neal stood out in sharp contrast to Coleman. His encyclopædic knowledge of the railway and arrogant authoritarianism made him classic CPR leadership material. No one ever expected that Coleman would fill Beatty's shoes, but everyone looked to Neal to continue the line and make the war-ravaged company strong again. But beneath Neal's armour-plated personality ran an unseen vein of weakness, and the burden of expecta-tion proved a catastrophically heavy load.

Known as Bill on the job and Billy by those who knew him best, Neal was born in Toronto on June 20, 1886, to William Merton and Elizabeth O'Neil.* He left school after grade five

William Neal

---

*While he was a young child, his Irish parents anglicized their name to Neal.

and spent several years stuffing pincushions in a factory before enrolling in a shorthand and typing course at Dominion Business College. In 1902, on his way to his first job interview at the Toronto Methodist Bookroom, he collided with the CPR's Toronto superintendent, Albert Price, who had just bought a book and was about to leave. After accepting the young man's profuse apologies, Price spent several minutes talking with him and was surprised by Neal's articulate poise, notwithstanding his grade five education. Price offered him a job on the spot as a CPR clerk.

As he moved steadily up the ranks and into the key transportation section of the company, co-workers and subordinates began to see a man with two distinct personalities. To some — especially to those in the lower ranks — he was warm-hearted, engaging and sympathetic. But to most others, particularly office staff, he was a "cold bastard, with a cruel streak," who bludgeoned subordinates for sloppy work or the slightest deviation from his strict code. Edward Beatty never allowed CPR employees to see the perplexing contradictions between his private and public selves. But Neal seemed to enjoy flaunting the lightning-swift alterations in his personality.

As vice-president of western lines from 1934 to 1942, Neal insisted on personally vetting every new employee, even labourers — a previously unheard-of practice. Once past Neal's stern inquiry, they were given a CPR rule book to memorize. Months might go by, and then Neal would suddenly materialize at some divisional point and quiz the new staffer about an obscure regulation. This sort of attention to minuscule detail also extended to his dealings with office staff. Company memos, he decreed, had to be typed according to exact specifications. Carbon copies were forbidden, so if copies had to be made, each one was typed separately — without errors. To enforce his dictum, Neal inspected the documents by holding up originals and copies to the light. If the periods and commas didn't line up, he ordered the whole lot redone. A tartar about punctuality, Neal sent employees home if they were late even by a few minutes, and docked them an entire day's pay.

He abhorred untidiness of any kind, and when a young clerk with a bad cold showed up one day wearing a sweater beneath his suit jacket, he was chastised and sent home.

But around his "boys," as he called the mechanics, firemen and engineers who actually worked on the railroad, Neal was a jovial companion, who insisted that the men's children call him Uncle Billy. Curtness gave way to easy banter as he inquired about their health, families and problems on the job. He addressed young apprentices as if they were childhood pals and was fond of boasting that he "always had time to talk to the poor section man." Some of his friendliness was genuine and some clever pretence. Jack Anderson, who rose to become vice-president of industrial relations, once accompanied Neal on an inspection trip. He vividly recalls being sent off in advance to surreptitiously collect crew names and details about their wives, children, misfortunes and successes, so Neal could commiserate, congratulate or inquire with all the pertinent information at hand.

The press adored him, for his comments always seemed candid and straightforward. "No hammer and chisel are required to penetrate through his plating," one writer commented. "The esprit de corps which exists in the C.P.R. system has resulted from the labors of such men as Mr. Neal. That sort of thing never develops under a tyranny, however restrained it may be."[2] Whenever newspapermen gathered together Neal was quick to invite them for a drink and he invariably insisted on picking up the tab. As western vice-president during the later years of the Depression, Neal had an unenviable job, but the local media sang his virtues constantly and Manitobans came to see him as a native. When he moved to Montreal in 1942 headlines mourned the loss of "one of our own."

NEAL SPENT FIVE YEARS TRAINING to become president and chairman and when an ailing Coleman turned the two jobs over to him in February, 1947, he attacked his responsibilities with fervour and enthusiasm. One thing Coleman impressed upon Neal was the importance of cleaning out and revitalizing many company departments where efficiency and productivity had sagged during the war. Mandatory retirement had been set aside since 1939 and it wasn't unusual to find managers and supervisors in their late sixties and early seventies happily clinging to old-fashioned methods. A seventy-four-year-old senior officer in the accounting department refused to allow his staff to use adding machines, insisting they do all sums by hand, and only used his telephone as a paperweight. It would have taken years to burrow through every department, and the company needed a fast facelift. Neal's solution was a steering committee empowered with responsibility to investigate the trouble spots.

It was a clever idea poorly executed, and Neal showed astounding insensitivity to the potentially devastating impact it could have on morale. Instead of staffing the committee with a representative mix of employees from different ranks and all parts of the country, Neal chose a handful of steely-eyed young turks from Windsor Station, including a keen lawyer by the name of Ian Sinclair and a brilliant engineer, R. A. Emerson, who as yet had little understanding of company tradition or respect for it.*

Committee members set to work with a will, poking and prying into all levels of the company's affairs, investigating departments, reporting on efficiency, even recommending personnel changes and generally running roughshod over anyone who got in their way. Respected men with decades of experience were forced to submit to their scrutiny. Feared and loathed, the powerful little band became known as Billy's Inquisition. "The committee generated some high drama, bad feelings and shaken morale," recalled Fred Stone, a committee member, forty years later. "Its demise gave rise to a general feeling of relief."[3]

---

*Even the committee members themselves weren't comfortable with their jobs, and those still living dislike speaking about it.

The opposition and antagonism to his steering committee surprised Neal, but he stubbornly refused to soften its thrust. Instead, he struck back at those who spoke against it, firing or demoting several senior officers. At first it appeared that he intended to use the committee as a harsh but necessary tool to scour away the CPR's dead wood and outmoded ideas. But when Neal began undermining his vice-presidents, it was clear that he had become nervous about the power of those beneath him. One morning William Mather, who held Neal's old job as vice-president of western lines in Winnipeg, came to work to discover that his empire had shrunk overnight by about a third. The whole province of British Columbia had been wiped off his map, and he was left with only the Prairies.

While Billy's Inquisition rolled like a juggernaut through the company, Neal faced his own personal ordeal. His initial enthusiasm began to fade as he came to realize the monstrous task that stretched before him. Rolling stock had to be up-graded, thousands of miles of long-neglected track had to be replaced and the steamship company, decimated by war losses, had to be rebuilt. The company's antiquated management structure, still rooted in the 1920s, needed a major overhaul and the growing wave of labour discontent brought on by inflation and higher American wages had to be quelled. And then, of course, there was Canadian Pacific Air Lines Ltd., set up in 1942 and by 1947 consisting of a higgledy-piggledy mishmash of routes and aircraft, some of which dated back to the first war.

Neal leapt upon the airlines with the kind of vigour reminis-cent of his days in Winnipeg. He hired the quirky but brilliant Grant McConachie and made him president of the airline, though he was only thirty-eight years old. By this point Neal was known as "Old Slaughterhouse" and employees tended to tiptoe past his door. Not so McConachie, who rode a bicycle to work and galloped through the CPR's inner sanctum like a young colt. When he wanted to see Neal, he'd roar past the secretary and hurl himself at the president's desk, saying, "And how are ya today, Mr Neal."[4] Together, McConachie and Neal persuaded C. D. Howe, minister of transport, to allow the airlines to operate in the west, the north, parts of Quebec and across the Pacific — but only because the government-owned Trans-Canada Airlines president didn't believe those routes could be profitable.

The airline was the only part of the CPR's operations that really excited Neal. As for the rest of the company, he felt no heady rush of exhilaration, no confidence that he could rebuild the wobbly structure. Instead, he suffered from the crushing weight of a crumbling colossus pressing on his shoulders.

IN THE SPRING OF 1947, NEAL went to England on the *Empress of Canada* for a round of getting-to-know-you meetings with the media and the CPR's European officials. Rolly Wilkes, who accompanied him as secretary, watched his superior grow steadily wearier as the insomnia that plagued Neal all his life became chronic. In his younger days, his robust physique allowed him to shrug off the lack of sleep, but now deep lines were etched in the sixty-one-year-old president's face and his former ruddy glow of good health gave way to a sickly pallor. He spent most of the return trip in his cabin bed with a severe cold.

Back in Montreal his condition went from bad to worse. Always a heavy social drinker, he began to arrive at work with whiskey on his breath. His complexion, alternately grey and flushed, aged him, and his nagging cold persisted. In June concerned directors urged him to spend a few weeks at the Seigniory Club at Montebello, Quebec, a posh resort frequented only by the wealthy and well-born. When he returned, still haggard but improved, Neal began a torrid affair with a young, shapely blonde. At first he was discreet enough to keep his "parties," as the scandalized employees dubbed them, private — often ordering his own business car hauled to odd places and parked, giving instructions for the engineer to return and collect him in the morning. But later he abandoned discretion and frequently squired his lover in public, lunching at an exclusive restaurant not far from Windsor Station.

Shortly after New Year's, 1948, Neal, Grant McConachie, Allan McDonald and Rolly Wilkes boarded a Northstar airplane for a demonstration flight to Jamaica. The plan was for Neal to assess the plane's performance and then stay on the island for a week to recuperate from his endless chest cold. And stay he did — but not just for one week. Half a month went by with nary a word from the president, and when George Walker, the senior vice-president in Montreal, sent a cautious query, he got no reply. Several more weeks passed with still no news of the president, though heads of various departments received the occasional letter or telegram with instructions or comments.

After nearly two months, Neal's absence had become an embarrassment, and with the annual meeting fast approaching the company needed him in Montreal. Philippe Brais, a senior board member and a friend of Neal, was delegated to investigate. Arriving in Jamaica, Brais was shocked to discover a man in the midst of a nervous breakdown. But far from being willing to resign, Neal maintained that he was running — and could run — the CPR just as well from Jamaica as from Montreal. Brais urged Neal to come back and see his doctor, but to no avail. Several weeks after Brais returned to Canada, Neal was still incommunicado. The whole fiasco came to a head at the end of February when Neal called first a board meeting and then the annual general meeting, both to be held in Jamaica.

The thunderstruck CPR directors finally realized they would have to act, but impeachment did not exist in the CPR vocabulary. The president was god and stayed that way until he died. Even though Edward Beatty had been virtually incapacitated during his last three years as president, the directors had only gingerly suggested that he resign as president — and no one dared even hint that he should step down as chairman. The prospect of firing Neal horrified the board, but with the annual meeting in the offing, they were forced to act.

On March 3rd, Philippe Brais and George Walker went to Jamaica, to either bring back Neal's head on a platter or at the very least persuade him to resign. Somehow they talked him into returning, but when the plane stopped for refuelling in New York, Neal slipped out and checked into a suite of rooms at the Waldorf Towers — and there he stayed, refusing to budge. He had become aware at last that the game was over, but withheld his resignation until the company offered him what he considered suitable retirement compensation.

On March 8, 1948, the CPR issued a press release announcing the president's retirement. "Mr. Neal, who has been recuperating in Jamaica this winter from an illness of some months' duration, tendered his resignation upon the insistence of his medical advisors. He asked, under the circumstances, to be relieved of his responsibilities immediately, a request which was acceded to with regret by the board of directors today."[5] Fred Stone and other CPR insiders marvelled then and later that not a hint of the story about Neal's "moral conduct" made it into the papers. It was all the more amazing, since so "many people inside Canadian Pacific knew or heard of Neal's condition and conduct in the months before his retirement."[6]

Neal eventually returned to Canada and quietly moved to Winnipeg with his wife, Frances. A few years later Stone met Neal by chance, on the train from Calgary to Winnipeg, and was astonished by the former president's relaxed manner and humorous asides about his new-found sobriety. "We talked for a couple of hours in the lounge car," Stone recalled. "He made many enquiries regarding developments in the Company and commented on some of them. He was quite rational, there was no evidence of rancour, and his sharp memory of various ongoing activities in the Company surprised me."[7] Neal, sixty-one when he retired, never worked again, but divided his time between Hawaii, Winnipeg and his summer home. He died at

Long Bow Lake near Kenora, Ontario, in 1961 at the age of
seventy-five.

FOR THE SECOND TIME IN FOUR YEARS, the CPR was left without
a proper successor. Fortunately, two men who complemented
each other like different sides of the same coin were ready to
take over the reins — at least until a new president could be
found. George Walker agreed to become chairman if William
Mather took on the presidency, and Mather said he would
serve as president, providing Walker became chairman. They
faced the same vast problems that Neal had encountered, but
neither had the benefit of even a moment of psychological
preparation for the job. What's more, Mather was near retirement at sixty-three and Walker was well past it at sixty-nine.
Nevertheless, theirs was an unbelievably fortunate pairing.
Although they were complete opposites intellectually and
temperamentally, Walker and Mather understood each other's
strengths and weaknesses. As a team they swung quickly into
action, officially assuming the presidency and chairmanship
on Monday, March 8, 1948, the same day that Neal's retirement notice was issued. By the end of the week, they had
abolished Neal's hated steering committee and sent out an
edict forbidding women to travel in the business cars.*

Before he married, George Walker distinguished himself as
a two-fisted drinker, closing down most law school parties and
often grabbing no more than an hour of sleep before tearing
off to class. He was also notorious for being able to swear for
ten solid minutes without repeating a single word. Walker, six
foot three inches tall, also had all the geniality and generous
spirit of a benevolent giant. Almost every CPR employee felt
free to approach him, and many times during his tenure as
senior vice-president and later as chairman he could be found,

---

*At the same meeting that ratified the Walker-Mather team, the board decided that the
positions of president and chairman would never again be held by one man.

his long form folded up in a cramped office, earnestly discussing some point with a junior officer.

The airline business fascinated Walker, and in a company where everything from hotels to mines was run by railway men, he went against tradition and ensured that Canadian Pacific Air Lines had veteran staff in the field. One of his favourites was McConachie, who preached the airline gospel with the entertaining flair of a stand-up comic and the passion of a missionary. After a session with McConachie, Walker would return to his office, fling himself back in his chair, put his feet on the desk and tell his secretary to hold all calls while he "demesmerized" himself.

Mather, in contrast, was a quiet man who disliked large gatherings and hated making speeches. Some thought him plodding and slow, but he was a careful, decisive thinker. When company officers brought him verbal or written reports, he rarely responded immediately, preferring to drop by their offices and casually detail his opinions. He had little vanity, and if he liked a suggestion, he simply scrawled "Yes" or "Do it" across the top of the page, allowing the junior officer to take responsibility and credit for the job.

Uncomfortable with social chit-chat, Mather was even more unhappy with the corporate bafflegab that began to infiltrate the business world after the war. "For heaven's sake, say what you mean!" was one of his most frequent expressions. Les Croteau, manager of an Alberta oil company of which Mather was a director once observed: "Mather does not say much; but when he asks a question, you don't try any end runs — you go right down the middle."[8]

Mather and Walker knew their job was to maintain the company and groom the heir apparent who had been selected years before, Norris Roy (Buck) Crump. Like Stephen, Van Horne and Shaughnessy, Crump had humble origins, yet he was strong-willed, ambitious, opinionated and intelligent. Any weaknesses were well sealed behind an air of invincibility. He had just the right amount of arrogance to set him apart from the general horde, yet his own labourer's roots and common-sense approach made him the most popular company president ever. At long last, Canadian Pacific again had a leader who could look the devil in the eye — and this one didn't need a good day to make him blink.

NORRIS ROY CRUMP CAME FROM a family that served the CPR for a total of 167 years. Crump's father, Thomas H., joined the company in 1890. A lad of eighteen with a mind of his own, he left the lush greenery of England for a job as a track labourer in Medicine Hat, Alberta. Landing in Quebec City and unable to find work, Thomas Crump headed west after hearing that the CPR needed trackmen, the most menial job on the line. It was brutal work — ten-hour days for a single dollar in wages.* From dawn to early evening the sweat poured off him and the dry, unrelenting Prairie sun parched his throat and lips. The roadmasters, responsible for forcing and cajoling work out of the track gangs, were the lowest-ranking bosses in the CPR hierarchy and sometimes seemed to be lowest on the evolutionary scale as well. By necessity and by temperament, they were often tyrannical dictators who ran their patch of track with all the sensitivity of chain-gang guards. The track crews, a thrown-together stew of immigrants, wanderers, remittance men and the odd fugitive, provided ideal fodder for the power-hungry. If a roadmaster didn't like the way one of his navvies spit, he fired him — no recourse, no separation pay, nothing.

Roadmasters kept a sharp eye out for troublemakers, ready to quash the slightest sign of disruptive individuality. When Thomas Crump's boss — a large man well known for his vile temper and propensity to solve even the slightest difference of opinion with his fists — saw the new arrival's jaunty cap, he

---

*During construction some labourers were paid as much as two dollars a day, but wages were quickly reduced when the demand for labourers declined after the last spike. There was also no consistency in what a navvy might be paid in British Columbia and in Ontario. Divisional heads simply tried to hire the best men for the least amount of money, taking advantage of labour surplus to reduce wages or perks like accommodation and food.

barked: "Get rid of that goddamned thing."* Crump had two
choices, to comply or be fired and left stranded, penniless, in
the middle of nowhere, but he didn't say a word, simply looking the man dead in the eye. An expectant hush fell over the
crew, who were sure that bloodshed was impending. Everything about the recent recruit — from the "don't tread on me"
set of his features to the relaxed but powerful expanse of his
shoulders, suggested the potential for massive retaliation. One
might defeat such a man in a fight, but at what cost?

For the first time in his career, the roadmaster backed down
to a labourer. Breaking the stalemate, he turned away abruptly
and went about his business for the rest of the day as if nothing
untoward had happened. Crump joined the road crew with his
cap, which became his trademark, still planted firmly atop his
head. You had to be hard in those days to survive the rigours of
life as a CPR navvy,† and Crump filled the bill. He had more
than just an intimidating gaze and broad shoulders to support
him. Though he was only five-foot-eight, he exuded an air of
granite-like immobility and unshakeable resolve that sapped
the will of even the most formidable challengers. As his frame
thickened and he topped two hundred pounds, the sinewy,
corded muscle made his already powerful chest massive and
gave him the strength to do jobs that often required two men.

Ruggedness was common coin on the road gangs; literacy
was not. So when one of the section officers learned that
Thomas Crump could read and write — in fact, had excellent penmanship — he immediately transferred him to the
Medicine Hat stores department. From there he became a
brakeman working the rail stretch between Medicine Hat

---

*Crump wore a typical English cap that made him look a bit of a dandy amidst the scruffy,
dirty labourers.

†Life as a navvy could also be bitterly lonely. The only people the road gangs saw from one
week to the next were the Mounted Police, who sometimes stopped to share a can of tea and
spin a few yarns, or the Blackfeet, who silently watched the rails being laid. One of the few
exciting events that Crump witnessed was Crowfoot's funeral procession. The tough navvy
stood leaning on his pick at Blackfoot Crossing as the procession, bearing the great chief's
body, wove slowly by.

and Canmore, gaining a singular reputation as someone who could solve problems, any problems. Crump's talent as a "clean-up man" didn't escape his superiors, who sent him from one hot spot to another, sorting out mistakes, smoothing the waters and investigating wrecks. Trouble shooters like Crump were worth their weight in gold, particularly in the mountains, where every twist and bend in the track, every steep grade and impossibly long trestle hid myriads of idiosyncrasies, all magnified by the extremes of weather.

But in all the mountains there was one stretch more treacherous than all the rest: the eighty miles that ran west from the Big Hill* at Field to the Rogers Pass. The reputation of this section was so fearsome that new recruits were warned they'd be sent there if they didn't measure up. Few returned unmarked, their tormentors would say, listing in grisly detail the accidents, the cold and the endless deluges of snow that could bury a man in an instant. And the stories were mostly true. In 1885, the same year that Donald Smith drove the last spike, more than thirteen metres of snow fell on the Big Hill. Rogers Pass was an equal hazard. In 1899 seven men were swept away by an avalanche that ripped apart the station roundhouse there.

The perilous mountain trackage cast a pall over the soul of even the most courageous. "The men are frightened," James Ross, western construction manager, warned Van Horne in 1883. "I find the snowslides on the Selkirks are much more serious than I anticipated, and I think are quite beyond your ideas of their magnitude and danger to the line." To make matters worse, the Hill's 4.4 percent grade was double that on any other section of the line. In comparison, the Peruvian National Railway, which cuts through the Andes at 15,670 feet above sea level, never exceeds a 4 percent grade.

After two decades of horrendously expensive maintenance, lost lives and equipment, and missed schedules, the CPR built the Spiral Tunnel. An engineering marvel, it was bored

---

*The Big Hill section is the legacy of Major Rogers' "new route" through the mountains. Running between Stephen and Field, the Big Hill climbs up the slopes of the Selkirks for over 1,100 feet, the steepest part covering just a few miles.

Clearing an avalanche on the CPR line in the Rogers Pass, 1910

through the mountains themselves and reduced the grade from 4.4 percent to an acceptable 2.2 percent. Construction began in 1906, and that year Thomas Crump, after holding numerous positions in the West, was transferred from Revelstoke to Field as trainmaster. During the three years it took to complete the tunnel, he contended with the coordination of freight and work crews on and off the four spur lines that had been set up for construction. He also had to make sure that trains got up and down the Hill safely—in itself no mean feat.

BUCK CRUMP SPENT HIS EARLY YEARS in the tiny settlement of Field, British Columbia. Life in the town centred entirely on the railway — the maintenance yards and the pleasant, clapboard Mt Stephen House, which drew tourists and adventurers until the company tore it down in the 1920s. Mt

Stephen House was a victualling stop for train passengers who could enjoy lunch there or wander about, surveying the magnificent scenery. As a little bonus for tourists, the CPR cleverly tethered a black bear near the hotel, so travellers could gawk or have their pictures taken next to an example of real Canadian wildlife.* Old Pete, a medium-sized beast of uncertain temperament, soon became one of Field's main attractions. When the trains drew in, Pete emerged from his den of railway ties and stalked around, never failing to draw a large crowd of entranced tourists.

As Old Pete prowled in circles, his chain wrapped around his pole, tightening his radius and drawing the tourists in ever closer. When he came to the end of his tether, the bear let out a huge roar and rapidly reversed course, scattering the frightened onlookers in every direction. "Pete got a big bang out of this," guffaws Crump. "My mother and the other natives would come out to watch — it was quite a spectacle." Aside from Pete's amusement value, locals considered him just

Old Pete at Mt Stephen House

---

*The bear was also a favourite of newspaper photographers eager to spice up their coverage of the CPR. When one of the first photos of a tourist and a CPR bear appeared in a London journal, the publication touched up the negative so the bear's chain was hidden. The caption read, "This Bear Is Not Stuffed!"

another part of the terrain, and children thought nothing of taking short cuts by and over his den.

Then one day, eight-year-old Crump, trailing along behind his older brother and friends, walked in front of Pete's den. As Crump passed the entrance, the bear cuffed him down with his huge, hairy paw and started dragging him inside. It would have been the end of the future railroad president if a kitchen worker at the hotel hadn't stepped out at just that moment to empty a bucket of slops. He saw the incident and in a flash dumped the scraps in front of Old Pete, who promptly released Crump, deciding that a boy was less appealing than leftovers. "Not many people can say they were saved by a pail of garbage," smiles Crump.*

After nine years of monotony at school Crump had had enough, and he quit. This left him with only two alternatives: he could head to Vancouver for a job on the road crews or he could work for the CPR at Field. So it was that in June, 1920, N. R. Crump hired on at forty cents an hour as a railway labourer. As the shortest (five-foot-seven) and youngest member of his crew, Crump seemed easy prey for the tough guys, especially since most suspected he only got the job through his father. Nepotism was running rampant in the CPR, where tradition slowed promotions to a snail's pace if you didn't have a family member or friend in some lofty place. Every little dirty job was shunted over to Crump. "The labour and all the repair people were Italian and I was the son of the trainmaster there and boy they really had it in for me," he says ruefully. But his readiness to use his fists and his unwillingness to be pushed even an inch earned him the nickname "Buck" which he has kept to this day.†

---

*Old Pete was shot a few months later when he badly mauled and nearly killed another young boy.

†For years Crump claimed not to know where his nickname came from but after many people asked, he offered the explanation that his mother dressed him in a Buster Brown outfit when he was a child. "All these enginemen up and down the Hill would see me and started calling me Buster. As I got a bit older it got shortened to Buck." But in western logging and railroad camps the toughest man on the crew, and often the most pugnacious, was usually called Buck.

ONE BRUTALLY HOT DAY THAT SUMMER, Crump and the rest of the track gang were wrestling to lift three-hundred-pound draw bars, part of the train's coupling mechanism, into place. With one man on either side of a short iron rod they heaved and struggled to move the bars. At that moment Crump was visited by an insight that changed his life. "We were packed close together," he grimaces as though it were yesterday, "and suddenly in the midst of that smell of sweat and garlic, I thought to myself: 'You aren't on the right track. You've got to get out of this.'"[10] Thinking he might like to be a mechanic, Crump discussed the possibilities with his father, who ruminated for a while before saying, "Well, that's your choice if you want to go into the shops." Then he added, "But don't go around with a monkey wrench hung on your watch chain," telling his son not to set his sights too low.

The next day Crump signed up for a five-year machinist apprenticeship program. But after a year in the locomotive pits, his doubts returned. Crump began looking wistfully at the spanking-clean engine wipers.* "One of my schoolmates did that and he wore nice clean overalls . . . and there I was struggling down in the pit." Though a wiper was among the lowliest of railway employees, those who stuck it out eventually reached the position of fireman and finally attained the exalted height of locomotive engineer or driver. Crump admired the mechanics, most of whom were Scottish or English and lived in a section of Revelstoke called Little Scotland. Still, he questioned whether he really wanted to stay in their trade. One day he was assisting Bob Miller, a journeyman mechanic in charge of air brakes. Miller sat in the cab operating the brakes while the apprentice worked in the filthy pit laboriously adjusting the turnbuckles, with oil and dirt dropping from the engine's underbelly into his face and eyes.

---

*The engine wipers' high standard of cleanliness was not duplicated in the United States. In later years if Crump wanted to insult a train crew, he'd say, "'the goddamn locomotive looks as if it belongs to the New York Central.' The Americans never looked after the locomotives, dirt and grease and grime — terrible! They never wiped them." On several occasions, as president, Crump ordered his own crews to clean an American locomotive that was especially filthy.

Periodically Miller came down to check on Crump's work and take a few illicit puffs on a sawed-off pipe he kept in his pocket. Crump had just finished calibrating the tender brakes when Miller appeared, lit his pipe and squatted in the corner of the pit, puffing away as he looked speculatively at Crump.

> "Why don't you go to university," he asked.
> "I can't go to university, I'm not qualified, I'm a grade nine drop out," responded Crump.
> "Well, you can go to night school," Miller retorted.

Crump mentioned the conversation to his father, who observed, "a degree saves a lot of explanation." In 1923, Crump transferred to Winnipeg, where he simultaneously finished his apprenticeship during the day and attended night school, taking only two winters to complete grades ten, eleven and twelve. Book learning never came easily to Crump, but over the course of his nineteen years, he had developed the ability to apply himself to any problem, making up in dogged slogging what he lacked in natural talent. Ironically, for a man who later took such pride in his rank-and-file origins, Norris Roy Crump expended a tremendous amount of energy to leave them far behind.

With every day that Crump spent in the roundhouses, he became more and more resolved to leave them forever. Winter transformed the cavernous structures into frozen fairylands with ice crusting into foot-thick layers on the walls and machinery. They became beautiful but hideously uncomfortable and treacherous refrigerators. Drafty and barn-like, the roundhouses were fitted with pathetically inadequate fans and heaters. Far from clearing the air, the system created steamy mists, so dense at times that workers could navigate their way past the pits only by edging along the walls. In summer, thick muggy banks of heat left workers drained and sodden after only a few hours. "The wonder is I'm alive," marvels Crump.

After finishing his apprenticeship in 1925, Crump enrolled at Purdue University in Lafayette, Indiana. For the next four years he studied every winter, returning to the CPR in

Buck Crump as a young mechanic

the summer months to work in the miserable roundhouses. Purdue was widely known as *the* trainman's university because the American Railroad Association tested all the latest equipment there and maintained a staff of eighty people for that purpose. It was at Purdue that Crump saw the first diesel engines, a discovery that was later to revolutionize the CPR and make Crump into an icon-smashing president. He recognized where the future of railroading lay, but twenty years passed before he could do anything about it.*

With his degree in hand, Crump returned to Canada, ready to take the first steps on his ladder out of the pits, but within three months he was laid off. Although his nine years' seniority should have insulated him from the cutbacks that hacked away several thousand jobs, the union ruled that because it hadn't granted him permission to leave the job for study, his last three years of work didn't count. "It never occurred to me to ask their consent; I had the consent of the Company. So they wiped out my seniority!" Crump snorts, still clearly riled fifty-nine years later. Like many young men, Crump saw all his training and work drain away overnight, and he was reduced to scrambling for enough money just to eat. He allowed himself a dollar a day for food, which he stretched to its maximum by eating chow mein for breakfast, lunch and dinner.

But Crump was one of the lucky ones. Prime Minister R. B. Bennett brought in railway subsidies in 1930 to stem the massive unemployment the country would face if the two major systems cut back their payrolls as much as they wanted. Six months after being laid off Crump was rehired as a night foreman in Saskatoon and one of the first things he did after he got the position was to get married. During the first eighteen years of their married life, the Crumps lived in twelve different cities and fourteen separate houses — some of them primitive to the extreme. In Wilkie, Saskatchewan, the company house they moved to in 1934 had no indoor toilet and no running water. The day they arrived it was so cold the veneer peeled right off their dining-room table.

Over the next few years Crump kept thinking about diesel engines. Canadian National had been quick off the mark, Sir Henry Thornton having put a lot of money behind a diesel

---

*Also at Purdue Crump met his wife Stella, a student at the library school there. The two came across each other thanks to Crump's part-time job shelving books in the library for twenty-five cents an hour.

program back in 1926. One of the CNR prototypes set a new transcontinental record when it sped 2,937 miles from Montreal to Vancouver in 67 hours. The company's two-unit locomotive, built in 1928, was larger and more advanced than any designed by either the German or the Russian pioneers. The CPR, however, was conspicuous in its lack of interest in the new technology.

After five years of work in the field, Purdue allowed graduates to submit a thesis for a professional degree. Crump chose diesels, tackling the complex subject with the tenacity of a bulldog. He worked for the CPR from seven at night to seven in the morning, as even with government subsidies, the company was badly understaffed. Then he staggered home, ate and fell into bed until four in the afternoon when he woke up, put in several hours of work on his thesis, ate dinner and headed back to the roundhouse. While he slept his wife took their baby out for long walks so the crying wouldn't disturb him. By 1936 when he finished his thesis, "Internal Combustion Engines in the Railroad Field," Buck Crump had become one of the leading experts on diesels in North America.

With his second degree completed, Crump advanced to division master mechanic in Regina and it was during this posting that his name began to circulate in the company's upper echelons. Part of his responsibility was the onerous job of keeping the railway's cantankerous gas-electric engines operating. "They were horrible things, always in trouble," he recalls. With too much car and not enough engine, the locomotives spent as much time in the shops as on the road. Their unreliability was an even greater hazard during the Depression because in those years every train that ran was loaded to maximum capacity. Eventually the gas-electric engines' ridiculous maintenance costs caused head office to question the value of their existence, and Crump was seconded to write a comprehensive assessment of their efficiency. Nuts and bolts suddenly gave way to "accounts," a subject which before and since has driven many a good railroad man to his knees. Nonetheless, Crump dived into the task and acquitted himself adequately enough for William Neal, then vice-president of western lines to turn his gaze on "that fellow Crump."

BY 1942 CRUMP HAD EARNED the imposing title of assistant to the superintendent of motive power and cars, western lines, but he still spent far more time in greasy coveralls, poking around the locomotives' entrails, than he did in an office — and he saw little chance of that ever changing. One evening he was under an engine checking for loose bearings when a call boy trotted over and told him he was wanted on the telephone. Pausing only to wipe the worst of the grease off his hands, Crump hurried to the phone, thinking that it had to be bad news. He'd been on the road inspecting equipment for six consecutive weeks. A call now meant either another assignment and more time away from home or a family emergency, as personal calls were strictly forbidden on company time. Instead, it was his superintendent with a mysterious order. "You're to report to Montreal in two days' time," he said in a peevish tone. "What's that all about?" asked Crump. "How do I know?" snapped his boss, aggravated at the peremptory instructions he'd received from head office and the prospect of losing his best man.

In those days a call to Montreal was tantamount to a royal summons and Crump left immediately, full of trepidation and accompanied by a suitcase packed with six weeks of dirty laundry.* Edward Beatty had just resigned, Coleman had been elevated to president and Neal to vice-president of the company. "Get me Crump," Neal had demanded, sending his secretary off puzzling about whether he meant a person or something to eat. Whispers and rumours flew around Windsor Station when it became known that Neal had taken on an obscure grease monkey — and a western one at that — as his senior assistant.

Inwardly Crump thought, "My god!" while outwardly he

*Crump would later say, "I'm the only guy that ever went down to Montreal with a bag full of dirty shirts and came back in a private car."

projected a calm façade. "That's very nice, sir," he said as Neal handed him the news. The jump from roundhouse pit to the executive wing was huge and unprecedented. "We were accustomed to wise men coming from the east," observes Florence Evans, a company stenographer at the time. Crump had no operational experience: he knew everything possible about fixing trains but nothing about running a system full of them. Windsor Station staff treated him as an interloper. "The knives were out," he remembers. "All the hatchet men were looking for me. A young mechanical officer from western Canada? Down in the jungle of the east? Hah!" Everyone waited for his first major slip. Confronted with myriads of subjects in which he had no training — law, public relations, personnel, and the jargon endemic to each — Crump had to swim a little faster than all the sharks in the executive pool. "I had to learn fast just to survive."

During Neal's six years in Windsor Station, he unearthed many talented young men, and a steady stream of them marched through his office between 1942 and 1948. He so prided himself on his talent-spotting ability that shortly after becoming president he boasted, "I could tell you right now who is going to be president of this company in 1981."[11] For Neal's hopefuls, however, the experience was little better than a baptism by fire. Many lasted only a few months, afterwards disappearing to far-flung posts like Hong Kong, London or Vancouver, never to be seen in Windsor Station again. "We used to take bets on how long these guys would last," chortles a former company secretary. "After a while we got it down to a science. I think we gave Crump about three months."

So it was back to school for Crump. After protecting his back and neck all day at Windsor Station, he headed home with a bulging briefcase to spend hours assiduously making himself into a well-rounded executive. The night before an important meeting Crump stayed up until the wee hours inscribing answers to every conceivable question on three-by-five-inch cards. Rare were the times that anyone caught him unprepared, and it wasn't long before he began to put his tormentors on the spot.

CRUMP COULD REMEMBER MANY ten-hour days tinkering in the bowels of a cranky locomotive with frozen and leaden fingers while a February blizzard whistled through every crack in the roundhouse wall. He soon learned that was child's play compared to a full day at Windsor Station. But there's an obstreperous "to hell with you" streak that runs clear as a vein of burnished copper through Buck Crump. He'd bulldozed his way this far through a combination of native intelligence and indomitable determination. No disapproving easterner with clean fingernails was going to get the best of him now. Crump had beat the odds just getting to Montreal, and after a year there, he was ready for more.

What attracted Neal to Crump was the young man's willingness to take a risk and express opinions that contradicted prevailing wisdom. At one point, Crump read a study recommending that an expensive centralized traffic-control system be installed to reduce escalating accident rates. He looked over the plans and point blank told Neal, who had already approved the recommendations, that it wasn't the right system and, in any case, it was too expensive. Crump then organized a two-week tour of North American railroads and signal makers, showing a surprising degree of political acuity by inviting the chief engineer of communications and the assistant engineer of signals to accompany him. The three of them found a system that was not only more effective but also far cheaper and easier to install. "That's where I first found out that you can get anything done if you don't care who gets the credit," recalls Crump after his idea was appropriated by senior officers and put into effect.

Pleased with his promising protégé's first year, Neal threw him to the wolves once again by making him general superintendent of the Ontario district, which included the worst section of track in the country: the Thunder Bay to Sudbury line. "That baby was a son of a bitch," reminisces Wally Richardson, a fireman during the early part of the war. "We used to call it purgatory. Some of the senior guys loved to throw scares into newcomers who messed up, telling them their punishment was sure to be a transfer there. Then we'd recite all these terrible statistics about train wrecks and disfigured bodies." Accidents were so frequent that one grimly humorous engineer tallied his mishaps with scratches inside his cab, like notches on a gunfighter's pistol.

Penny pinching during the war and diversion of equipment and men had left the section understaffed and in a state of deterioration. The problems were exacerbated by several devastating winters of wildly fluctuating temperatures, and the vicious cycle of freeze and thaw took care of anything that managed to survive the neglect. In the early spring of 1943 two drivers came across a colleague sitting on an upended carton holding his head between his hands, sunk in deep misery. "What's the matter?" one of them asked. "Number three!" the stricken one replied, contemplating his third derailment in less than a year. "Oh," his fellows commiserated, adding, "Cheer up, after three accidents around here you get promoted."

Then Buck Crump moved in and such things were no longer matters of jest. "It was terrible," Crump recalls, shuddering slightly at the memory. "You had unskilled men running the locomotives. Our safety record was unbelievably bad. We didn't have enough room on the map to put all the flags indicating accidents. . . . The first thing I did was fire a number of people, to get a little discipline in the place." Crump's housecleaning was so decisive and swift that behind his back employees dubbed him "the Janitor." "I don't think anyone called him that to his face," says Richardson, "but it wasn't completely disrespectful. Everyone was fed up with how lousy things had gotten."

After his success as a general superintendent, Neal used Crump like a human fire extinguisher, dousing fires wherever they ignited. He spent more time on the line than almost any general superintendent in the system, and at every stop he continued to propagandize the superiority of diesels.

Most company officials recognized that the future lay with the diesel engine, but some powerful opponents were implacably opposed to conversion. H. B. Bowen, who had been the CPR's chief of motive power since 1929, was a resolute proponent of steam.* In 1929, the year that Canadian National unveiled the world's largest diesel road unit for testing, Bowen designed his own brain child, a massive three-chamber steam engine intended to prove the superiority of steam once and for all. The 8000 rolled out of the Angus shops in 1931 to much fanfare. A prodigy of power, its oversized high-pressure boiler could build up 1,750 p.s.i. of steam, about twice the normal 850 p.s.i. But despite extensive field trials the 8000 proved to be so mechanically complex and pernickety it could never leave the shop without at least one motive power specialist going along to make quick adjustments. Testing stopped in 1935 and the 8000 sat in the yards, gradually being stripped for its parts until it was officially decommissioned and dismantled in 1941.

In 1948, Mather and Walker made Crump senior vice-president of the company. Twenty years after he had seen the first diesel prototypes at Purdue, he was finally in a position to fulfill his dream. Immediately he cancelled all orders for steam engines, though he had to take delivery of two in 1949. In 1947, when the company operated 1,800 engines, all but 55 diesel yard switchers were steam. By 1954 every transcontinental passenger train was diesel, and by 1958 CPR diesel engines outnumbered steam 944 to 776. The conversion took twelve years altogether and cost $250 million. But the railroad's operating expenses were cut by millions. Whenever the public or a reporter bemoaned the loss of romance as

---

*Bowen was loathed by mechanical crews for building streamlined locomotives with all the vital parts covered and tucked out of reach. "They looked nice but they were hell to maintain," snorts one oldtimer in remembrance. "Bowen never operated a locomotive in his life."

the grimly utilitarian diesel took over, Crump invariably responded with his memorable line: "When people talk to me about the lonely cry of the steam whistle in the middle of the night on the Prairie, I say bullshit!"

Crump served his apprenticeship as vice-president for six years, and then, in 1955, the board officially made him president, though he had been the de facto president for at least a year. An aging Mather remained as chairman, but to everyone it was clear that the new strong man had arrived at last. A few days after Crump took his place behind William Van Horne's desk, a reporter asked him for the secret of his success and Crump replied, "You have to work like the devil — and then be around when the breaks happen."[12] The little tough guy who started out with a #2 shovel was ready to haul the CPR into the modern age at last.

CHAPTER 13

THE LAST RAILROADER

*"I've always made it a practice to meet a guy halfway,
but if he doesn't want to come halfway, then . . .
I'll kick his teeth in, one way or another."*

— Buck Crump

With one notable exception, the CPR has always been able to produce the right leader at the critical moment. In the beginning it was William Van Horne who rode in at the eleventh hour to save the otherwise doomed company. Similarly, when Buck Crump came on the scene, Canada's largest corporation was a decrepit hulk, once again on the brink of failure.* Along with Van Horne and J. J. Hill, he ranks among the great railroaders of all time.

Though Crump disparaged his own intelligence and often played up his lack of sophistication, no other CPR president could match him for preparation.† Not only did he have operational experience to equal Van Horne's, but he was the best-educated president as well. Crump commanded respect because no one, from track labourer to engineer, doubted he could do their job as well, and probably better, than they themselves.

---

*Things were so bad that Crump, when he took over, privately told several people that if Canadian Pacific was still a publicly listed company when he retired, he would consider his life a success.

†Crump's deprecatory comments about his own capabilities were often delivered to put opponents off guard — somewhat like throwing a handful of dirt in an opponent's face before administering a groin kick.

Crump inherited the CPR's highest debt since 1941, the highest fixed charges since 1948 and the lowest return on investment since 1922. The source of the problems was the railroad itself. Although the company had sunk $600 million since 1951 into improvements, mostly on equipment and track, the influential *Fortune* magazine dismissed the company as "encrusted with tradition" and estimated that it would have to spend a further $1.5 billion just to bring itself into the middle of the twentieth century. Share prices languished as the return on capital investment shrank to a paltry 4 percent, compared to 30 and 40 percent in the glory days. Crump faced a classic Catch 22: the railroad couldn't attract investment because it wasn't profitable and couldn't become profitable without massive investment. And there was a devilish kicker, the notorious 1897 Crow Rate ("the bane of our existence"), which froze grain rates — the largest component of rail revenue — at artificially low levels.

Any advances the CPR made in increased efficiency and earnings were undercut by prices that had risen by more than 110 percent since the early part of the war. Labour, once malleable in the overlord's hands, had become restless, and new wage demands, formerly rare events, cropped up with distressing regularity. In 1955 Crump reigned over 87,000 people, few of whom were willing to allow the good old days of feudal rule to continue.

Compounding the CPR's problems was the transportation revolution. Cars, trucks and airlines had swooped in to siphon off large portions of freight and passenger business. Gone were the days when the company could thwart a competitor simply by slapping down a spur line to service one mine. "I'll be damned if I'm going to build a branch line every time some guy digs a hole in the ground," Crump retorted when a reporter asked him how he intended to serve the burgeoning mining industry. "If we build it we have to make sure it's going to pay. We'll serve them all right but I don't call a money-losing handout service."[1]

Crump was determined to make every facet of the CPR pay

and pay well. He realized the only way to raise money to finance modernization and save the railroad, which would not be profitable for years, was to take a giant can opener to it, pry it apart and drag out its potential. With millions of acres of undeveloped land, not to mention mineral rights in rich mining and oil districts, the company had been sitting on a chest of gold for decades, but had shortsightedly used their non-rail assets only as loss leaders to build up rail traffic.* "We have as freight customers oil companies with whom we don't want to compete," said one executive, explaining why the CPR had the lowest oil-lease rates in the industry. "We do all right."

The CPR held 600,000 acres of timberland on Vancouver Island and only sold the timber to a handful of insiders — "people we like to do business with," in the words of a company spokesman. No purchase bids were ever submitted by the mills, which merely negotiated a price, the company being content in the knowledge that no outside competitor could muscle in. "We're not in it for the last cent," explained one of the CPR's managers. "We consider how long a mill has been doing business with us. In return, the mills do the best they can to give us freight."[2] "Stupid," was Crump's assessment of these nice comfortable little deals. "More than stupid, plain wrongheaded."

CRUMP INTENDED TO PUT THE CPR through some massive changes, but the first thing he did as president was set off on a tour of the road. That wasn't unusual — all the presidents surveyed their domain — but only in the spring, summer or early fall. "You couldn't get those buggers out of Montreal once the leaves dropped," he snorts. "When you saw them it was at a distance. They were like gods." Crump pointedly made a second trip that first year in the dead of winter, something no

---

*In 1955 the CPR owned the oil rights to 10 million acres. Its trackage was 21,834 miles and air mileage 37,991. In addition to 16 hotels and 21 steamships, the company's interests included mines, telegraph operations, stockyards, slaughterhouses and grain elevators.

president had done since Van Horne. He put up with the fanfare that always accompanied executive tours the first time, but the winter tour was a working trip, and superintendents who were expecting to talk in glowing, self-congratulatory generalities were shaken when Crump demanded specifics and insisted on inspecting everything first-hand. When he wasn't in his business car, the *Laurentian*, poring over maps and monitoring the train's performance on the specially installed instruments,* he was in the cab with the engineers, as often as not taking a hand at the controls.

Crump in the cab of a CPR engine

---

*In his private car, Crump monitored the train's progress by means of a speedometer, a system of mirrors placed so that he could see the signals and a special high-powered searchlight to allow him to inspect the track at night.

Senior officers quickly learned that Buck Crump wouldn't tolerate even the most impressive-sounding claims without hard facts backing them up. And only something he could see or touch or taste was a fact as far as Crump was concerned. During one western tour he concentrated on evaluating the use of diesels between Calgary and Revelstoke, his old stomping ground. In his hands was a report by Fred Stone and Frank Haney of the research department stating that diesels were habitually underloaded and could haul several hundred more tons.

"Thomson," Crump suddenly barked to the vice-president in Winnipeg, who was riding with him, "I want a diesel test from Calgary to Revelstoke and back." "Yes, sir," Dave Thomson replied. "Normal tonnage?" "Like hell," Crump shot back. "We're going to put on the tonnage that these damn guys have put in the blue book." Crump punctuated the order by vigorously thumping the blue department of research report.

With Crump, Stone, Haney and Thomson on board, everything went as smooth as silk to Revelstoke, including the treacherous descent down the Big Hill. The return was just as uneventful until they reached the middle of the Spiral Tunnel. Then the diesel began to labour and slip. Speed dropped to two miles per hour, and the train crew were faced with the mortifying prospect of having to back down the mountain with all the brass on board. Thomson, who was in the lead unit with Crump, observed, "I bet Fred Stone is sitting on the edge of his seat back there." Crump's lips stretched a fraction as he said, "Well, if we don't move, I bet his bowels do."

Crump served in numerous miserable roundhouses during his career with the CPR and professes to have hated every one. But as president, he was clearly drawn to them. Whenever his schedule slackened on a tour, his aides always knew where to find him — down in the roundhouse "jawing" with the workers. Crump could tell a risqué joke with the best of them, especially if the punch line came at his own expense. He frequently bet on hockey or football games, invariably returning to pick up his winnings or settle the debt. In 1959 a young mechanic spotted Crump wandering around outside the Regina roundhouse, bundled up to his eyebrows against the bitter chill. "Who the hell is that fool?" he asked his supervisor. "Oh, that's just Crump," came the response. "He always does that. Don't worry, he'll come in when he's seen enough or froze himself clear through."

The same week that Crump took charge at Windsor Station, he presided over the launching of his pride and joy, the *Canadian*, the culmination of his determination to win back train passengers. With the sleek outlines of a rocket, the *Canadian* drew global attention. Railway publications described it as one of the world's great transcontinental trains, placing it beside such immortals as the Orient Express. Though there's hardly a sentimental bone in Buck Crump's thickset frame, he couldn't avoid an emotional comment when he introduced his revolutionary stainless steel train. "She's a beauty," he admitted to a reporter who asked for his opinion.[3] Certain that the *Canadian* would attract badly depleted passenger traffic, Crump joked, "If you've got time to spare, go by air," mocking an airline industry plagued by flight delays, mechanical breakdowns and slow baggage service. Destined to serve the transcontinental passenger route, the *Canadian* enjoyed a solidly booked inaugural season, with long waiting lists.

But Crump's fight to save passenger service was doomed before it had even begun. Today he calls the $250 million dollar *Canadian* a colossal mistake. "That was my train! I still think it was the best goddamn long distance train in the world. [But] the *Canadian* was too late. The public left us. It took 123 damned employees to run from Montreal to Vancouver and we couldn't charge rates commensurate to pay the expenses. I made up my mind. To Hell with this! Let's get out of the passenger service." True to his word, by the end of 1955, he had eliminated or reduced the frequency of fifty passenger trains. By the 1960s Canadians had cut down their train travel by 50 percent from the war years. Despite these figures, many saw passenger service as a sacred trust and thought Crump's abandonment of it akin to treason. But with thirty-five years of

The Canadian *crossing Stoney Creek bridge in the Selkirks*

railroading experience under his belt before he claimed the president's office, Crump was uniquely positioned to still the tremors within the company as he smashed tradition after tradition and charted an entirely new course.

IN THE 1950S THE CPR needed something it had never required before: a good labour man. Tough and unyielding, Crump could put a strident union leader on the defensive without even trying. He never failed to open a meeting without a little figurative suspender snapping, casually challenging the labour bosses to put their experience as real workers on the table. "I wore overalls a hell of a lot longer than any of the labour leaders I know," he reminded them at key moments.[4] Nor did he neglect to needle them for their excesses. Prior to one round of negotiating in Ottawa, Crump pulled into the Parliamentary parking lot with Frank Hall, long-time railway union boss, in a brand-new Olds 88, right behind him. Getting out of his well-used Pontiac, Crump said, "By God, Frank, if I work for this company long enough maybe I can own an Olds 88!"[5]

When it came to blunt talk no one could be blunter than Crump. He once stared down the jowly, bonebreaking Hal Banks ("that goddamn Hal Banks"), then president of the Seafarers' International Union, who was trying to organize the part of the CPR's shipping fleet that ran under the British flag. "At one point, there were three of our *Empress* vessels tied up in Liverpool," recalls Crump. "It got so you couldn't tell whether you were going to sail or not." Banks met with Crump and immediately raised the president's hackles with a thinly veiled threat. "Banks was a hard bastard, a very big husky guy. I said, 'Look, Hal, I'm an old gun man and in my fraternity there's an old saying. God created man but Colonel Colt made them equal and any goddamn time you want to start anything I'm all set.' We got along fine after that."*

When it came to negotiation, as in life, Crump's philosophy was simple: "I've always made it a practice to meet a guy halfway, but if he doesn't want to come halfway, then, goddamn it, I'll kick his teeth in, one way or another." Despite his ball-busting talk, Crump usually solved his labour problems with finesse. His frustrated partner on many such occasions was Frank Hall. "The President [had] the name of being a fine character and very thoughtful towards his employees and all the rest of us," recalls Hall.

> He would meet us at the door and shake hands with each of the five members of the committee and ask us to sit down and inquire as to the well-being of our families and the rest of it. We'd finally get down

---

*Crump's main hobby over the years — other than reading and being a dedicated amateur historian — has been his gun collection. At its peak, his collection contained several hundred prize weapons including cross-bows, Gurkha "kukris," Arabian sash guns, blunderbusses and flint-lock pistols, all lovingly restored and maintained in his elaborate basement workshop. Crump, who doesn't even belong to a gun club, gets no thrill out of firing the guns. What he enjoys is the guns' historical value and "doing something with my hands — you can read only so long." Though he no longer repairs his guns, his workshop is kept in immaculate condition. Not a speck of dust or rust is visible, every cutting edge is sharp and every tool is in its place.

to talking business and he'd ask us to say what it was we were there
for. . . .

We outlined the character of our case. We said that we thought we
had some money coming to us, we didn't get anywhere with the wolf
pack. The wolf pack are the personnel officers and the vice-president
who were assigned to meet with us and try to convince us that we
should have a decrease instead of an increase.

And the president sat there and he became quite emotional . . .
tears came in his eyes and he was touched undoubtedly, emotionally
that is, not money wise. Then he would say, "Well, gentlemen, I wish
there was something I could do for you, but I can't. I've got to
consider the widows and the orphans who've got their dollars and
their quarters and their dimes invested in this railroad." So by the
time we'd got to that routine, we knew we'd had it and we retired.[6]

Shortly after Crump became president, he warned the
unions that if they hoped for a bit of mollycoddling because
one of their own held the reins of power, they were mistaken.
"It is the boast of most Canadians that they came up the hard
way. Let us not forget that Canada, too, came up the hard way.
It wasn't built on the 40-hour week. . . ."[7]* In 1956, the major
North American railroads banded together and announced
their determination to drop firemen from diesel locomotives
because their real function dated back to the days of steam.

On January 3, 1957, pickets ringed Windsor Station.
Crump, whom many of the firemen had known when his
fingernails were still dirty, told them he was prepared for a
tough fight. But then he watched in disgust as the other
railways tucked their tails under and slunk away to a safe spot
on the sidelines. He told reporters he didn't intend to act as a
bell cow for the industry: "They'll stick behind the CPR right
down to the CPR's last dollar," he growled with contempt. "Let
them look after themselves."[8] Like every railway strike until
that point, this one was short-lived.† Crump roared up to

---

*Crump was referring to the 1950 agitation for pay increases and a reduced work week, from
forty-four hours to forty. After a nationwide strike and arbitration, the unions were awarded
their demands.

†At that point no Canadian rail strike had lasted more than a few days. So dependent was the
country's economy on trains that governments invariably stepped in to force a settlement.

Ottawa and, eschewing tedious tribunals and depositions from labour, government and industry, made a bargain with Prime Minister Louis St Laurent to end the walkout. Though Crump agreed to put a hold on plans to get rid of the firemen while a royal commission under Justice R. L. Kellock studied the issue, he didn't intend to sit and twiddle his thumbs waiting for a decision. As Kellock deliberated, Crump ordered an impromptu inspection of every fireman's seat on the line. What the investigators found were hundreds of pounds of comic books. Driving the point home further, Crump complained to reporters that firemen spent so much time reclining that their boots were scratching the diesel windshields.

When Kellock determined that the fireman's job had become disposable, the union walked out again, claiming a breakdown in negotiations between themselves and the company. Crump believed his terms were fair and proclaimed he would "run the damn railroad" with secretaries if he had to. The CPR pressed every retiree and supervisor into action to keep the trains rolling. To underline their determination, rail management rounded up hundreds of desk jockeys, gave them vision tests and allocated each a standard railway watch so they could step in as replacements. At first, 3,200 men were off the job, but union members began returning to work at a surprisingly fast rate. The split in the ranks provoked some nasty threats, including a number of anonymous phone calls to engineers, telling them they might find themselves running down the track at night with the switches against them and no warning lights.

The strike wobbled through three days before it became patently obvious that even members of the firemen's union had doubts about the wisdom of their protest. In the middle of the third day Crump called up H. E. Gilbert, president of the Brotherhood of Locomotive Firemen and Engineers, and told him he had until nine o'clock that evening to settle up or Crump would withdraw his promise to honour all seniority up to 1956, lay off no one and give every displaced fireman a job of equivalent stature elsewhere in the organization. In the end,

Gilbert had no choice. Crump's settlement was generous — in fact, several U.S. railroads criticized him for being too soft. There were only two people at the negotiating meeting. "The final settlement was made between the head of the fire-men and me — alone," emphasizes Crump. "Nobody else. Nobody."

Norris Roy Crump was the most remarkable of all the CPR presidents because, in many ways, he was the most ordinary of the lot. He couldn't boast of awesome intelligence, overwhelm-ing shrewdness or even a larger-than-life personality. But he did have the rare ability to recognize his own weaknesses and to compensate for them. He also used his intense will to wring every scrap of potential out of himself. Crump's strength did not come from absolute rule. While his predecessors ran the company like feudal lords, Crump understood that the age of the railway baron was gone. What's more, he knew he couldn't possibly carry the rapidly diversifying company on his own shoulders. "Very early I realized that I wasn't very bright and that I needed a lot of help. I searched our company when I was made vice-president in 1948 for the best intellects I could find because I thought I'd have to have somebody to prop me up if I was going to get by."

As a mechanic, Crump knew the value of having the finest tools at hand, and he had the same attitude toward people. Also on his mind was the problem of succession. He had seen first-hand the heavy price the CPR paid for Edward Beatty's failure to provide an heir, and the tragedy of W. M. Neal proved to him the danger of trusting the future to a single man. By 1955 Crump had gathered four men around him, including R. A. (Bob) Emerson and Ian D. Sinclair. Crump, Emerson and Sinclair ruled the CPR as a corporate oligarchy for more than a decade.

BORN INTO A RAILROADING FAMILY, Bob Emerson's grand-father drove a wood-burning locomotive out of Winnipeg during Van Horne's presidency. His father managed the CPR

Crump and Emerson

station at Plum Coulee, Manitoba, a tiny oasis marked only by a grain elevator and a stand of wild plum trees growing along the river bank. Even as a boy, Emerson's quick mind distinguished him from others. To amuse himself, he created a game based on the memory training described in Rudyard Kipling's book *Kim*. The contest started with a handful of objects and the teams had a few seconds to memorize what was there. After each round they added another item to the pile. Emerson, by himself, took on any group of children he could gather together. Despite the uneven odds, Emerson's opponents never had a chance, and he eventually abandoned the game because he couldn't find anyone to last more than a few rounds with him.

Though Emerson initially showed no particular aptitude for school, his sponge-like mind absorbed numbers with the ease of a natural mathematician. During his early railroading days as a rod man on a CPR survey crew, he challenged fellow employees to memory contests, each trying to recite the numbers on rolling stock as they whizzed by. Emerson always kept reciting long after the others ran dry.

Working for the CPR allowed Emerson to finance a University of Manitoba engineering degree, which he finished in 1930, a terrible time to graduate. Because the company had no work for him, he spent a year as a lab demonstrator for the university. Impatient with the tedious routine and itching to get back in the field, Emerson managed to land a position as a locating engineer with the Ontario government. He spent most of the next two years wandering around the northern Ontario bush until the Strathcona Memorial Fellowship Foundation selected him for post-graduate study at Yale. It was a long way from Plum Coulee to the Ivy Leagues, and though Emerson often felt like a working-class bumpkin compared to his rich and privileged classmates, he had little difficulty matching wits with the best brains on campus.

After Emerson left Yale he rejoined the CPR as a transit man, the only job he could find during the last years of the Depression. Once war was declared, he vaulted through the ranks, advancing faster than any other company executive since Edward Beatty. From engineer of track in 1948 he shot steadily upward to chief engineer in 1951 and vice-president of operations and maintenance in 1955. Finally, Crump made him vice-president of the entire company in 1958. During the interminable government hearings and commissions of the fifties, Emerson evolved into an excellent expert witness for the CPR — becoming so adept at fielding questions that opposing lawyers simply gave up cross-examining him. "Men with lesser minds tended to freeze in confrontation," commented Fred Stone years later.[9]

Not since the days of William Van Horne and Thomas Shaughnessy had there been two men at the top of the CPR with such skill and experience, but Crump wasn't content: he added a third, Ian David Sinclair. Crump recognized that if he was to haul the CPR into the modern era and diversify it at the same time, he needed a powerful, trustworthy ally to battle the royal commissions and freight-rate hearings that settled on the company like a pestilence after the war. Though some of his most respected colleagues were lawyers, Crump considered the profession to be full of poseurs and time-wasting nit-pickers. "The first course they take in law school is dramatics because they are always putting on an act," he says derisively.

Fortunately, he had Ian Sinclair, a man with a formidable legal mind, who could pose and nitpick with the best of them.

IAN SINCLAIR WAS BORN in Winnipeg on December 27, 1913, and graduated from high school just as depression and drought were taking their greatest toll in the West. His father held a modestly paid but decent job as a test rackman for the CNR. Everyone loves a bootstrapper, and the minute Sinclair made a name for himself in corporate circles, many journalists extolled his "rise from poverty," a fairy tale Sinclair won't tolerate. "We were not poor," he emphasizes. "I don't come from a poor family. My father was never on relief."

Scholarships buttered his way through university, but since they weren't enough to pay all his costs, he had to work too. Jobs were rare and precious in those days, particularly for young, unmarried men with few measurable skills. Sinclair took anything he could find to pay his way through an Economics degree: delivering papers, selling milk and making binder canvases for farm equipment at seventeen cents an hour. The last was a dreadful job. He worked from 7 A.M. to

Sinclair as a boy in Winnipeg

9 P.M. in a warehouse used to store tires that gave off a sickening odour. Sinclair hated the job but never failed to show up. "Every morning it used to bother me; there were people lined up in case someone didn't turn up for work. That was really tough."

After he graduated with a BA in Economics in 1937, Sinclair settled for law school because there was no business school in Winnipeg. Fifty years ago Canadian law schools operated on the now-extinct clerk system: students studied in the morning and worked with a firm in the afternoon. Sinclair also spent every summer building up his savings for the next term. His most interesting job came in the summer of 1940 when, on the recommendation of a friend, he landed a bit part as an RCMP corporal in the British film production, *The 49th Parallel*.

The CPR has a long association with the film business, but Sinclair was the first would-be president ever to appear in one. Movie extras don't usually become accountants, but when the opportunity presented itself he grabbed it. "They found out I could look after money so I got paid for that too," he says, still wryly amused fifty years later. "Some of these people had no more damn idea of money than they could fly." He discovered the production company was overdrawn, although the crew still gaily wrote cheques and paid for hotel bills as if the account was fat with cash. Sinclair soon sorted the mess out, and by the time the summer ended he was the company's de facto business manager and accountant.

Sinclair read law with the Winnipeg firm Guy Chappell & Co. It was an extremely fortunate choice for him, because litigation, the firm's forte, gave him an intense introduction to the court room lawyer's craft. After graduating in 1941, Sinclair spent a year teaching torts at the university before joining the CPR's Winnipeg law department as a junior solicitor. It wasn't long before word of his drive, energy and encompassing knowledge reached the right ears in Windsor Station, and four years later he gathered up his wife, Ruth, and their two young children and moved to Montreal, where he became company solicitor.

Sinclair playing the role of an RCMP *corporal
in the film* The 49th Parallel

Sinclair couldn't have chosen a better time than the early
fifties to take root and bloom. The transportation revolution
and labour unrest created a lawyer's paradise on Parliament
Hill. Between 1947 and 1959, Sinclair technically lived in
Montreal but he spent most of his time in Ottawa. He never
stopped preparing briefs and questions and grooming witnesses. To labour he pushed the CPR's case that it couldn't
afford continual raises. To the royal commissions, the Board of
Railway Commissioners, the Board of Transport and the Ses-
sional Committee of the House of Commons he argued that
the artificially low Crow Rate squashed profitability and didn't
allow CPR shareholders a fair rate of return. Sinclair's opponents came and went, but he never tired, growing stronger
in his conviction that the Crow Rate could be beaten and

realizing that the CPR's land and other non-rail assets promised a glittering future for whoever led the way in developing them. By the time Crump became president, Sinclair had been dubbed the Perry Mason of railway law.

At that point Sinclair was by no means the CPR's ranking legal officer. He simply acted as if he was. During one freight-rate case an inexperienced company witness ran into difficulty on the stand, and the CPR's senior counsel let him flounder without intervening. When the court adjourned for lunch, Sinclair berated his superior in front of the legal team, denouncing him for not protecting the witness and repeatedly threatening to resign if the failing wasn't corrected. That afternoon, the senior officer vigorously defended his witnesses against all attacks.

Crump abhorred executive excitement, but with Bob Emerson on one side of him and Ian Sinclair on the other, he denied himself a peaceful or unchallenged reign. Emerson never had Sinclair's eloquence, but the two jousted well and often. When they disagreed vehemently on a certain point, which happened frequently, Crump was invariably in the middle, straight-arming his two right-hand men as they swung at each other. "I always got the feeling that Mr Sinclair and Mr Emerson respected each other, but when the two of them went at it, the whole of Windsor Station knew," recalls one former company secretary. "I'd go in with some papers for Mr Crump to sign and I could tell something was going on between Mr Emerson and I.D.S. because Mr Crump would be really grumpy and just snap at me, which he almost never did. I never heard them shout at each other, but the atmosphere changed."

Although Crump detested disorder and unexpected problems, he viewed the constant wrangling between Emerson and Sinclair, which inevitably came to involve him, as an irritating but creative process — essential in that time of change. "The three of us worked very closely together and I think Canadian Pacific certainly benefited through tough times. But you had to keep your throat covered all the time or . . . ," he says, making a vigorous slashing motion. "If you were wrong or someone thought you were out on a limb then, boy, you'd get cut down in a hurry."

Emerson and Sinclair often sparred with each other during the preliminary rounds and then united to turn on Crump for the main event. But no matter how persuasive they were, once Crump made up his mind, nothing could change it. "If he gave us a hearing and decided against what we wanted to do, that was it," says Sinclair. "I remember once in particular when Bob and I were very much on one side and he didn't agree with us. We were very unhappy about the fact because we thought it was a very bad decision that was being made, but he was the Boss." No matter how weary Crump became with the constant in-fighting, he never tried to rein his lieutenants in. If their ambitions and competitiveness spilled over, he let Darwin's theory sort it out. "Some of the things we did I'm sure caused him concern," Sinclair acknowledges, "but he gave us responsibility and he gave us accountability and he let us go."

BY 1959 CRUMP WAS FED UP with commissions, freight-rate cases and hearings. They cost the company millions of dollars and absorbed key people's time, including his own, as witnesses. In May of that year, after a freight-rate dispute, John Diefenbaker's neophyte government appointed yet another royal commission to investigate "inequalities in the freight-rate structures."[10]* It seemed like more of the same, but Sinclair convinced Crump that this commission was different. "I saw the order-in-council setting it up and thought about it. It appeared to me to give us a fantastic opportunity because the thing was broad . . . . Here was an opportunity, if you developed it properly, to have a breakthrough in regard to regulation, to finally put to

---

*The commission came to be known as the MacPherson Commission after its chairman M. A. (Murdo) MacPherson, former attorney general of Saskatchewan.

bed the whole question of other income."* Crump gave his chief lawyer carte blanche to mount an assault on Ottawa, with the front lines drawn in the Department of Transportation building.

In one of those fortunate confluences of events, everything lined up in 1959 to allow Ian Sinclair a virtually free hand in shaping the direction of the railways' case. Donald Gordon, then head of the CNR, was preoccupied defending himself against political attacks on his presidency. Yet another royal commission ranked far down on his list of priorities.† Despite improvements in the road, increased traffic and $1.89 billion spent over the previous decade, Gordon had not been able to produce an operational surplus. With missionary zeal, Diefenbaker's government zeroed in on the $2 billion debt the company dragged behind it like a ball and chain.

Gordon's term as president was due to expire shortly before the royal commission began, and the House of Commons Railway Committee went after his throat like a hungry wolf pack. In an uncanny reprise of Thornton's last days, the committee members picked apart his regime, even questioning whether the kerosene for his summer cottage had been paid for by the company and scrutinizing the issuance of railway passes.

Unlike Thornton, Gordon fought back. "If you have come to the conclusion that we are not an efficient management, for God's sake tell us so and fire the lot of us," he dared the committee after a long, tedious and pointless session in the hot

---

*"Other income" meant all the non-rail revenue earned from hotels, shipping, airlines, trucking, telecommunications and the like. The CPR had always argued that only rail revenue should be considered when determining both freight and wage rates. Also, if rail revenue were allowed to stand on its own, it would become strikingly obvious that the Crow Rate was making that part of the company's operations barely profitable.

†Gordon was a banker who suddenly became a railroader in 1949 when the job of running the CNR fell into his lap. A man with the same kind of cheery bonhomie as his predecessor, Henry Thornton, Gordon disarmingly admitted to detractors and supporters that he knew nothing about the business. Before potentially hostile audiences of long-time railway men he confessed in his best Scottish burr to be "a chiel among ye, takin' notes." (Stevens, *History of the Canadian National Railways*, p. 425)

seat.[11] When the accusations didn't abate, he rose to his feet and spent twenty-five minutes taking the committee apart limb by limb and defending his company. "This," he bellowed, stabbing his finger in the direction of the committee, "is designed to disturb the morale of our employees, which is the ultimate aim of a campaign against anyone charged with duties that call for action or for decisions which effect changes in old-established methods and customs."[12]

Fighting for his job, Gordon was too distracted to pay much attention to Diefenbaker's new royal commission, which his advisors told him was insignificant anyway. Picking up his cue, everyone in the CNR legal department fought to avoid being seconded to an apparently ho-hum affair offering few opportunities to earn promotional points. The two men Gordon chose to prepare the company's case were Archie MacDonald, a small, elderly CNR regional lawyer with a serious heart condition, and Bob Bandeen, a twenty-eight-year-old with a brand-new PhD degree in economics from Duke University and not one iota of railway experience. "They didn't want to waste good talent on a weak commission and therefore they decided that I should head it," laughs Bandeen, who went on to become CNR president from 1974 to 1982. "That was a great way to start you off."

CANADIAN NATIONAL'S ATTITUDE to the CPR is a curious mixture of dislike and respect. Employees joke that their compatriots at Windsor Station — which they and the unions call "The Kremlin" — speak a different language, walk differently, dress differently and generally consider themselves to be above the common muck. The CNR lawyers called Sinclair, already infamous for his rousing courtroom style, "Ian the Terrible" — a label his own staff thought deadly accurate. "Sinclair didn't move obstacles if they got in his way; he mowed them down," observes Stu Eagles, now chairman of Marathon Realty, a CP subsidiary, and then a member of the CPR's research team.

Traditionally, before any important hearings or commissions, the two railways met to sort out their interests and form a common strategy where possible. Though fierce competitors for traffic, when it came to freight rates, subsidies and labour negotiations, CN and CP circled their wagons. Sinclair arranged for the meeting to be held at Windsor Station, and though his own spacious office was perfectly adequate, he selected a more intimidating backdrop for the first, and to his mind, critical, consultation between the two lines. A firm believer in the value of sets, props and environment to enhance a performance, Sinclair aimed to completely dominate the CNR. The dark, massive table in the company's law library, with its walls of leather-spined books and great, dusty piles of documents, provided the perfect backdrop to his offensive.

In truth, Sinclair hardly needed tricks to cow his opposition. Beside his hulking six-foot-one, 240-pound frame, the tall and lanky Bandeen looked like a callow high school student, and it appeared that a good sneeze could do away with the grey and withered MacDonald, let alone a Sinclair volley. The two men arrived at 2 P.M., and before they'd even settled themselves, Sinclair began to talk, and talk and talk. Sinclair's voice is another weapon in his imposing arsenal. One moment it can be soft, melodious and confidential and the next, a sudden peal of thunder. When he was preparing to make a key statement, his voice took on great clarity and force, rising and intensifying until it had the momentum of a wrecking ball whistling through the air.

For the next two-and-a-half hours, MacDonald industriously scribbled notes in his binder, though Bandeen couldn't for the life of him imagine what there was in Sinclair's rambling worth writing down. "It was interesting," he remembers, "but it was getting to be 4:30 or quarter to 5, and we hadn't done anything germane as far as I could see except listen to him." At five o'clock precisely, MacDonald, under doctor's orders to work no more than eight hours a day, decisively snapped his binder shut, got up and put on his coat. Nodding to Sinclair, he said to a startled Bandeen, "Bob, you carry on."

Those who liked to keep regular schedules found Sinclair's work habits a strain, as he often got down to his real work after supper. Bandeen was dismayed at being left alone to begin the organization of CN's case but he soon realized that once Sinclair got rolling, he only had to hop on board and Sinclair would pull the whole train by himself. Their non-stop session lasted until nearly midnight as Sinclair dictated and Bandeen busily copied down the guts of what was to be the most important commission in the history of Canadian railroading.

When the hearings began, Sinclair had his army briefed and loaded down with enough documentation to fill a library. Compared to the CPR's huge contingent, which at times swelled to thirty, the CNR team, with only five members, was pathetically small.* The hearings rarely finished before 4:30 P.M. and, as Archie MacDonald's wife came to pick him up each day promptly at five, Bandeen and the others were left with only thirty minutes to discuss the next day's strategy with him. "It soon got to the point where CN's lack in the legal area was embarrassingly obvious. Ian was aggressive, so we worked out a method of working together that benefited us both." Once Sinclair had an opening, he didn't hesitate to move into it, and before long he was, for all intents and purposes, lawyer for both railways.†

---

*Sinclair's opponents, from the provinces to the farm organizations, were all self-styled "little guys." He didn't want the CPR to be an easy target, so he made his team keep a low profile. Staff ate as many meals as possible in their rooms and were called to the hearing room only as needed. He even went so far as to quarter some lucky ones in private rail cars so no one would know the CPR group's true size.

†Though young and unschooled in the railway world, Bandeen had a brilliant and creative mind for the esoteric field of statistics. Along with CPR economist John Stenason, he brought fresh and compelling expertise to the issue of freight rates. Until the MacPherson Commission, economic analysis of railways rivalled paint-by-numbers for its lack of sophistication. "In the late forties and early fifties, they had seventeen classifications in freight traffic and the seventeenth was bigger than the others all together," says Sinclair. "The reason it was big was because we didn't know how to break it down and you had to finish up with 100 at the bottom of the column." Bandeen spearheaded the introduction of techniques like multiple regression analysis to bolster Sinclair's argument that artificially low grain rates were killing the railways.

The CPR's staff had a difficult and often dreary job, made worse by the knowledge that the slightest foul-up would earn them a Sinclair tongue lashing, guaranteed to be more painful than a session on the rack.* One night after the CPR foot soldiers had been labouring over the day's testimony, Sinclair called Bob Bandeen and his small crew in for a consultation. "He relied on us because we didn't have any allegiance to him or any need to be afraid of his wrath," points out Bandeen. "We could just get up and walk out." On that night the CPR team presented some conclusions that Bandeen wouldn't accept, and "instead of being diplomatic about it we just said we didn't think the results were accurate." The CNR's criticisms infuriated Sinclair, but he carefully directed none of his anger towards them. "He wiped the floor with his own staff in front of us, just tore them to shreds," recalls Bandeen. In particular, Sinclair singled out John Stenason, a taciturn but talented CPR economist, ridiculing his degrees and dismissing his experience.

Horrified and embarrassed, Bandeen tried to leave, but Sinclair, surprised at his sensitivity, threw a beefy arm over his shoulders and dragged him into the adjoining room, where he proceeded to dispense his secrets of handling people. "Evaluate their strengths and weaknesses, then go to work on the latter," he told Bandeen, who recalls it as a "fascinating" half-hour. But it all sounded a little too close to the tricks of a master torturer for his taste. Completely unsettled, Bandeen gathered his little band and went off to get gloriously drunk.†

During the testimony, the CPR team lined up behind a long

---

*The CPR staff, while commiserating over beers late one night, jokingly made up a story about an unfortunate statistician who neglected to attach his conclusion to an analysis requested by Sinclair. After being called into The Presence to be told of his sins, the man was so devastated he went home, divorced his wife, sold his dog and took a job running a worm farm in Florida.

†Despite the legendary stories of Sinclair's tongue lashings, he rarely lost his temper, keeping his staff in line more by the force of monumental expectations than through fear of recrimination. Even when his fury was unleashed, it often seemed to be a deliberate strategy to keep his subordinates off balance and running hard to please.

table and a bank of hefty tomes, prepared to provide last-minute information for the lawyers and supporting details for the company witnesses. On one occasion, Sinclair asked a question of his own witness, who confessed he didn't have the answer. Stu Eagles pounced on the right book and was just about to offer up the information when he felt a heavy hand thud down on his shoulder. Sinclair kept talking, expounding on this point and that, all the while patting and kneading Eagles all over as if he were a lump of dough, to make sure he didn't let out the answer that Sinclair didn't want.

FOR EIGHTEEN MONTHS SINCLAIR cajoled and terrified witnesses from every professional field. At once dramatic, flamboyant and subtle, he paced and stalked the polish right off the transport building floor in his obsession to make his points. Brandishing a pair of black, heavy-framed glasses like a pirate sword, he stabbed them at witnesses or even at MacPherson himself, who more than once locked wills with Sinclair. When the hearings dragged, he swooped in to make ringing denunciations or stunning declarations in his deep, gravelly voice, frequently backing up his statements with information he'd absorbed only moments before.

The first volume of the MacPherson Commission's landmark report appeared in the spring of 1961, the second a year later. They contained the seeds of the CPR's transformation. MacPherson's recommendations eventually resulted, more than twenty years later, in the abolition of the detested Crow Rate and gave official blessing to Crump's plan to separate rail and non-rail assets. The MacPherson report also laid the groundwork for the eventual deregulation of the entire industry, allowing the CPR to compete, for the first time on an equal basis, with its new, hungry rivals: the pipelines, trucking companies and airlines.

MacPherson's report came not a moment too soon. Calling the CPR "a crippled titan," one publication declared that the company was headed for "economic suicide,"[13] with returns on rail investment hovering around 2.8 percent, while other large industrial concerns averaged 9 to 12 percent. Crump cautiously praised the report but any joy he felt soon turned to frustration as the government delayed turning the recommendations into a promised new transportation act.* In the meantime, the CPR limped from one interim payment and subsidy to another, all designed to make up for freight rates that had been frozen when the royal commission began.

But Crump could do something to improve the balance sheet — phase out passenger traffic. Since the *Canadian* had been introduced, the CPR's passenger revenues had declined by 35 percent. The biggest bugbear was the transcontinental service, and when Crump admitted in 1965 that he intended to drop it as soon as possible, a roar of indignation reverberated across the country. Many outraged citizens brought up the 1881 contract clause which stated that "the company shall thereafter and forever efficiently maintain, work and run the Canadian Pacific Railway," but passenger service isn't mentioned anywhere in the contract. Many suggested that if the CPR dropped passenger service it should give back its land grant.

Crump was unmoved. He had spent the past decade slowly and carefully pushing the company toward diversification and competitive profit centres, and he had no intention of shackling the railway with money-losing passengers, just for the sake of some ancient, unspecified obligation. "If I can't see any prospect of getting a net [profit] out of them, then I get rid of them," he said bluntly. "By God, you can't live on sentiment."[14]†

Crump had realized that the CPR was a sleeping giant long before *Fortune* magazine put that description into print in 1955. In 1956 he began the long process of cataloguing, in some cases discovering, the extent of the company assets.

---

*The National Transportation Act was finally passed in 1967.

†Crump makes a great deal out of his lack of sentiment but is so attached to the Empress Hotel in Victoria that he promises to take a shotgun to anyone who tries to tamper with the hotel's beautiful interior.

Though the task took nearly ten years to accomplish, Crump didn't wait until he had the inventory list in his hand to start pushing the CPR on to new horizons. In 1962, hard on the heels of MacPherson's recommendation that the railway be allowed to separate its rail and non-rail assets, Canadian Pacific Investments Ltd. (CPI) was formed to administer the company's non-transportation assets. One of the best things about CPI was completely unseen: it gave Crump an epic challenge to hand over to the impatiently ambitious Ian Sinclair.

THE CRUMP, EMERSON, SINCLAIR TROIKA was magic for the CPR, but it worked only because Crump played an interme-diary role — something that couldn't continue forever. Ham-pered by emphysema, which made him infuriatingly short of breath and forced him to quit his beloved cigars, he had long ago resolved to retire at the age of sixty-five. When he did retire in 1972, he said, "I feel like a wind-broken cayuse," but it was evident that he'd been feeling that way for some time. Crump believed that the CPR needed both Sinclair and Emerson, but only one could take his place, and Emerson had long been the chosen one. Satisfying Sinclair presented a problem.*

Crump always had tremendous respect for his number two man, but he had his reservations. "Sinclair in most ways, *and I emphasize in most ways,* is one of the most able men I've ever known." He believed Sinclair was often too rambunc-tious, thrust himself forward too much and treated employees harshly. But his main reason for preferring Emerson for the presidency was that Sinclair wasn't a railroader.

Even in today's world of professional managers the railroad is the CPR's touchstone. Some alchemy imparts an aura of competence merely by experience on the rails. Until recently, the company's philosophy was "If something is wrong, get a railroad man in to fix it." Sinclair had no time and less patience

---

*Though Emerson, as vice-president of the company, was nominally Sinclair's superior, they treated each other as equals.

for tooling around in his business car, gladhanding and jawing with the operations men. Many from the rank and file to the senior officers believed he couldn't effectively assume (and more precisely didn't deserve) the president's chair because they felt he didn't understand the railroad. Once, during a heated cost-cutting session with the chief rail executives, Sinclair needled them for poor earnings until one finally blurted out, "Well, I really object. If it was the airline you wouldn't go after us." Sinclair's head whipped up from the displeasing documents he was studying and his eyes and lips narrowed and pursed in harmony. "I may not be in the railway," he boomed, "but I fly over it enough and every time I do the damn tracks are empty."*

With the formation of CPI, a limitless vista opened up to Ian Sinclair. "I think his eventual goal was to split CPI off from Canadian Pacific entirely," observes a company executive. "Then as president of that company he'd report directly to the board of directors, not to Emerson. I'm sure he expected and planned to overshadow CP completely, in earnings and every other way." With the creation of CPI, the CPR, which Crump once likened to a mammoth ocean liner with a full head of steam, began to alter its course.

Diversification† hit the company like a bomb. It had been a familiar, cozy relationship, everything being part of the railway, and suddenly the prospect of being flung out on the cold

---

*On the rare occasions that Sinclair lowered his bulk into a seat in his business car "you could see the track shake from Saint John to Vancouver," observes Ron Swan, now sales manager of the Royal York. "I.D.S. knew the railway. He didn't work in it but he knew it from the rate cases. He probably knew the track and knew the equipment better than some of the railroaders."

†CPI was intended as a supervisory vehicle to maximize the profitability of each non-resource company and to ensure that none was treated as a sideline. The first two companies sold to CPI by the parent company, in exchange for capital stock, were Canadian Pacific Oil and Gas Limited and Pacific Logging Ltd., which held the company's 500,000 acres of land on Vancouver Island. CPI then formed two operating subsidiaries, Canadian Pacific Hotels Limited, to manage the company's hotels and Marathon Realty Company Limited, to manage the company's 900,000 acres of agricultural lands and 1,000 acres of town sites, in conjunction with CP Rail. In 1963 Consolidated Mining and Smelting Company, Cominco, was transferred into CPI.

world to compete for profits like everyone else was a frightening one. "The atmosphere was incredible," recalls Ron Swan, then a clerk. "All of a sudden we weren't going to be a railway anymore. We were going to be more than a railway. People got very upset, everyone started looking over their shoulders, no one really knew what direction we were going in." One senior officer in the trucking department was so upset when he discovered that his division was to operate on its own, he bolted into a nearby washroom and vomited. When he returned, pale and shivering, his shocked secretary asked, "What's the matter?" "I'm fifty-eight," he replied in a shaky voice. "I've been working for this company since I was fourteen, and I feel like my wife of forty-four years has just asked me for a divorce."

WITH SINCLAIR FULLY OCCUPIED setting up CPI, Crump made his old friend Bob Emerson president of the CPR in October, 1964.* It was the culmination of a lifelong quest for the clever and dedicated executive, but the pressures of the job quickly leeched out the pleasure of accomplishment. Outwardly Emerson was the essence of toughness, a completely unemotional and unsympathetic man. "In the company, people believed he made decisions by his slide rule," recalls Jack Anderson, former vice-president of industrial relations. But those closest to him had a completely different picture.

When Anderson's wife Doris was pregnant for the fourth time, Emerson insisted that she hire a helper and charge the salary to the company. Florence Evans, Emerson's secretary, remembers a host of little kindnesses that he quietly dispensed. Shortly after she bought her first car Emerson beckoned her into his office and, chortling like a child with a secret, hauled out a large bag and said, "Here, I think these will help you." It was full of automotive gadgets and supplies, all of which he had purchased personally.

---

*Crump retained the position of chairman and chief executive officer.

Every Sunday Emerson dutifully attended service, then walked across the street to Windsor Station to work for several hours. The ladies of the church knew a good thing when they saw it and pounced upon him as a likely candidate for church supper donations. Emerson always obliged, sending down to Windsor Station's Alouette Room for a large roast, which he paid for himself and carefully inspected before sending it across the street. Anderson also recalls several occasions when Emerson asked a group of staff to work overtime on short notice. "At the end he'd go out and get his chauffeur and send him to the liquor store for bottles of Chivas or wine and some cards." Each staff member received his handwritten thank-you and a bottle.

At heart, Emerson had warmth and great sensitivity, and the hard decisions about firings, track abandonment and the like began to eat away at him. Never an outgoing or exuberant man, he became ever colder and more withdrawn. At the same time, he began to see Ian Sinclair not as a sparring companion, but as just another irritant. On one occasion, Emerson and Fred Stone, by then a vice-president, were meeting to put the finishing touches on a complicated hotel deal. After hours of discussion, they had finally settled on a plan when Sinclair burst in "unannounced and uninvited." With barely an acknowledgement to either, "he joined in the discussion and raised questions which prevented our reaching a conclusion in the matter," observed Stone. "I felt that Sinclair was being more troublesome than constructive, and I imagine Emerson felt the same way."[15] Frustrated by such incidents, Emerson wrote several letters to Crump, complaining that relations between Sinclair and himself weren't making his job any easier.

On a Monday morning in March, 1966, Bob Emerson was found dead on the floor of his garage at his home in Montreal's affluent Mount Royal district. He died on Saturday, but wasn't found for two days because his wife, a native of Georgia who detested the bleak Quebec climate, was visiting relatives in the United States. Though there was a high proportion of carbon monoxide in his blood, the coroner's verdict was death by heart attack. Because of the circumstances, Emerson's obvious preoccupation and the unrelenting pressures, many assumed his death was suicide. "A lot of bunk," spits out Sinclair dismissively. "I had been with him on the Saturday. . . . We worked Saturday afternoon on a situation and I was meeting him Monday morning."

It is impossible to know how Emerson and Sinclair would have worked together once Crump left the chairmanship, but one thing is certain: there was genuine respect and fondness between them. Sinclair's grief over Emerson's death was evident at the funeral, the only time anyone in his family ever saw him cry.

The CPR has never been a company that adapts well to change. Employee morale, so delicately tied to the manœuvrings that take place in Windsor Station — variously called the Marble Hall, Peacock Alley and the Holy of Holies — was pole-axed by Emerson's death. Crump, still chairman, calmed the fears by briefly reassuming the presidency. Meanwhile, the very foundations of the company shivered with anticipation as employees speculated about who would be the next sovereign. Crump, distraught over the loss of his friend, was still a very practical man. Company plans, not to mention his own, were suddenly flung out of orbit, and annoyance gnawed at the edge of his distress. Returning from vacation, Fred Stone stopped by Crump's office to offer a word of condolence, "which I intended to be one of sympathy for the loss of a most competent associate. He stared coldly and sternly at me without saying a word. I was puzzled and slightly taken aback. I thought about this a good deal and often wondered if his reaction was not related to the fact that Crump disliked too much 'executive excitement.'"[16]

Shortly after the funeral, Florence Evans was mournfully cleaning out Emerson's desk when Crump walked in. "Don't break your neck on that," he told her bleakly. "Nobody will be moving in after this meeting." At the time, Evans was baffled by the remark, but word sped through Windsor Station like a Prairie bush fire that for the first time in the company's history, the board of directors would not ratify the chairman's choice for the presidency, Ian Sinclair. "Some of the directors objected to his manner and ways of negotiating," recalls Lucien Rolland, a board member at the time.

THE MEETINGS TO CHOOSE the next sovereign took on the secrecy and ambience of a papal conclave.* Sinclair had his supporters, but many names were put forward as alternatives, including some from outside the company. Crump was implacable, however, refusing even to consider the heretical suggestions. "His pony was Sinclair," says Rolland, "and he backed him to the limit." Despite his own reservations, Crump believed that Sinclair deserved to be the next president and was convinced he was the best man for the job. But it was only after Crump threatened to resign from the company that the board buckled under. In April, 1966, the directors finally elected Ian Sinclair as the tenth president of the CPR.

Norris Roy Crump resigned as chairman of the CPR in 1972, only three years after his sixty-fifth birthday. Much had been accomplished during his seventeen years in charge. The company was still firmly and profitably in private hands — and now no one doubted that it always would be — but most important, it was finally clear of its archaic methods and preconceptions. "It's a slow process changing a company's course," he'd once explained to *Forbes* magazine. "It's like reversing direction on an ocean liner when it's underway. It takes a long time and for a long while nothing seems to be happening."[17] Crump's proudest accomplishment was "repatriating" the company. In 1946 Canadians held only 6 percent of the stock, but by 1972 they owned 60 percent.

Today, the only railway Crump controls is the contraption that lowers him down the thirteen steps to his basement office. "Crump's Railroad," he calls it. "Twenty-two seconds travelling

---

*Word on the candidates did leak out, however, and CN employees even set up a pool, with odds posted on whom the directors would choose.

time." Even at the age of eighty-four, humiliatingly tethered by a forty-foot leash of transparent green oxygen hose and forced to wear gardening gloves to warm his neuritis-chilled hands, Buck Crump is unmistakably a CPR president. Toughness, combativeness and determination bristle like porcupine quills from the last railroader.

CHAPTER 14

THE BUCCANEER

I don't get heart attacks . . . I give them.

— Ian Sinclair

Not since the Terror of Flat Krick stood the railroad on its end had such a combination of intellect, physique and bravura ruled the CPR. Ian David Sinclair, tenth president of the company, had the same voracious appetite for work, the same predilection to lead by conspicuous example and a larger-than-life persona. He shared many of Van Horne's strengths and a few of his weaknesses, often using a bludgeon when a whisk would do and at times letting his joie de combat push him beyond the bounds of good sense.

At six-foot-one and more than 240 pounds, Sinclair dominated and intimidated by his existence alone. With a huge, lumpy chest and booming baritone, whose range an opera singer would kill for, Sinclair enjoyed the effect his presence had on lesser beings, and used it to good advantage. He's never been known for his elegance or sartorial splendour. Even in a Savile Row suit, Sinclair looks like he's wearing a kapok life preserver under his suit jacket instead of a vest. Allan Fotheringham once called him a "fleshy dracula . . . a linebacker who stumbled into the chairman's suite by mistake."[1] But Sinclair was far more like a corporate Paul Bunyan charging through effete boardrooms and scattering directors in his wake like saplings.

When Buck Crump was toiling away in the greasy pits, no one could have guessed that he would become the CPR's president. But many would have bet on the young Sinclair's chances. "I knew in 1947 that he was going to head the whole thing," his successor Fred Burbidge states emphatically. "A whole bunch of others did, too." The earliest CPR pictures of Sinclair reveal a faint but unmistakable smirk. Some colleagues charitably called it a twinkle. But beneath that subtle interaction of facial muscles lay the suppressed glee of a hunter with his prey firmly sighted. However, it wasn't the kill he relished, but the chase.

When he took over the presidency, Sinclair soothingly told

Ian Sinclair in 1964

employees not to "expect too different a team operation than [they'd] been accustomed to in the past."[2] But it was soon clear there would be no Crump-style troika of power for Sinclair, though he talks a good line about the value of teamwork and collegial decision making. "Look, if you are going to run something, you're a team person to start with," he's fond of saying. "That's absolutely essential. There's nobody alive smart enough to run things by himself." But no one who has ever worked with him believes those words for a minute. And even Sinclair himself admits the philosophy only goes so far. "When you make a decision to move and if you're running the team, *you* make that decision. . . . You listen to things and then you say, 'Goddammit, this is what we're going to do,' and everyone supports you or gets off the team."[3]

Sinclair's presidency ushered in an era of unprecedented change, but nothing had a greater impact on the CPR than his personality and style. Crump had been an all-powerful leader but a quiet and relatively self-effacing one. Within a few years of succeeding Emerson, Sinclair's image overshadowed the company to such an extent that many people believed he actually owned it.

Though he could be a delightful and entertaining companion, Sinclair on the job was a study in total concentration, eliminating and brusquely ignoring anything not pertinent to the issue at hand. On many occasions senior executives rode up the Windsor Station elevator beside him without getting even a nod of recognition. "I like to say that we don't go to work; we report for duty," was one of his favourite comments — said only half in jest.[4] Florence Evans, Emerson's former secretary, found the new approach unsettling. "I was used to going in first thing in the morning and getting a smile. But with Mr. Sinclair you were lucky if he even looked at you. No chit-chat, just do what you came in for and leave." The president often startled her by abruptly lurching out of his chair, flinging himself out of his office and pacing up and down the corridor of the executive wing, never talking or pausing — moving silently and relentlessly like a great white shark on the prowl. Then, just as suddenly, he would return to his desk.

Many have interpreted Sinclair's concentration and focus as rudeness or callousness. But family members who have felt its cold, hard edge know otherwise. When his daughter Susan missed the school bus, she had to walk up the road to wait for the regular transit. If Sinclair drove by he wouldn't pick her up or acknowledge her with a honk or a wave. "Part of the reason he never gave me a ride was, no doubt, to teach me a lesson," she explains. "But I think the deeper reason was once he got into the CPR car with the CPR chauffeur, he was on CPR business and picking me up wasn't CPR business."

When Buck Crump became president, he wrenched the company off its tottering footings and laid a new foundation. Sinclair took the foundation and built a castle, frequently adorned with idiosyncratic embellishments that sometimes only he could appreciate. Many long-time employees, forgetting Van Horne's flamboyant promotional style, mourned the

Sinclair at a press conference

end of company dignity when the CPR began running catchy television commercials and sponsoring Canadian Football League games. "We're a railroad not a soda pop," spat an operations officer in disgust after watching one of the prime time spots. The new advertising was the suggestion of Lippincott & Margulies International Ltd., a trendy New York "image maker" whose ad men described the CPR's previous image as dragging "somewhere back of the caboose."[5]

IAN SINCLAIR WAS DETERMINED that no aspect of Canadian Pacific — image, performance or size — would lag behind anyone or anything. He strode through the expansionary optimism of the late 1960s and 1970s like a colossus pushing, pulling and bludgeoning the company from $2.1 billion in assets in 1966 to a staggering $16.3 billion in 1981, when he retired as chairman of CP Ltd. The propellant for this rocketing growth was Canadian Pacific Investments Ltd., the company Crump had formed to keep Sinclair out of mischief back in 1962.

In its first five years of existence, CPI appeared to be little more than an anonymous holding company. The 1962 annual report devoted a bare five sentences to it, and in 1963, it merited only a small section, including the names of the six companies it controlled, but no breakdown of their individual earnings.

In 1967 CPI suddenly shed its chrysalis with the announcement of a $100 million public share issue, then the largest in Canadian history. Financial jaws dropped from one coast to the other. Sinclair had been working on the offering for months with a team of advisors, but not a word had leaked out. The prospect of CPI, which was supposed to be just a management tool, striking out with that much money in its pocket had more than a few industries nervously checking their backs. The shares went on the market at par, $20, and were almost immediately snapped up as eager investors bid them up to $23.75.

Sinclair had a vision for the CPR that crystallized back in 1956 when Crump instigated the massive decade-long cataloguing of the company's dormant assets. In addition to continuing Crump's exploitation of these resources, Sinclair was eager to expand into industries that would counteract Canadian Pacific's cyclical earnings pattern. In many ways the CPR was balanced like a giant, upside-down pyramid; a bad year for grain, timber or steel and the whole thing teetered dangerously as earnings of the railway and key subsidiaries plummeted.

By the end of 1967 he had taken a large step toward fulfilling the first part of his plan. CPR freight cars were carrying sulphur produced by Canadian Pacific Oil and Gas (CPOG) to CPR-owned Cominco, where it was turned into fertilizer, which was then transported by company rails, barges and trucks to Canadian Pacific Air Lines planes, and sprinkled over CPR-owned forests on Vancouver Island.*

But shipping freight didn't satisfy Sinclair. What he really wanted to do was *make* the goods as well as transport them. The company had an entrée into the mining industry and its spinoffs with Cominco, but that was only a start. When he took over from Emerson, Sinclair had promised "aggressive diversification" and he intended to deliver. The tools at his disposal were considerable: 21,300 miles of railway track, 18,000 miles of truck routes,† an 18,000-mile telecommunications network, 25 passenger and freight liners, 11 hotels, and 17 aircraft, as well as 845,000 acres of western agricultural land leased to 3,000 tenants, nearly 400,000 acres on Vancouver Island and

---

*There is a company yarn about an Englishman who arrived in Canada aboard a CP ship and took a room at the Château Frontenac, a CP hotel. He went to the desk to send a Canadian Pacific Communications cable, which he paid for with a Canadian Pacific traveller's cheque. Upon leaving, he asked the clerk, "What time is it in Vancouver?" The man replied, "It's 11 A.M. Canadian Pacific time." "Good heavens," said the startled tourist. "Don't tell me you own *that* here too!"

†With trucking companies snatching up every bit of the CPR's cargo business that wasn't nailed down, Crump had earlier decided that the company had to get its own foothold in the new industry. After he swooped in and purchased a huge trucking firm, Smith Transport, CP Trucks was on its way to becoming the largest trucking business in Canada.

Sinclair doing an advertisement for CP Air cargo services

substantial holdings in the heart of most of Canada's major cities. Functioning almost like an agency, the CPR had always sold timber leases, mineral rights and farmland in order to get the freight traffic that resulted from development. But after eighty years, the cozy relationship with other industries had begun to destroy the company's competitive fibre. "We decided, no more!" Sinclair booms out like an evangelist denouncing promiscuity. "We're going to start running this ourselves." "Santa Claus is disrobing," observed one reporter when he declared there would be no more giveaways. The decision caused a major shakeup in the timber and mineral industries, and the iconoclastic CPR president relished every minute of it.

Sinclair's biggest incursion into areas the CPR had traditionally left to others came in the oil and gas business. A passive land bank that had been incorporated in 1958, Canadian Pacific Oil and Gas exploded into production by the end of 1967 with 431 producing wells and nearly $20 million invested in exploration of over 14 million acres in the West and North. Central-Del Rio Oils Ltd., purchased in the late sixties, provided CP with another 1.5 million acres of mineral-rich land in Saskatchewan. In 1971, CPOG and Central-Del Rio were merged to form Pan Canadian, which held rights to 20 million acres in Canada, as well as extensive interests in South America, Africa and Indonesia.

During Sinclair's first years as CPR president, the effects of his promised "aggressive diversification" weren't always obvious. Many companies like Marathon Realty appeared to grow very little, and descriptions of their activities were relegated to a few obscure columns in the annual reports. But what the figures didn't show was Sinclair's manœuvring as he positioned the company for the dazzling expansion push of the seventies. Through CPI he slowly acquired and increased the CPR's investment in areas that interested him: pipelines, forest products, mines and manufacturing.

OF ALL THE COMPANIES Sinclair ruled, his favourite was the airlines. In comparison to the frequently staid and tradition-bound railway, the airline industry attracted an intriguing collection of oddballs and eccentrics, like twenty-cigar-a-day Canadian Pacific Air Lines president Grant McConachie, who carried an inflatable globe around with him on his lifelong mission to sell air travel.* Though Sinclair steadfastly claimed to be governed by nothing but the bottom line, he was rarely happier than when he could squeeze his bulk through the narrow cockpit door of a plane and stand swapping stories with the captain and his crew. In the seventies, the corporate jet had become a symbol of success and nearly every major enterprise in the country had one — except Canadian Pacific. Sinclair, who travelled 100,000 miles annually, said, "I don't need a company plane. I have a whole airline."

One day in 1975 a *Financial Post* reporter caught sight of Sinclair towering above a group of passengers as he waited in line to check his bags like any other ordinary citizen. When the reporter voiced his surprise that Sinclair would stand in line, let alone see to his own bags, the president responded, "Well, sometimes you can only see what's really going on when you queue up with the rest of the folks." Gesturing toward the agent as she took his ticket, the reporter said, "Is she going to think you're just one of the folks?" Sinclair let go a sabre-toothed grin, "She'd better not!"

Sinclair hated to be kept waiting, even for a moment, though he occasionally held others up to ensure he arrived on time. A prominent Toronto businessman recalls boarding a CP flight with his wife for a skiing holiday. "We got on and just sat there and sat there. They kept coming up with some excuse why they couldn't take off. Then I happened to be looking out the window, and out of the terminal came a little cart with this great big man in it. Ian Sinclair. We took off pretty soon after that."

Sinclair's beloved airline was not an easy child. Ever since Beatty formed Canadian Pacific Air Lines in 1942, the company had to battle the government and Air Canada for every air mile it added to its route. In 1967 CPA still had only one

---

*McConachie died of a heart attack in 1965, only fifty-six years old. In his last years he complained mightily about the various concoctions his doctors forced him to take. "One day I emptied the whole selection, one day's dose, into a glass of water," he told a friend, "and do you know what happened? It exploded!" (Keith, *Bush Pilot with a Briefcase*, p. 313)

transcontinental flight. When Sinclair became president, the company faced one of the most disastrous periods in its history. "This airline has been running on a mixture of glamour and gasoline for twenty years. Now we've got to inject a strong dose of economics, or else," he warned.[6] But the injection didn't work, and almost immediately CPA went into a downward spiral. Net income plummeted from a high of $7.4 million in 1966 to a paltry $1 million in 1970.

Many believed that the well-managed CPA might have been far more profitable if it could have cajoled more lucrative routes out of the miserly transport bosses in Ottawa, who kept the most profitable ones for Air Canada. Then and now, some blame Sinclair's impatience with politicians in general and with Jean Marchand, minister of transport, in particular, for the airline's misfortune. "He and Marchand hated each other," insists John Hamilton, a lawyer often retained by CPA.* "Sinclair rubs people the wrong way," a civil servant told *Business Week* magazine. "He lectures them. In official circles he is regarded as a total disaster. CP handles its affairs here very badly." A Cabinet aide added, "Sinclair acts on the presumption that everyone in government is stupid." Even Sinclair himself bluntly admitted that his relations with Ottawa could have been better. "If big corporations can influence government," he told one reporter, "then I've been singularly unsuccessful."[7]

Many politicians and bureaucrats viewed Sinclair as "brusque, abrasive, demanding, pushy and argumentative," but former transport minister Jack Pickersgill found his approach refreshing. "You know, this town is so full of bootlickers, it's terrible. Sinclair isn't that way. He is totally honest with people. He is

---

*Years after Marchand left politics, Hamilton attended a meeting where the two old adversaries were present. He was astonished to see Sinclair taking uncharacteristically small steps to keep pace with the shorter Marchand, who was walking at his side. The big man's arm was slung across the shoulders of the former Cabinet minister and the two were chatting like old school buddies. "Ian, how can you do that?" Hamilton asked as soon as he had a chance to draw Sinclair to one side. Cracking one of his toothsome grins, Sinclair shrugged, "Different times, different place."

tough and aggressive and says what he means. But you can talk back to him. He doesn't care."[8] Sinclair was always comfortable with his well-publicized conflicts in Ottawa because they protected his dozens of valuable contacts and kept them out of the limelight. He spent decades patiently eroding the political obstacles against abolishing the Crow Rate and getting Prime Minister Pierre Trudeau and Minister of Transport Jean-Luc Pepin "on side." Though the hated grain rate wasn't chopped until 1983, during Fred Burbidge's CPR chairmanship, Sinclair deserves a large measure of credit for seeing it into the grave.

REINFORCING SINCLAIR'S POLITICAL connections were unparalleled conduits into the most important companies in the country. Before "networking" became a cliché, he was its premier practitioner, giving Canadian Pacific a huge window on

Sinclair and Trudeau

other business and industrial sectors and extending the company's influence. While other executives played racketball or "did lunch," Sinclair dominated boardrooms across the nation. At the height of his power in the mid-1970s he sat on twenty-two of Canada's most powerful boards, including those of the Royal Bank of Canada, The Seagram Co. Ltd., Simpsons Ltd., Sun Life Assurance Co. of Canada Ltd. and Union Carbide Canada Limited. As with anything he came near, Sinclair was never an idle spectator.*

"Sinclair rules every damn board he sits on," says one colleague who sat in his shadow on four of them. "Trouble is, he tends to know more than anybody else, so it's tough to challenge him. It can be quite scary when you are trying to oppose someone with that much power and that kind of mind."

The sixties and seventies ushered in the age of analysts, specialists and management teams to report on various aspects of corporate activities. Sinclair eschewed all that, especially within Canadian Pacific. "He reported on everything, and brilliantly. You name it, he was ready to report," recalls former company director Lucien Rolland. That meant Sinclair was likely to know his subordinates' business better than they did themselves — so working for him was no joyride. Once Sinclair had embraced the facts and figures of an enterprise or a department, he committed them to memory and shelved them within easy reach. "I don't think he's forgotten anything he's ever learned," muses his current secretary, Pat Brock. "He never has to see anything twice." Sinclair's memory was a curse to many CP officers, who often felt they had two bosses wrapped up in one: Ian Sinclair and The

---

*In a congratulatory telegram he sent to Sinclair on the occasion of his retirement from Canadian Pacific Enterprises on April 12, 1984, Trudeau referred to Sinclair's multiple corporate involvement:

I had often wondered why Ian switched from the academic world to the corporate offices of Canadian Pacific. I am told that somebody once asked him this question, to which he responded, "I always wanted my own railroad." I don't dare ask him why he became a director of the Royal Bank.

Memory. And the second boss was as tough as the first: it never seemed to forget a promise, a decision, a threat or even a casual remark from a past conversation. Of course, Sinclair did forget some things, but who would be foolish enough to point it out?

SINCLAIR CULTIVATED HIS REPUTATION as a tyrant and carried it conspicuously strapped to his hip like a gunfighter's six-gun — ready for instant use but most valuable as an ever-present threat. Even vice-presidents drew deep breaths, sucked in their stomachs and squared their shoulders before entering his enclave. Sinclair punctuates even casual conversation with the drumlike thudding of his thick, meaty fingers against whatever surface is available. He also has the disquieting habit of suddenly flinging himself forward across the blotter as if to grasp the person opposite by the throat and throttle him. It came as a pleasant shock, especially to junior officers, when they found the lion could actually be approached without loss of limb. "On a couple of occasions a case would come up and someone wanted him to do something," smiles John Cox of public affairs. "He'd ask me my opinion and I thought, 'Well, he's just going to go and do what he wants,' and then I found that he had accepted my advice. It was a great surprise."

Much of the difficulty in working for Ian Sinclair stems from the simple fact that he flourishes with a level of stress and confusion that would give anyone else an ulcer. "I don't get heart attacks . . . I give them," he once quipped. Fred Burbidge sardonically observes, "If there wasn't a crisis going he'd create one!"

Another aspect of Sinclair's ogre boss persona which pains those with tender sensibilities is his sharp and often rather wicked sense of humour. Like his predecessor, Sir William Van Horne, he especially likes jokes that come at the expense of someone else. A young articling student named David Flicker was once doing some work for the law department when he came across a matter that required Sinclair's immediate attention. He rushed off to inform the chairman's secretary about the problem. To his surprise, the woman insisted that he tell Sinclair personally. Flicker protested, but the secretary, enjoying his discomfort, was adamant. Before the aspiring lawyer realized what was happening, she opened the office door and, with the help of another woman, literally pushed the young man inside, quickly shutting the door.

The inner sanctum seemed to stretch for acres with Sinclair seated at his desk, in the middle, outlined by a halo of bright lights suspended from the ceiling. For a few seconds Flicker stood paralyzed like a mouse caught in the deadly gaze of a snake. The chairman stared at the intruder quizzically. Finally finding his tongue, Flicker explained in his best junior apprentice voice what the problem was and offered his solution. "Fine," shot back Sinclair, "Do that."

"Oh, heady glory," thought Flicker. "I've impressed the chairman." His career was assured, riches awaited, nothing could stop him now. Sinclair abruptly returned to his work, indicating the interview had ended. But getting out of the room presented a problem. "You just don't turn around and walk out of Sinclair's office. You don't do it with Kubla Khan and you don't do it with Ian Sinclair." Flicker genuflected, backed down the long expanse of carpet, and when his hand made contact with the door knob, he opened it and swept out.

For several panicky moments Flicker wrestled with a dreadful feeling of disorientation. Unexpectedly he found himself in a very small and very dark cubicle. "You idiot!" he said to himself. "You went into his closet and he *saw* you do it." Flicker had entered a long-disused phone booth. He considered staying until Sinclair went home, but that wouldn't work because the chairman had watched Flicker go in. Feeling his future ooze away and deciding he couldn't make things any worse, the young man opened the door a crack. "Please, Mr. Sinclair, tell me I'm not the first one to do that," he said sheepishly, trying to salvage some honour from the débâcle. "No," conceded the chairman, barely suppressing his laughter. "But you are the first to go in and close the door behind him."

Sinclair loved to drive an elbow into his colleagues' ribs, but he simply adored the prospect of making an ass out of an outsider. Shortly before becoming president, he and a group of CPR executives were having dinner at the Empress Hotel in Victoria when a businessman with ties to W. A. C. Bennett's British Columbia Social Credit government invited himself to their table. He had a few too many under his belt. Sinclair eyed the unwelcome guest and decided to have a little fun. With a wink at the others, he began to talk as if he were a CN executive with a particularly close relationship to the company's president, Donald Gordon, extolling the virtues of public ownership and speaking proudly of CN's tremendous deficit.

The businessman protested belligerently, declaring that the "people's railway" deficit was an abomination and his friend W. A. C. Bennett certainly didn't operate British Columbia that way. Sinclair ignored him and boomed on: "Donald and I have an objective." "Whassat?" slurred the tipsy guest. "A hundred million," stated Sinclair. "A hundred million for what?" exclaimed the other. "We are going to get that deficit up to a hundred million dollars — or die in the attempt."

The next day the businessman indignantly reported the conversation to Premier Bennett. "Who told you that?" the premier asked suspiciously. "Well, I think his name was Sinclair, Ian Sinclair." Bennett roared with laughter. "Sinclair was just giving you a lesson in public relations. He's a Canadian *Pacific* vice-president."

HISTORICALLY, CPR PRESIDENTS have always receded into the background when they moved up to the chairman's position. But Ian Sinclair was different. In 1972 he had only begun to fulfil his vision for the company. Though Fred Burbidge* became president that year, Sinclair, as new chairman and CEO, ran the show publicly and privately. The winds of change that whistled through the company in 1966 began to blow again. A

---

*Fred Burbidge was also a lawyer and another of the "Manitoba Mafia" as Crump liked to call it, a group of high-ranking CP executives who came from that province.

year earlier the CPR had applied to Parliament to drop "Railway" from the company's name, and when a Toronto *Daily Star* reporter asked Sinclair about it, he received the curt reply, "I am not motivated much by nostalgia."[9]*

The year Sinclair became chairman was not an auspicious one for railways. Six American railroads had gone bankrupt in the previous six years, the most prominent being Penn Central, which had attempted to diversify into non-transportation areas. Then along came Ian Sinclair, declaring he was interested in anything that made a profit, from textiles to meat packing, if it bolstered the highly cyclical earnings of many of CP's current interests.

At the end of 1972, Sinclair's first year in complete control, the railroad's net income of $57.6 million still overshadowed CPI's $44.3 million, but by 1974, the balance sheet had changed drastically. That year CPI's net income of $114.2 million was more than three times as great as the railroad's $35.8 million. The child had overwhelmed the parent. Sinclair was behind it, launching an astonishing acquisition binge that lasted for nearly a decade. Though he portrayed himself as a manager and barrister, in his heart lurked the zeal of a hard-core entrepreneur. At no time was this more obvious than when he put on his negotiating hat. Like Van Horne, Sinclair had a reputation as a bull in the china shop, excelling at frontal assaults. But he was equally capable of sidling into a match with nonchalance and supreme outward indifference.

OF SINCLAIR'S HUNDREDS OF NEGOTIATIONS, the one that has assumed legendary status is his 1973 purchase of Algoma Steel Corporation,† a prey he'd been watching for years with

---

*When Crump was asked about the value of the traditional name, he answered, "I like it as long as you make money. But if it's a choice between money and tradition, to hell with tradition."

†Algoma, Canada's third-largest steel producer, controlled a vast amount of coal and iron reserves, owned Algoma Central Railway and 43 percent of Dominion Bridge, a group of steel fabricators.

the patience of a cobra. At the time, the massive West German conglomerate Mannesmann AG had a 25 percent interest in the company, but Algoma was proving to be a thorn in the side of Egon Overbeck, Mannesmann's chief executive, a decorated German general staff officer and one of the most feared industrialists in Europe. Originally, the investment had been a natural offshoot of Overbeck's expansion plans, but he had become disenchanted with the whole business because of the restrictions imposed by the Foreign Investment Review Agency, set up in 1973. He was also aggravated by Algoma's irritating habit of ignoring his directives.

Overbeck approached investment dealers Burns Brothers & Denton Ltd. of Toronto to find a buyer. "We had a list of twenty-two potential people," remembers Latham Burns. "CP really caught our eye, so we approached Ian Sinclair." Algoma really caught Sinclair's eye too, but he reacted with the inscrutability of a sphinx. "He played a little cat-and-mouse game with me," chuckles Burns. "But then we started talking about the price, and there was a considerable difference." Sinclair offered $19 a share (Algoma was trading at 18⅞), refused to pay interest on the promissory notes and insisted that all cash be in Canadian dollars. Overbeck demanded that the notes bear an interest rate of 12½ percent and that the cash be in deutsche marks. Burns knew that only a face-to-face showdown would consummate the sale. The problem was getting Sinclair to Germany.

"There's no point in him coming if he's not going to pay interest," Overbeck snapped to the German press. After Overbeck's remarks, Sinclair pointedly cancelled his CP flight to Germany, telling reporters who called that he had plans to spend the weekend with his family at his summer home in the Eastern Townships. Suddenly thrown off balance, Burns scrambled to revive the deal. He anxiously checked with CP Air to see if Sinclair had re-booked his flight, but each time he made the request, the answer came back, no. At the last minute, Sinclair, with a great show of reluctance, let himself be persuaded to fly to Germany. Only later did Burns learn that the president had secretly booked a seat on KLM.

The CP chairman had wanted to be on Overbeck's turf all along. "When you are going to negotiate with a fellow, always go to his place because then he thinks he's got you at a disadvantage. Most people are kind and relaxed then." Overbeck fêted Sinclair at his eighth-century castle, Schloss Hugenput, near Düsseldorf. The one-upmanship began in earnest over a roast venison dinner, with Overbeck pointedly mentioning that the castle had been built seven hundred years before Europeans even set foot in North America and Sinclair countering with his own remarks about stagnation and entropy.

The next morning both teams met. A single aide accompanied Sinclair, while Overbeck surrounded himself with four of his own executives and three from Burns. The two unmatched groups laid immovable positions on the table and spent several hours wrestling over minor details. Throughout it all, the principals watched each other, silently trying to gain the psychological upper hand. Unable to compete with Overbeck's six-foot-four stature or his ramrod military posture, Sinclair countered by hunching forward like a massive, belligerent bulldog.

Suddenly, without warning or visible communication between them, Overbeck and Sinclair got up and left the room, leaving their retinues staring out over the Rhine, muttering pleasantries to each other. When they returned, Overbeck's long, proud face was set. "Gentlemen, we have sold our shares to Mr Sinclair for $20 and I'm not the least bit happy about it." The price was exactly what Sinclair had already decided he would pay before he even left Canada, including the provision of half the price in deutsche marks. "They wanted some marks, so I said sure. All we did was hedge them." In return, Sinclair got precisely what he was after: the balance of payment in short-term notes with no interest attached. It was a spectacular coup, but Sinclair scoffs at that description and at the suggestion he used any particular technique to pull it off.

"A coup? No, you don't have coups. Technique is knowing what the other fellow is going to do."

AFTER JUST FOUR YEARS as chairman Sinclair had turned CP into a starkly different company from what it had been just a decade before. Between 1972 and 1981, the company's assets mushroomed from $2.4 billion to $16.3 billion, and the railway operations contributed only 30 percent toward profits of $174 million. From a largely transportation-based company, CP had been transformed into a multinational conglomerate with interests stretching from South America to the Arctic and from Prince Edward Island to Iran. CP Hotels constructed or leased hotels in West Germany, Israel, Quebec, Halifax and Thunder Bay. Mining acquisition and expansion included Steep Rock Iron Mines, Fording Coal — set up in 1972 — and the Rubiales zinc-lead mine in northern Spain. Sinclair purchased Baker Commodities, a rendering company; Rothsay Concentrates Ltd., an animal and vegetable waste recycling plant; Syracuse China Corporation in New York; Canadian Freehold Properties with a large portfolio of land and buildings; and Maple Leaf Mills, a large food-processing and distribution concern.

In the past, Canadian Pacific had always sold land, but now Sinclair began buying it at such a pace that it seemed he intended to replenish the company's original land grant. Marathon Realty which, in its early years, had concentrated on developing CP's own land, suddenly began acquiring raw real estate, office buildings and shopping centres in Edmonton, Toronto, Ottawa, San Francisco and Atlanta to name a few. Huge development schemes in Vancouver, Peterborough, Montreal and Calgary sprang up. No sooner had Sinclair digested one major project or takeover target than he swallowed another. *Business Week* magazine called him "one of North America's most powerful, fiercely autocratic industrialists [with an] eat-'em-alive style."[10]

Nicknamed Big Julie, after the wheeler-dealer/crapshooter in the musical *Guys and Dolls*, Sinclair appeared invincible. But he did occasionally fail, most notably during his highly publicized 1978 attempt to take over MacMillan Bloedel, the giant British Columbia forest products firm. CP had been acquiring MacBlo shares for years, and the relationship between the two companies was frequently stormy, as first Crump then Sinclair upbraided the executives for inefficient operations and low profits. But with only 13.4 percent of the shares, they could do little more than complain. After a disastrous few years in the mid-seventies, the MacBlo board hired Calvert Knudsen away from Weyerhaeuser Company, an Oregon-based forest products company, to drag B.C.'s largest employer back into the black. Bringing an American in provoked considerable controversy, but Knudsen proved to be exactly the kind of medicine MacMillan Bloedel needed.

SINCLAIR HAD HAD HIS EYE ON the company at least since 1976 when he airily told *Business Week*, "We might take over MacMillan Bloedel some day,"[11] but Sinclair wasn't the only suitor. Late in 1978 Domtar made a bid for control, and MacBlo retaliated by going after Domtar. Though he preferred to be courted rather than the other way round, Sinclair found MacBlo too appetizing to be coy, especially with Domtar in the picture. The MacBlo board met his initial approach with a firm no. But the directors might just as well have said nothing. "Guys like Ian Sinclair don't back off that easily," says Sinclair himself. The more MacBlo resisted a takeover, the more persistent Sinclair became until an exasperated Knudsen called him a "loose cannon on a deck."[12]

During one board meeting Ernie Richardson, then MacBlo chairman, politely asked Sinclair, who was a director, to leave the room while the other board members discussed the proposed takeover. Sinclair merely glowered darkly and sat there like a boulder, as if daring anyone to oust him. Richardson then told him that if he didn't leave he was going to adjourn the meeting. At that point Sinclair heaved himself to his feet, cast his eye around the room and growled, "All right! I will leave. But if you bastards do anything while I'm out of the room, you'll regret it for the rest of your life!"

Throughout December, 1978, in a series of moves, counter-moves and feints, MacBlo, Domtar and CP whirled around in a takeover free-for-all. Thwarting hostile buyouts usually involves the appearance of a white knight to snatch the prey away from the hunter. In this case the white knight was not another corporation, but B.C. premier Bill Bennett. The premier didn't like the idea of Canadian Pacific wielding any more control over the province's economy than it already had. More to the point, he didn't like Ian Sinclair. Bennett preferred to be stroked, cosseted and flattered, and he found Sinclair's arrogance and his assumption that what was good for CP was good for B.C. intensely annoying. Hot words flew back and forth between Victoria and Montreal. During one heated phone conversation Sinclair roared, "Well, how much can I buy?" Bennett, flushed to the roots of his hair, shouted back, "Not one more share! Nothing!"

Bennett made a barnful of political hay over the issue, playing up the West's legendary dislike of Canadian Pacific. "It was viewed as David versus Goliath . . . at last somebody was standing up to CP," recalls John Arnett, then premier Bennett's press secretary. The media seized the opportunity of cutting Sinclair, and by definition CP, down to human size. "It was an uplifting experience because the general feeling was that Sinclair felt bigger than anybody and that no premier was going to tell him what to do,"[13] said Arnett. But the barbs and insults bounced off Sinclair's hide like so many paper darts off a rhino's skin. "Hating the Canadian Pacific is good winter sport in the West," he told a *Business Week* reporter. "It gets cold and you can't go outside and you've got to take a shot at someone."[14]

Bennett, however, took the game seriously, and he had a card up his sleeve that not even Ian Sinclair could trump. It was the 1978 Provincial Forest Act, which allowed the government to back out of timber rights agreements if a takeover of a B.C. company did not meet with Cabinet approval. Since 80 percent of MacBlo's timber rights were held by the government, cancellation of them would carve the heart right out of the company. After a secret meeting in early 1979, Bennett placed his ace on the table and within days both CP and Domtar dropped their bids. Bennett had won, and he basked in the sunshine of his victory, trumpeting, "British Columbia is not for sale" — a proclamation that earned him a cover story in *Maclean's* and a lot of air time across the country. As the dust cleared, the *New York Times* observed drily, "Canadian Pacific . . . has withdrawn its bid for MacMillan Bloedel, which has withdrawn its bid for Domtar Inc., which has withdrawn its bid for MacMillan Bloedel."[15] Ironically, fifteen months later, MacMillan Bloedel fell to Noranda, based in Toronto and owned by Brascan Ltd., the epitome of establishment money.

Many chortled at the buccaneer's setback and hoped the experience would chasten him. Far from it. Sinclair merely shrugged off the defeat. "You can't kiss all the girls," he replied to numerous reporters' questions. "You've got to lose sometimes." When he emerged from the 1979 secret meeting with Bennett, he looked neither disappointed nor chagrined, but inexplicably content.

LOST IN THE HUE AND CRY over Sinclair's MacMillan Bloedel defeat was his intriguing purchase of Reed Paper Ltd. in Dryden, Ontario. In that deal, the buccaneer displayed a subtle and delicate style. With a Canadian head office in Toronto and the parent Reed International in England, Reed Paper's primary asset was its pulp and paper mill in Dryden and 6,900 square miles of timber. Suffering from the twin blights of ill-conceived expansion and sloppy absentee management, the company was in poor shape in the late seventies, losing $27 million in 1977 and writing off another $47 million. The company president, Robert Billingsley, had surrounded himself with opulence, including a private chef and a corporate jet, as he embarked on an expensive five-year buying frenzy, purchasing furniture, drapery and wallpaper interests.

In 1977 Billingsley abruptly resigned, leaving the company's management in complete disarray. Head office ordered Donald MacIver, the new president, to cut costs and sell off everything he could. Unfortunately, the directive was made publicly, robbing him of any bargaining chips, and forest companies across North America salivated at the prospect of snatching up the troubled Dryden mill at a fire sale price. But complicating any takeover attempt was the fact that the Dryden mill had been polluting a northern Ontario river with mercury. No one knew how much the pollution-related claims would cost, an intangible that frightened away many prospective buyers.

Ironically, the most ardent suitor was none other than MacMillan Bloedel. Early in 1978, Cal Knudsen conducted a thorough appraisal of the mill, and it was widely believed that a deal had been struck. There was only one problem: Ian Sinclair. He also wanted Reed, which would be a perfect fit with nearby Great Lakes Paper Company, 56 percent owned by Canadian Pacific. In curious harmony, shortly after Sinclair backed away from his MacBlo takeover attempt in early 1979, Knudsen announced he couldn't reach agreeable terms for Reed Paper.

With MacBlo unexpectedly out of the picture, Reed Paper was left alone in the ring with Sinclair. In September, 1979, Reed International categorically declared that the company was not for sale. "We're in business in Dryden, and we intend to stay in business in Dryden," MacIver was instructed to say.[16] Then, exactly six weeks later, Reed International made MacIver look like a fool when it sold the Dryden mill and surrounding timberlands for $80 million to Ian Sinclair and Great Lakes Paper. Some critics claimed that Sinclair had paid a ridiculous price, but they ignored two little sweeteners he'd negotiated with the Ontario government, which desperately wanted a strong Canadian company to replace Reed International. To the astonishment of all observers, he induced the Tory government to cover any pollution claims above $15 million — effectively capping a cost that some estimated could run to the tens of millions.* Before closing the deal, Sinclair also ensured that the government would honour a controversial agreement, signed four years earlier, to open up 19,000 square miles of undeveloped timber for the company's use.

"It was a very ingenious approach," raves Knudsen in retrospect. "You had to be someone like Ian even to ascertain whether such a deal was possible. We didn't have those kinds of connections. It never even crossed our minds to try." Sinclair vigorously denies that his attack on MacMillan Bloedel played even the slightest part in the Reed Paper takeover, or that any deal was made by the B.C. government or MacMillan Bloedel. Nevertheless, there are some interesting coincidences.

Around the same time that Canadian Pacific purchased Reed Paper, it also sold its shares in MacMillan Bloedel to the British Columbia Resources Investment Corp., a creature of the B.C. government, for a $13 million dollar net profit, even though the value of the shares had plummeted since their initial purchase. That deal may explain why Sinclair emerged from the 1979 secret meeting with Premier Bennett looking more irrepressibly pleased than crushed. Despite his arrogance and bravado, Sinclair was always willing to swallow his pride if it meant a $13 million profit and a clear shot at a deal he really wanted.

AS SINCLAIR SIGNED THE REED purchase he was at the height of his power and, at the age of sixty-five, nearing the end of his reign. Despite CP's reputation as a stodgy corporation still bound by an antiquated emphasis on seniority, there were many top-flight executives in the upper echelons. The trouble was they all paled beside Sinclair, who hung onto control with

---

*The actual claims payments came to $16.7 million, of which Great Lakes paid $6 million. The balance was paid by Reed Paper Ltd. and the Ontario government.

an unshakable grip. "In Canadian Pacific there's Ian, and everyone else is a secretary," remarked one department head. Though Sinclair loathed sycophants, "servile" best describes the relationship between him and many of his subordinates. Rod Sykes, who worked to set up Marathon Realty before becoming Calgary's mayor, said, "Sinclair is a Roman emperor with consuls and pro-consuls but too few governors. It would be a disaster for CP if anything happened to Sinclair." Directors worried that no single man could ever replace him.

In 1981 Ian Sinclair turned sixty-eight and became the oldest chief executive officer in the history of Canadian Pacific.* As head of both CP Ltd. and CPE,† he carried a staggering load, and all agreed that two men should take his place when he stepped down. However, I.D.S. seemed in no hurry to hand over the reins, although the board had already requested that he submit a proposal of succession.

For Sinclair to leave at that point would be like a fullback handing over the football to a teammate a few inches from the goal line after having carried it the entire length of the field. Canadian Pacific controlled or had interests in over three hundred companies worldwide, many purchased during Sinclair's reign. Boasting assets of $16 billion, Canadian Pacific was the largest Canadian-owned company in the country. Canadian Pacific Enterprises, Sinclair's passion, had grown from its inception in 1962 into a massive $8 billion empire. On its own, it was Canada's fifth-largest company.

But that wasn't enough. With 14 percent of CPE's assets in the United States, Sinclair still had some distance to go to reach his target of 25 percent U.S. assets. And he didn't yet have the market share he wanted in finished goods, food services or the forestry industry. Though Sinclair's Canadian Pacific projects had helped redraw the face of many Canadian cities, potential

---

*William Mather at seventy and George Walker at seventy-five were actually older, but both acted more as consultants and advisors to Crump than as operating officers.

†Canadian Pacific Investments had changed its name to Canadian Pacific Enterprises (CPE) in 1980.

multibillion-dollar projects on Toronto and Vancouver's waterfronts still tantalized him. His last big splash was CPE's 1981 $1.1 billion U.S. purchase of Canadian International Paper (CIP). A tidal wave of criticism both in and outside the company met the announcement. The price was considered at least 50 percent too high, in view of CIP's $1.5 billion debt. Sinclair merely smiled knowingly at the naysayers, pointing to CIP's 1.4 million acres of forest, mostly in Quebec and New Brunswick, and cutting rights to another 9.3 million acres of government land. He assured everyone that one day the purchase would be a veritable jewel in Canadian Pacific's crown.

In the end, of course, Sinclair did have to retire, but he did it on his own terms, relinquishing control piece by piece. He handed over the jobs of chairman and CEO of CP Ltd. to sixty-two-year-old company president Fred Burbidge in 1981, but stayed on as chairman and CEO of Canadian Pacific Enterprises. He also retained the chairmanship of CP's powerful executive committee, scandalizing many inside Canadian Pacific, as that spot traditionally belonged to the company chairman, now Fred Burbidge.

THOUGH SINCLAIR DID give up the CEO post of Canadian Pacific Enterprises in 1982, he hung onto the chairman's spot, despite being chosen that summer by federal finance minister Allan MacEachen and Prime Minister Pierre Trudeau to head a twelve-member private-sector "6 and 5 committee," established to encourage business to keep prices down and labour to moderate wage demands. The enthusiasm with which Sinclair flung himself into the task was reminiscent of the days of the MacPherson Commission. Week after week he toured the country, browbeating business and labour. Though the only tool he had was the power of persuasion, Trudeau later credited him with being a major force in bringing inflation down from 11.2 percent to 5.4 percent in 1983.

The Sinclair twinkle

On December 23, 1983, four days before his seventy-first birthday, Trudeau offered him a place in the Senate. Opponents accused the PM of "paying off" Sinclair for his part in the 6 and 5 committee, a suggestion Sinclair met with some characteristically ominous words: "You don't pay off Ian Sinclair."

There was little change in the arrogant, autocratic and bull-like man who had ruled Canadian Pacific for so long. As always, he thrived on confusion and chaos, and there was plenty of that swirling through the Senate when Sinclair was appointed. Though still a rookie, he took on the chairmanship of the Standing Committee on Banking, Trade and Commerce, long regarded as the most important Senate committee, and used that perch to launch tirade upon tirade against the evils of allowing families like the Bronfmans and the Reichmanns to gather so much financial power to themselves.

Sinclair finally severed his last formal tie with Canadian Pacific in May, 1984, when he resigned as chairman of Canadian Pacific Enterprises. The new crew that followed him is steadily dismantling many of his proudest achievements, and he continues to have a legion of detractors inside and outside the company. For them all he has a simple answer: "Nobody ever accused the public of Canada of loving Canadian Pacific and I never thought I was going to get them to love it. But I was desperately trying to make sure they respected it."

An imperious aura of authority still halos Sinclair. Bowing and scraping follow him everywhere. Even the mighty enjoy basking in the reflected glow. "I love having lunch with Ian at the Royal York," gloats Senator Keith Davey. "It's the closest thing to a prime ministerial reception I've ever seen."

Sinclair is facing retirement from the Senate in December on his seventy-fifth birthday and, like the president he most resembles, William Van Horne, he's looking for yet another career — perhaps a stint at university in hard-rock geology or, who knows, maybe another railroad company. A former CP director recently met Sinclair by chance in an elevator and asked, "How are you doing, Ian?" The senator flashed a carnivorous grin and replied, "I am fighting the world and the world is receding." The Sinclair twinkle — or smirk — is firmly in place, and behind it lurks a man who's still having the time of his life.

EPILOGUE
A LORD IN THE MAKING

O n May 6, 1981, the changing of the guard began. Fred Burbidge, nearly sixty-four, had spent nine long years in Ian Sinclair's shadow as president of Canadian Pacific. Now, as chairman and chief executive officer, he finally had control of the kingdom but only a few years to enjoy the throne. A perfect example of the extremely capable and intensely loyal men who have quietly subjugated themselves to Canadian Pacific, Burbidge, as second-in-command to Sinclair, uncomplainingly played the good cop to his superior's irredeemably bad cop — soothing ruffled brows, tidying up details and reconciling divergent interests.

Widely known as an approachable "gentleman" and a "nice guy," people called Burbidge "Fred" without asking, and subordinates felt comfortable chatting with him in the elevator. No one would have dreamt of taking such liberties with any other company president.* Almost everyone, from typists to

---

*Fred Stone, a former CP vice-president and long-serving employee who had known N. R. Crump for more than fifty years, didn't dare call him "Buck" until he was invited, even when both men were in their eighties and long retired. Ian Sinclair inspired similar respect — or trepidation. Recently one of CP's most senior executives grandly offered to introduce a visitor to "Ian." But once in the retired president's office, the executive was transformed into a fawning clerk, stammering twice and calling Sinclair "Sir" six times in two minutes before he was dismissed.

vice-presidents, has a story about his kindness or interest in the rank and file. He also endeared himself to employees by his straight talking, clear thinking and dislike of obscure jargon. The CPR euphemistically refers to train accidents as "affairs," a parlour-room word at odds with the horrific tangle of men, machinery and track that even the simplest derailment can produce. One day Burbidge was working quietly in his office when his assistant brought news of a bad "affair" in the west. After hearing the details Burbidge exclaimed, "Affair! That's not an affair. That's a goddamn train wreck!"

Burbidge's penchant for simple words gives the impression of a simple man. In fact, he has a razor-sharp intellect and classic CP presidential toughness, accented by a tart, sarcastic manner which he lets loose only on rare occasions. If he seems unimposing, it is only because he has always placed the overall good of the company before his own considerable pride and ambition. Particularly effective in dealing with Ottawa's politicians and bureaucrats, Burbidge had many quiet achievements — in 1983 he put the finishing touches on the historic removal of the Crow Rate, the agreement that had been plaguing the company since 1897.

Though not a caretaker leader like Coleman, Mather or Walker, one of Burbidge's most important jobs in his short time as chairman and CEO was to train and test the next CP strong man, William (Bill) Stinson.

Born on October 29, 1933, into a railroad family, Stinson's career followed the classic pattern of those who achieve high rank in the company. Still, he was really a dark-horse candidate for the presidency. Though he held the number two spot as senior executive officer of CP Rail,* Stinson wasn't elected to the CP board of directors until he became president — not an unprecedented occurrence, but rare indeed in company history.

---

*The position of vice-president of the company, which had formerly been the most powerful job next to the presidency, no longer existed.

Even after Stinson was appointed to the company's top post in 1981, many Canadian Pacific insiders privately doubted his presidential mettle. Over the years, the pressures of the job had crushed one president, bent another and eliminated untold candidates. But those closest to Stinson knew that he had what it took to be a CP president. "Cold" and "hard" are adjectives that come quickly to associates' lips when speaking of Stinson. The words are shaded with intonations of respect and not a little fear. "You're lucky if you can get a smile out of him and you never know what he's thinking," emphasizes one former vice-president. "But if he decides to tell you, he'll tell it straight."

In the coming years, Stinson would need to be every bit as tough as his legendary predecessors. Between 1981 and 1985 the company drifted, hit particularly hard by the recession and chained to money-draining subsidiaries like CP Air and CP Ships, Algoma and Canadian International Paper. In 1985 CPE and CP Ltd. were merged, a move that appeared to repudiate all that Sinclair had strived for since the early sixties.

In 1986, Stinson added the title of CEO to that of president,* in time to take responsibility for the unthinkable — an $80 million loss, the first in the company's entire 107-year history.† Presiding over the CP annual meeting at which the humiliating loss was announced, Stinson, looking even more dour than usual, was the picture of unspoken determination, but many still doubted his ability to restore the fortunes of the faltering empire.

Dark and balding, Stinson is the most innocuous-looking of CP's presidents. He is able, and apparently content, to pass unnoticed among the flannel-suited sharks of the corporate world, and he has never made much of an impression on the media. Press accounts of the previous ten years have given him

---

*Though this was the first time the president also held the CEO title, it signalled a return to the CP tradition of making the president the real power in the company.

†A large measure of the 1986 loss is attributable to a $260.9 million write-down of CP Ships and a $75 million write-down of Algoma.

a wide range of first names, from Michael to Harry, and he is often described as short, though he is actually five feet ten inches tall.

But like his six most powerful predecessors, Stinson had merely bided his time until he had enough control to burn his own unique brand onto the company hide. In a flurry of activity, matched only by Sinclair's acquisition spree of the seventies, Stinson hacked away at the company. Gone were a host of subsidiaries: the flight kitchens; Château Insurance; Maple Leaf Mills; Express Airborne (a division of CP Trucks); an office building in London, several assets controlled by AMCA, an equipment-manufacturing firm; and Steep Rock Resources Inc. Even Algoma Steel Corp., which had lost money between 1982 and early 1987, was rumoured to be on the block.

Stinson didn't shy away from the controversial or emotional decisions either. In 1986 he sold CP's 52.46 percent share in fabled Cominco Ltd., the company's oldest subsidiary, to Teck Corporation and Metallgesellschaft AG of Germany for $472.1 million. Often called "the Republic of Cominco" by CP employees, it had been like the young child in the nursery rhyme for ninety years: when it was good it was very, very good and when it was bad it was horrid. That year, too, Stinson dropped nineteen bulk tankers from CP's Bermuda-based fleet of twenty-six. The cruellest blow came in 1987 when Pacific Western Airlines gobbled up CP Air for $300 million. "There wasn't a wet eye in the house," Stinson proudly proclaimed to a group of London investors.[1]

There may not have been any "wet eyes" but there were certainly some narrowed ones. "It is an awful lot easier to sell assets than it is to build or buy them," Sinclair commented in 1988 in the quiet, reasoned tones of a father passing judgment on errant sons who haven't quite measured up. "And the most difficult thing for a man who runs a company is to make sure you don't get carried away by selling things because that's easy. . . . Burbidge and Stinson never had an identification with two areas — mining or air — and as a result, both those areas are gone."

After eighteen months of mighty slashes with his machete, Stinson had reduced CP's massive debt of $6.2 billion to $3.8 billion, but he'd also shrivelled the company's $21.3 billion in assets to a paltry $18 billion. Like the strongest CP presidents before him, however, Stinson aspired to building his own uniquely styled empire. He was merely clearing a site to lay the foundations.

At the 1988 annual meeting, Stinson presided over a transformed company. The loss had been eradicated, cauterized and buried by a record $800 million profit. Though he issued a rare smile — more a grimace than anything else — he still did not have the look of contentment that might be expected after such a triumph. Impatient and jumpy, he seemed as if he had left a dozen jobs half finished and could barely restrain himself from leaping off the stage and tearing back to his office to complete them. A few days after the meeting, Stinson dropped a bombshell with the announcement that CP had purchased controlling interest in Laidlaw Transportation Ltd. for nearly $500 million in cash and shares. North America's largest school bus company and third-largest in the waste disposal industry, Laidlaw was one of the country's most profitable corporations, with 1987 revenue of $1.2 billion.

Untold numbers of North American railroads have come and gone, but Canadian Pacific has endured 107 years. The secret of its longevity and power isn't the short-lived monopoly, the original government subsidy or even the massive land grant. The company has survived because of its ability to find, with amazingly few exceptions, the right leader at the right time, from George Stephen to Ian Sinclair. Bill Stinson's bold strokes suggest that the dynasty has not ended — there may be another Lord in the making.

Illustration Credits

p. 4 Glenbow Archives, Calgary, Alberta/NA-1494-6; p. 8 Notman Photographic Archives, McCord Museum, McGill University; p. 14 Courtesy CN Archives; p. 23 William Notman/National Archives of Canada/NA-143226; p. 31 Minnesota Historical Society; p. 33 James Jerome Hill Reference Library; p. 39 Minnesota Historical Society; p. 42 William (attrib.) Notman/National Archives of Canada/C-08315; p. 47 National Archives of Canada/C-27255; p. 49 James Jerome Hill Reference Library; p. 54 Department of Geography, University of Toronto; p. 67 Notman Photographic Archives, McCord Museum, McGill University; p. 69 National Archives of Canada/C-78599; p. 74 CP Rail Corporate Archives; p. 78 National Archives of Canada/NA-26412; p. 80 Manitoba Archives; p. 94 Notman Photographic Archives, McCord Museum, McGill University; p. 97 Notman Photographic Archives, McCord Museum, McGill University; p. 100 Circus World Museum, Baraboo, Wisconsin; p. 105 Courtesy Canadian Railway Museum, Van Horne Collection; p. 117 Notman Photographic Archives, McCord Museum, McGill University; p. 120 Notman Photographic Archives, McCord Museum, McGill University; p. 131 CP Rail Corporate Archives; p. 134 CP Rail Corporate Archives; p. 139 CP Rail Corporate Archives; p. 141 Courtesy Canadian Railway Museum, Van Horne Collection; p. 147 CP Rail Corporate Archives; p. 150 CP Rail Corporate Archives; p. 156 Department of Geography, University of Toronto; p. 158 Courtesy Canadian Railway Museum, Van Horne Collection; p. 163 CP Rail Corporate Archives; p. 175 CP Rail Corporate Archives; p. 177 CP Rail Corporate Archives; p. 185 CP Rail Corporate Archives; p. 192 CP Rail Corporate Archives; p. 194 CP Rail Corporate Archives; pp. 195–96 Department of Geography, University of Toronto; p. 201 James Jerome Hill Reference Library; p. 211 Minnesota Historical Society; p. 220 Glenbow Archives, Calgary, Alberta/NA-1023-1; p. 229 Courtesy Canadian Railway Museum, Van Horne Collection; p. 241 Notman Photographic Archives, McCord Museum, McGill University; p. 247 Drawn by Benny Van Horne; p. 249 Notman Photographic Archives, McCord Museum, McGill University; p. 255 Hudson's Bay Company Archives, Provincial Archives of Manitoba; p. 260 Notman Photographic Archives, McCord Museum, McGill University; p. 273 CP Rail Corporate Archives; p. 275 CP Rail Corporate Archives; p. 277 CP Rail Corporate Archives; p. 282 H. R. Charlton/National Archives of Canada/NA-020516; p. 291 CP Rail Corporate Archives; p. 294 CP Rail Corporate Archives; p. 302 CP Rail Corporate Archives; p. 307 CP Rail Corporate Archives; p. 309 Courtesy Lord W. G. Shaughnessy; p. 322 CN Archives; p. 335 From a cartoon by Arch Dale. Courtesy of the Winnipeg Free Press; p. 339 Courtesy McGill University Archives; p. 348 CP Rail Corporate Archives; p. 352 CP Rail Corporate Archives; p. 358 CP Rail Corporate Archives; p. 363 CP Rail Corporate Archives; p. 366 CP Rail Corporate Archives; p. 379 Whyte Museum of the Canadian Rockies, Banff, Alberta — Byron Harmon, collection photographer; p. 380 Whyte Museum of the Canadian Rockies, Banff, Alberta — Frank W. Freeborn, collection photographer; p. 384 CP Rail Corporate Archives; p. 396 CP Rail Corporate Archives; p. 399 CP Rail Corporate Archives; p. 404 CP Rail Corporate Archives; p. 406 Courtesy I. D. Sinclair; p. 408 Courtesy I. D. Sinclair; p. 426 CP Rail Corporate Archives; p. 428 CP Rail Corporate Archives; p. 431 CP Rail Corporate Archives; p. 435 CP Rail Corporate Archives; p. 451 CP Rail Corporate Archives.

Endnotes

For full bibliographical details concerning the shortened references given in these endnotes, see the Bibliography. Abbreviations of archival collections used in these endnotes are as follows:

BL — Beatty Letterbooks, CP Rail Corporate Archives; CP Archives — CP Rail Corporate Archives; DP — Dafoe Papers, National Archives of Canada; JJHP — James J. Hill Papers in the James Jerome Hill Reference Library, St Paul, Minnesota; KHP — Katherine Hughes Papers, National Archives of Canada; LP — Laurier Papers, National Archives of Canada; MP — Macdonald Papers, National Archives of Canada; NAC — National Archives of Canada; SL — Shaughnessy Letterbooks, CP Rail Corporate Archives; SP — Shaughnessy Papers, National Archives of Canada; VHL — Van Horne Letterbooks, CP Rail Corporate Archives; VHPC — Van Horne Private Correspondence, Canadian Railroad Historical Association.

All unattributed quotations in the book are from personal interviews conducted by the authors.

PROLOGUE
1. Shaughnessy to Vaughan, May 8, 1920, SP.
2. Ibid.

CHAPTER 1 THREE MEN AND A DREAM
1. Freeman Hubbard, *Encyclopedia of North American Railroading*, p. 130.
2. Quoted in Walter Vaughan, *The Life and Work of Sir William Van Horne*, p. 131.

3. Winnipeg *Manitoban*, October 31, 1885.
4. *Aberdeen Daily Free Presss*, August 22, 1901. Quoted in Heather Gilbert, "Mount Stephen: A Study in Environments," *Northern Scotland* (Centre for Scottish Studies, University of Aberdeen), vol. 1, no. 2 (1973): 179.
5. Quoted in Beckles Willson, *The Life of Lord Strathcona and Mount Royal*, p. 141.
6. Andrew T. Drummond in the *Monetary Times*, December 16, 1921.

7. Quoted in Michael Bliss, *Northern Enterprise: Five Centuries of Canadian Business*, p. 186.

8. John Murray Gibbon, *Steel of Empire*, p. 121.

9. Quoted in Willson, p. 139.

10. George Stephen to J. J. Hill, August 23, 1897, JJHP.

11. Quoted in Willson, p. 50.

12. Quoted in Willson, p. 57.

13. George Simpson to Donald Smith, 1845. Quoted in Shirlee A. Smith, "A Desire to Worry Me Out: Donald Smith's Harassment of Charles Brydges, 1879–1889," *The Beaver* (December 1987–January 1988): 4.

14. Stephen to William Van Horne, October 1, 1914, VHPC.

15. Quoted in Willson, p. 65.

16. W. T. R. Preston, *Strathcona and the Making of Canada*, p. 265.

17. Willson, p. 85.

18. Beckles Willson, *From Quebec to Piccadilly and Other Places*, p. 187.

19. *Harper's New Monthly Magazine,* April-May, 1861.

20. Andrew T. Drummond in the *Monetary Times*, December 16, 1921.

21. Albro Martin, *James J. Hill and the Opening of the Northwest*, p. 45.

22. William E. Wellington to Hill, March 28, 1865. Quoted in Martin, p. 49.

23. Hill to Joseph Howe, April 22, 1870. Quoted in Martin, p. 75.

24. *St Paul Daily Press*, April 29, 1871. Quoted in Martin, p. 80.

25. George H. Ham, "Mount Stephen, Pioneer, Passes," *MacLean's Magazine*, January 1, 1922.

CHAPTER 2 THE MINNESOTA GOLD MINE

1. Norman W. Kittson to George Stephen, September 17, 1877, JJHP.

2. J. J. Hill to Kittson, July 31, 1877, JJHP.

3. Joseph G. Pyle, *The Life of James J. Hill*, vol. 1, p. 205.

4. *Farley* v. *Kittson et al.*, 1888, Testimony of George Stephen. Quoted in Albro Martin, *James J. Hill and the Opening of the Northwest*, p. 144.

5. *Farley* v. *Kittson et al.*, 1888, Testimony of George Stephen. Quoted in Heather Gilbert, *Awakening Continent*, vol. 1 of *The Life of Lord Mount Stephen*, p. 42.

6. George Bliss to Charles Rose, September 17, 1879. Quoted in Dolores Greenberg, "A Study of Capital Alliances: The St Paul & Pacific," *Canadian Historical Review* (March, 1976): 35.

7. Stephen to Hill, telegram, February 7, 1878, JJHP.

8. Donald Smith to Kittson, January 8, 1878, JJHP.

9. Hill to Stephen, January 16, 1878, JJHP.

10. Stephen to Sir Arthur Bigge, 1908. Quoted in Heather Gilbert, "The Unaccountable Fifth," *Minnesota History* (Spring, 1971): 176.

11. Hill to Stephen, October 28, 1878, JJHP.

12. John S. Barnes. Quoted in Martin, p. 184.

13. Hill to Stephen, January 6, 1879, JJHP.

14. Stephen to Frederick C. Billings, November 26, 1878. Quoted in Martin, p. 188.

15. Hill to Stephen, January 6, 1879, JJHP.

16. Donald Smith's remarks to the Winnipeg Canadian Club. Quoted in Pierre Berton, *The National Dream, 1871–1881*, p. 334.

17. John Turnbull to William Secombe, June 26, 1883, JJHP.

18. Hill to John S. Kennedy, April 13, 1881, JJHP.

19. Clara Hill Lindley, *James J. and Mary T. Hill*, pp. 134–35.

20. Hill to Stephen, October 19, 1878, JJHP.

21. Hill to Stephen, June 23, 1878, JJHP.

22. Hill to Stephen, January 6, 1879, JJHP.

23. Hill to J. Kennedy Tod, June 8, 1883, JJHP.

24. Hill to Willis James, February 6, 1885, JJHP

CHAPTER 3 THE RELUCTANT RAILROADER

1. George Stephen to Sir Joseph Pope, May 10, 1914, CP Archives.

2. R. B. Angus to Stephen, September 15, 1880, JJHP

3. Stephen to Sir John A. Macdonald, January 23, 1881, MP.

4. Alexander Galt to Mrs Galt, June 23, 1867, Sir A. T. Galt Papers, NAC.

5. Richard J. Cartwright, *Reminiscences*, p. 211.

6. From the prospectus dated January 9, 1872, CP Archives.

7. Macdonald to Sir John Rose, January 11, 1872, MP.

8. Hugh Allan to General G. W. Cass, July 1, 1872, *Report of the Royal Commissioners*, 1873, pp. 211–12.

9. Sir George Etienne Cartier to Hugh Allan, July 30, 1872, *Report of the Royal Commissioners*, 1873, pp. 136–37.

10. Macdonald to Allan, August 26, 1873, *Report of the Royal Commissioners*, 1873, p. 118.

11. Sir George W. Ross, *Getting into Parliament and After*, p. 72.

12. W. T. R. Preston, *My Generation of Politics and Politicians*, p. 92.

13. Ross, p. 72.

14. Beckles Willson, *Lord Strathcona: The Story of His Life*, p. 149.

15. Quoted in Gustavus Myers, *History of Canadian Wealth*, p. 241.

16. Willson, p. 149.

17. Donald Creighton, *John A. Macdonald: The Old Chieftan*, p. 189.

18. J. S. Willison, *Reminiscences: Political and Personal*, p. 36.

19. Toronto *Mail*, March 28, 1876.

20. Quoted in O. D. Skelton, *Life and Letters of Sir Wilfrid Laurier*, vol. 1, p. 249.

21. Montreal *Gazette*, November 3, 1879.

22. Alexander Campbell to Macdonald, July 15, 1880, MP.

23. Stephen to Macdonald, July 9, 1880, MP.

24. J. J. Hill to Angus, July 8, 1880, JJHP.

25. Hill to Angus, October 19, 1880, JJHP.

26. Hill to Angus, October 19, 1880, JJHP.

27. Sir George Ross, p. 116.

28. Hansard, 1880–1881, p. 77.

29. Stephen to Rose, December 16, 1880, MP.

30. Stephen to Macdonald, January 23, 1881, MP.

31. Sir Wilfrid Laurier, Speech to the House of Commons, December 21, 1880.

32. Stephen to Macdonald, May 5, 1881, MP.

33. Tupper to Macdonald, July n.d. 1881, Tupper Papers, NAC.

34. Pope to Macdonald, January 5, 1885, Sir Joseph Pope Papers, NAC.

CHAPTER 4 GEORGE STEPHEN'S NIGHTMARE

1. George Stephen to Sir John A. Macdonald, January 24, 1881, MP.

2. Stephen to Macdonald, January 23, 1881, MP.

3. Stephen to Macdonald, November 4, 1881, MP.

4. Harold A. Innis, *A History of the Canadian Pacific Railway*, p. 104.

5. Henry Labouchere, "The Canadian Dominion Bubble," *Truth*, September 1, 1881.

6. Stephen to Macdonald, December 13, 1881, MP.

7. Stephen to Macdonald, February 26, 1882, MP.

8. Stephen to Macdonald, April 18, 1882, MP.

9. Stephen to Macdonald, May 8, 1881, MP.

10. J. H. E. Secretan, *Canada's Great Highway: From the First Stake to the Last Spike*, p. 187.

11. *The Engineering News Record*, March 28, 1935. Quoted in John Murray Gibbon, *Steel of Empire*, p. 265.

12. Albert Rogers in A. O. Wheeler, *The Selkirk Range*, vol. 1, Appendix E.

13. Hill to Van Horne, December 16, 1881, JJHP.

14. Secretan, p. 184.

15. Hill to Stephen, April 6, 1882, JJHP.

16. George H. Ham, *Reminiscences of a Raconteur*, p. 51.

17. Hill to Stephen, October 19, 1881, JJHP.

18. Hill to Stephen, undated. Quoted in Walter Vaughan, *The Life and Work of Sir William Van Horne*, p. 74.

19. D. B. Hanna, *Trains of Recollection*, p. 40.

20. Vaughan, p. 212.

21. Van Horne to Billy Van Horne, 1914. Quoted in Vaughan, p. 12.

22. S. Macnaughton, "Sir William Van Horne," *Cornhill Magazine*, February, 1916.

23. Ibid.

24. Ibid.

25. Vaughan, p. 18.

26. S. Macnaughtan, *Cornhill Magazine*.

27. Vaughan, p. 20.

28. Ibid., p. 26.

29. *Cyclopædia of Canadian Biography*, p. 234.

30. Edgar Andrew Collard in the Montreal *Gazette*, April 21, 1984.

31. Edmonton *Bulletin*, October 6, 1934.

32. Vaughan, p. 46.

33. Beckles Willson, *From Quebec to Piccadilly and Other Places*, p. 56.

CHAPTER 5 VAN HORNE TO THE RESCUE

1. R. K. Kernighan, Winnipeg *Sun*, June 10, 1882.

2. J. J. Hill to George Stephen, April 6, 1882, JJHP.

3. Hill to R. B. Angus, January 3, 1882, JJHP.

4. Hill to William Van Horne, June 20, 1882, JJHP.

5. Hill to Van Horne, June 22, 1882, JJHP.

6. Hill to Stephen, June 30, 1882, JJHP.

7. Hill to Van Horne, April 6, 1882, JJHP.

8. Hill to J. S. Kennedy, October 5, 1882, JJHP

9. Van Horne to E. T. Talbot, *Railway Age*, November 26, 1883.

10. J. H. E. Secretan, *Canada's Great Highway: From the First Stake to the Last Spike*, pp. 103–4.

11. Secretan, p. 105.

12. Stephen to Sir John A. Macdonald, November 21, 1882, MP.

13. Stephen to Macdonald, December 13, 1882, MP.

14. Kennedy to Hill, January 16, 1883, JJHP.

15. Kennedy to Hill, January 16, 1883, JJHP.

16. Hill to Angus, January 10, 1883, JJHP.

17. Kennedy to Hill, May 28, 1883, JJHP.

18. Kennedy to Hill, May 28, 1883, JJHP.

19. Hill to Angus, February 14, 1883. JJHP.

20. Hill to J. Kennedy Tod, March 6, 1883, JJHP.

21. Hill to Kennedy, May 4, 1883, JJHP.

22. Hill to Angus, May 3, 1883, JJHP.

23. Hill to Willis James, July 25, 1883, JJHP.

24. Hill to James, July 26, 1883, JJHP.

25. Stephen to Hill, July 14, 1883, JJHP.

26. Hill to Tod, August 11, 1883, JJHP.

27. Hill to Stephen, August 10, 1883, JJHP.

28. Hill to Stephen, November 7, 1883, JJHP.

29. Harold A. Innis, *A History of the Canadian Pacific Railway*, p. 119.

30. *The Wall Street Daily News*, November 17, 1883. Quoted in Heather Gilbert, *Awakening Continent*,

vol. 1 of *The Life of Lord Mount Stephen*, p. 142.

31. A. T. Galt to Macdonald, January 9, 1883, MP.

32. Macdonald to Sir Charles Tupper, November 22, 1883. MP.

33. Stephen to Macdonald, December 15, 1883, MP.

34. Stephen to Macdonald, January 22, 1884, MP.

35. Toronto *Globe*, February 19, 1883.

36. Stephen to Macdonald, June 18, 1884, MP.

37. Macdonald to Stephen, July 18, 1884, MP.

38. *Money*, December 8, 1884.

39. Stephen to Macdonald, November 11, 1884, MP.

40. Stephen to Macdonald, February 9, 1885, MP.

41. Macdonald to Tupper, March 17, 1885, Tupper Papers, NAC.

42. Stephen to Pope, April 16, 1885, MP.

43. Stephen to Macdonald, April 15, 1885, MP.

44. *Financial Times*, March 13, 1885.

45. Beckles Willson Papers, NAC.

46. Shaughnessy Papers, NAC.

47. Stephen to Macdonald, July 23, 1885, MP.

48. *Money*, April 8, 1885.

49. *Anglo-American Times*, September 25, 1885.

50. Dalton C. Coleman, "Lord Mount Stephen." Address to the Newcomen Society of England, American Branch, New York, 1945.

CHAPTER 6 SHAUGHNESSY BACKSTOPS VAN HORNE'S BIG PUSH

1. D. C. Coleman, "Rt. Hon. Lord Shaughnessy, K.C.V.O." An address to

the Officers' Luncheon Club, Montreal, March 18, 1936.

2. Ibid.

3. Quoted in John A. Eagle, "Baron Thomas Shaughnessy: The Peer That Made Milwaukee Famous," *Milwaukee History* 6 (Spring, 1983): 33.

4. John A. Eagle, "Baron Thomas Shaughnessy: The Peer That Made Milwaukee Famous," *Milwaukee History* 6 (Spring, 1983): 32.

5. Thomas Shaughnessy to Walter Vaughan, May 8, 1920, SP.

6. Shaughnessy to Archer Baker, November n.d., 1882, SL.

7. Shaughnessy to John Egan, October 16, 1884, SL.

8. Shaughnessy to Baker, August 18, 1884, SL.

9. R. G. MacBeth, "Sir William Whyte: A Builder of the West," *Canadian Magazine*, July, 1914.

10. Shaughnessy to William Whyte, August 16, 1884, SL.

11. Shaughnessy to Whyte, December 22, 1884, SL.

12. Shaughnessy too W. K. Kelson, March 25, 1883, SL.

13. Shaughnessy to Kelson, December 21, 1885, SL.

14. Shaughnessy to Whyte, January 26, 1885, SL.

15. Shaughnessy to Baker, August 12, 1884, SL.

16. Shaughnessy to Whyte, June 4, 1884, SL.

17. Shaughnessy to F. R. Brown, October 2, 1884, SL.

18. Shaughnessy to J. Harris and Co., April 29, 1884, SL.

19. Shaughnessy to Barney Smith Manufacturing Co., July 17, 1885, SL.

20. Shaughnessy to James McIntire, October 4, 1884, SL.

21. Shaughnessy to Bell, Lewis and Yates Co., November 11, 1884, SL.

22. Shaughnessy to John Ross, February 16, 1884, SL.

23. Shaughnessy to John Ross, March 5, 1884, SL.

24. Shaughnessy to Watts and Co., October 23, 1884, SL.

25. Simon Blanchette to Shaughnessy, January 21, 1885, Shaughnessy Incoming Correspondence, CP Archives.

26. Shaughnessy to McIntyre, Woods and Co., November 10, 1884, SL.

27. Shaughnessy to Frank Smith, January 14, 1885, SL.

28. Shaughnessy to Thos. Muir, April 20, 1885, SL.

29. Shaughnessy to H. Abbott, February 12, 1885, SL.

30. More than a dozen identical letters were sent out on July 24, 1885, SL.

31. Shaughnessy to Conner and McLennan, September 7, 1885, SL.

32. Shaughnessy to Conner and McLennan, September 7, 1885, SL.

33. Shaughnessy to Kelson, August 24, 1884, SL.

34. Omer Lavallée, *Van Horne's Road*, p. 144.

35. John Ross to William Van Horne. Quoted in Omer Lavallée, *Van Horne's Road*, p. 147.

36. Shaughnessy to Van Horne, November 21, 1885, SL.

37. Shaughnessy to Van Horne, November 21, 1885, SL.

38. Shaughnessy to Van Horne, November 21, 1885, SL.

39. Walter Vaughan, *The Life and Work of Sir William Van Horne*, p. 130.

CHAPTER 7 CLASH OF THE TITANS

1. George Stephen to William Van Horne, KHP.

2. *Financial News*, January 17, 1891.

3. J. J. Hill to George Stephen, May 11, 1886, JJHP.

4. Hill to Stephen, May 18, 1886, JJHP.

5. Stephen to Hill, May 23, 1886, JJHP.

6. Hill to Stephen, May 27, 1886, JJHP.

7. Stephen to Hill, May 31, 1886, JJHP.

8. Albro Martin, *James J. Hill and the Opening of the Northwest*, p. 289.

9. Hill to Stephen, October 5, 1886, JJHP.

10. J. S. Kennedy to Hill, February 11, 1887, JJHP.

11. Stephen to Hill, July 16, 1888, JJHP.

12. Stephen to Hill, August 4, 1888, JJHP.

13. Stephen to George M. Grant, February 11, 15 and 29, 1888, Grant Paper, NAC.

14. Letter to CPR Shareholders, August 7, 1888, CP Archives.

15. Hill to Stephen, May 10, 1889. JJHP.

16. Martin, p. 376.

17. Stephen to Hill, June 19, 1889, JJHP.

18. Stephen to Hill, June 19, 1889, JJHP.

19. Van Horne to Sir John A. Macdonald, January 13, 1890, MP.

20. Walter Vaughan, *The Life and Work of Sir William Van Horne*, p. 158.

21. Stephen to Van Horne, March 31, 1893, VHPC.

22. Hill to Stephen, cable, March 2, 1890, JJHP.

23. Van Horne to Stephen, early 1891. Quoted in John Murray Gibbon, *Steel of Empire*, p. 339.

24. Quoted in Gibbon, p. 339.

25. Van Horne to Stephen, February, 1891. Quoted in Vaughan, p. 222.

26. Stephen to Van Horne, March 2, 1891, VHPC.

27. Van Horne to Thomas Skinner, March 2, 1892, VHL.

28. Hill to E. T. Nichols, September 26, 1892, JJHP.

29. Hill to E. T. Nichols, September 26, 1892, JJHP.

30. Notes on draft manuscript, KHP.

31. Notes on draft manuscript, KHP.

32. Notes on draft manuscript, KHP.

33. Stephen to Van Horne, January 23, 1893, VHPC.

34. Stephen to Van Horne, January 24, 1893, VHPC.

35. Stephen to Van Horne, January 18, 1893, VHPC.

36. Stephen to Hill, June 19, 1889, JJHP.

37. Notes on draft manuscript, KHP.

38. Stephen to Van Horne, March 31, 1893, VHPC.

39. Stephen to Van Horne, March 14, 1893, VHPC.

40. Van Horne to Stephen, June, 1893. Quoted in Vaughan, p. 231.

41. Stephen to Van Horne, January 5, 1893, VHPC.

42. Van Horne to Stephen, February 16, 1894, (two letters) VHL.

43. Van Horne to Stephen, June 20, 1894, VHL.

44. Van Horne to Gaspard Farrer, June 18, 1894, VHL.

45. "Special News Bulletin," Dow, Jones Company, March 2, 1894.

46. Hill to J. P. Morgan and Company, November 8, 1898, JJHP.

47. *Statist*, June 23, 1894.

48. Heather Gilbert, *The End of the Road*, vol. 2 of *The Life of Lord Mount Stephen*, p. 80.

49. Van Horne to Stephen, July 27, 1894, VHL.

50. Quoted in Vaughan, p. 237.

51. Stephen to Lord Shaughnessy, December, 1894. Quoted in Shaughnessy to Vaughan, n.d., SP.

52. *Statist*, December 22, 1894.

53. Quoted in Shaughnessy to Vaughan, n.d., SP.

54. *Bullionist*, October 10, 1905.

55. Farrer to John Sterling, May 14, 1895. Quoted in Gilbert, *The End of the Road*, p. 82.

56. R. M. Horne-Payne to Katherine Hughes, July 24, 1917, KHP.

57. Donald Smith to Hill, September 28, 1898, JJHP.

58. Van Horne to Skinner, April 17, 1896, VHL.

59. Quoted in Vaughan, p. 254.

60. Hill to J. P. Morgan and Company, November 8, 1898, JJHP.

61. Martin, p. 470.

CHAPTER 8 THE LAST OF THE TITANS

1. C. F. Paul, "The Discredited Interview," *Canadian Magazine*, March, 1904.

2. C. Lintern Sibley, "Van Horne and His Cuban Railway," *Canadian Magazine*, August, 1913.

3. Ibid.

4. Gonzalo de Quesada, "The Iron Horse in East Cuba," *The Gulf Stream*, October, 1929. Gonzalo de Quesada Y Arostegui Papers, NAC.

5. C. Lintern Sibley, "Van Horne and His Cuban Railway," *Canadian Magazine*, August, 1913.

6. Ibid.

7. Walter Vaughan, *The Life and Work of Sir William Van Horne*, p. 288.

8. William Van Horne to John Fraser, December 8, 1886. Quoted in Allan Pringle, "William Cornelius Van Horne: Art Director, Canadian Pacific Railway," *The Journal of Canadian Art History*, vol. 8, no. 1(1984): 61.

9. Fraser to Van Horne, January 8, 1887. Quoted in Allan Pringle.

10. Fraser to Van Horne, March 1, 1887. Quoted in Allan Pringle.

11. Edward Colonna to Van Horne. Quoted in unpublished manuscript on Windsor Station by Dave Jones of CP Rail, Montreal.

12. Edgar Andrew Collard, "Sir William Van Horne as an Art Collector," *Montreal Yesterdays*, p. 250.

13. Howard Mansfield, "My Reminiscences of Sir William Van Horne," VHPC.

14. S. Macnaughtan, "Sir William Van Horne," *Cornhill Magazine*, February, 1916.

15. S. Macnaughtan, "Sir William Van Horne," *Cornhill Magazine*, February, 1916.

16. Edgar Andrew Collard, "Sir William Van Horne as an Art Collector," *Montreal Yesterdays*, p. 260.

17. From personal interviews in St Andrews.

18. From personal interviews in St Andrews.

19. Vaughan, p. 182.

20. Robert Thorne to Van Horne, February 24, 1905, VHPC.

21. Van Horne to Acton Burrows, August 31, 1914, VHPC.

22. Lord Northcote to J. J. Hill, May 2, 1896, JJHP.

23. Northcote to Hill, May 2, 1896, JJHP.

24. George Stephen to Hill, August 23, 1897, JJHP.

25. Gaspard Farrer to Hill, October 16, 1897, JJHP.

26. Quoted in Heather Gilbert, "Mount Stephen: A Study in Environments," *Northern Scotland* (Centre for Scottish Studies, University of Aberdeen), vol. 1, no. 2(1973): 196.

27. Beckles Willson to Stephen, September 28, 1914, VHPC.

28. Stephen to Van Horne, October 1, 1914, VHPC.

29. Shaughnessy to Van Horne, November 23, 1914, VHPC.

30. Stephen to Van Horne, November 17, 1914, VHPC.

31. John Sterling to Hill, November 9, 1898, JJHP.

32. George Stephen Trust Settlement Balance Sheet, April 20, 1906. In the possession of Alexis Reford, Montreal.

33. Montreal *Gazette*, April 20, 1906.

34. Lady Mount Stephen to Queen Mary, December 4, 1921. Quoted in Heather Gilbert, *The End of the Road*, vol. 2 of *The Life of Lord Mount Stephen*, p. 394.

CHAPTER 9 THE GOLDEN ERA OF THE SYSTEMS MAN

1. Thomas Shaughnessy to H. E. Dunning, December 20, 1893, SL.

2. Shaughnessy to Dunning, December 24, 1893, SL.

3. D. C. Coleman, "Rt. Hon. Lord Shaughnessy, K.C.V.O." An address to the Officers' Luncheon Club, Montreal, March 18, 1936.

4. Shaughnessy to William Whyte, July 8, 1896, SL.

5. Shaughnessy to Mr Olds, Memo, April 3, 1886, SL.

6. John Murray Gibbon, *Steel of Empire*, p. 352.

7. Cable to CPR offices, Liverpool, England, July 22, 1909, CP Archives.

8. Inspector Dew to H. G. Kendall, Cable, July 29, 1910, CP Archives.

9. *The Daily Telegraph* (London), August 4, 1910.

10. The Make-up Man, "Shaughnessy, the Efficient," *MacLean's Magazine*, September 1, 1921.

11. George Musk, *Canadian Pacific: The Story of the Famous Shipping Line*, p. 22.

12. Musk, p. 22.

13. Saint John *Daily Telegraph*, October 8, 1909.

14. Vancouver *Province*, February 19, 1901.

15. Victoria *Daily Colonist*, May 23, 1903.

16. Shaughnessy to E. B. Osler, December 21, 1899, SL.

17. The Make-up Man, "Shaughnessy, The Efficient," *MacLean's Magazine*, September 1, 1921.

18. Newton MacTavish, "George Ham: Sketch of a Gentleman on Whom the Sun Never Sets," CP Archives.

19. Ibid.

20. Ibid.

21. Ibid.

22. Ibid.

23. Beckles Willson, *From Quebec to Piccadilly and Other Places*, p. 94.

24. "Home Counties: How Two Londoners Went to Canada," *World's Work*, November, 1906.

25. Ibid.

26. Lord Minto to Shaughnessy, (date obscured) 1900, Minto Papers, NAC.

27. D. J. Hall, *Clifford Sifton: The Lonely Eminence, 1901–1929*, p. 89.

28. Manitoba *Free Press*. Quoted in Hall, p. 1.

29. D. B. Hanna, *Trains of Recollection*, p. 150.

30. Shaughnessy to C. S. Mellen, May 21, 1900, SL.

31. Shaughnessy to W. D. Matthews, February 22, 1901, SL.

32. Victoria *Daily Colonist*, November 25, 1902.

33. G. R. Stevens, *History of the Canadian National Railways*, p. 221.

34. The Make-up Man, "Shaughnessy, the Efficient," *MacLean's Magazine*, September 1, 1921.

35. Hanna, p. 229.

36. *Bullionist*, August 5, 1906.

37. *Financier*, July 5, 1907.

38. Van Horne to Manvel. Quoted in Albro Martin, *James J. Hill and the Opening of the Northwest*, p. 569.

39. R. G. MacBeth, *The Romance of the Canadian Pacific Railway*, p. 192.

40. The Make-up Man, "Shaughnessy, the Efficient," *MacLean's Magazine*, September 1, 1921.

41. *Westward Ho! Magazine*, September, 1908.

42. Shaughnessy to Walter Vaughan, SP.

43. D. C. Coleman to Victor Odlum, 1946, Odlum Papers, NAC.

44. George H. Ham, *Reminiscences of a Raconteur*, pp. 280–82.

45. Ham, pp. 277–78.

46. Ibid.

47. W. J. Shaughnessy to his wife, June 26, 1918, SP.

48. Shaughnessy to Sir Thomas Gratton Esmonde, January 6, 1921, SP.

49. *Railway Digest News*, December 26, 1923.

CHAPTER 10 THE YOUNGEST BARON

1. John Murray Gibbon, *Steel of Empire*, p. 104.

2. D. H. Miller-Barstow, *Beatty of the CPR*, p. 13.

3. Miller-Barstow, p. 16.

4. Gibbon, p. 386.

5. Winnipeg *Evening Tribune*, February 4, 1928.

6. Miller-Barstow, p. 17.

7. "Yes, I'd Go Back to College," *MacLean's Magazine*, October 15, 1927.

8. Victoria *Daily Colonist*, August 14, 1927.

9. "Mr. Beatty," *Maclean's Magazine*, July 1, 1933.

10. Ibid.

11. *MacLean's Magazine*, October 15, 1927.

12. Ibid.

13. Beatty to Freddy (no last name), June 21 and August 30, 1921, BL.

14. Miller-Barstow, p. 19.

15. Hector Charlesworth, *Candid Chronicles*, p. 156.

16. Miller-Barstow, p. 22.

17. Thomas Shaughnessy to W. C. Van Horne, June 27, 1890, SL.

18. Gibbon, p. 384.

19. Freeman Hubbard, *Encyclopedia of North American Railroading*. p. 389.

20. D. B. Hanna, *Trains of Recollection*, p. 261.

21. Beatty to Charles Bishop, October 8, 1920, BL.

22. Beatty to J. J. Warren, September 23, 1920, BL.

23. Beatty to W. R. MacInnes, July 28, 1921, BL.

24. Memo, June 13, 1921, BL.

25. Gibbon, p. 386.

26. C. P. Pyper, in the Winnipeg *Evening Tribune,* February 4, 1928.

27. Beatty to William Allison, August 23, 1921, BL.

28. *New York Chronicle,* December 24, 1921.

29. *Financier,* February 3, 1919.

30. Hanna, p. 306.

31. Beatty to Sir John Eaton, May 28, 1921, BL.

32. Memo to W. R. MacInnes, August 19, 1921, BL.

33. Beatty to D. B. Hanna, November 11, 1921, BL.

34. Hanna, p. 268.

35. Sir Joseph Flavelle to J. W. Dafoe, October 24, 1922, DP.

36. D'Arcy Marsh, *The Tragedy of Henry Thornton,* p. 97.

37. Marsh, p. 95.

38. G. R. Stevens, *History of the Canadian National Railways,* p. 310.

39. Beatty to L. J. S. Brown, February 10, 1920, BL.

40. Beatty to (first name obscured) Hebert, October 24, 1923, BL.

41. Beatty to G. Frank McFarland, May 1, 1924, BL.

42. Miller–Barstow, p. 46.

43. Beatty to Hanna, November 1, 1922, BL.

44. Beatty to W. R. MacInnes, September 23, 1923, BL.

45. Beatty to John Imrie, October 20, 1921, BL.

46. Stevens, p. 317.

47. Beatty to R. G. MacBeth, October 14, 1924, Memo to John Murray Gibbon, December 15, 1924, BL.

48. Beatty to J. L. Counsell, December 15, 1924.

49. Miller-Barstow, p. 46.

50. Memo to W. R. MacInnes, September 23, 1923.

51. W. Kaye Lamb, *History of the Canadian Pacific Railway,* p. 313.

CHAPTER 11 THE MAN WHO WED THE CPR

1. Mrs Henry James to G. R. Stevens. Quoted in G. R. Stevens, *History of the Canadian National Railways,* p. 348.

2. D'Arcy Marsh, *The Tragedy of Henry Thornton,* p. 265.

3. Sir Henry Thornton to J. W. Dafoe, January 21, 1933, DP.

4. Thornton to W. S. Thompson, February 10, 1933, DP.

5. *Financial Times,* February 23, 1934.

6. Edgar Andrew Collard in the Montreal *Gazette,* April 2, 1977.

7. D. H. Miller-Barstow, *Beatty of the C.P.R.,* pp. 6 and 43.

8. Collard in the Montreal *Gazette,* April 2, 1977.

9. Edward Beatty to Sir Charles Gordon, December 30, 1919, BL.

10. Stanley B. Frost, *McGill University: For the Advancement of Learning,* vol. II, p. 202.

11. David Lewis, *Political Memoirs, 1909–1958,* p. 34.

12. Lewis, p. 35.

13. Ralph L. Curry, *Stephen Leacock: Humorist and Humanist,* p. 168.

14. Beatty to Stephen Leacock, December 14, 1935. Quoted in Curry, p. 249.

15. Toronto *Star,* December 8, 1984.

16. Collard in the Montreal *Gazette*, June 21, 1975.

17. Beatty to Dr. C. Stanley, November 9, 1936, BL.

18. Beatty to W. T. Jackman, December 24, 1936, BL.

19. Beatty to Jackman, December 24, 1936, BL.

20. Beatty to Gordon, December 29, 1936, BL.

21. Miller-Barstow, p. 165.

22. Victoria *Daily Colonist*, August 14, 1927.

23. Miller-Barstow, p. 168.

24. Dr F. Cyril James to Edgar Andrew Collard. Quoted in Edgar Andrew Collard, "Voices from the Past." CP Archives (Edward Beatty Biographical Files).

25. Ibid.

CHAPTER 12 CRISIS, CONFUSION AND CRUMP

1. *Financial Post,* October 13, 1934.

2. "Mr W. M. Neal," *Wilton's Review,* January 5, 1935.

3. Fred Stone Papers, CP Archives.

4. Ronald A. Keith, *Bush Pilot with a Briefcase: The Happy-Go-Lucky Story of Grant McConachie,* p. 237.

5. CPR press release, March 8, 1948, CP Archives.

6. Fred Stone Papers, CP Archives.

7. Fred Stone Papers, CP Archives.

8. Fred Stone Papers, CP Archives.

9. John G. Wood, *The Snow War,* p. 4.

10. "Last of a Line," *Time,* May 15, 1972.

11. "Pin Boy to President," *Time,* February 3, 1947.

12. Montreal *Star,* May 7, 1955.

CHAPTER 13 THE LAST RAILROADER

1. "Vanishing Trains," CBC *Newsmagazine,* October 26, 1958.

2. "The Canadian Pacific: Overdue," *Fortune,* August, 1955.

3. Montreal *Gazette,* May 6, 1955.

4. Montreal *Gazette,* August 18, 1970.

5. Speech at N. R. Crump's retirement, 1972, CP Archives.

6. Speech at N. R. Crump's retirement, 1972, CP Archives.

7. Montreal *Gazette,* March 20, 1956.

8. Montreal *Gazette,* July 4, 1957.

9. Fred Stone Papers, CP Archives.

10. W. Kaye Lamb, *History of the Canadian Pacific Railway,* p. 417.

11. *Canada Commons Railway Committee Report,* 1959, p. 369.

12. *Canada Commons Railway Committee Report,* 1961, p. 291.

13. "The Case of the Crippled Titan," *Executive,* February, 1961.

14. "How to Ride the CPR Even If It Has No Trains," *Time,* Canadian edition, January 28, 1966.

15. Fred Stone Papers, CP Archives.

16. Ibid.

17. "Canadian Pacific," *Forbes,* May 15, 1964.

CHAPTER 14 THE BUCCANEER

1. "Shall We Dump 'em, Mr. Sinclair? The Pleasure's Mine, Mr. Clyne," *Maclean's,* April 19, 1976.

2. Montreal *Gazette,* May 7, 1966.

3. Peter C. Newman, *The Canadian Establishment,* p. 204.

4. "Not So Much a Railway as a Way of Life," *Time,* Canadian edition, November 24, 1967.

5. *Time,* Canadian edition, November 24, 1967.

6. Ronald A. Keith, *Bush Pilot with a Briefcase,* p. 306.

7. "Highballing into Bigger Profits via the U.S.A.," *Business Week,* February 23, 1976.

8. *Business Week,* February 23, 1976.

9. Toronto *Daily Star,* June 3, 1972.

10. *Business Week,* February 23, 1976.

11. Ibid.

12. Peter C. Newman, *The Acquisitors,* p. 16.

13. Susan Goldenberg, *Canadian Pacific: A Portrait of Power,* p. 61.

14. "Canada Frees the Reins on Its Railroaders," *Business Week,* June 24, 1967.

15. Quoted in "A Dubious Acquisition," *Executive,* March, 1980.

16. *Executive,* March, 1980.

EPILOGUE

1. Harvey Enchin, "Leaner and Meaner: CP's William Stinson," *Report on Business Magazine,* July, 1987.

Selected Bibliography

Books

Bain, D. M. *Canadian Pacific Airlines: Its History and Aircraft*. Calgary: Kishorn Publications, 1987.

Barret, Anthony A., and Rhodri Windsor Liscombe. *Francis Rattenbury and British Columbia*. Vancouver: University of British Columbia Press, 1983.

Barthe, Ulric. *Wilfrid Laurier on the Platform 1871–1890*. Quebec: Turcotte and Menard's Steam Printing Office, 1890.

Berton, Pierre. *The National Dream: The Great Railway 1871–1881*. Toronto: McClelland and Stewart, 1983.

—————. *The Last Spike: The Great Railway, 1881–1895*. Toronto: McClelland and Stewart, 1983.

—————. *The Promised Land: Settling the West, 1896–1914*. Toronto: McClelland and Stewart, 1984.

Bliss, J. M., ed. *Canadian History in Documents, 1763–1966*. Toronto: The Ryerson Press, 1966.

Bliss, Michael. *Northern Enterprise: Five Centuries of Canadian Business*. Toronto: McClelland and Stewart, 1987.

Borden, Robert Laird. *Robert Laird Borden: His Memoirs*. Toronto: Macmillan, 1938.

Bowman, Charles A. *Ottawa Editor: The Memoirs of Charles A. Bowman*. Sidney, B.C.: Gray's Publishing, 1966.

Cartwright, Sir Richard J. *Reminiscences*. Toronto: William Briggs, 1912.

Charlesworth, Hector. *Candid Chronicles: Leaves from the Note Book of a Canadian Journalist*. Toronto: Macmillan, 1925.

—————. *More Candid Chronicles: Further Leaves from the Note Book of a Canadian Journalist*. Toronto: Macmillan, 1928.

Chodos, Robert. *The CPR: A Century of Corporate Welfare*. Toronto: James Lorimer, 1973.

Collard, Edgar Andrew. *Montreal Yesterdays*. Toronto: Longmans Canada, 1962.

Creighton, Donald. *John A. Macdonald: The Old Chieftain*. Toronto: Macmillan, 1955.

Curry, Ralph L. *Stephen Leacock: Humorist and Humanist*. New York: Doubleday, 1959.

Cyclopædia of Canadian Biography. Toronto: Hunter-Rose, 1919.

Dempsey, Hugh, ed. *The CPR West: The Iron Road and the Making of a Nation*. Vancouver: Douglas & McIntyre, 1984.

Dorin, Patrick C. *Canadian Pacific Railway: Motive Power — Rolling Stock — Capsule History*. Saanichton, British Columbia: Hancock House Publishers, 1974.

Ford, Arthur R. *As the World Wags On*. Toronto: Ryerson Press, 1950.

Francis, Diane. *Controlling Interest: Who Owns Canada?* Toronto: Macmillan, 1986.

Frost, Stanley B. *McGill University: For the Advancement of Learning*, vol. II. Montreal: McGill-Queen's University Press, 1983.

Gibbon, John Murray. *Steel of Empire: The Romantic History of the Canadian Pacific, the Northwest Passage of Today*. London: Rich & Cowan, 1935.

Gilbert, Heather. *Awakening Continent.* Vol. I of *The Life of Lord Mount Stephen.* Aberdeen: Aberdeen University Press, 1976.

—————————. *The End of the Road.* Vol. II of *The Life of Lord Mount Stephen* (1891–1921). Aberdeen: Aberdeen University Press, 1977.

Goldenberg, Susan. *Canadian Pacific: A Portrait of Power.* Toronto: Methuen, 1983.

Greber, David. *Rising to Power: Paul Desmarais and Power Corporation.* Toronto: Methuen, 1987.

Grodinsky, Julius. *Transcontinental Railway Strategy, 1869–1893: A Study of Businessmen.* Philadelphia: University of Pennsylvania Press, 1962.

Gwyn, Sandra. *The Private Capital: Ambition and Love in the Age of Macdonald and Laurier.* Toronto: McClelland and Stewart, 1986.

Hall, D. J. *Clifford Sifton: The Lonely Eminence, 1901–1929.* Vancouver: University of British Columbia Press, 1985.

Ham, George H. *Reminiscences of a Raconteur between the 40s and 20s.* Toronto: The Musson Book Co., 1921.

Hanna, D. B. *Trains of Recollection.* Toronto: Macmillan, 1924.

Hart, E. J. *The Selling of Canada: The CPR and the Beginnings of Canadian Tourism.* Banff: Altitude Publishing, 1983.

Hubbard, Freeman. *Encyclopedia of North American Railroading: 150 Years of Railroading in the United States and Canada.* New York: McGraw-Hill, 1981.

Hungry Wolf, Adolf. *Rails in the Canadian Rockies.* Invermere: Good Medicine Books, 1979.

Innis, Harold A. *A History of the Canadian Pacific Railway.* Toronto: University of Toronto Press, 1923.

Keenleyside, Hugh, and Gerald S. Brown. *Canada and the United States: Some Aspects of Their Historical Relations.* New York: Alfred A. Knopf, 1952.

Keith, Ronald A. *Bush Pilot with a Briefcase: The Happy-Go-Lucky Story of Grant McConachie.* Don Mills: Paper Jacks, 1972.

Lamb, W. Kaye. *History of the Canadian Pacific Railway.* New York: Macmillan, 1977.

Lavallée, Omer. *Van Horne's Road: An Illustrated Account of the Construction and First Years of Operation of the Canadian Pacific Transcontinental Railway.* Toronto: A Railfare Book, 1981.

Legget, Robert F. *Railways of Canada.* Vancouver: Douglas & McIntyre, 1973.

Lewis, David. *Political Memoirs: 1909–1958.* Toronto: Macmillan, 1981.

Lukasiewicz, J. *The Railway Game: A Study in Socio-Technological Obsolescence.* Toronto: McClelland and Stewart, 1976.

MacBeth, R. G. *The Romance of the Canadian Pacific Railway.* Toronto: Ryerson Press, 1931.

MacKay, Donald. *The Square Mile: Merchant Princes of Montreal.* Vancouver: Douglas & McIntyre, 1987.

Macnaughtan, S. *My Canadian Memories.* London: Chapman and Hall, 1920.

Marsh, D'Arcy. *The Tragedy of Henry Thornton.* Toronto: Macmillan, 1935.

Martin, Albro. *James J. Hill and the Opening of the Northwest.* New York: Oxford University Press, 1976.

McDougall, J. Lorne. *Canadian Pacific.* Montreal: McGill University Press, 1968.

McKee, Bill, and Georgeen Klassen. *Trail of Iron: The CPR and the Birth of* the West, 1880–1930. Vancouver: Douglas & McIntyre, 1983.

Mika, Nick, and Helma Mika. *Railways of Canada: A Pictorial History.* Toronto: McGraw-Hill Ryerson, 1972.

Miller-Barstow, D. H. *Beatty of the C.P.R.: A Biography.* Toronto: McClelland and Stewart, 1951.

Mowat, Grace Helen. *The Diverting History of a Loyalist Town: a Portrait of St. Andrews, New Brunswick.* Fredericton: Brunswick Press, 1976.

Musk, George. *Canadian Pacific: The Story of the Famous Shipping Line.* London: David & Charles, 1981.

Myers, Gustavus. *History of Canadian Wealth.* Chicago: Charles H. Kerr, 1914.

Neatby, Blair H. *William Lyon Mackenzie King: 1924–1932 — The Lonely Heights.* Toronto: University of Toronto Press, 1963.

Newman, Peter C. *The Distemper of Our Times.* Toronto: McClelland and Stewart, 1978.

————————. *The Acquisitors.* Vol. II of *The Canadian Establishment.* Toronto: Seal Books, 1982.

————————. *The Canadian Establishment,* Vol. I. Toronto: Seal Books, 1983.

Pope, Sir Joseph. *Public Servant: The Memoirs of Sir Joseph Pope,* ed. Maurice Pope. Toronto: Oxford University Press, 1960.

Preston, W. T. R. *My Generation of Politics and Politicians.* Toronto: D. A. Rose Publishing Company, 1927.

————————. *Strathcona and the Making of Canada.* New York: McBride, Nast & Company, 1915.

Pugsley, Edmund E. *The Great Kicking Horse Blunder.* Vancouver: Evergreen Press, 1973.

Pyle, Joseph. *The Life of James J. Hill.*

Toronto: McClelland and Stewart, 1917.

Reksten, Terry. *Rattenbury.* Victoria: Sono Nis Press, 1978.

Ross, Sir George W. *Getting into Parliament and After.* Toronto: William Briggs, 1913.

Sanford, Barrie. *McCulloch's Wonder.* Vancouver: Whitecap Books, 1977.

————————. *The Pictorial History of Railroading in British Columbia.* Vancouver: Whitecap Books, 1981.

Schull, Joseph. *Edward Blake: Leader and Exile, 1881–1912.* Toronto: Macmillan, 1976.

Secretan, J. H. E. *Canada's Great Highway: From the First Stake to the Last Spike.* London: John Lane, 1924.

Skelton, Oscar D. *Life and Times of Sir Alexander Tilloch Galt.* Toronto: McClelland and Stewart, 1966.

————————. *The Day of Sir Wilfrid Laurier: A Chronicle of Our Times.* Toronto: Glasgow, Brook & Company, 1920.

————————. *Life and Letters of Sir Wilfrid Laurier,* Vol. I. Toronto: Oxford University Press, 1921.

————————. *Life and Letters of Sir Wilfrid Laurier,* Vol. II, 1896–1919. Toronto: McClelland and Stewart, 1965.

————————. *The Railway Builders: A Chronicle of Overland Highways.* Toronto: Glasgow, Brook & Company, 1920.

Smith, Goldwin. *Reminiscences,* ed. Arnold Haultain. New York: Macmillan, 1911.

Stacey, C. P. *A Very Double Life: The Private World of Mackenzie King.* Toronto: Macmillan, 1976.

Stevens, G. R. *History of the Canadian National Railways.* New York: Macmillan, 1973.

Tebbutt, H. R., and K. J. Cooksley. *The Crow's Nest Agreement.* Edmonton: Alberta Pool, 1978.

Thompson, Norman, and J. H. Edgar. *Canadian Railway Development: From the Earliest Times.* Toronto: Macmillan, 1933.

Tupper, Sir Charles Hibbert, ed. *The Life of Sir Charles Tupper.* Toronto: Ryerson Press, 1926.

Vaughan, Walter. *The Life and Work of Sir William Van Horne.* New York: The Century Co., 1920.

Wheeler, A. O. *The Selkirk Range.* Ottawa: Department of the Interior, Government Printing Bureau, 1905.

Wilbur, Richard. *St. Andrews Remembered.* St Andrews, New Brunswick: St. Andrews Civic Trust Inc., 1984.

Willison, J. S. *Reminiscences: Political and Personal.* Toronto: McClelland and Stewart, 1919.

Willson, Beckles. *From Quebec to Piccadilly and Other Places: Some Anglo-Canadian Memories.* London: Jonathan Cape, 1929.

————————. *Lord Strathcona: The Story of His Life.* London: Methuen & Co., 1902.

————————. *The Life of Lord Strathcona and Mount Royal G.C.M.G., G.C.V.O. (1820–1914).* London: Casse' and Company Ltd., 1915.

Wood, Charles R. *The Northern Pacific: Main Street of the Northwest.* Seattle: Superior Publishing Company, 1968.

Articles, Pamphlets, Government Reports, Commissions and Company Publications

All newspaper and magazine articles, pamphlets and government documents directly quoted in the text are fully cited in the endnotes. The references listed below are articles that we found useful, but did not quote in the text. Not listed here, but invaluable, were the dozens of bound volumes containing thousands of clippings recently uncovered by the CP Rail Corporate Archives. CP's annual reports and in-house magazine *Spanner* also provided a wealth of statistics and details on company operations.

Baden-Powell, Sir George. "To The East, Westwards!" *The English Illustrated Magazine,* February, 1891.

General Publicity Department. *Canadian Pacific Facts and Figures.* Canadian Pacific Foundation, 1937.

Gilbert, Heather. "King Edward's Hospital Fund for London: The First 25 Years." *Social and Economic Administration* (University of Exeter) vol. 8, no. 1 (1974).

Greenberg, Dolores. "A Study of

Capital Alliances: The St. Paul and Pacific." *Canadian Historical Review* (March, 1976).

Masters, D. C. "Financing the C.P.R., 1880–1885." *Canadian Historical Review* XXIV (1943).

McCready, J. E. B. "When the World was Young." *Canadian Magazine*, October, 1906.

Moorhouse, Hopkins J. "The Building of a Railway." *Canadian Magazine*, June, 1904.

Northcote, H. Stafford. "Canada's Highway to the Pacific." *The Nineteenth Century* (January, 1882).

Ramsey, G. G. "Over the Rocky Mountains by the Canadian Pacific Line in 1884." *MacMillan's Magazine*, December, 1884.

Roe, F. G. "An Unsolved Problem of Canadian History." *Report of the Canadian Historical Association.* Toronto: University of Toronto Press, 1936.

Thomson, T. Kennard. "The Canadian Pacific Railway." *Engineering* (December, 1891).

Waiser, W. A. "A Willing Scapegoat: John Macoun and the Route of the CPR." *Prairie Forum*, the journal of the Canadian Plains Research Center, vol. 10, no. 1 (Spring, 1985).

Woods, John G. *Snow War: An Illustrated History of Rogers Pass Glacier National Park, B.C.* The National and Provincial Parks Association of Canada and Parks Canada, 1983.

Yeats, Floyd. *Canadian Pacific's Big Hill: A Hundred Years of Operation.* Calgary: The Calgary Group of the British Railway Modelers of North America, 1985.

Unpublished Manuscripts

Armstrong, Gerald W. "The Mount Stephen Club," M.A. thesis, McGill University, Montreal, 1959.

Crump, T. H. "Recollections: His Service with CPR, 1890–1934."

Crump, N. R. "Stirrups."

Griffiths, Alison. "Climbing Discovers Canada: A History of the Development of Mountaineering in Canada."

Jones, David. Untitled manuscript on Windsor Station. In his possession, CP Rail, Montreal.

Kilpatrick, T. "Some Reminiscences of Railroading on the Canadian Pacific in the Mountains of British Columbia, and of Some Important Improvements on the Line That Could Have Been Made." CP Archives, 1935.

Stevenson, John. Untitled paper on Lord Mount Stephen. In the possession of Alexis Reford, Montreal.

Stone, F. V., recorder, Omer Lavallée, editor. "Crump's Chronicles: No. 1."

Tuck, Hugh. "W. C. Van Horne and the 'Foreign Emissaries': The C.P.R. Trainmen's and Conductors' Strike of 1892." CP Rail Corporate Archives, 1979.

Unauthored. "Stephen." 1929. In the possession of Alexis Reford, Montreal.

Walker, Willa. Untitled manuscript on St Andrews, New Brunswick. In her possession.

Archives

Large volumes of material directly relating to the CPR and its presidents exist in the National Archives of Canada; the Glenbow Archives (Calgary, Alberta); the Archives of the Canadian Rockies (Banff, Alberta); the Canadian Railroad Historical Association Archives (St Constant, Quebec); the McCord Museum, McGill University; McGill University Archives; the James Jerome Hill Reference Library (St Paul, Minnesota); and in provincial archives across the country. Also, the libraries of most major Canadian cities contain useful information on the company. Papers in the National Archives of Canada filed under the following names were not directly quoted but proved very useful.

Governor General Aberdeen – MG 27 IB5

A. T. Galt – MG 27 ID8

Lomer Gouin – MG 27 IIIB4

Lord Lorne – MG 27 IB4

C. A. Magrath – MG 30 E82

George Parkin – MG 30 D44

Joseph Pope – MG 30 E86

Gonzalo de Quesada Y Arostegui – MG 30 A12

George Stephen – MG 29 A30

Lord Strathcona – MG 29 A5

Charles Tupper – MG 26 F

Beckles Willson – MG 30 D5

Index

Page numbers in italics refer to photographs and maps.

the national bestseller

N E T
WORTH

EXPLODING THE MYTHS
OF PRO HOCKEY

David Cruise & Alison Griffiths

"...spellbinding, virtually from cover to cover... the anecdotes
are positively delicious... Hardly anybody's reputation
escapes unscathed. It's a marvellous read."
— *The Globe and Mail*

In December 1990, a group of NHL old-timers — including
Bobby Hull, Bobby Orr, and Gordie Howe — met secretly in a
hotel meeting room. Here, in this one room, were some of the
greatest players of all time. What brought them together? A
refusal to play in the Old-Timers' All-Star game and a plan to
sue the NHL to reveal the corruption they had all witnessed —
and suffered — while in the league...

A PENGUIN BOOK